*Fact
into
Fiction*

English literature and the industrial scene 1750-1850

Ivanka Kovačević
Professor of English Literature
University of Belgrade

Fact

into

Fiction

Leicester University Press / University of Belgrade
1975   Faculty of Philology

First published by Leicester University Press/
Faculty of Philology, University of Belgrade, 1975
Distributed in North America by Humanities Press Inc., New Jersey

Designed by Arthur Lockwood

Set in 'Monotype' Plantin and Scotch Roman
Printed and bound in Great Britain by
W. & J. Mackay Limited, Chatham
ISBN 0 7185 1130 1

Contents

Part 2   Anthology

Foreword

When the Victorian Studies Centre was established in the University of Leicester in 1966, one of the problems of scholarship in this period which it identified was the relative inaccessibility of many significant texts, out of print and not easily available through second-hand catalogues. As a result, the Leicester University Press has been publishing, since 1969, the Victorian Library, a series of reprints, all introduced by a scholar of some standing. Professor Ivanka Kovačević's anthology of literary items bearing on nineteenth-century British industrialism does not appear in this series because she includes much pre-Victorian matter; moreover, for reasons which she explains, she does not always reprint items in their entirety (as is the policy of the Victorian Library). Professor Kovačević's aims, however, are in line with those of our series, and it was because the Press publishes the Victorian Library that, when seeking a publisher in the English-speaking world, Professor Kovačević submitted her proposals to us. We are happy to be thus making available a selection of texts on this topic, all of which are difficult to come by and all of which are very well worth reading, in the context of the editor's exposition and argument. No other collection, we believe, assembles such a variety of items on this topic from the minor fiction of the first half of the nineteenth century: and, as a glance over the Contents will show, the authors selected, though minor, are by no means nonentities. The interest of this reprinting is greatly increased by its editor's substantial Introduction and prefatory notes, which in effect constitute a valuable monograph on this subject.

Professor Kovačević is happily placed, in Yugoslavia, to make the best of what (belatedly and provincially perhaps) one still tends to think of as two worlds, those of Eastern and Western Europe. A wide-ranging student of English literature, as her Introduction shows, she had the salutary experience of pursuing her postgraduate research, at Oxford, under the direction of Humphry House, a scholar whose zest, range and humanity were memorably conjoined with a daunting severity if ever a student failed to be aware of all the relevant evidence or showed signs of indulging in loose or opinionated thinking. Since 1950, Professor Kovačević has been on the staff of the Department of English at the University of Belgrade, where she is now Professor of English Literature. Thus she has had access to a range of scholarship and a mode of interpretation of which her Western colleagues are not always sufficiently aware. Her view of history and of the social bearings of literature owes much, it is clear, to Marxist thinking, and she is knowledgeable about recent Soviet scholarship in the area of her present collection. As such works as Y. V. Kovalev's *Anthology of Chartist Literature* (Moscow, 1956) remind us, more work has been done recently in the Soviet Union than in the Anglo-Saxon countries on several such phases and kinds of English literature. Anglo-Saxon scholars are not always as familiar as they might usefully be with Eastern European scholarship and critical discussion (and, as a non-reader of Russian, let alone Polish, Hungarian or Serbo-Croat, I can no more plead not guilty than most of my colleagues). Professor Kovačević has the advantage over us of being as aware of the relevant Eastern scholarship as she is of the Western. Her pre-eminent qualification for her task, however, is her manifest frequentation of English literature of the eighteenth and nineteenth centuries, major and minor, and her sense of critical perspective which (as her preliminary discussion shows) prevents her making inappropriate claims for the items which she is presenting. These, as she avers, come from minor fiction; they have merit, intrinsic or representative, but she does not confuse them with major literary feats, some of which she discusses and all of which are of course sufficiently familiar and available.

One more of Professor Kovačević's virtues may be mentioned, if I may do so without becoming patronizing. She is her own translator: or rather she wrote her editorial matter in English – and so well that, when her typescript arrived at our Press's offices, one of its staff remarked that he wished that many other authors, native to Britain, who send offerings to the Press would write with such literacy and felicity as this Yugoslavian scholar commands. Professor Kovačević insists that some of the credit for this should go to her friend Professor Maren-Sofie Røstvig, of the University of Oslo, who has helped her to revise her manuscript. "Our Language is Difficult. Ours is a Copious Language, and Trying to Strangers", Mr Podsnap emphatically remarks during his attempt to make the Foreign Gentleman glimpse the sundry Blessings of the British Constitution. Professor Kovačević, in alliance with Professor Røstvig, has long since triumphed over any Difficulties she may initially have encountered, and her knowledge of our society and its history as well as its literature is so ample that she could certainly discourse, in more detail as well as with more critical detachment than Mr Podsnap, on Our Constitution too.

I welcome this addition to the Press's list of nineteenth-century British titles, and am sure that many readers will be grateful, as I have been, for Professor Kovačević's scholarship and discrimination, and for this opportunity to read a number of texts which, if minor events in the history of literature, are fascinating documents in the history of ideas and of sensibility.

PHILIP COLLINS
University of Leicester

Part I

Introduction

Preface

This book has been written to trace the development of the industrial theme in English imaginative writing from the time of its first appearance, when it had all the charm of novelty, to the middle of the nineteenth century, when the process of industrialization was more or less completed. Such a survey enables one to see much more clearly how the so-called social novel came into being, and to observe the gradual growth of the social conscience which inspired the reformist zeal of Charles Dickens and his contemporaries. Yet another gain is a better understanding of the reasons for the bias shown in fictionalized accounts of social problems – a bias against working-class organizations and their actions.

That such a survey should include an anthology of some of these fictionalized accounts has its obvious advantages; it permits the reader to relish the full flavour of the kind of writing that gradually came to acquire some literary merit. Existing studies of this subject have a limited usefulness as they seldom consider the industrial subject as a whole or as a subject in its own right, touching on it only incidentally in connection with other issues. For this reason the treatment is necessarily casual and fragmentary, and it is particularly regrettable that the early stages of the tradition in the eighteenth century have been virtually ignored. It has been my purpose, therefore, to provide a more reliable perspective by beginning at the beginning and not as it were in mid-stream.

In view of the great complexity of my subject, I have decided to focus attention on some carefully selected aspects of it and to study these with greater thoroughness than would be possible in a more comprehensive survey. An investigation of this kind is bound to touch on issues whose highly controversial character has been retained or even increased with the passing of time, and it will be difficult and perhaps impossible to achieve complete objectivity in the selection and evaluation of material. Another very real difficulty is that no one scholar can hope to grasp fully, let alone do complete justice to, the total literary output of the period considered here. The sheer bulk of the works that touch on various aspects of the process of industrialization is as intimidating as its variety is kaleidoscopic. I have nevertheless attempted to survey the forest despite its innumerable trees. I realize that the necessity of having to simplify highly complex issues may result in an impoverished account of the literary milieu, but I hope that I may have erred no more than is inevitable in a project of this kind. Although we no longer need fear the myopia which so often impairs the vision of contemporaries, our own period imposes its own preconceptions and attitudes so that scholarly detachment may be as hard to achieve today as during the Industrial Revolution itself.

It is an important part of my purpose to relate the fictional representation of social problems to political and intellectual trends. A study of such trends, however, is no easy task since it would entail more than a mere compilation of facts bearing on economic and social history. It is generally recognized that the pattern of ideas in this period was a complicated one: concepts derived from widely disparate traditions, some of them old and some quite recent, were combined or fused, sometimes with complete disregard for logical consistency. In the course of its progress from the original springs or well-heads, the stream of thought meandered to such an extent that it is almost impossible to trace its progress in any specific direction. Scholars who have tried to map some of the intellectual traditions of this period have achieved more or less successful syntheses, and although the merit of their studies is indisputable, further research is undoubtedly indicated to supply the insights needed for a reliable analysis of the kind of fiction which is my concern. But it is no part of my purpose to submit an analysis purely in terms of a history of ideas – I shall touch on the subject from time to time, however, in an effort to straighten out certain ideological cruxes. For the student of literature the genesis of certain ideas will be less interesting than the way in which such ideas can be seen to group themselves around certain social problems reflected in the fiction of the day.

It was only to be expected that it would take some time before the general public became aware of the various problems posed by a society in the process of industrialization. The process was a gradual one, and the focus of attention can be seen to shift from one set of problems to another according to their importance at the moment. Variety is the outstanding characteristic – variety of attitudes and variety of literary modes and genres. Some writers were profoundly serious and deeply concerned, while others were content to exploit the commercial value of the new subject matter. Then, too, the same kind of social problem could provoke widely different reactions. To survey the field properly, virtually all the conventional genres must be included; relevant material can be found in didactic poetry, in propagandist fiction and in leading periodicals as well as in the penny press. On the one hand we must consult the doggerel of the mere rhymester and anonymous tracts composed by hack writers, and, on the other, true poetry and social fiction of considerable literary merit. Some of the sources I have drawn on lie entirely outside the sphere of literature proper – diaries, for example, and biographies, regional histories, chapbooks, travel books and historical documents of various kinds. Some of the records consulted are of such obscurity today that they have been entirely forgotten. Nevertheless these records are often so revealing that I have quoted from them on several occasions to illustrate different aspects of my theme, although I am aware of the fact that this may create an impression of repetition.

Complete coverage is obviously impossible. Like the sociologist, the historian must be content to base his study on an adequate number of samples; the selection, therefore, must be fairly liberal to ensure a reliable assessment of the way in which literature can be seen to reflect the tremendous change wrought by the Industrial Revolution in the pattern of daily life and in the mind of the nation.

It is, perhaps, somewhat disappointing to discover that so few authors focus their attention directly on the process of industrialization. This is of course why literary histories pay such scant attention to this particular literary theme – a neglect which contrasts very strongly with the attention bestowed upon other subjects. But it is understandable that the age itself should largely ignore the issue. England, after all, was engaged in a pioneering venture and had no experience to draw on so as to understand the course of events, let alone control them. The wisdom to understand the nature and import of social changes as they occur is given to few, and the number of those who can envisage future developments is even less. Most of us must be content to approach the problems of the present with concepts and attitudes inherited from the past, and this applies to literature as well: traditional themes and styles have a habit of persisting despite the growth of new concerns calling for new forms and techniques for adequate expression. During the period considered here the material or physical basis of daily life was undergoing constant change, but no similar modernization manifests itself in the thought habits of artists or intellectuals – certainly not to the same extent or at the same time. The political thinkers erred, like the general public, in their analysis of the problems involved in matters of social and political organization, and this was largely due to the survival of outmoded ways of thinking incapable of meeting the challenge of capitalist competition and mechanized methods of production. This is shown with startling clarity in the works of minor and major writers alike.

The works that I shall refer to will often possess little or no artistic merit, but the novelty of the industrial theme is a redeeming feature.

Works that deal with the industrial scene are relatively few in number but they are significant because many things are mentioned and many questions formulated for the first time. From its very beginning the age of industrialization puzzled would-be authors who had no ready formula for transposing it into fiction; freshness of response, however, was guaranteed by the newness of the phenomenon. Hence the mediocre quality of much that was written during the generation that fostered James Watt is atoned for by a freshness of vision completely lost to later generations as a consequence of their familiarity with an industrialized environment.

My revaluation of the literary scene will not affect the major writers, whose achievement will only seem the greater by being contrasted with the minor fiction and sub-fiction of the age. This minor fiction itself nevertheless possesses an intrinsic merit that should not be ignored. Its literary quality is far from negligible, and its historical relevance should be obvious. This kind of literature enjoyed the widest possible circulation at the time and so must be of considerable interest in the study of the history of ideas in this period. To the student of literature it represents the first important stage in the shaping of a tradition that was to achieve considerable eminence – and notoriety – in the second half of the nineteenth century.

The works included in the anthology are virtually unobtainable and can be consulted only by readers with access to the great libraries in the English-speaking world. In an attempt to meet the needs of the general student as well as the specialist, I have also reproduced two or three texts that will be familiar to English readers, perhaps, but not to readers on the Continent or in more distant parts of the globe. And since the process of industrialization will be in its early stages in some of these parts, these accounts of the early stages in England may be felt as more directly relevant than they can possibly be in Western Europe.

My selection has been guided by two considerations: (1) that the works included should be reproduced *in toto*, and (2) that the whole formal and thematic range of this type of fiction should be represented. The only exception to the first rule is the section reproduced from William Godwin's novel *Fleetwood* (1805), but these four chapters constitute a separate episode that may be considered as a self-contained unit. To keep the Anthology within reasonable limits I have had to exclude poetry in general and short stories or poems written by the Chartists. This selection, therefore, cannot pretend to provide an adequate basis for a thorough study of working-class literature. Before such a study can be attempted, more research is indicated along the lines traced by Professor Y. V. Kovalev, whose *Anthology of Chartist Literature* (Moscow, 1956) is the most authoritative study to have appeared so far.

The seven items in the Anthology represent various types of writing which reflect the impact of the Industrial Revolution during the period which started with the French Revolution and terminated with the Great Exhibition of 1851, and I have prefaced each with an introduction about its author. I have chosen the tract and the short story (except in the case of *Fleetwood*) as they appear quite as characteristic of this type of literature as the much longer novel; furthermore, these shorter works have the additional distinction of being least accessible to the modern reader. All of them, if not otherwise stated, are reproduced from first editions. Obvious spelling errors have been corrected.

My indebtedness to other scholars will appear from my bibliography and, of course, from my footnotes. What cannot be inferred in this manner, however, is my extensive indebtedness to various institutions and persons who have supported my project and contributed substantially to its realization. Thus the Department of English in Belgrade University has permitted leave of absence on several occasions, and my visits to various research libraries in Great Britain and the United States have been financed by liberal grants from the Ford Foundation, the British Council, and the Faculty of Philology in my own university. I owe a debt of gratitude for services promptly rendered by the following libraries and their staff – the Bodleian Library in Oxford, Cambridge University Library and the Huntington Library in San Marino, California.

My greatest debt is to Maren-Sofie Røstvig, Professor of English Literature in the University of Oslo, whose professional assistance was as freely offered as her moral support. I must thank her in particular for her careful reading of the first draft of my manuscript, and for all the time she has devoted to improving my text with regard to style and presentation. I also wish to thank Mrs Mary Stansfield Popović of Belgrade University who has taken a keen interest in my research from its very beginning a number of years ago. After reading the manuscript she made a number of valuable suggestions for revisions.

My thanks are also due to Professor Ada Nisbet of the University of California, Los Angeles, for encouragement and advice, and to Diana Dixon, then bibliographer in the Victorian Studies Centre of Leicester University, for assistance in the checking of references. I thank our librarian, Mrs L. Stanić, for her competent assistance. Finally let me add that I am profoundly grateful to Mrs Jean Charnley of San Marino, California, and to Mrs Madeline House of Cambridge, for friendly encouragement during some particularly trying stages in the preparation of this book.

I dedicate this book to my mother, Bosa Ćuković.

I.K.
Belgrade
27 March 1973

Chapter I

Genesis of a New Theme

1. The Mechanical Muse

The word 'smog' has been coined fairly recently, but the phenomenon itself is much older. It was described as early as 1661 when John Evelyn published his *Fumifugium, or the Inconvenience of the Aer and Smoake of London dissipated*. This curious pamphlet addressed to "his Sacred Majestie, and the Parliament now Assembled" was a petition for government action with a view to improving the air in London. And improvement was certainly needed; the air was full of smoke and fumes issuing from the chimneys of brewers, dyers, soap-boilers and lime-bakers. The sun itself was eclipsed by clouds of sulphur and the atmosphere was saturated with foul smells. This complaint which was to become so typical of fictionalized accounts concerned with the process of industrialization was echoed and further amplified by Timothy Nourse in his 'Essay upon the Fuel of London' included in his *Campania Foelix* (1700). Even at some miles' distance from the town one may see, feel, smell and taste the effect of "great Heaps, or Mountains, rather, of Cole-Dust" which "upon the least puff of

Wind . . . invade and cover all Places". And in the summer "when Men think to take sweet Air" what they suck into their lungs is a "Sulphurous stinking Powder, strong enough to provoke Sneezing in one fall'n into an Apoplexy. From whence comes all those Rheums, Coughs, and Consumptions, which so universally afflict the Inhabitants of this place." The very casements are eaten away by this hellish smoke that "works it self betwixt the joins of Bricks, and eats out the Mortar; so that what was Fresh and Beautiful Twenty or Thirty years ago, now looks Black and Decay'd."[1] When Evelyn's *Fumifugium* was reprinted in 1772, the editor underlined the fact that conditions had become even more intolerable through the unchecked growth of factories: "We have a great increase of Glass-Houses, Foundries, and Sugar-Bakers to add to the black catalogue; at the head of which must be placed the Fire-Engines."

Today this sort of complaint is only too familiar, but it is important to realize that the history of environmental pollution antedates the Industrial Revolution, so that an already existing problem was strongly aggravated in the course of the eighteenth century.

The history of the process of industrialization is so well known that the briefest of summaries will suffice. When the so-called revolution was initiated, manufacturing processes were already highly organized in terms of division of labour, specialization and large-scale production – all of which had been inherited from the Tudor period. The great change occurred when the skilled workman and his tools were replaced by machines capable of setting tools in motion by means of man-controlled mechanical power, first based on water and then on the steam-engine. When this development became a reality, the chief characteristics of industrial society grew equally apparent: capital investment on a large scale, organized production, a complex technology, and regimented labour.

One comes across industrial themes in English literature even in the period prior to the technological revolution, and during this early phase the attitude is one of universal and unqualified approval. The first visible signs of the great innovations – the building of factories and canals and machines incorporating various technical inventions – were acclaimed with a mixture of wonder and patriotic pride as evidence of England's leading position among the nations. Most authors took it for granted that economic prosperity conduced to universal happiness.

As the eighteenth century progressed, poets paid increasing attention to the process of industrialization as manifested in town and countryside.[2] The appropriate genre for descriptions of this kind was, of course, the Virgilian Georgic poem, one of Virgil's major themes being praise of the Roman empire and its civilization.[3] Virgil inspired many an eighteenth-century poet to praise "our noble cities and all the work of our hands", to quote an anonymous poet who submitted a poem entitled 'A Journey to Nottingham' to *The Gentleman's Magazine* for 1743. In the course of his journey the poet arrives at Newport, and, prompted by mercantile enthusiasm, acclaims "pleas'd *Industry*":

> Now Newport meets us rising from the wave,
> Whose busy mart surrounding waters lave;
> Here pleas'd *Industry* smiling o'er her race,
> Directs the bobbin, and designs the lace.[4]

This exaltation of hard toil and "mechanic arts", to borrow a phrase from James Thomson's *The Castle of Indolence* (1748),[5] is an innovation. The homage paid to the independent husbandman by Virgil, as by Horace,[6] must not be associated with this eighteenth-century praise of industrial productivity: the Augustan poets undoubtedly used the Georgic tradition as their point of departure, but they turned in a totally different direction when they introduced the theme of industrial labour – of work organized by capital, carried on in factories and performed by labour-saving machines as well as men.

Some of the poets who gloried in the spectacle of economic prosperity were quick to recognize the significance of machines even before these had reached their final form. Thus the first description, in poetry, of a mining pump dates from 1710, long before James Watt was to provide his crucial contribution to the construction of steam-engines. Similarly John Dyer's description of textile machinery in *The Fleece* (1757) appeared before the major inventions connected with spinning and weaving. Dyer tried to write honestly about an object of vital concern to the nation, and he succeeded in avoiding the affectation which so often mars the efforts of those who tried their hand at this sort of poem. His description is factual and precise: he admires the efficiency of the machinery and the subtlety of the invention:

> But patient art
> That on experience works, from hour to hour,
> Sagacious, has a spiral engine form'd,
> Which on an hundred spoles, an hundred threads,
> With one huge wheel, by lapse of water, twines,
> Few hands requiring; easy-tended work,
> That copiously supplies the greedy loom.
> . . . We next are shown
> A circular machine, of new design,
> In conic shape; it draws and spins a thread
> Without the tedious toil of needless hands.
> A wheel, invisible, beneath the floor
> To every member of the harmonious frame
> Gives necessary motion. One, intent,
> O'erlooks the work: the carded wool, he says,
> Is smoothly lapp'd around those cylinders,
> Which, gently turning, yield it to yon circque
> Of upright spindles which with rapid whirl
> Spin out in long extent, an even twine.

(III, 79–85 and 291–302)

Dr Johnson disliked the poem largely on the score of its subject matter. Dyer's efforts were defeated by "the meanness naturally adhering, and the irreverence habitually annexed to trade and manufacture."[7] Dyer's nineteenth-century editor, George Gilfillan, disagreed because he felt that any object, if idealized, may "become fit for the purpose of poetry". A shuttle and loom may be "very prosaic" but become poetic the moment they are seen as emblematic of human existence ("the mingled yarn of human life"). On the other hand it is admitted that boiling vats "can hardly yield much of the Hippocrene of imagination", nor can one extract poetry from "that chaos of whizzing facts, the wheels of a cotton mill."[8] Dyer's realism, then, remained unappreciated by later ages as by his own, but it is this very realism that makes him so interesting from our point of view. Then, too, the poem's obvious weaknesses are atoned for by Dyer's pride in the triumph of human intelligence as it utilizes the power latent in inert matter. It may have been this quality which inspired Wordsworth to dedicate a sonnet to Dyer, and even the Romantic poet could not have failed to appreciate his successful description of the intricate structure of the textile machinery, so precise in its smooth and swift rotation and in its carefully timed movements. Among the poems from the mid-century that describe the new technical inventions, Dyer's *The Fleece* is undoubtedly the most interesting.

During the 1770s the poetry concerned with industrial themes entered on a new phase largely as the result of the increasing use of machinery. The very appearance of the countryside was affected by the stark outlines of factory chimneys, foundries, waterworks and iron bridges. The Midlands and the northern counties acquired considerable economic importance, and from these regions issued poetry characterized by pride in the local industries. The topographical poem lent itself to themes of this kind, and almost every region had its rhymester.

One of the first poems to describe in detail an industrial landscape appeared in 1767 when Richard Jago published his *Edge-Hill*. The poet's muse considers the "wise Artificers / In Brass, and Iron" busily at work in the Midlands:

> Here, in huge Cauldrons the rough Mass they stowe,
> Till, by the potent Heat, the purer Ore
> Is liquified, and leaves the Dross afloat.
> Then, cautious, from the glowing Pond they lead
> The fiery Stream along the channel'd Floor;
> Where, in the mazy Moulds of figur'd Sand,
> Anon it hardens, and, in Ingots rude,
> Is to the Forge convey'd; whose weighty Strokes,
> Incessant aided by the rapid Stream,
> Spread out the ductile Ore, now tapering
> In lengthen'd Masses, ready to obey
> The Workman's Will, and take its destin'd Form.
>
> (III, 507–18)

Bars of iron are carried over the "Furrow'd Pavement" of Birmingham and distributed to innumerable hands that fashion a variety of objects from the metal: knives, scissors, buttons, buckles, seals, rings, pins, needles, printer's type or engraver's plate. The concluding lines proudly extol the hard and sustained labour of these workmen and the trade which "makes the Treasures of each Clime her own."

Another poet who celebrated the Birmingham area was Anna Seward, who spent her whole life in the Midlands. Her poem on 'Colbrooke Dale', written some 20 years after Jago's *Edge-Hill*, employs mythological imagery even in the description of an industrial site. She begins by deploring the process of industrialization which has banished the sylvan race from her Derbyshire home, invaded now by clanging engines and countless fires while troops of dusty and noisy artisans inhabit the once peaceful valleys. This nostalgia, however, gradually yields to expressions of pride in her country's achievement. Since she was the friend of Dr Erasmus Darwin and a member of his circle, Anna Seward knew about the achievement of James Watt and did not fail to admire the works in Birmingham ('Soho') where Watt's patent for the steam-engine was executed and the first machines produced for sale. Her inspired panegyric on the new industrial age constitutes what I believe must be the first poetic description of an expanding industrial town:

> While neighbouring cities waste the fleeting hours,
> Careless of art and knowledge, and the smile
> Of every Muse, expanding *Birmingham.*
> Illum'd by intellect, as gay in wealth,
> Commands her aye-accumulating walls,
> From month to month, to climb the adjacent hills;
> Creep on the circling plains, now here, now there,
> Divergent – change the hedges, thickets, trees,
> Upturn'd, disrooted, into mortar'd piles,
> The streets elongate, and the statelier square . . .

The diction conveys an impression of triumphant achievement; the "streets elongate" are juxtaposed with the "statelier square" without a sense of incongruity.

Dr Darwin, the grandfather of Charles Darwin, dedicated some of his verses to what he calls the "Mechanical Muse" – an admirable term for the kind of poetry reviewed in this chapter. Though medicine was his profession, it was not his only interest. Such was his insatiable curiosity and his comprehensive knowledge of natural science, philosophy and psychology, that he became the *spiritus movens* of the Lunar Society Club, whose members formed an intellectual élite including some of the pioneers of big industry: Boulton, Watt, Keir, and Wedgwood. These industrialists were his personal friends, and it is no wonder that his poetry occasionally exploited industrial themes. Darwin's chief claim to fame rests on his *Botanic Garden* (1789–91) – a singularly inappropriate title for a poem that deals with almost every conceivable topic including the present state of scientific studies and various aspects of industry. Dr Darwin was surprisingly well informed about industrial matters,

for he took the trouble to ascertain the facts. When he decided to
include a description of the steam-engine, he wrote to James Watt
for information, and although Watt failed to see "how steam engines came among the plants", he nevertheless provided the
information required. Darwin used some of this material for additional notes on the construction of the engine. The poem itself
presents a fairly conventional description of clanging iron and
ponderous beams (I, i, 259–62), but Darwin differs from other
bards of machinery in his wider outlook. He believed in the future
importance of the steam-engine:

> Soon shall thy arm, Unconquered Steam! afar
> Drag the slow barge, or drive the rapid car;
> Or on wide-waving wings expanded bear
> The flying-chariot through the fields of air.
>
> (I, i, 289–92)

This vision of the future is startling in its prophetic accuracy but
the poet's imagination failed to grasp the implications of elec-
tricity as a source of power; to him it was of interest merely as a
natural phenomenon (I, i, 335–88).

The Botanic Garden describes a number of industrial machines
and activities: the air pump (I, iv, 127–42), the manufacture of steel
(I, i, 183–92), Wedgwood's 'Etruria' pottery works (I, ii, 291–96),
and the construction of canals (I, iii, 349–56). His fondness for
personifications and for animating the scenes that he describes
invests his lines with a kind of wit that must have been unintended:

> So now the Derwent rolls his dusky floods
> Through vaulted mountains, and a night of woods,
> The Nymph, *Gossypia*, treads the velvet sod,
> And warms with rosy smiles the watery God;
> His ponderous oars to slender spindles turns,
> And pours o'er massy wheels his foamy urns;
> With playful charms her hoary lover wins,
> And wields his trident, – while the Monarch spins.
> – First with nice eye emerging Naiads cull
> From leathery pods the vegetable wool;
> With wiry teeth *revolving cards* release
> The tangled knots, and smooth the ravell'd fleece.
>
> (II, ii, 85–96)

This passage, which is typical of Darwin's style, prefaces his account of cotton manufacture. He had little feeling for decorum, but would assemble basically incompatible subjects and proceed to adorn them with all the flowers of a pompous rhetoric. To his eye the pumping machine becomes an infant sucking its mother's breast – and the simile prompts the advice that ladies ought to nurse their own children. No wonder, therefore, that such an incongruous potpourri sparked off a number of parodies.[9]

Stereotyped ornament similarly clogs the description of Staffordshire industries in *The Vale of Wever* (1797) by John Gisborne. And the level of poetic achievement is even lower in the grandiloquent passages adorning the commercial guide to Birmingham written by the self-taught poet James Bisset, an engraver by trade. Bisset began his poetic career in an effort to attract customers by means of versified advertisements, and his success encouraged him to attempt an elaborate panegyric on the business of the city. The poet takes Apollo, Hermes and Bacchus on a conducted tour of factories producing buttons, guns, buckles, and toys, and in the end the visiting deities agree to award the prize to 'Soho'. It seems odd that Bisset should boast of the "purity of air" at a time when complaints of pollution were quite common, but he was apparently determined to ignore all negative aspects of the industrial scene. A more honest anonymous poet writing in 1743 had compared the smoky atmosphere to a cloud "which buries thousands in its sooty shroud",[10] while another mid-century poet deplores the "Thick dark'ning clouds" whose "sooty Stench the Earth and Air annoys, / And Nature's blooming Verdure half destroys."[11] Similar sentiments were expressed by Anna Seward, and John Gisborne too was bothered by the blackening volumes of smoke hanging in the air like curtains and dimming the radiant green of the countryside. But such protests must by no means be taken to indicate a negative attitude to industry: as already stated, the prevailing view was one of complete approval – and, as the next part of this chapter will show, a study of similar descriptions presented in eighteenth-century non-fictional prose confirms this conclusion.

2. Prose Quarries

Since eighteenth-century fiction ignores the process of industrialization and related issues, one must consult the non-fictional prose of this period to ascertain the prevailing attitudes. Passages selected more or less at random confirm the impression that the educated classes on the whole were favourably impressed by the growth of industry until the time of the economic crisis caused by the Napoleonic wars. The malaise remained vague and unidentified until the last few years of the eighteenth century when the anxiety that was to become a virtual obsession in the Victorian period first manifested itself.

Expressions of unqualified approval may be found in Daniel Defoe's *Tour Thro' the Whole Island of Great Britain* (1724–7), as in Arthur Young's *A Six-Month Tour through the North of England* (1771). The former praised the clothing trade of Leeds as "a more genuine source of wealth than the mines of Peru", while the latter's keen eye for detail resulted in excellent reports on various industries such as the spinners of Manchester, the miners of Craven, the clothiers of Durham, the hosiers of Kendal and the cutlers of Sheffield. Young accompanies his descriptions by statistical data in order to encourage further industrial development.

When James Boswell paid a visit to Birmingham, the sight of the great Soho Works made him wish for the presence of Dr Johnson: "The vastness of the contrivance of some of the machinery would have 'matched his mighty mind'. I shall never forget Mr. Boulton's expression to me: 'I sell here, Sir, what all the world desires to have – POWER.' He had about seven hundred people at work."[12] But the spectacle of these hundreds of labourers elicited no more than a casual remark; it was the captains of industry that engrossed the attention of Boswell as of other observers. The note of approval is equally apparent in John Throsby's *Memoirs of the Town and County of Leicester* (1771). The author informs us (p. 26) that the chief manufacture is stockings,

which has abundantly increased within these fifty years. Most of the first people of Leicester employ their wealth in this business; and large fortunes have been rapidly obtained by it, in that place. There are hosiers here, who may be said to employ, including the dependants upon the *Comber* and the *Stocking-Market*, near a thousand manufacturers.

And this is the praise bestowed upon the Duke of Bridgewater's canals in the anonymously published *Sketch of a Tour into Derbyshire and Yorkshire* (1778):

These undertakings are truly stupendous, and strongly mark the spirit of enterprise which is so much the character of the present age. The advantages to trade are immense, and in other respects are very great to the country thro' which the canals pass.

In his description of a day of celebration in Lombe's silk mill the same author comments on the survival of old country customs among the workers:

The money given by strangers is put into a box, which is opened the day after Michaelmas Day, and a feast is made; an ox is killed, liquor prepared, the windows are illuminated, and the men, women and children, employed in the work, dressed in their best array, enjoy dancing and decent mirth on a holiday, the expectations of which lightens the labour of the rest of the year.[13]

This record of the collective entertainment of industrial workers – an entertainment reminiscent of an almost feudal relationship as described for example by Thomas Deloney in his *Jack of Newbury* (1597) – is an extremely rare phenomenon. Since those who wrote about the industrial proletariat wanted to enlist public support, logically enough they would describe scenes of misery rather than the occasional celebrations. Scenes of gloomy horror therefore were *de rigueur* in the social novels of the next century.

A few additional quotations from descriptions of industrial areas will illustrate the positive enthusiasm which persisted almost throughout the eighteenth century. At the end of his five-hundred-page *Tour* the Rev. Shaw Stebbing exclaimed: "But what will not the genius of Britain aspire to and sucessfully perform!"[14] R. J. Sullivan in his *Observations Made during a Tour* found Birmingham "really wonderful, it strikes one with enchantment".[15] The Dean of Cambridge was delighted with the success of Boulton's Soho Works in Birmingham.[16] The coal mines of Newcastle and their steam-engines provoked a positive response in another observer, John Brand,[17] and so did the city of Birmingham as seen through the eyes of William Hutton, a prosperous citizen who arrived without a penny and fought his way from rags to riches.[18]

Lancashire was described so frequently that a mere listing of titles would require several pages, and it would be more rewarding to take a closer look at one of the more interesting items, Richard Ayton's *A Voyage round Great Britain 1813* (London, 1814), a work in eight volumes dedicated to Sir Walter Scott and illustrated by William Daniel. Ayton had been sent to Manchester to study law, so that he was quite familiar with the area, but he pursued no professional career, preferring the leisurely existence of a gentleman who takes a semi-professional interest in the world of letters. He tried his hand as a writer of plays and miscellaneous pieces, and his dramatic sense manifests itself also in his *Voyage*. This is a work which compares favourably with the better-known fictional accounts of industrial workers, and the second volume is particularly interesting. Ayton took a genuine interest in the Lancashire mechanics as people and not merely as social cases, and he had no marked political prejudice over and above such as were only to be expected among men of his class and upbringing. Ayton wrote at a time when the social conscience of the nation had not as yet been stirred, and his attitude is pleasantly unselfconscious when he reports on the habits and living conditions of the Lancashire workmen. He was in a position to draw on personal observation and not merely on material presented in government Blue Books in the manner of some social novelists; his account, therefore, may be considered as reliable, and it is of unusual interest since it describes exactly those aspects that were omitted by condition-of-England novelists in the decades that followed – to wit the social life of the workers.

Ayton's "manufacturers" are a sturdy and resistant race; they are never crushed by oppression despite their poverty and hard work. For this reason he helps us to understand the independent spirit of the English working class – the same class that in the next generation was to rise under Chartist leadership to fight for emancipation. Ayton's very real appreciation of this spirit of independence nevertheless could not prevent him from feeling that the spectacle of accumulated wealth was a good omen for the future. Thus he characterizes the port of Liverpool as "certainly the most noble and animated sight that we had seen during our tour, not only grand and picturesque, but possessing *a high moral interest*, as it brought before our minds the country in the pride of its industry and enterprise, and under the most striking signs of its wealth and power." (Vol. II, p. 80.) Ayton's description of the port, by the way, anticipates the one given by Elizabeth Gaskell in *Mary Barton* (1848).

Ayton had travelled in the poverty-stricken areas of Wales, so that he was pleasantly surprised to find on arriving in Lancashire that the villages were inhabited by people who seemed reasonably well provided for, and

enjoying many little comforts and luxuries that give grace to their domestic life . . . The cottages of the poorest class are well built, and invariably distinguished by extreme neatness and cleanliness. The people in their external appearance are equally well-conditioned, and bear about them the same comfortable signs of ease and competency.

(vol. II, pp. 120–1)

Ayton observed that factory workers were attracted to Blackpool as a holiday resort, where they would begin the day with "a draught of salt-water" washed down with gin and beer. The rest of the day would be spent on a beach "darkened with clusters of people full of motion and continually splashing in and out of water." Three or four days spent in this manner were supposed to be good for the health; a longer stay was out of the question for those who worked at the loom. Their holiday accommodation was extremely poor, but they seem to have thought nothing of "five or six beds [being] crammed into each room and five or six people into each bed". The beds were used in turn during the hours of the night, but sleep was anyway what these holiday-makers were least in need of. They enjoyed copious evening meals and indulged freely in liquid re-freshments and in singing and dancing. The women were "gaily attired", and the men enjoyed witty repartee; ale was served "till order was entirely confounded, and all was talking, and singing, and laughing, all together." Ayton adds that this entertainment was entirely new to him, and that he found it "more amusing than the ponderous decorum of higher company." Ayton shows his sym-pathy with his Blackpool companions when he fails to disapprove of their riotous recreation, praising it instead as a break from their sedentary occupation:

An occasional riot that does absolute violence to every part of the body, and turns the whole order of it topsy-turvy, may be of some service to persons leading sedentary lives; and certainly no more effectual plan of general disturbance can be conceived than the annual course of walking, drinking, dipping, and lodging, submitted to by these patient manu-facturers.

(vol. II, p. 103)

Ayton felt completely exhausted merely as a spectator. On other occasions, however, Ayton could write as a social superior. He notes, for example, that workers who earn a lot tend to become "saucy and arrogant". They are aware of the importance of the work they are doing "and take their reward as a matter of simple right; looking upon any expression of thanks as an unworthy sign of inferiority and dependance." Indeed, they are "quite satisfied with themselves, and not at all disposed to regard anyone as more than an equal." (Vol. II, p. 118.)

Ayton was not content merely to record; he tried to analyse the situation in terms of cause and effect:

The great manufacturing system is without doubt the first cause of all the distinctions that I have noticed; this collects people in crowds together, and putting more money into their pockets than is necessary to their support, furnishes them with the means and opportunities of dissipation . . . Much vice and profligacy necessarily prevail among them; but while their morals are corrupted, the powers of their minds are called forth, they become lawless and unprincipled, but quick, cunning and intelligent . . . By constant exercise of reasoning or quarrelling, or bantering among themselves they gain an unusual shrewdness and great readiness and volubility of expression.

(vol. II, p. 119)

But these people who spend their leisure and all their money in pubs or ale-houses cannot actually be blamed. It is sad "to see people of so much intelligence the slaves of such brutal profligacy", but "there can be no chance for them as long as their first step from the nursery is into the manufactory, and their education picked up there and at the alehouse." (Vol. II, p. 120.)

At the time of Ayton's tour the Corn Laws were still two years in the future, which means that the working class had not as yet begun to feel the disastrous effect of the rising price of wheat. The tour was conducted during a short interval of relative prosperity after the end of the blockade. The workers still believed that Parliament would see to it that they were given a 'living wage', the agitation for the Factory Act of 1815–19 had not yet begun, nor had the radical agitation which terminated in the Peterloo massacre. After these events a detached treatment of working-class conditions in the manner of Ayton was inconceivable. This increases the importance of an account whose intrinsic interest is considerable. It provides a useful perspective on the fictional or semi-fictional accounts of authors like Hannah More. The generation that was contemporary with Cobbett at the turn of the century came to witness the first stage in the most severe social crisis in modern English history – a crisis pregnant with the threat of revolution. It was no longer possible to pen poetic descriptions of industrial processes and inventions in the manner of John Dyer or Dr Darwin, nor could the process of industrialization be discussed in a prose marked by a dispassionate, let alone confident, tone of voice. The triumphant feeling of achievement was beginning to fade in the face of grave apprehensions concerning the many negative effects on the life of the nation. As we shall see in the chapter which follows, a doctrine of self-help was gradually evolved in an effort to meet the challenge of the Industrial Revolution.

Notes

1. Quoted from M.–S. Røstvig, *The Happy Man. Studies in the Metamorphoses of a Classical Theme*, vol. II; 1700–1760 (Oslo, 2nd edn 1971), 31f. [NB. Only places of publication outside London are given.]
2. For a discussion of this poetic tradition, see my essay on 'The Mechanical Muse: the Impact of Technical Inventions on Eighteenth-Century Neoclassical Poetry', *The Huntington Library Quarterly*, XXVIII (1965), 263–81.
3. For one recent account, see John Chalker, *The English Georgic* (1969).
4. *The Gentleman's Magazine*, XIII (1743), 491ff.
5. Thomson, *The Castle of Indolence*, II, xix.
6. See the works referred to in footnotes 1 and 3.
7. *Lives of the English Poets* (1783), IV, 321.
8. From 'The Life of John Dyer' in *The Poetical Works of Armstrong, Dyer and Green*, ed. George Gilfillan (Edinburgh, 1858), 113f.
9. Two anonymous poems illustrate the reaction: *The Loves of the Triangles* published in *The Anti-Jacobin* for 23 April and 7 May 1798, and *The Art of Candle Making* in *The European Magazine*, XLII (1802), 424.
10. 'A Journey to Nottingham in a Letter to a Friend', *The Gentleman's Magazine*, XIII (1743), 491f. (ll. 29–32).
11. William Goldwin, *A Description of the Ancient and Famous City of Bristol. A Poem* (1751).
12. *Life of Dr. Johnson* (Friday 22 March 1776).

13. [William Bray], *Sketch of a Tour into Derbyshire and Yorkshire* (1778), 57, 64.
14. *A Tour of the West of England* (1789), 539.
15. [Sir R. J. Sullivan], *Observations Made During a Tour through Parts of England, Scotland and Wales* (1780), 141f.
16. [Edward Clarke], *A Tour through the South of England, Wales and Parts of Ireland, Made during the Summer of 1791* (1793), 373f.
17. John Brand, *The History and Antiquities of the Town and County of Newcastle upon Tyne* (1789), vol. II, 685.
18. *An History of Birmingham* (Birmingham, 1795), *passim.*

Chapter 2

The Gospel of Self-Help

The ideal of self-help – that is, the belief that the fate of the individual is in his own hands – is as important for a proper understanding of the evolution of modern society as a knowledge of Christianity must be to the student of the Middle Ages. This ideal is the moral concomitant of the economic principle of *laissez-faire*, the two being closely connected and of equal importance to the new class of industrialists that gradually replaced the traditional moneyed class.

Although the *Oxford English Dictionary* traces the term self-help no further back than to the year 1831, the principle is, of course, much older. The Puritans of the seventeenth century and the pious Nonconformists of the eighteenth firmly believed that prosperity was a sign of divine approval and hence a sign of election to salvation. Daniel Defoe's *Robinson Crusoe* (1719) epitomizes the spirit of self-help; seldom has the creative activity of man been presented with greater imaginative appeal than in this story of the isolated individual who, in the face of heavy odds, nevertheless masters a hostile environment so that it becomes subservient to his needs. But this is made possible because the hero turns his heart to

God in his hour of dire need. The invigorating optimism of Defoe's narrative helps to explain its lasting popularity. The Victorian parable of self-help – Dinah Craik's *John Halifax, Gentleman* (1856) – may be an inferior performance when compared with Defoe's masterpiece, but the moral lesson is the same. By the time of Dinah Craik, however, the moral principle entailed had been consciously evolved in an effort to cope with the serious social problems of the time.

The years between the publication of these two novels witnessed the transformation of a largely agrarian society into an industrial one, but the social ethos remained unaffected by the change. Certain basic concepts retained their absolute validity, and none more so than the idea of private enterprise. The theory of political economy associated with Adam Smith was almost universally accepted, which meant that capitalism was recognized, tacitly or explicitly, as the only basis for a prosperous society. There were, of course, a few dissenting factions. Thus the obsolete ideal of neo-feudalism enjoyed a short-lived revival in the movement known as Young England, but its appeal was strictly limited. Another minority group that had too few members to constitute anything like a challenge to the existing orthodoxy consisted of a handful of writers with an anti-capitalist bias; among them were men like Robert Owen (*A New View of Society*, 1813) and William O'Brian. Since the new social philosophy based on the needs of the working classes was only beginning to be formulated, it was incapable of making itself felt, so that the entire nation was more or less convinced that there was no workable alternative to the capitalist system.

Although it was quite obvious that England did not represent the best of all possible worlds, the belief nevertheless prevailed that near-perfection could be achieved on the basis of a *laissez-faire* policy. Various shortcomings were only too apparent, but would-be social reformers were incapable of going beyond the generally accepted view of social economy. They argued, instead, that if the individual could achieve success by dint of hard work, then why not society as a whole? This line of thought prompted the public-spirited to engage in activities the purpose of which was to mend already existing social mechanisms, or to adjust them somewhat to the needs of the new age. And in the course of the process of adjustment the principle of improvement through self-help was transferred from the sphere of the individual to that of society as a whole.

Fully confident as they were of the efficacy of this principle, the middle classes never doubted that the evil aspects of their industrial society would ultimately be completely eliminated. This optimistic attitude explains the great fervour of the benevolent reformers who never tired of hammering home what they considered the vital lesson. Their concern for the welfare of the nation was undoubtedly prompted by class-interest – that is, self-interest – but it was also inspired by a sincere belief in a general progress that would benefit all levels of society. Alexander Pope had written that "God and Nature link'd the gen'ral frame / And bade Self-Love and Social be the same" (*An Essay on Man*, 1733–4), and succeeding generations applied a similar prescription for the cure of all social ills: a mixture of self-love, self-help, and social love. And the cure was partly effective. Evangelical reformers, ultra-conservative Tories, Utilitarians and others may have approached the condition-of-England problem from totally different points of view so that their interests were possibly at cross purposes, but their philanthropic and reformist efforts did in fact constitute an effective counter-attack on the worst evils of the existing social system. This capacity for improvement would appear to be inherent in the capitalist system itself. While the diverse capitalist interests are engaged in competition with each other, the principle of self-help would seem to operate within the social system *as a whole*. In other words, the self-help resources of a capitalist society can be seen to conduce to its own evolution in a favourable direction. The competitive system, however, eventually over-reaches itself by engendering anti-capitalist forces embodied in a militant working-class organization whose ultimate purpose is to reorganize society on another basis.

During the period of industrialization one may clearly observe the impact upon the working classes of the middle-class ideal of self-help. Two different reactions may be perceived: some workers were inspired to try to reach a higher social level, while others found that the principle provided a basis for their own class consciousness. The progressive optimism engendered by the tremendous energy released by the process of industrialization in its turn made the working classes feel a new confidence in their future importance, which explains why they came to adopt the self-help principle as part of a proletarian ideology. The trade unions, for example, came to employ as their slogans the very phrases associated with this principle – fortitude, perseverance, diligence. It was lifted to a higher moral level, however, by being associated with the collective interests of the working classes rather than with the necessarily selfish ambition of a single member. Also it was strongly argued by Chartist leaders dedicated to the cause of the proletariat that it should be possible to organize society without recourse to oppression and exploitation, a belief which grew ever stronger and more widely accepted with the passing of time.

Insofar as the principle of self-help can induce large-scale co-operation, it may be invoked even today when our very existence as a species is threatened by conflicting interests on a global scale. To resolve these supra-national conflicts mankind must rely on that collective self-help instinct which may help us to survive. And it seems to me that the instinct for preservation which is connected so closely with the principle of self-help is actually urging our generation towards solutions dimly perceived by the disinterested and public-spirited fighters for social justice in the age of Chartism. It is not at all unrealistic, therefore, to believe that a non-capitalist social organization will eventually prevail.

An anthropologist would no doubt classify the motive power of self-help as one of the positive human urges stimulating the individual to sustained effort of the kind that we have come to regard as the basis for all improvement in our human condition. But every good, when taken to excess, will produce evil, and during the period of the primary accumulation of capital, the principle of self-help was certainly taken to an extreme. During the reign of the Tudors and Stuarts economic progress was the consequence of the bitter struggle between free-traders and the monopoly of state-protected interests. This struggle, because of its ruthlessness, be-queathed to the subsequent capitalist competition a relentless spirit of brooking no compromise and tolerating no defeat. Later on in the eighteenth century the *laissez-faire* economists professed that as each man sought his own best interest, a 'natural law' would ensure that all members of society would achieve the state they desired. When combined with capitalist competition, this self-complaisant social philosophy resulted in a very crude application of the self-help principle from which the class that possessed no capital at all was bound to suffer most. If every man's duty is to be successful, and if he has no responsibility at all for his fellow men, it follows that he will crush the weak whose interests conflict with his own.

The man of business had no conception of social responsibility that might compel him to consider the welfare of those whom he employed. The issue of social responsibility was felt to have no connection with the conduct of one's personal affairs; it manifested itself instead in the zeal of the philanthropists and the reformers. This sharp distinction between a private and a public ethos allowed the middle classes to entertain an exaggerated notion of their own moral rectitude. With the greatest show of dignity and solemnity the profit-makers expended all their energy to carry on their business and to accumulate capital as if by so doing they were fulfilling their obligation to God and to society. To them the self-help principle was something of a gospel, but a gospel which made them close their ears to the grievances of the poor. Indeed, they would often use the Gospel as a weapon to be brandished against the socially dissatisfied, just as they rejected the complaints of the poor with the 'irrefutable' argument that poverty is the punishment for being lazy.

If a worker should protest that his life was nothing but dreary drudgery, few would try to persuade him otherwise. Life at the bottom of the social ladder was necessarily miserable, but the argument of the moneyed classes was simply that the road to the higher levels was open to all, and the worker was invited to join the ranks of the masters. This may be illustrated by a quotation from Elizabeth Gaskell's novel *North and South* (1855), in which a factory owner argues that it is "one of the greatest beauties of our system, that a working-man may raise himself into the power and position of a master by his own exertions and behaviour" (chap. X). This argument, however, is effectively refuted in the pages of Charles Kingsley's *Yeast* (1848), by a labourer who knows only too well that the gap between theory and practice cannot be bridged:

Men that write books and talk at elections call this a free country, and say that the poorest and meanest has a free opening to rise and become prime minister, if he can. But you see, Sir, the misfortune is that in practice he can't . . . Day-labourer born, day-labourer live, from hand to mouth, scraping and pinching to get not meat and beer even, but bread and potatoes; and at the end of it all, for a worthy reward, half-a-crown a week and a parish pay – or the workhouse.

(chap. XIV)

This was the kind of 'dialogue' which took place, on different occasions and not always peacefully, between the 'two nations', as Disraeli called them in his famous condition-of-England novel, *Sybil, or the two Nations* (1845).

Firmly convinced as they were that economic progress depended on personal effort, the capitalist class strove to impress their own views on the rest of the nation. As they saw it, progress was possible only on the basis of social inequality. The great physicist, Humphry Davy, referred to inequality as a source of power: "The unequal division of property and of labour, the difference of rank and condition amongst mankind, are the source of power in civilized life, its moving cause, and even its very soul." During the earlier phases of industrialization, however, the so-called lower orders could feel no concern for a "moving cause", let alone the "soul" of "civilized life". They were perforce limited to grumbling about social injustice and to trying to cope with their own day-to-day existence. The process of converting the working classes to a capitalist frame of mind was necessarily a slow one, but in the end it succeeded, and so the modern 'consumer society' was created. The traditional static view of the social hierarchy gradually yielded to a more dynamic concept based on the desire for change, and at the same time the spirit of private enterprise penetrated the ranks of the working classes so that these, too, became converted to the self-help ideal. This attitude became general at the time when the transformation from an agrarian to an industrial nation had been fully achieved. When the Chartists were defeated by the industrialists, a spirit of conciliation became dominant at the same time that the gradual adoption by the working classes of the principle of self-help turned this principle into a highly effective weapon against political radicals. The effectiveness of this weapon has suffered no diminution with the passing of time; it is almost as potent today as in the age of Queen Victoria.

1. The Reluctant Labourer

By the middle of the eighteenth century economic theorists were becoming concerned because factory hands were unwilling to meet the demand for sustained, hard labour. The new factories were badly in need of workers whose ceaseless efforts would ensure maximum production, but owners were faced instead by labourers who were extremely reluctant to work every day of the week. They preferred irregular but well-paid employment that would leave enough time for leisure and sufficient money for the ale-house. It was obviously desirable for industrialists as well as political economists that these habits should be changed.

This need for more man-power is registered in essays on economic issues, and occasionally in literature proper. John Dyer, for example, devoted a passage in *The Fleece* (1757) to a complaint that the slackness of the weavers reduced their output. The traders are defeated by the reluctance of the "giddy rout" of labourers to bend to their task: their own industry is defeated

> when cease
> The loom and shuttle in the troubled streets;
> Their motion stopp'd by wild intemperance,
> Toil's scoffing foe, who lures the giddy rout,
> To scorn their task-work, and to vagrant life
> Turns their rude steps; while misery, among
> The cries of infants, haunts their mouldering huts.
>
> (III, 227–33)

Some authors, however, were ready to excuse such behaviour, and one of them is Josiah Tucker, Rector of St Stephen's church in Bristol. He explains in his *Instruction for Travellers* (1757) that this is a consequence of the fact that they have no prospect of advancement:

The Motives of Industry, Frugality and Sobriety are all subverted by this one Consideration, *viz*. that they shall always be chained to the same Oar, and never be but Journeymen. Therefore their only Happiness is to get Drunk, and to make Life pass away with as little Thought as possible.

Some of Tucker's ideas seem to anticipate views that were to be advanced some 20 years later by Adam Smith in his *An Inquiry into the Nature and Causes of the Wealth of Nations* (1776). Tucker affirms, for example, that a man will contribute to the welfare of his community by pursuing his own ends, and he reveals a startlingly modern attitude to production and consumption when he writes that "Almost the whole body of the people of Great Britain may be considered either as Customers *to*, or Manufacturers *for*, each other." And Tucker realized the importance of machines even before the introduction of the steam-engine. Machines would provide more employment for more workers, and would "enable the

Generality of a People to become Purchasers of the Goods."
Tucker's publication, therefore, is one of the more interesting of
those that favour the doctrine of self-help.

Arthur Young, the economist, realized that the progress of
industrialization depended on the availability of man-power, and
he was disturbed by the fact that the workers were so unwilling to
provide what was needed. Young's account of his *A Six-Month
Tour through the North of England* (1771) comments on the fre-
quency with which complaints were voiced concerning the
"scarcity of hands". A Darlington manufacturer assured him that
he could provide employment for many more workers, but that it
was impossible to persuade "the idle part of the poor of the town"
to "turn industrious". Hence "numbers of hands capable of
working remain in total idleness." And in Kendal it was stated that
all workers could obtain constant employment if they so wished.

Before the technological inventions of the century had become
fully operative, the problem, therefore, was not unemployment but
rather how to attract more workers into the factories. Arthur
Young gave serious attention to this problem, and he was, of course,
pleased to observe the increasing interest taken in the principle of
self-help. He underlined (p. 175) the attraction of better pay,
recommending an increase to tempt the 'lazy' to become 'industrious':

Two shillings and sixpence a day will undoubtedly tempt some to work
who would not touch a tool for one shilling . . . In a word, idle people
are converted by degrees into industrious hands . . . Thus a new race
of the industrious is by degrees created, and its increase is proportioned
to its creation . . . Money will at any time make men.

Since Young constantly urged the workers to earn more money in
order to be able to buy more, he must be considered as one of the
founders of the modern consumer society.

The contrast between Arthur Young and a man like Jonas
Hanway is a contrast between a utilitarian and a philanthropist. It is
an interesting point that their conflicting philosophies nevertheless
permitted an identical attitude to the poor; both authors discuss the
poor as they might another species. Hanway was an indefatigable
champion of the 'needy', who dedicated his energy and his fortune
to the foundation of philanthropic institutions, yet he was incapable of realizing that poverty could be abolished. As he puts it

in his didactic book, *Virtue in Humble Life* (1774): "Misery there is and misery there will be, here and in all countries" (p. 199). This 900-page treatise consists of 209 conversations between a father and his daughter on a number of social and moral issues, and as one works one's way through this rather confusing material one realizes that Hanway did not recommend self-help as a universal remedy. Hanway was not familiar with the vigorous industrial enterprises of the North and the Midlands; his experience was limited to London, where there were few opportunities to climb from the bottom of the ladder to higher levels. This is clearly why Hanway did not try to stir the ambition of the poor beyond a certain minimum level of achievement; it must have seemed more realistic to recommend, as he did, such virtues as would serve to reconcile the poor and the miserable to their lot: devotion, fidelity, patience, obedience, humility, meekness. Hanway, in other words, tried to help the poor by teaching them to bear their poverty, and he seems to have struck a responsive chord. During the first six years no less than ten editions of his work were called for, some of them complete, some enlarged, and some abridged. And 60 years later, in 1835, parts of the book were published as separate tracts by the Society for the Diffusion of Christian Knowledge. At this time – just prior to the Chartist movement – Hanway's dialogues were eminently suited to serve as propaganda ensuring the continued passivity of the socially discontented. But this was no part of Hanway's purpose, just as he never favoured the theory of a beneficent self-interest. Instead he denounced what he called "a blind and partial self-interestedness" which, "for the love of a *paltry gain*", tempts so many "to do a thousand hurtful and ruinous things" (p. 273). This sentiment is anti-industrial and anti-self-help, and it recalls the Christian hostility to worldly riches, but since the author had acquired his own wealth by trade it is difficult to take his condemnation entirely seriously.

During the early phase in the history of industrialization only a small minority of the poor would be employed in factories. Those who addressed themselves to the poor as preachers or philanthropists would therefore be thinking of an undistinguished mass of poor people in town and country. Before the technological revolution effected by the introduction of steam-power the majority of the poor would have little or no opportunity to improve their condition, which is why the self-help slogan is seldom encountered before the age of James Watt. This is also why the preachers tried to reconcile the poor to their position in the manner of Hanway. Farm labourers formed perhaps the largest grouping among the destitute; the enclosure movement and the introduction of modern technology in agriculture caused a growing unemployment. The number of the unemployed finally became so large that little difference was felt when thousands of families migrated to industrial areas; the majority remained behind to plough the fields that did not belong to them. The squalor of their lives inspired little compassion; with the waning of interest in pastoral or rural themes even the poets turned their backs on the simple rustic. Among the honourable exceptions is Oliver Goldsmith, whose social sensibility prompted his poem on *The Deserted Village* (1770).[1] Goldsmith explains, in his dedicatory epistle to Sir Joshua Reynolds, that when he regrets the "depopulation of the country", he is attacking "the increase of our luxuries". And he adds that "so much has been poured out of late on the other side of the question, that, merely for the sake of novelty and variety, one would sometimes wish to be in the right." Goldsmith is unmoved by the spectacle of the flourishing state of English trade; instead he deplores the change that this trade had brought about and joins the classical poets in their denunciation of "the rage of gain". A nation, "Though very poor, may still be very blest" if possessed of "native strength", while "trade's proud empire hastes to swift decay" (11.424–7). And when George Crabbe wrote about the poverty-ridden peasantry in *The Village* (1783) his sympathy is patently sincere. The spectacle of wealth increases the misery of the poor:

> When plenty smiles – alas! she smiles for few –
> And those who taste not, yet behold her store,
> Are as the slaves that dig the golden ore –
> The wealth around them makes them doubly poor.
>
> (11.136–9)

Like Goldsmith and Crabbe, William Cowper, too, was hostile to that enthusiasm for profit-making which is so typical of the middle classes. Cowper did not mince his words when, in the course of *The Task* (1785), he considers the spectacle of "charter'd boroughs" and their "burghers". These wealthy men may be "unimpeachable of sin / Against the charities of domestic life", but, "once combin'd" or "incorporated", they become "hurtful to the main". Disclaiming "all regard / For mercy and the common rights of man", they "Build factories with blood", "dyeing the white robe / Of innocent commercial justice red" (IV, 679–83).

But this indignant condemnation is a relatively rare phenomenon. The minor poets hailing from the lower classes felt no urge to dwell honestly on themes fetched from their own sphere of life. This is true of would-be poets like William Newton, Stephen Duck, Anne Yearsley, and even of John Clare, all of whom courted acceptance by their social superiors. It was fashionable for some time to discover poetic genius among the poor, and it is not surprising that some of them tried to attract notice by composing poems. The professional critics, however, seldom failed to expose the poverty of the verse written to solicit patronage. As one reviewer put it, "Certain journey-men . . . presumed to make rhymes and discharge them upon the public" (*The Monthly Review*, 1778).

Apart from a few honourable exceptions, therefore, the muses were silent spectators of the misery of the poor.

2. Divine Aid

Illiteracy may have been widespread, but it was not general. Young villagers could learn to read in Sunday school, where philanthropic teachers encouraged them to read edifying tracts as well as the Bible. The tracts were usually given to the pupils, many of whom took them home to be read by the parents as well. For this reason the writing of tracts for simple readers became a worthy task for clergymen and pious ladies and gentlemen who usually took the opportunity to stress the necessity of subordination. Today it seems somewhat callous that the farm labourer should be promised, in return for faithful service, a reward after death only. The premiss leading to this conclusion is found in the sentiment that everything on earth is "sordid and vile" and "unworthy of our care and affection" compared to Heaven and its happiness. Hence it does not matter "in what rank or garb we pass our few days here". "What is any loss, any disappointment in this world to us who have the hope of being partakers of the perfect and endless joys of eternity?"[2] All addresses to the working class should endeavour to "prompt the love of God in every Heart" to use a phrase coined by Hanway in his *Manual of Devotion* (appended to his *Virtue in Humble Life*), a work designed "for the *meek* and *upright*".

The Christian message is complex and capable of many interpretations; but it is significant to discover that those who addressed the poor in the name of Christ gave expression only to such doctrines as were likely to induce a state of mind that they considered beneficial. We find no mention of the supposed equality of men or of the perils of wealth: instead the authority of God is cited to refute the claims of the weak and poor. If there is inequality, this is the will of God, and man's first duty is to respect the station where he has been placed by God.

But the story of the collaboration between the church and the ruling classes with a view to preserving the existing social order is too well known to require more than a brief mention. Of greater interest to my present argument is the connection between free-trade and Christianity and the problem posited by the attempt to reconcile the principle of self-help with Christianity. One might easily think that the two would be incompatible, but this is not so, as we see from the history of the Puritans, on both sides of the Atlantic. As already stated, the dissenters tended to consider worldly prosperity as a sign of divine favour and a proof of election to grace, and the Bible provided many a text capable of yielding moral lessons in support of this view. Thus everyone has been commanded by Christ to labour in the vineyard and to use the talents entrusted to him; to spend one's life in indolence was a sin against God who favoured the diligent. Long before the Industrial Revolution got under way, generations of preachers had conditioned their poor parishioners to accept, without questioning, the socio-religious moral code of a nascent capitalistic system.

A notice to the effect that a hundred copies would cost only four guineas "to such as give them away to journeymen Weavers" adorns the title-page of Benjamin Fawcett's tract *The Religious Weaver, or Pious Meditations on the Trade of Weaving* (1773). This dissenting minister advised the weavers to rely entirely on their own efforts; a weaver "may begin with a very little stock" and yet prove successful "with some good degree of application and ingenuity". He notes, optimistically, that it is "commonly observed, that those who begin with the least stock in trade, generally raise the best estates", while conversely "If the mind is not urged by necessity, it usually abates of its natural vigour". Next to the blessing of the Almighty, the poor weaver must put his trust in his own "industry, discretion and frugality", just as "It will much contribute to his success if he has in some measure an inventive and pushing genius". His condemnation of the idle is as absolute as it is solemn: 'The idle person is the only one for whom a bountiful God has made no provision" (pp. 100–10 *passim*).

Fawcett was writing for hand-loom weavers who had been organized for centuries, but his attempt to dissuade them from combining is marked by a spirit of patient tolerance; he even advises the masters to try to understand their journeymen. These friendly admonitions contrast very strongly with the furious invectives so typical of later generations of hostile pamphleteers.

The attempt to indoctrinate the industrial proletariat commenced with the factory children the moment that they began to attend Sunday school. However, to the author of an article in *The Gentleman's Magazine* for 1797 education itself was suspect. His "modest proposal" is quite simply that some kinds of labour are so mean and servile that they can be performed only by workers whose minds are soothed by the balm of ignorance, and for this reason society must see to it that such workers remain ignorant. Then, too, this ignorance will make them impervious to "the pernicious doctrines of seditious writers". The argument is so callous and yet so logical that it recalls Swift's *A Modest Proposal*:

The laborious occupations of life must be performed by those who have been born in the lowest station; but no one will be willing to undertake the most servile employment, or the meanest drudgery if his mind is opened, and his abilities increased by any tolerable share of scholastic improvement . . . The man whose mind is not illuminated by any ray of science, can discharge his duty in the most sordid employment without the smallest views of raising himself to a higher station . . . His ignorance is a balm that soothes his mind into stupidity and repose, and excludes every emotion to discontent, pride and ambition . . . While those who are qualified by a tincture of superficial learning and have imbibed the pernicious doctrines of seditious writers, will be the first to excite rebellions, and convert a kingdom into a state of anarchy and confusion.

(*The Gentleman's Magazine*, Oct. 1797, 819f.)

One imagines that sentiments like these could be entertained by some, but why publish them abroad? How could such appalling frankness fail to provoke a reaction among those condemned to ignorance for the most selfish of reasons ? But little or no risk was actually entailed. A quality periodical like *The Gentleman's Magazine* was accessible only to the upper classes. To common wage-earners the price would be prohibitive and few of them would have the leisure time for reading. The half-literate members of the lower classes had perforce to remain content with cheap trash issued by enterprising publishers intent on exploiting a market whose large numbers more than made up for the fact that each could afford only a penny or two. In this manner a new kind of 'popular' literature was created, consisting largely of almanacs and chapbooks that provided unpretentious amusement or sensational accounts of crime and violence. Their triteness and vulgarity apparently caused little concern, since no one took the trouble to improve the quality of these publications. But a keen interest in the reading habits of the masses manifested itself the moment that more liberal and radical ideas began to be entertained. Such ideas can be traced back to the period before the French Revolution; the Spitalfields riots of the silk-weavers in 1768 reveal the latent social discontent that was to be more clearly revealed after 1789 with the spread of egalitarian and atheistic ideas from France to England. Thomas Paine's revolutionary pamphlet on *The Rights of Man* (1791-2) gained a wide circulation; mild as it may seem to modern readers, it nevertheless provoked alarm at the time of its appearance. Paine's ideas were also presented in popular and simplified versions for the less well educated: imitators hurried to emulate him, enemies to refute him. A tract published in 1792 before the proclamation of the French republic has the suggestive title *A Word in Season to the Traders and Manufacturers of Great Britain*, and an equally suggestive origin, since it was printed "at the expense of the Society for Preserving Liberty and Property against Republicans and Levellers". The author tries to persuade his readers that their constitution is a glorious one, and that the English are "the most prosperous people in the world". As was only to be expected, the threat of a possible revolution at home compelled the privileged members of society to take an interest in the state of mind of their inferiors. The wave of philanthropic fervour which animated the Evangelicals and other humanitarians resulted in the creation of a joint project for the dissemination among the poor of such reading matter as would unobtrusively teach them the virtues of piety, subordination and contentment. Other philanthropists would undertake a similar task on their own; to counteract what they considered as 'pernicious tendencies', they would invent short stories or sketches designed to convey to the reader the desired moral lesson. These publications constitute the first phase in the history of the exploitation of fiction for propaganda purposes, and throughout this phase the connection with religious sermons is obvious. The new kind of fiction written for the masses was religious in form and conservative in spirit. During the ninteenth century this kind of fictionalized propaganda experienced a tremendous increase in scope and popularity, its staple argument being that the capitalistic system offers equal opportunities to all if they are sufficiently pious and self-reliant.

The first true specimens of fictionalized propaganda were created by Hannah More, not because she was the first to turn fiction to this use, but because she was the one who truly popularized the genre, if genre it may be called. Before the days of Hannah More the Society for the Promotion of Christian Knowledge had engaged in continuous, but rather slack, editorial activities of a similar kind, nor must one forget the Wesleyan tracts of her contemporary Sarah Trimmer. Sarah Trimmer's purpose is made explicit in the title and subtitle of the periodical that she edited: *The Family Magazine, or the Repository of Religious Instruction and Rational Amusement* to counteract the pernicious tendency of immoral books which have circulated of late years among the inferior classes of people (1788-9). The didactic short stories printed in this magazine over a number of years were published in a collected edition in 1810 with the title *Instructive Tales*. Two sentences may be quoted to illustrate the moral lessons: "Prosperity is usually one of the worst enemies men have to encounter", and "There is no life preferable to a happy death."

To make this new genre truly popular, more was obviously required than sentiments of this kind, and it was Hannah More who provided what was needed. The "Old Bishop in petticoats", as William Cobbett called her, thoroughly understood the business side of her venture; she provided and organized funds, authorial collaborators, publishers and distributors. Even so it is surprising that her large-scale publishing enterprise dating from 1795 – *The Cheap Repository Tracts* – should have reached the fabulous circulation of over two million copies by March 1796.[3] Part of the secret of this first example of a publication 'explosion' is found in Hannah More's literary acumen. The tales in prose and verse which filled the pages of her tracts, copied the form and even the appearance of the broadsides, chapbooks, and flyers so far produced for the entertainment of the lower classes. They were printed on coarse paper and illustrated with plain woodcuts. Her tales of humble people were told with sufficient artistry to catch the attention of readers and thus to secure a positive reception for whatever doctrine they might convey. Hannah More's social philosophy boils down to the simple formula that one should fear God and the king, but, practical as ever, she also taught her readers how to get on in life by putting the principle of self-help into practice. A more detailed account of Hannah More's work is offered in the chapter devoted to her.

Hannah More's philanthropic work was largely carried out during the decades that succeeded the French Revolution. This disintegration of an existing social structure induced public-spirited men and women to take some kind of action to prevent the spread of revolutionary ideas across the English Channel. It was, of course, the traditional role of the clergy to feel responsible for the morals of their parishioners, and the sermons published at this time again and again hammer home the importance of being *content*. A sermon by the Rev. John Liddon of Hertfordshire from 1792 may be quoted by way of illustration. Liddon consciously and explicitly extends the message of the Gospels to apply to society as a whole; the Gospels abound with precepts "which enjoin diligence, obedience, and contentment", but "this contentment and subordination" should not be taken to be "confined to private families". They must "extend themselves to society at large". Christianity is typically seen as the best safeguard against the demolition of the class-structure, since "Christian knowledge has a tendency to establish the peace of society by teaching each individual to fill up the place which Providence has assigned him." The sermon concludes with the argument that religious principles will ensure prosperity by begetting "habits of virtue" such as frugality and industry: "Temperance which religion inculcates, enables the frugal to save what in time accumulates, and raises them to superior stations. Hence it is that there are so many opulent persons professing Godliness who have risen from very small and unpromising beginnings." (p. 11.)

The socio-religious doctrines presented in William Paley's treatise *Reasons for Contentment* (1792) gained considerable popularity; the pamphlet became something of a best-seller, but modern readers are bound to be shocked by its obvious class hypocrisy.[4] Further examples can be cited to indicate the general trend. The title of the following sermon written by the Rev. Thomas Biddulph of Bristol is self-explanatory: *Seasonable Hints for the Poor on the Duties of Frugality, Piety and Loyalty* (1797). Direct advice to "shun the company of the reformers" is given by William McGill of Ayr in his sermon *On the Fear of God and the King* (1795), at the same time that he condemns to eternal damnation all those who resist what he calls "the ordinance of God".

The clergymen referred to here are typical examples of the trend to use the pulpit to stem the tide of liberal ideas. The social doctrines embedded in sermons like these can be found in works of fiction as well, and more or less travestied in popular tracts, dialogues or sketches. Edifying stories for the poor were invented solely with a view to presenting the same moral and political lessons. This in itself was nothing new; the parables of Christ served a similar purpose, and many of the events narrated in the Old Testament had been repeatedly glossed by exegetes so as to convey moral and political doctrines. The Bible, therefore, as expounded by the theologians, must have encouraged many writers of religious works to use fictional devices for the purpose of persuasion. This is undoubtedly why the traditional hostility of the pious against literature did not extend to this kind of fiction; it was felt to have Biblical sanction.

It is an interesting point that even those who did not subscribe to pious sentiments on their own behalf nevertheless felt obliged to support the arguments advanced in the works considered here. Arthur Young, the economist, for example advocated the building of churches in densely populated industrial areas. Young's anti-Jacobin sentiments pervade his *An Enquiry into the State of the Public Mind among the Lower Classes in a Letter to W. Wilberforce* (1798); thus those who sympathized with the French revolutionaries are characterized as "the Frenchified disciples of Satan". More churches and highly qualified preachers therefore are required so that the poor may "learn the doctrine of that truly excellent religion which exhorts to content, and to submission to the higher powers." (p. 19.)

While the religious tone in publications of this sort remained essentially the same in the nineteenth century, the sugar-coating of the social message became somewhat more sophisticated. As a genre the sermon became more completely integrated with fiction in order to promote politically conservative points of view. Theology, one might say, became the handmaiden of politics through this affiliation. A new element can nevertheless be perceived which marks the nineteenth century in contrast to the late eighteenth century. An unexpected fusion occurred between two kinds of sermon: the one written for evangelical purposes, and the strictly utilitarian sermon. The paradoxical alliance between Christian and economic doctrines is one of the strange Victorian 'muddles'. As we see from Robert Owen's autobiography, social respectability was identical with, and dependent on, religious professions and practices. When he writes that the profession of religion and the attention to religious forms and ceremonies "were the foundation on which Scotch character and society were formed", this applies with equal justness to England and the English.[5] This belief was so ingrained that even Harriet Martineau – the champion of utilitarianism and an avowed atheist – had nothing but praise for the respectable working-class woman who on Sundays would take her children to church dressed in their best clothes.[6]

It is less well known, perhaps, that Elizabeth Gaskell, too, contributed her share to the promotion of the gospel of self-help. This is somewhat unexpected, since her social novels *Mary Barton* (1848) and *North and South* (1855) may be said to attack the complaisance engendered by it. Nevertheless her short story 'Hand and Heart' – written shortly after *Mary Barton* and before *North and South* – reads almost like one of Hannah More's tracts. Its principal characters are a poor widow and her eight-year old son. The son is taught to despise luxury – that is, to refrain from tea, sugar, and his Sunday meat – and when the mother dies and he is adopted by a family, he exerts a powerful, religious influence on its members. In another of her stories Mrs Gaskell preaches subordination and submission to providence: "And never you neglect the work clearly laid for you by either God or man . . . God knows what you are most fit for" ('Bessy's Troubles at Home', 1852). In these stories Mrs Gaskell comes very close to the spirit of Miss More's *Cheap Repository Tracts*. Both of these women authors addressed the lower classes as they might children and they were in complete agreement on what was good for them. They urged the young members of the working class to adopt the principle of self-help as their life philosophy, and at the same time they taught them to be humble. It is clear that the half century which separates Miss More from Mrs Gaskell brought but little change in the fictionalized didacticism intended for the 'lower classes'.

Similarly, Samuel Smiles, author of the famous book on *Self-Help* (1859), unhesitatingly subscribed to the traditional social philosophy despite the fact that he was a social reformer. He calls it "the ordinance of God" that "there should be a class of men who live by their daily labour", adding that it is doubtless "a wise and righteous one". One must not attribute to Providence, however, the fact that this class "should be otherwise than frugal, contented, intelligent, and happy," since this "springs solely from the weakness, self-indulgence, and perverseness of man himself" (pp. 218–26).

The thesis so forcibly expressed by Samuel Smiles – that Heaven helps those who help themselves – could appropriately be used as a heading characterizing the content of the didactic literature produced during the nineteenth century. The poor were at the receiving end of a veritable shower of tracts impressing upon them various socio-religious doctrines often conveyed through short stories. The publication figures are truly staggering, but this does not necessarily mean that the tracts were popular, nor can we assess the extent to which the indigent were actually converted to the principle of self-help. Certainly the more intelligent members of the working classes must have resented the patronizing and condescending attitude and the all too obvious motive prompting the authors of these tracts. Then, too, the trite little stories were so utterly devoid of imaginative appeal that it is hard to believe that they would have been appreciated as stories. This absence of imaginative power is understood when we recall that the evangelical authors would have nothing to do with literature proper; their concern was with the moral and religious welfare of the poor.

3. The Villager

As the Industrial Revolution gained momentum, purely religious propaganda embodied in popular fiction became increasingly ineffective for the simple reason that the religious sensibility of the poor was blunted as a consequence of the changes that were taking place. The application of steam-power to industry accelerated the process of change within the social structure, at the same time that the so-called poor no longer constituted an undistinguished mass of dumb sufferers driven in one moment by despair to occasional rioting, only to subside in the next into listless resignation. One begins to perceive various clearly defined groups; the industrial workers were becoming increasingly class-conscious, while the rural population lagged behind with regard to political activity as well as class-consciousness. For this reason the propagandist fiction addressed to industrial workers would carry a different message from what was found suitable for farm labourers. The distinction is felt most strongly whenever the principle of self-help is advocated, but it goes without saying that the attitude to the working class in general would be identical, and so would the religious message conveyed, if any.

The nineteenth-century didactic tale designed for the rural population recommends the spirit of self-help either in a much diluted form, or not at all. There would be no point in recommending industry and thrift to farm labourers subsisting on poor relief. For them the prospect of rising from the bottom of the social ladder was virtually non-existent; no farm hand could possibly hope to rise to the status of the landed gentry through his employment. Then, too, the assistance extended to the poor tended to keep them idle; their inadequate wages were supplemented by money taken from the poor rates.[7] To the extent that the legal system tried to safeguard the landed interest, it tended to oppress the farm labourers, as is seen for example in the case of the Enclosure Acts which deprived them of the use of the common.[8] And the Speenhamland Act of 1795 provided farm labourers with a dole rather than a living wage, while the Corn Law of 1815 contributed its quota of misery for the poor by keeping up the price of bread. The Game Laws forbade the farm-hand to help himself to a meal from the wild birds and animals that surrounded him, or from the fish in pond or river. The Poor Law, moreover, provided relief only for persons born in the parish, which effectively prevented migration to places where employment might be found. Hedged around as he was by all these restrictions, the indigent rural labourer experienced a rapid process of deterioration and increasing degradation; it was virtually impossible for him to rely on his own efforts. This helps to explain why he could be described as no better than a kind of animal, as we see from one of the first novels concerned with the social condition of villages, G. R. Gleig's *The Chronicles of Waldham* (1835). One of the characters in this novel speaks contemptuously of the day-labourer's inability to make, or even wish to make, "large strides upwards in the scale of humanity". He hates innovations and is content to "do in all things what his father did before him". "The young agriculturist is, for the most part, half a savage – one whose very movements resemble those of the overgrown beast whom he drives or leads." (p. 409.) These words are spoken in anger after the failure of a scheme to relieve the poor by giving them allotments of land. Such allotment schemes were very popular at the time; in 1816 Jane Marcet recommended that all benevolent landowners allot small vegetable gardens to their labourers, a scheme that may be characterized as a diluted version of the self-help principle.[9] Mrs Marcet argues that the hours that otherwise might have been spent in the ale-house should be used to raise "an additional stock of wholesome food", and the money saved "may form perhaps the beginning of a capital, and in process of time secure a little independence for himself and his family." Similar sentiments are expressed by Charlotte Elizabeth Tonna (*The Perils of the Nation*, 1843), when she states that "the poor, helpless, hopeless day-labourer, just subsisting on seven shillings per week" would become "at once sober, frugal, and most industrious" if given "half an acre of land, at a moderate rent". And another condition-of-England novelist, Fanny Mayne (*Jane Rutherford or the Miner's Strike*, 1854), hopefully maintains that "the true rights of property" will remain inviolate if the rural labourer, although he might continue as such on a weekly wage, by means of "strength of mind, forethought, and self-denial" could become proprietor of a freehold (p. 225). Support for the allotment system can be found even among the ranks of the Chartists; the more moderate group at the centre of the movement, headed by O'Connor, rejected Socialism, advocating instead a kind of independence for the individual achieved through a modified version of the allotment project.

But the didactic writers suggested further remedies based on a combination of philanthropic assistance and the exertions of the individual labourer. In so doing they drew a sharp line of division between the 'deserving' and the 'undeserving' poor. Because relief could be provided only by charitable institutions or benevolent masters, the indigent labourer had perforce to distinguish himself by displaying those virtues that the givers of alms recommended. This was his only chance of attracting attention to himself so as to be singled out from among the mass of his fellow-sufferers. A poor person who appeared self-reliant and religious would be more likely to soften the heart of donors. This kind of situation was fictionalized again and again, and nowhere, perhaps, more typically than in Hannah More's tract 'The Shepherd of Salisbury Plain', the sterotyped pattern being that of the philanthropist who appears suddenly, like a *deus ex machina*, to rescue worthy sufferers. Various versions of this fixed situation are found in the pages of those innumerable Victorian novels where the lady of the manor is portrayed as visiting the homes of the village poor.

The extent of this philanthropic activity should not be minimized. Large numbers were involved, as we see from the fact that a special periodical was published for the benefit of those who operated in the countryside: *Cottagers' Monthly Visitor* (1821–56). Periodicals of a similar kind often contained both practical instruction for the would-be philanthropist and didactic fiction designed to be handed out to the village poor. Some of them, however, contained no fiction at all. A complete list of these periodicals would be a very long one, and so it is sufficient to mention just a few: *Family Prize Magazine* (1854), *The Half-Penny Library* (1832), *The Labourer's Friend* (1834–84), *The Labourer's Friend* (1844–5), *The Labourer* (1847–8), *The British Farmer's Magazine* (1826–74), *The Farmer's Magazine* (1832–3), *The Cottage Magazine* (1812–47), and yet another *Cottage Magazine* (1832–3).

Cottagers' Monthly Visitor, which appeared without a break for more than 30 years, may serve as an example. Each number, which cost sixpence, would be filled with articles on topical subjects and amateurish literary efforts in the form of letters, dialogues, sketches, and so forth. 'The Account of Thomas Simpson' is entirely typical of the genre. This sketch relates the story of a village lad whose behaviour was so exemplary that his master employed him as a groom. Tom's virtues are such as are suited to his station – he is humble, industrious and pious – and he marries a girl possessed of similar perfections. They produce a large family and lead lives as happy as they are unblemished. By way of contrast is presented the picture of another groom in the same stable who differs from Tom in every respect, and so, of course, "everything went wrong with him". This black-and-white picture dramatizes the over-simplified account of virtue and vice as conducive to happiness or misery in this life.

The 'undeserving' cottager was by definition dissatisfied with the place assigned to him by divine Providence for his own good, nor did he work hard and respect his master. His attitude to the church would be a negative one, and he was always ready to listen to seditious agitators. So far from trying to become a 'respectable' villager, he preferred, instead, to rebel against his betters and to violate the laws of the realm. 'A True Story' (*The Cottage Magazine*, 1843) develops its plot along these lines. A London shoemaker who entertains socialistic ideas settles in a village; because he has some education and a command of speech far superior to those around him, he soon succeeds in spreading the poison of sedition among his new neighbours. Contaminated by his Satanic doctrines, an honest young man, John Pert, resorts to drink to pacify his conscience for having given up his practice of praying. But one day on returning from the ale-house late at night, he sees his own little daughter kneeling in pious prayer to redeem her erring father. This touches him to the heart so that he is instantly reformed and scorns the company of the shoemaker who had led him to abandon his God. A less naive plot is developed in a story from 1835, 'The Mospits', by S. Hall. A rebellious villain persuades his law-abiding friend to set fire to the barns of his master, and as a consequence of this deed the latter is sentenced to death. In another story, 'The Incendiary' by G.E.S. (*Bradshaw's Manchester Journal*, 1842), we find a detailed description of the effect of the Corn Laws on the condition of farm labourers. Because the attack on the landowners in this Manchester journal was aimed at educated readers, the social criticism contained in 'The Incendiary' must have been beyond the reach of simple cottagers. The editor opposed the landed interest and wished to expose the vicious practices of the landlords, while the landlords on their side were equally loud in their denunciation of the factory system. Each party tried to promote their own interests by attacking the other side.

The four stories summarized here indicate quite clearly that little or no attention was paid to the problem of how to improve the social position of these labourers. As already stated, it would have served no purpose to urge farm labourers to exert themselves; instead they were persistently encouraged to be contented and pious. The propaganda effort was intensified during the Chartist riots of the 1830s and 1840s, when the upper and middle classes alike feared lest agricultural workers should join forces with factory hands to initiate a social revolution. Of the two, the latter constituted the gravest threat to the safety of the existing social order.

4. The Industrial Proletarian

As R. H. Horne reminded his readers in his novel *The Dreamer and the Worker* (serialized in 1847), the working classes "are rapidly rising, and more particularly the mechanic and artisan class who are, comparatively, the most advanced of any other class in the world."[10] Such a class quite obviously could not be talked into subordination by tract-distributing ladies; more sophisticated measures were required to cope with intelligent men who put questions to which they expected plausible answers. And among the industrial workers the number of such men was steadily growing. This explains the striking difference in quality between publications designed for villagers and those addressed to factory workers. While the agricultural labourer could entertain no hopes for the future, those who were employed in factories formed a dynamic and mobile class whose intelligence was favourably affected by contacts with fellow-workers. The political awareness of factory workers is touched on by W. M. Thackeray in *The Newcomes* (1854-5) in an authorial comment on a discussion between a banker and an industrial worker. The factory worker is said to have "a good cause" and to be "a far better master of debate than our banking friend, being a great speaker among his brother operatives, by whom political questions are discussed, and the conduct of political men examined with a ceaseless interest and an ardour and eloquence which are often unknown in what is called superior society." (chap. LXIX.) Although one must make some allowance for Thackeray's desire to be satirical at the expense of "superior society", his praise of the political activities of factory workers undoubtedly has a factual basis.

Despite the fact that the industrial proletariat was an indispensable part of an industrialized society, the members of this class had to live under conditions that made a civilized existence hardly possible. As long as the principle of *laissez-faire* was universally accepted, no pressure was exerted to bring into harmony the interests of capitalists and those of the workers. The men and women who worked in factories and mines had no influence at all on their own living and working conditions, and, as we know, even children were cruelly exploited during several decades. Low wages, expensive food, bad housing, poor education and other disadvantages inherent in their mode of living gradually engendered a growing feeling of discontent, and under the pressure of their miserable condition the workers gradually acquired a consciousness of constituting a separate class with distinct interests. During its initial stage the attempted organization of labourers had a predominantly economic programme; what the trade unions did was to negotiate for better working conditions. After the suspension of the Habeas Corpus Act of 1794 the trade unions were driven underground as illegal organizations. The discontent which smouldered below the surface erupted into violence in the Luddite riots after the end of the Napoleonic Wars, while the riots provoked by the Corn Bill of 1815 involved various ranks among the poor and not just factory-workers. At the same time that these disturbances occurred, radical politicians campaigned for a reform of Parliament, and the left wing of this radical movement consisted of working-class members who aspired to some measure of political representation in the House of Commons. But the first Whig government after 1832 effectively barred all such aspirations so that the political activity of the industrial proletariat once more was channelled in the direction of the programme of the trade unions. The Grand National Consolidated Trades Union founded by Robert Owen in 1833 counted roughly half a million members, so that its strength was impressive. Owen's programme, however, was hopelessly utopian; he wanted socialism at once and without the use of violence. Such a programme had to fail, but the effort was not entirely futile; it helped to disseminate sceptical assessments of the capitalist system as basically inefficient, and the radical view that a class struggle was inevitable.

By the end of the 1830s Britain was again agitated by nationwide unrest, and this time through the Chartist movement. Although it failed to implement its six-point programme, this movement effected something of a revolution in the social consciousness of the nation; the privileged classes began to feel differently about labour. It is largely due to the work of the Chartists that labour was given a place of honour as a creative factor – a truly revolutionary development in view of the contemptuous attitude to manual work which had prevailed so far. It is also largely due to the Chartists that the industrial proletariat gained a new importance by showing the potential power of large numbers when united in an organization, and that the theory of identical class interests was shown up as false.

Faced by tendencies at once so powerful and so extreme, the middle-class writer was appalled and at a complete loss how to encounter working-class complaints. As the antagonism between the classes increased in strength, the novelist was confronted by the awkward dilemma: should he try to justify the social system under which he lived, or rather censure it for its obvious failures? It was only to be expected that the majority simply ignored the issue, thus refusing to meet the challenge of their environment. A considerable number nevertheless sided with the social critics by exposing the abuses of the factory system, and these are commonly referred to as the condition-of-England novelists. Not only did these novelists fail to take an interest in the principle of self-help, they often denounced it as spurious. Those who still defended this principle also defended the theory of *laissez-faire* and the capitalist system. A worker, so they thought, who relied on his own efforts alone would scarcely feel inclined to join strikers, and he would also approve of the profit motive subscribed to by the middle classes, while at the same time he would accept the doctrine of identical class interests. A capitalist society needed such men; it could use enterprising individuals to organize further industrial developments. From the point of view of the latter, it would be a very bad thing indeed if the workers were controlled by anti-capitalist influences. Their satisfaction must have been great when the majority of the English workers ultimately abandoned Owen's dream of a socialistic society and instead became converted to the ideal of private enterprise. As a consequence the trade unions were content, throughout the second half of the nineteenth century, to pursue very modest aims which they gradually achieved. Many causes combined to make the working-class organizations abandon the revolutionary programme of the 'hungry forties', but one thing is certain: the mass media of the day – the pulpit and the cheap press – played no small part in the process.

Let us therefore consider the role of the cheap press. Writers had to bear in mind that as reading could not be an important activity in the life of a working man, since no worker could afford to buy books or current periodicals, the cheap press necessarily became the most appropriate vehicle for literary material aimed at the working classes. And so conservatives and liberals alike had to turn to the cheap press to enlist the support of the popular reader. A quotation from the *Family Prize Magazine* (1854) illustrates one of the basic arguments. Being industrious "leads to independence and enjoyment"; as soon as the workers "begin to accumulate, they feel an interest in the right of property, and an attachment to those institutions under which they live and flourish." Suitable fables were invented to dramatize this philosophy, much in the manner of the early morality plays where allegorical characters conveyed specific lessons. In the "morality plays" based on factory life, Everyman is tempted by Laziness, Intemperance, Discontent and Sedition, and his true friends are Industry, Frugality, and Thrift. The description of the class struggle follows a familiar set pattern: those who strike are invariably workers who refuse to be thrifty and industrious, preferring to better themselves by extorting higher salaries from their masters. Loyal workers are industrious and thrifty, they always save against a rainy day and expect no rise in wages. And during strikes these loyal workers carefully protect the property of their master. When the strike is over, every one is rewarded according to merit – the strikers lose their jobs and their leaders are sent to trial in a court of law, whereas the model workers obtain a rise in wages. An additional message can be found in the tales invented by evangelical authors: the working-class reader must pray to God and read his Bible besides being industrious. He must not take to drink nor must he indulge in frivolous pleasures and entertainments, and he must take great care to avoid men who profess revolutionary principles. Whoever follows these counsels of perfection will be rewarded by a pleasant sensation of self-righteousness permitting him to look down on everybody else. Readers of Hannah More's tracts from the late eighteenth century will remember these set situations and sentiments only too well, but what is new is the tremendous proliferation of this type of didactic fiction.

The modern reader is bound to feel repelled by the overt class partiality of this literature and may therefore be inclined to dismiss it all as too artificially contrived to be worthy of notice. One cannot deny that the stories were indeed contrived, but on the basis, one presumes, of examples from real life. Charlotte Brontë, for example, could rely on the experience of her father when she wrote *Shirley* (1849), as he had been very active on the side of the authorities during the Luddite riots. Then, too, she had some knowledge of working-class people in Haworth itself. But Charlotte Brontë was prompted by no didactic purpose; she had not witnessed the Luddite riots, but she had travelled around the country and had met the sons of the rioters. *Shirley* presents a faithful picture of the social situation. It shows, for example, that the age was so saturated by religious sentiments that a certain socio-religious pattern had to be established if the different social classes were to co-exist with reasonable amity. Between the destitute weavers and their employers the clergy must serve as mediators, and peace would follow with the threefold pattern of (1) loyal worker, (2) benevolent master, and (3) superintending clergyman. One of Charlotte Brontë's episodes develops this set situation. One William Farren is employed in a factory, where things come to such a head that machinery is destroyed. Farren is quite content to ply his trade; he feels no jealousy at the spectacle of his master's wealth, and he disapproves heartily of the breaking of the machinery. The problem is that Farren is embittered by privation; his family is half-starved, the best part of their furniture has been sold, and they are on the very brink of complete disaster. At this junction the author sends a minister to the rescue of these most deserving poor people. Because he is familiar with Farren's impeccable moral character, the minister has obtained a loan on behalf of Farren to enable him to begin work as a gardener. At the same time his wife receives a small gift of money with which to start a shop in the village. The solution, in other words, is to enable Farren and his wife to help themselves. But this is no real solution, as the author must have felt herself. Very few labourers could obtain the capital required to become independent. Capital was not available for the masses; even the most benevolent of clergymen could not command the means to assist all those who wanted to destroy the machines that had deprived them of their jobs in the textile factories in the North and the Midlands. The money offered to Farren in Charlotte Brontë's story was a bridge enabling him to cross to the side of the masters, and so it quenched his incipient revolt. Thus the man whom we meet for the first time in the story while he has a sharp argument with the owner of the factory where he works, abandons his occupation and his social class to become a member of the lower middle classes – a *petit bourgeois*. That the crucial role of saviour should have been given to a clergyman reflects the importance attributed to the clergy at this time as distributors not only of the Gospel but also of more worldly charities.

If religion was one powerful agent, education was another. Both exerted a lasting and a decisive influence on the mind of the average working-man. Popular education figured as an essential item in the political programme of social reformers, as one would expect. Only educated workers would be able to take part in politics, and more or less complex machinery could not very well be left in the hands of illiterates. Ignorance was indeed an insurmountable obstacle to the improvement of a worker's private economy. Because the state did virtually nothing to ensure free education for the children of workers or for the children employed in factories, it was left to the Church and the various sects to provide some rudiments of education for the poor. But the literacy achieved by means of once-a-week courses was necessarily very modest. Various Mechanics' Institutes, however, offered courses where the most ambitious among the working classes could mix with members of the lower middle classes and imbibe their social philosophy. The various biographies of industrialists written by Samuel Smiles present a trustworthy, albeit somewhat idealized, account of that thirst after knowledge which proved the main motive behind many successful careers. Smiles wrote these biographies because he felt, to quote the *Dictionary of National Biography*, that "Concrete examples of men who had achieved great results by their own efforts best indicated the true direction and goal of social and industrial progress". The titles of many of Smiles' works proclaim his concern with the moral issues: *Self-Help, with Illustrations of Character and Conduct* (1859), *Character* (1871), *Thrift* (1875), *Duty* (1880), and *Life and Labour* (1887). The moral arguments presented, often by means of edifying examples fetched from the careers of successful men, reveal a somewhat facile social optimism. Among key words that occur over and over again are energy, courage, accuracy, method, dispatch, temperance, self-denial, self-control, self-culture and self-respect.

The sphere of influence of books like these extended beyond the boundaries of Great Britain; the middle classes in other countries too drew hope and encouragement from these popular English manuals of self-help. Thus the first Yugoslav translation of Smiles' *Self-Help* (Zadar, 1871), was followed by a number of translations of other of his works and many of these ran into several editions. This vogue persisted for a considerable time, the last of these translations appearing as late as 1930. Further bibliographical research would undoubtedly yield interesting information about the extent to which these books were current on the Continent of Europe.

The works of Samuel Smiles represent the culminating point in the history of an important Victorian trend. This climax occurred during the second half of the century, but one comes across similar moral counsels before the turn of the half-century, for example in a cheap weekly magazine, *Eliza Cook's Journal*. In the issue published in June 1849, we may read that the hard-working man "who is studious and industrious arrives with all moral certainty at two great sources and means of power – knowledge and wealth." One assumes that many workers turned to books purely to satisfy a thirst for knowledge. And as we learn from Elizabeth Gaskell's *Mary Barton* (1848), the books read could represent a very high intellectual level. Mrs Gaskell is well aware of the fact that the reading habits of labourers were largely unknown to her contemporaries, and that her account would be doubted by many. Workers of this kind, however, could be found not only in Manchester, but "scattered all over the manufacturing districts of Lancashire." There are weavers in the neighbourhood of Oldham, she writes, "common hand-loom weavers, who throw the shuttle with unceasing sound, though Newton's *Principia* lie open on the loom, to be snatched at in work hours, but revelled over in meal times, or at night." And "many a broad-spoken, common-looking factory-hand" would study mathematical problems "with absorbing attention", just as "the more popularly interesting branches of natural history" found "warm and devoted followers among this class." (Chap. V.) But science did not prevail at the expense of the humanities; Stephen Morley in Benjamin Disraeli's *Sybil* (1845) was well read in politics and sociology, and Alton Locke in Charles Kingsley's novel of the same name (1850) was an outstandingly gifted intellectual. In his study of *Le roman social en Angleterre* (Paris, 1903) Professor Louis Cazamian commented on the similarity between Kingsley's Alton Locke and Thomas Cooper, the Chartist. Another Chartist poet – Bedford Leno – feels that "the hero of that story (*Alton Locke*) resembles myself".[11] But long before the days of Chartism, the poet and distinguished eighteenth-century radical John Thelwall can be seen to bear a striking similarity to Alton Locke. Both had some experience of tailoring in their youth, and both were very much against the use of physical force to solve political conflicts. Kingsley could also have found inspiration for the character of Alton Locke in the biography of Samuel Bamford, although it must be noted that while Bamford turned conservative in his later years, Alton Locke was converted to Christian socialism. Yet Kingsley would scarcely have been in need of such specific examples from the past, since there were many men of the calibre of Alton Locke among the Chartists.

Education, however, was not without its hazards. By adopting the cultural heritage of the privileged classes Alton Locke found himself in an ambiguous position. Although a revolutionary, he was sorely tempted to abandon his political principles because a revolution would have disturbed, perhaps even destroyed, the culture which he had come to love. The problem was a very real one. As we know from the history of the working-class movement, the majority of the intellectuals among the proletariat gradually came to reject the use of physical force to gain their objectives. And by slow degrees they aligned themselves with middle-class intellectuals until complete fusion was achieved. Only a minority persisted in their refusal to join the ranks of the capitalist class. A case of this kind is described by R. H. Horne (*The Dreamer and the Worker*), when he lets one of his characters – a worker well read in philosophy, history and other subjects – proclaim that one ought to remain within one's own class in an effort to raise their general level. This is how he puts it: "I have come to feel a new kind of emotion. If I could set a good example to my own class of being much more in themselves than they are at present, I think I shall do a thousand times more good by staying among them, than if I rose as an example of how to leave them. And I never *will* leave them" (chap. XII). These idealistic sentiments are admirable, but could scarcely hope to compete with the attraction of acquiring property and being in a position to exploit the opportunities presented by a capitalist and imperialist society in its ascendence. Most workers were content to provide examples of how to leave

their class, and once this elevation had been achieved, they identified their own interests with those of the middle classes rather than
the class they had left. Charles Dickens, the great friend of the
underprivileged, would never have thought of wishing to be counted
as one of them.

To rise in the world did not necessarily mean to become an
employer; the primary aim was simply to achieve what was referred
to as 'independence', which meant being released from the necessity
of engaging in manual work to gain a livelihood. The mill-owner
Thornton in Mrs Gaskell's *North and South* (1885) puts it rather
neatly when he remarks that everyone who is decent, sober, and
attentive to his duties, "comes over to our ranks". He may not
always do so as a master, "but an overseer, a cashier, a book-keeper,
one on the side of authority and order." Even a minor rise within
the industrial hierarchy could entail considerable improvement in
living conditions, and so it was towards this goal that these educationalists directed their best efforts to stir the ambition of their
humble readers. Fictionalized propaganda along these lines can be
illustrated by reference to the six-chapter story 'How to Get on in
the World' published anonymously in 1848 in *The Family Economist*. The setting is the workshop of a Birmingham blacksmith who
forges nails, his only assistant being his eight-year-old son Peter.
Although Peter wields the hammer for 10 or 12 hours a day, he
attends school as well to qualify for more profitable employment.
Nobody encourages the boy in his efforts, but by dint of hard work
and because he "keeps his character" he eventually obtains a post
as draughtsman at a salary of £300 per annum.

5. The Self-Made Industrialist

The sympathy of the underprivileged tends to be on the side of the
fairy-tale heroes who, on the strength of their own valour and
cunning, obtain the princess and half the kingdom. The appeal of
the Cinderella story has remained undiminished through a succession of untold generations, and it is still possible to feel the
attraction of medieval romances with their accounts of the young
and unknown knight whose chivalrous deeds make all Christendom
resound with his fame. But some measure of legendary fame adhered
also to more humble stories of success like that of Jack of
Newbury, a cloth manufacturer, and Richard Castelar, a shoemaker

who lived in early Tudor times. These were glorious figures, as we see from the account of their rise to fame and riches written by Thomas Deloney towards the end of the sixteenth century.[12]

Since men like Jack of Newbury and Richard Castelar made their fortune in trade, one would have thought that a similar aura of glamour would have surrounded some of the young men who rose so spectacularly from poverty and obscurity to wealth and fame during the Industrial Revolution. But this was not so. The career of a man like Sir Richard Arkwright is just as remarkable as those of his fifteenth-and sixteenth-century predecessors, but it failed to stir the imagination of his contemporaries. Originally a barber by profession, Arkwright invented the spinning machine and in 1771 established the first English cotton-spinning mill driven by water-power, the reward of his inventive genius and his industry being the acquisition of great wealth and a knighthood. That the careers of men like Sir Richard Arkwright failed to provoke general enthusiasm can be ascribed to the increasing alienation between the common people and the successful industrialist, however humble his origin. During the eighteenth century the prevalent feeling among the poor was that their class interests were distinct from, and opposed to, those of the higher classes. This hostile attitude to the rich industrialists is found also among the traditional privileged classes – the landed gentry, for example – and it is reflected in literature as well. A factory owner could not very well figure as a hero in a novel or short story, much less as a glamorous one. I have come across no example of the fictional presentation of mill-owners in the eighteenth century, whereas this type figures prominently in non-fictional prose. One such prose composition written by a clergyman in 1757 comments very judiciously on the reason for the unpopularity of practically every mill-owner. The latter is "tempted by his Station to be proud and overbearing, to consider his People as the Scum of the Earth, whom he has the Right to squeeze whenever he can; because they ought to be kept low, and not to rise in Competition with their Superiors."[13]

The haughty demeanour of the aristocrat was taken for granted by his social inferiors, but when men of very low origin presumed to lord it over their working-men, this was bound to be resented. It was of course the fondest dream of the *nouveaux riches* to be accepted as socially superior to those who but a few years since had been their equals. Moreover these rude industrialists had little education and less refinement, so that their behaviour towards those who worked for them would be harsh and anything but sympathetic. This can be illustrated by a few quotations from the memoir of a working-class man referring to the period around 1800. The author relates how the owners of a cotton-spinning mill – Ellis Needham of Highgate Wall in Derbyshire and his son – treated the parish apprentices employed in their factory with the greatest cruelty. The young master was a tyrant and an oppressor of the boys, and the girls fared even worse, as they were treated "with an indecency as disgusting as his cruelty was terrific."[14] Half a century later a character in Elizabeth Gaskell's *North and South* (1885) tries to explain the mentality of the early 'cotton lords':

"Seventy years ago what was it? And now what is it not? Raw, crude materials came together; men of the same level, as regards education and station, took suddenly the different positions of masters and men, owing to the mother-wit, as regards opportunities and probabilities, which distinguished some, and made them far-seeing as to what great future lay concealed in that rude model of Sir Richard Arkwright's. The rapid development of what might be called a new trade, gave those early masters enormous power of wealth and command. . . . There can be no doubt, too, of the tyranny they exercised over their work people. You know the proverb, Mr. Hale, 'Set a beggar on horseback, and he'll ride to the devil,' – well, some of these early manufacturers did ride to the devil in a magnificent style – crushing human bone and flesh under their horses' hoofs without remorse."

(Chap. X)

Even Harriet Martineau, an avowed friend and admirer of the industrialists, created not a single fictional example of a lovable industrialist. Her long short story 'A Manchester Strike' stresses the arrogance of a young factory owner, and at the same time clearly reveals the absence of any spirit of conciliation among workers and employers alike shortly before the Chartist riots. In another of her stories one of the masters – the grandson of a manual labourer – answers a delegation of workers that he will never "carry on the business under the control of those who depend on our capital for substance ('The Hill and the Valley', chap. VII). He would rather choose the lesser evil of having to return whence he came. Similar sentiments, only more harshly put and in a more insulting manner, are expressed by one of the characters in Charlotte Brontë's *Shirley* (1849, chap. VIII). Even after the experience of the Chartist riots many masters persisted in refusing to grant any of the requests advanced by the workers. This attitude is illustrated in the anonymously published novel *Hugh Vernon, the Weaver's Son* (1853), when an angry master dismisses a skilled worker because the latter has dared to criticize the factory system and the political principles of the British Constitution. If he were not to dismiss the worker, the master feels that he would lose all authority so that he would become a mere "plaything", "tool", or "servant", "instead of being as now, the obeyed and respected master of three hundred English workmen."[15]

Frances Trollope's *Jessie Phillips* (1844) describes a member of the Poor Relief Board in a country village who had originally made his fortune by manufacturing buttons, and so had "become a *county gentleman.*" When an old woman applies to the Board on behalf of her destitute daughter-in-law and her five grandchildren, this worthy gentleman blames her daughter-in-law for having produced "a litter of brats" and then attempting to make honest and thrifty people pay for their maintenance:

"Shame! shame! shame! . . . to come and ask the active, honest, intelligent, thrifty part of the population to rob themselves and their own children (honestly brought into the world, with consciousness that there was power to maintain them) . . . to ask their money out of their pockets, in order to feed this litter of brats that you know in your own heart and conscience ought never to have been born at all. Get along!

(Chap. IV)

Because they failed to understand that these evils were inherent in the factory system of their day, novelists frequently criticized factory owners for showing such a disregard for the workers and their problems.[16] They believed, somewhat ingenuously, that a good relationship between masters and men was a matter of showing good will. Thus Elizabeth Gaskell attributes the violent activities of John Barton – the Chartist portrayed in *Mary Barton* (1848) – to his experience of the lack of humanity on the part of his masters. At the time when he had lost his only son whose death was largely caused by slow starvation during a period of economic depression, he had seen the wife of his employer shopping in the most expensive store in Manchester. Many years later further bitterness was accumulated when his master Carson refused to assist the family of a worker who was dying from a virulent fever.

In the end John Barton is driven to the extremity of actually killing his young master. This happens after a confrontation between a delegation of workers and their masters, when young Carson is responsible for the breakdown of the negotiations. The desperate workers decide to kill him and the task of performing this act falls to the lot of Barton. The author's portrait of young Carson is that of an overbearing master, prepared to deride the working men and to seduce their pretty daughters.

The doubtful character of the principle of self-help so enthusiastically advocated by contemporary industrialists was brought out most clearly by Charles Dickens in *Hard Times* (1854). Dickens's satirical portrait of the rich industrialist Bounderby presents a type rather than an individual. He is seen as the embodiment of the self-help principle, who constantly, from an excess of inverted snobbery, boasts of his low origin in order to show the magnitude of an achievement based entirely on his own unaided efforts. When two admiring subordinates discuss the merit of the self-help principle, one of them remarks with great complacency: "'Now, look at me, Ma'am. I have put by a little, Ma'am, already. That gratuity which I receive at Christmas, Ma'am; I never touch it. I don't even go the length of my wages, though they're not high, Ma'am. Why can't they do as I have done, Ma'am? What one person can do, another can do.'" (Bk. II, chap. I.) In the authorial commentary Dickens adds that in Coketown any capitalist "who had made sixty thousand pounds out of sixpence always professed to wonder why the sixty thousand nearest Hands didn't each make sixty thousand out of sixpence".

The most successful among the industrial magnates felt that their wealth entitled them to membership of the privileged upper classes. This is the ambition of the factory owner described in Robert Blincoe's *Memoir* (1828), in Frances Trollope's *The Life and Adventures of Michael Armstrong, the Factory Boy* (1839–40) and in *Hugh Vernon* (1853) by an anonymous author. These are all men of mean descent who tried to gain an entry into polite circles by an ostentatious display of wealth. Their neighbours accept their lavish hospitality, but with a feeling of contempt for their vulgar hosts. Those of the second generation usually lack the tremendous energy of their fathers and are often ashamed to acknowledge the source of their wealth, as we see in the case of the Vincy brother and sister in George Eliot's *Middlemarch* (1872). In Catherine

Gore's *Men of Capital* (1846) a very rich manufacturer builds a magnificent mansion in the countryside after retiring from business in Manchester, but in his case the social gulf is bridged when his son falls in love with the local squire's daughter.

Political ambitions were just as common, as we see for example in William Paley's fictionalized tract *Equality, a dialogue between a Master-Manufacturer and one of his Workmen* (1793). The master-manufacturer explains how he began his life without a penny, and goes on to sketch his plans for his sons. One, the eldest, will carry on the business, another will study Law, a third is destined for the Navy. "It is from such as these that Lords are made; the first pursues trade, purchases land, his son becomes a Squire, is returned to Parliament, and if he has abilities may justly pretend to a Peerage."[17] Charles Kingsley's *Yeast* (1848) relates the success-story of Lord Mitchamstead who rose from poverty to great wealth at the time when the manufacture of cotton was greatly increased by the exploitation of steam-power. Subsequently he purchased coal mines, steam-boats and railway companies, and became an important banker among whose creditors dukes and kings were included. His large estates in half-a-dozen counties secured a peerage for him, and this honour is seen as the climactic point of his amazing career (chap. 4). But not even such a character commanded the sympathy of his author; the novelists as a rule showed a general dislike of wealthy manufacturers.

Yet these men had qualities which could command respect if not love. This was realized by Elizabeth Gaskell, who spent her married life in Manchester and met many industrialists. In her first social novel, *Mary Barton, a Tale of Manchester Life* (1848), she approaches the problem from the proletarian point of view, and depicts the two Carsons, father and son, without any embellishment. But in her second novel on that subject, *North and South* (1855), she tried to be fair to the industrialists and made her hero a young factory owner in order to do justice to certain qualities in men of Thornton's calibre, qualities usually overlooked by the writers of social novels. She understood that in the character of such men the mere love of money was not the principal motive. His unbending spirit, his single-mindedness, his dedication to his enterprise gave Thornton the fortitude to persevere in the bitter competitive struggle which animated the world of business. At the same time, Thornton's sturdiness and self-reliance made him scorn those who were not prepared to make sacrifices and who possessed insufficient strength of purpose and character to fulfil their ambition. Of a similar stamp are Robert Moore and Hiram York in Charlotte Brontë's *Shirley* (1849), and John Withers in Geraldine Jewsbury's *Marian Withers* (1850–1). John is rescued from the gutter by a benevolent lady who puts him in a workhouse from which he is sent as a parish apprentice to a cotton mill. The author omits all mention of John's experience in the mill, concentrating instead on his self-reliance. Having taught himself to read, John fixes his mind on an important technical invention. For this reason he gives up his job in the factory, but when his meagre savings are spent, he is exposed to great privation; he lives on scraps picked up in the market, and when his invention is finally completed, he collapses from exhaustion. He recovers, however, after three months in hospital, and sells his patent to a manufacturer. From then on his road to success offers no obstacle, and he becomes a prosperous Manchester manufacturer.

The moral lesson summarized by the author – that a "spirit of self-help does lie at the bottom of all success" – may serve as a fitting conclusion to this chapter. As Geraldine Jewsbury had been brought up in Manchester she understood the mentality of these industrial pioneers and their "barbaric strength", and she honoured their achievement. They "need education, they need civilising; but they will change the face of the world", she said; and so they did.

Notes

1. Goldsmith's poem deplores the condition of the rural poor, and in one couplet he contrasts the weaver and the courtier: "Here while the courtier glitters in brocade, / There the pale artist plies his sickly trade."
2. 'Reflections and Maxims', *The Family Magazine* (November 1788).
3. M. G. Jones, *Hannah More* (Cambridge, 1952), 142.
4. For further information, see p. 135.
5. *Life of Robert Owen by Himself* (1920), 85.
6. 'A Manchester Strike', chap. 2.
7. Since the reign of Queen Elizabeth I to provide for the poor was a duty incumbent on all rate-payers.

2 The Gospel of Self-Help

8. The common was an area of undivided land shared by all the inhabitants of a village. Formerly the village poor could let their sheep and cows graze on the common, but the Enclosure Acts deprived them of this traditional privilege.

9. The allotment system was recommended as early as 1795 by the anonymous author of an article on 'An effectual Method of relieving the Poor', *The Gentleman's Magazine* (1795), 824. The author recommends that small allotments of ground be given to the poor villagers, and he concludes by stating that "True charity to the poor, honest labourer is to enable him to *become* rich."

10. Douglas Jerrold, *Shilling Magazine*, chap. 12.

11. P. B. Davis, *Industrial Fiction 1827–1850* (unpublished doctoral dissertation, Wisconsin, 1961), 423.

12. Thomas Deloney (?1543– ?1600) was a weaver by profession; he is known today as the author of popular ballads and a series of prose stories concerned with various craftsmen. *Jack of Newbury* relates the story of a young weaver's apprentice who marries his master's widow and becomes the prosperous proprietor of a shop with two hundred looms. Richard Castelar's story is told in *The Gentle Craft*; he lived at the time of Henry VIII and bequeathed his fortune to the poor.

13. Josiah Tucker, *Instruction for Travellers* (1757), 25.

14. *Original Biography, Memoir of Robert Blincoe* by John Brown, published anonymously in *The Lion* (a weekly paper) for the period 25 January to 22 February 1828.

15. This attitude is illustrated in chap. III of Harriet Martineau's 'A Manchester Strike', see our Anthology.

16. In *The Life and Adventures of Michael Armstrong, the Factory Boy* (1839–40), Frances Trollope accuses Dowling of outright malice and cruelty; Charlotte Elizabeth Tonna (*Helen Fleetwood*, 1839–40) denounces mill-owners for violating the principles laid down in the Factory Laws, just as Benjamin Disraeli (*Sybil*, 1845) exposes the culpability of employers by drawing on the more impressive passages in the Blue Books.

17. See our Anthology, 142.

Chapter 3

Towards a New Sensibility

The spectacle of human suffering cannot be supposed always to elicit an immediate response from artists whose eyes are focussed on the contemporary scene. The mere fact of social injustice, however great, is not enough to provide the inspiration for works of fiction, nor can it guarantee that such works will have outstanding artistic merit. No consistent pattern of cause and effect can be traced. Much the same is true of the creation of public opinion, as we realize on considering the fact that exactly the same kind of social abuse, in different countries or during different historical periods, fails to provoke the same reaction. Although the slaves of Greece and Rome may have suffered more than the American Negro in more recent times, the literature of Antiquity has no counterpart to Harriet Beecher Stowe's *Uncle Tom's Cabin* (1852). The decisive factor is the general state of mind in a particular society at a given time; this it is which accounts for the presence, or absence, of a social sensibility. That this is indeed so can be inferred from a study of literary references to the human suffering caused by the Industrial Revolution. Public opinion was much less sensitive to this suffering in the period preceding the introduction of steam-power into industry, than afterwards, for reasons that I shall try to explain. Nor had the centuries prior to the development of the factory system witnessed a more humane treatment of the common labourer; he had fared just as badly then, if not more so. It may seem a strange paradox that condition-of-England fiction should become popular at the time when the working classes no longer formed a suppressed and largely inarticulate group, and when some of them received better wages than ever before, but the reason is obvious: what had happened was a change in popular sensibility.

In periods dominated by a static view of society one will usually find a placid or stolid acceptance of the fact of social injustice. When the structure of society is believed incapable of change except for the worse, its continued existence must be ensured by all means. Since the rich and the poor had always been there, their co-existence must have seemed like something of a natural law, and such was the prevalence of this social fatalism that hunger and pain were seen as inherent in our human condition. It required the tremendous pressure engendered by the process of industrialization for the traditional, static view to be replaced by a more dynamic one based on the idea of social equality. Those who watched the process often sensed the fact that a decisive change was taking place. One anonymous contributor to *The Gentleman's Magazine* for the year 1800 expressed extreme bewilderment at the speed with which everything had happened. It is impossible, he writes, "not to be filled with a degree of astonishment to find that one single century has made such changes, when so many had passed over before without leaving almost any trace or alteration."[1] As increasing numbers grew aware of the fact that the very ground on which the social structure rested was shifting, the static view had to be abandoned. And the moment that all aspects of society were examined and assessed, the existing class structure could no longer be regarded as sacrosanct. Deficiencies in the existing order were denounced, at the same time that it became more and more generally recognized that poverty could be overcome. Since change was the outstanding feature of the nation's economic life, changes for the better could be envisaged in other areas also, such as the legal system and public institutions, so as to protect the interests of *all* classes. Thus the acceptance of social injustice as a necessary evil was replaced by an increasing effort to secure some degree of equality with respect to the basic necessities of life. Today there is universal agreement that everyone is entitled to these basic necessities, and it is no coincidence that this attitude can be traced back to the decades that witnessed the spectacular changes wrought by the great technological inventions. With the successful introduction of machines in the process of production an economic basis was created for social improvements of various kinds. Now that the resources were actually available, writers no longer had to envisage utopian frameworks for their schemes of social reform; they could plead for justice within the existing economic and political framework.

Before this could be achieved, however, the old idea of 'every-man-performing-his-duty-as-assigned-to-him-by-Providence' had to be exchanged for 'every-man-performing-that-task-for-which-he-is-best-suited'. This new philosophy entails a new social sensibility, in that any person, man, woman, or child, who is denied full development of his or her natural capacities is considered to have been sacrificed to a system whose viciousness is thereby exposed. Since the victimization of children is particularly pathetic, it was bound to affect the social sensibility most profoundly. The violation of our inborn instinct to protect the young is a sign of the onset of moral decay in society as well as in the individual, but during the eighteenth century this is exactly what happened when very young children of both sexes were used as workers in factories and mines. Although they performed the same work as adults, they received only one-fourth of the wage, and their working hours were from early morning to late evening and sometimes into the hours of the night.

What is so surprising today is the fact that no one seems to have been particularly alarmed by the situation of these children; writers even greeted it with approbation, since it enabled the destitute to earn a living. Thus Daniel Defoe had noted with satisfaction that there was hardly a child "above four Years old, but his Hands are sufficient to itself."[2]

1. A Choir of Larks

William Hutton was probably born in the year when Defoe published his *Tour thro' the whole Island of Great Britain* (1724). At the age of seven he worked as an apprentice in a silk mill, a fact which in those days was not at all remarkable. But what was indeed exceptional was that the experience of this factory child should be preserved for posterity, since Hutton left a written record of his life and career.

Hutton served two seven-year periods as an apprentice – first in the silk-mill and then in a workshop for the manufacture of stockings. At the end of these 14 years, however, he was still unqualified for a trade. It is amazing that Hutton in his memoirs never once censures the system to which he had been exposed for so many years, but he wrote at a time when he had been a well-to-do and respected citizen for a considerable period. Then, too, the age was marked by widespread unemployment caused partly by the enclosure movement and partly by a sudden increase in the population, so that starvation was a very real threat. No wonder, therefore, that many were so worried that they considered it a blessing when a child found employment. Indeed, for many children there was simply no alternative; if they remained idle they were doomed to perish. This explains the attitude of approval of child labour shown throughout the eighteenth century, and it is important to keep this in mind before passing too harsh a judgment on writers whose views must seem unnatural and cruel to twentieth-century readers.

The poet John Dyer was one of those who expressed positive pleasure at seeing children at work in textile factories visited during the 1750s. To him the machines were a real blessing, and the work easy:

> The younger hands
> Ply at the easy work of winding yarn
> On swiftly circling engines, and their notes
> Warble together, as a choir of larks:
> Such joy arises in the mind employed.
> (*The Fleece*, III, 281–85)

It is not difficult to imagine the kind of persuasion employed to induce children to join this warbling "choir of larks" rather than to run freely about in the suburbs where they lived. Educationalists expected as a matter of course that the poor should accept their poverty as a Providential design to test their moral and spiritual fortitude, and whenever they failed to accept their yoke in a proper spirit of Christian humility, they were told that they would surely provoke the wrath of God. All this is sufficiently familiar, but it is important to add that these religious educationalists realized that they had to begin with the children, if their lesson was to be fully accepted. According to Josiah Tucker, Rector of St Stephen's in Bristol around the mid-century, the great advantage of child labour was that it "trains up children to an Habit of Industry, almost as soon as they can speak."[3] And a dissenting minister, Benjamin Fawcett, wrote in 1773 that the best provision for the children of the poor was to train them up "in such a manner, as constantly to exercise their diligence and industry, their care and caution, their prudence and frugality and above all, in the *nature* and the *admonition of the Lord*".[4] Sarah Trimmer, too – the well-known religious writer for the poor – favoured the view that the children of paupers should be trained to perform manual work. Children who lived in the workhouse should be profitably employed in charity schools:

If for instance there was a school for spinning flax, girls of five years of age might be employed at it; and the yarn might easily be manufactured into white or striped linen and checks; and by the time each little spinstress had worn out the clothes with which the parish or private benefactors should at first have furnished her, she might earn sufficient to entitle her to linen and other necessaries.[5]

This quotation is taken from Sarah Trimmer's *Address to Ladies Concerning Sunday-Schools* (1787), where she extends her scheme by proposing that schools for the carding and spinning of wool should be established and conducted on the same principles, since such schools would become self-supporting in a short time. She was delighted to discover the existence of a spinning machine that was so easy to manage that "the least child can, with the smallest touch, disengage and set going any one of the wheels without any interfering with another." (p. 72.)

Many reports of travellers contain approving remarks on the industry of child labourers. The anonymously printed *Tour of Derbyshire and Yorkshire* (1778) says of the potteries that "Happily, many very young [hands] are enabled to earn a livelihood in the business."[6] And in 1780 Sir Richard Sullivan wrote that the spirit of industry was so prominent in Birmingham "that not a person is seen, not even children, without being employed in some kind of business or other."[7] A German traveller recorded that seven-year-old children "are employed in some manufacturies, and many earn half a crown a week, which in some respect accounts for the cheapness of things manufactured, and how it is that families, notwithstanding the apparently small wages of their labour, can maintain themselves."[8] In 1793 yet another traveller observed that at Barnstaple in Devonshire he saw the silk-mills, the machines of which were so simple that "boys and girls conduct with ease the chief part of the work."[9]

When Parliament debated the First Factory Bill in 1802, a Select Committee was appointed to report on the use of child labour. This report is a useful source of reliable information, and it leaves no doubt in the reader's mind that the children of paupers were often treated no better than slaves. Thus parentless and abandoned children left in the charge of the parish were 'ceded' to mill-owners in the North of England. And when industrialists built their factories in sparsely populated valleys next to the rivers that provided a source of power, they bargained with various parishes for pauper children. These were bound to them as 'apprentices' for seven years, and during all this time they usually received no wages. The work was exhausting and monotonous and the hours long, and yet they were taught no trade. All they got was food and lodging of the poorest kind, and hence the mortality rate was appalling. It was nevertheless possible for Sir Richard Sullivan, in his *Observations* (1780), to describe the parish apprentices as happy. A fairly long quotation is required to indicate his attitude and tone of voice:

> Mr. Strutwell originally projected this manufactury from a benevolent desire of employing so many unprotected beings from their infant state. Women he appoints to take care of them; and they are fed and clothed, at his expense, until they are capable of work, when they are entered at the looms, and receive a regular stipend for their daily labours. Delighted at this unusual, but sensible exertion of charity, we begged the permission of the people to let us see the children. We were accordingly admitted into a room, where we observed a party of them gathered round their old mistress, decently dressed, with health and cheerfulness sparkling in their countenances. The sight was affecting – we could not refrain from expressing it; and we thereby gained the blessing of the venerable matron. "God bless you!" says she, "they are poor, it is true, but still they are lovely little innocents. God protects them; and sure I am, He will reward their generous benefactor with peace and happiness hereafter!" Happy man! thought I, the feelings of thy own heart must afford thee ample recompense in this life; and, in that to come, blessings attend thee and all thy generation! Amen.[10]

Sir Richard Sullivan's concluding peroration calls to mind the religious hypocrites so often described by Charles Dickens, and one is tempted to repeat Dr Johnson's scornful comment on the exaggerated cult of benevolence. When Boswell regretted his inability to feel for others "as sensibly as many say they do", Dr Johnson's retort was as follows: "Sir, don't be duped by them any more. You will find these very feeling people are not very ready to do you good. They *pay* you by *feeling*."[11] One suspects that Sir Richard's journey, like that of Laurence Sterne, must have been a sentimental one. He must have wanted to describe the reaction of his heart on observing acts of benevolence, and so the children had to be "decently dressed, with health and cheerfulness sparkling in their countenances".

2. Deceptive Good

A bondage lurking under shape of good.
(Wordsworth, *The Excursion*, IX, 189)

On leaving the eighteenth century and turning to the nineteenth, one discovers that the position of child labourers became even more difficult. With the introduction of steam-power factories were built in towns rather than distant valleys, and in these towns the un-employed were more than willing to send their children into factories. This resulted in the employment of children on a scale which continued to increase. By 1835 the cotton industry alone employed 28,771 children under the age of 13, 27,251 boys and girls between 13 and 18, and of females over 13 years no less than 106,059. Most of these 'females' would be young girls. Since the population was only about 17,000,000 in 1835,[12] the proportion of child labourers was indeed great, which helps to explain why the nineteenth century, unlike the eighteenth, could ill afford to ignore the problem, let alone consider it with any degree of optimism.

The first signs of a change in attitude can be perceived before the turn of the century in the poetry of William Blake, the first great poet to denounce the exploitation of children. This denuncia-tion, however, is part of his general attack on modern society for having sacrificed true human values to false ones, so that the youth of the nation "spend the days of wisdom" "In sorrowful drudgery":

> Intricate wheels invented, Wheel without wheel,
> To perplex youth in their outgoings & to bind to labours

Of day & night the myriads of Eternity; that they might file
And polish brass & iron hour after hour, laborious workmanship,
Kept ignorant of the use that they might spend the days of wisdom
In sorrowful drudgery to obtain a scanty pittance of bread.[13]

One must turn to Blake for the most powerful and poetically moving expression of a feeling of revulsion, but since our concern is with specific details rather than general sentiments, other sources must be consulted, for example the pamphlet published by a group of medical men in Manchester in 1784 on the condition of factory children. These are said to be overworked and underfed and hence liable to infectious diseases, thus endangering the city as a whole. It was solely to reduce this danger that these doctors recommended that the working hours of children be limited to ten, and the argument was sufficiently powerful to induce the city magistrates to issue a regulation along these lines. However, since the regulation never took effect, it is of historical interest only, as an indication of the nature of the concern felt for these children. Their own plight provoked no comment; what mattered was the fact that they represented a potential health hazard to the rest of the population.

The same problem was considered by another member of the medical profession in Manchester, John Aikin, in his *Description of the Country from Thirty to Forty Miles around Manchester* (1795). Although Aikin was a great admirer of the new industries, he could not but realize that thousands of factory children in the area lived under very unhealthy conditions. Writing as he did before the introduction of steam-power, the child labourers with whom he is concerned would primarily be parish apprentices, these being still in the majority during the 1790s. As he explains, many of them had been "transported in crowds" from the London workhouses to the factories:

In these children of very tender age are employed; many of them collected from the *workhouses* in *London* and *Westminster*, and transported in crowds, as apprentices to masters resident many hundred miles distant, where they serve unknown, unprotected, and forgotten by those to whose care nature or the laws had consigned them. These children are usually too long confined to work in close rooms, often during the whole night: the air they breathe from the oil, &c. employed in the machinery and other circumstances, is injurious; little regard is paid to their cleanliness, and frequent changes from the warm and dense to a cold and thin atmosphere, are predisposing causes to sickness and disability, and particularly to the epidemic fever which so generally is to be met with in these factories. It is also much to be questioned if society does not receive detriment from the manner in which children are thus employed during their early years.

(pp. 221f.)

Aikin makes a point of the fact that the girls who have to work in factories are prevented from learning how to become good house-keepers and mothers, and he deplores the bad influence to which many of them are exposed so that they lose their respect for religion and become improvident. He notes, too, that their education is neglected, and concludes with a firm statement to the effect that the public "have a right to see that its members are not wantonly injured, or carelessly lost."

As far as I have been able to ascertain, this was the first expression of the humanitarian argument that was to become so common in the decades which followed. After the turn of the century, when the towns and cities of the North were increasingly thronged by children hurrying to their work at dawn or returning home at night, middle-class observers became more and more concerned on noticing their emaciated frames and haggard expression. But very little was actually done for them during the first decade of the new century, largely because the attention of the public was focussed on issues connected with the Napoleonic wars. The block-ade had a negative effect on trade, an economic crisis followed, and then the Luddite riots, so that it was not till 1815 that Parliament once more considered the problem of the legal protection of factory children. Parliament was not alone in its neglect of this issue; there are very few fictional accounts of the lives of these unhappy members of society, one of the first being William Godwin's novel *Fleetwood, or the New Man of Feeling* (1805), four chapters of which are devoted to this subject.[14] And ten years later Thomas Love Peacock touched on the problem of child labour in his *Headlong Hall* (1816). His reference, it is true, is casual and short, but his sentiments are emphatic and outspoken. He admits that the children are doomed to death "from their cradles":

Wherever this boasted machinery is established, the children of the poor are death-doomed from their cradles. Look for one moment at midnight into a cotton-mill, amidst the smell of oil, the smoke of lamps, the rattling of wheels, the dizzy and complicated motions of a diabolical mechanism; contemplate the little human machines that keep pace with the revolutions of the ironwork, robbed at that hour of their natural rest, as of air and exercise by day: observe their pale and ghastly features, more ghastly in that baleful and malignant light, and tell me if you do not fancy yourself on the threshold of Virgil's hell.

(chap. VII)

This new vision of Hell also engaged the pen of William Wordsworth as he wrote Books VIII and IX of *The Excursion* (1814), but the subject failed to kindle his poetic genius. A few quotations will illustrate the fervent if pedestrian character of these passages that describe how children are "offered up" to "Gain, the master-idol of the realm" as a "Perpetual sacrifice":

> an unnatural light
> Prepared for never-resting Labour's eyes
> Breaks from a many-windowed fabric huge;
> And at the appointed hour a bell is heard, . . .
>
> A local summons to unceasing toil!
> Disgorged are now the ministers of day;
> And, as they issue from the illumined pile,
> A fresh band meets them, at the crowded door − . . .
>
> Men, maidens, youths,
> Mothers and little children, boys and girls,
> Enter, and each the wonted task resumes
> Within this temple, where is offered up
> To Gain, the master-idol of the realm,
> Perpetual sacrifice. . . .
>
> Economists will tell you that the State
> Thrives by the forfeiture − unfeeling thought,
> And false as monstrous! Can a mother thrive
> By the destruction of her innocent sons
> In whom a premature necessity
> Blocks out the forms of nature, preconsumes
> The reason, famishes the heart, shuts up
> The infant Being in itself, and makes
> Its very spring a season of decay!

The boy is a prisoner in a factory, excluded from all schooling:

> His raiment, whitened o'er with cotton-flakes
> Or locks of wool, announces whence he comes.

Creeping his gait and cowering, his lip pale,
His respiration quick and audible;
And scarcely could you fancy that a gleam
Could break from out those languid eyes, or a blush
Mantle upon his cheek. . . .

    – Can hope look forward to a manhood raised
on such foundations? "Hope is none for him!"
The pale Recluse indignantly exclaimed,
And tens of thousands suffer wrong as deep.

(Book VIII, 11.167–336 passim)

If the process of industrialization is taken too far, it may become a curse rather than a blessing, "A bondage lurking under shape of good" (IX, 189).[15] But the issue cannot have engaged the poet at all deeply, since his voluminous correspondence contains no reference to it, except in a brief note to a friend explaining that he had himself supported Robert Southey's campaign on behalf of factory children. This note was written in reference to Sir Robert Peel's attempt to enlist the aid of Parliament in an effort to restrict the use of child labour. The elder Peel was himself an owner of large textile factories, but he declared that the sharp competition did not permit him to shorten the working hours, however much he may have wished to do so. The consequence of such a measure would have defeated its purpose, since his factories depended for their existence on customers who naturally would prefer the lower price levels made possible by the exploitation of children. For this reason one factory owner alone could never hope to achieve a reform; this had to be left to the nation acting through Parliament. And a prolonged debate did take place in the House of Commons; as one would expect, the advocates of Free Trade disputed the principle of state intervention in the relationship between masters and workers, but Commissions were nevertheless appointed, witnesses heard, reports written and various proposals submitted and rejected. A new Factory Act was finally passed in 1819 which represented a distinct improvement as compared with the Act of 1802, although it failed to provide protection for all children by being limited only to those who worked in cotton mills. A step had nevertheless been taken in the right direction, and the many debates had succeeded in stirring the conscience of the more privileged classes. The extent to which public opinion was engaged can be inferred from the many articles which appeared in the years from 1815 to 1819 in newspapers and periodicals. Among the writers of such articles, the two Romantic poets Robert Southey and S. T. Coleridge took the lead. Southey had been a friend of the French Revolution in his youth, but like so many of his generation had become a thorough conservative by 1815. His Tory bias made him hostile to the new industrial 'lords', so that he was more than ready to join the ranks of their enemies. As the chief target for his attack he chose the exploitation of child labour in factories, a topic to which he dedicated his *Essays Moral and Political* (first collected edition, 1832). These essays, originally written prior to the passing of the Factory Act of 1819, constitute an early example of Tory attempts to enlist public support by embracing the cause of factory workers. Southey's political purpose is fairly obvious, but one nevertheless receives a strong impression of genuine sincerity. His account of the shameful trade in pauper children is moving as well as informative; the children are trained "as soon as their little fingers can twirl a thread, or feed a machine". Even the "slave-trade itself was scarcely more systematically remorseless". Indeed, "a new sort of slave-trade was invented" when "London work-houses supplied children by waggon-loads" to factory-owners; "child-jobbers travelled the country, procuring children from parents whose poverty was such as would consent to the sacrifice". Because the machinery required a 24-hour service, "one set of these poor children worked by day, another by night; and when one relay was relieved, they turned into the beds which had been vacated by the other, warm as the others had left them."[16]

Southey's close friend, S. T. Coleridge, published two articles on this subject in 1818 at the height of the controversy. Coleridge's indignation is great; in a factory the child is "employed on tasks the most opposite to its natural instincts", and these tasks are performed "in a heated, stifling, impure atmosphere" and with "limbs and spirit outwearied". After ten hours the child still has three, four or even five hours of further work to look forward to, so how can "the poor little *sufferer* be brought to believe that these hours are mere trifles – or the privilege of going home not worth his thanks?"[17] These sentiments are expressed in Coleridge's first circular letter, and in a second such letter he invites his readers to examine their conscience and to consult their common sense concerning the reasonableness of forcing children to work for 13 or 15 hours a day.[18] One of Coleridge's private letters explains that the poet had felt this concern for a long time. Despite his severe indisposition, he writes, "I have yet been doing my best on behalf of the poor Cotton Factory Children, whose condition is an abomination which has weighed on my feelings from earliest manhood". And he adds that he has himself "been indeed an eye-witness of the direful effects."[19]

As a rule, political radicals focussed their attention too exclusively on the issue of Parliamentary reform to feel much concern for the fate of factory children, an interesting exception being Richard Carlile. Carlile was a well-known reformer and an uncompromising radical who spent more than nine years in prison for having written and published seditious pamphlets. Among his publications is the sixpenny weekly, *The Lion* (January 1828–December 1829), in which he serialized John Brown's biography of an orphan boy entitled *Original Biography, Memoir of Robert Blincoe, an orphan boy, who with others, was sent from the workhouse of Saint Pancras, London, to one of the horrible cotton-mills and cotton masters in Nottinghamshire.* The first instalment appeared in the issue of 25 January 1828, the last on 22 February the same year. The biography – possibly semi-fictional – was published again in 1832 in Manchester with a slightly different title (*A Memoir of Robert Blincoe, an orphan boy sent from the workhouse of Saint Pancras, London, at seven years of age to endure the horrors of a cotton mill*), the publisher being John Doherty, the well-known Lancashire trade union leader of Irish extraction. Doherty was a printer and bookseller as well, and a café proprietor.

As John Brown tells the story, Robert Blincoe was born in a London workhouse towards the end of the eighteenth century; the exact date of his birth and the names of his parents were not registered by the careless officials of the workhouse. These officials sent him to a cotton factory in the North, where he was bound apprentice for 15 years. Eighty apprentices were sent off to this factory from the same London parish, packed together like cattle. The journey took four days, but on finally arriving their misery was increased rather than relieved. They had been induced to go on the strength of false promises and obvious lies; their new life was even worse than their previous existence. The food consisted of boiled potatoes, porridge, rye bread and milk diluted with water; the dormitories were crammed full, two children sharing the same bed, and they had to work for 14 hours a day, sometimes even 16. Because Robert was very short, it was difficult for him to follow all the movements of the machinery so that he provoked the anger of the overseer. On attempting to run away, he was caught and returned to his master by a hypocritical Methodist who was given a reward of £5. The hunger of the apprentices was such that they plundered the fields at night, thus earning a very poor reputation among the farmers. Nevertheless their condition was not entirely hopeless, they did not become cripples and were even allowed some time for playing in the open air. They were occasionally taken to visit a church on Sundays, and were not actually locked within the gates of the establishment. However, when the mill was shut down, Blincoe was transferred to a new master under whom he suffered "excess of toil, of filth and hunger", as a result of which the child labourers fell victim to contagious fevers. On the least provocation a child would be thrown on the floor to be kicked and beaten until the tormentor tired of the exercise. The children were allowed to wash only once a week, but without soap, and Robert's head was covered with vermin and dirty wounds. Often their food would be spoilt and so infested with worms that even the hungriest child would be unable to eat. They would faint from hunger as they worked, and those who died were buried in secret, and a fresh supply of parish apprentices brought in as replacement. When Robert escaped from the factory to try to enlist the support of the local magistrate, he was advised to return to his master and was obliged to do so. By then he was a grown boy who was sufficiently well informed to comment on the inadequacy of the Factory Act of 1802, since it was actually after this Act had been passed that he had been exposed to the greatest suffering. When his 'apprenticeship' was finished, Robert tried several masters, but finally succeeded in establishing himself as a retail dealer in waste and raw cotton.

This pathetic biography elicited comments from the editor as well as various readers. Carlile stated that when it was being published, Blincoe was languishing in a debtors' prison, while the author of a letter to the editor, one Samuel Davy, confirmed the veracity of Blincoe's account. Davy, too, had been sent from London to the North to work in a factory near Preston, where child labourers were cruelly exploited and ill-treated. One boy – Richard Goodall – was "entirely beaten to death" by a master who habitually used a rod of iron for the purpose of punishment, and Davy's own brother was exposed to similar treatment.[20] John Joseph Betts, who had worked as an apprentice in the same mill as Blincoe, wrote to the editor offering to provide a full account of the suffering of these young apprentices, if the editor would correct his grammar.[21] A correspondent who insisted on preserving his anonymity had lived next to the mill where Robert had suffered most and he confirmed that the beds consisted of sackcloth stuffed with straw and crawling with maggots during the summer months. Moreover, "the young girls were often prostituted to the cruel lust of the young master."[22] A contributor who signed himself "A friend at Manchester" wrote that Blincoe was personally known to him: "He showed me various scars on his head and face, which had been inflicted upon him, and the backs of his ears were covered with scars, which had been caused, as he told me, by the pincers . . . which his merciless task-master applied to his ears to punish him."[23] To make this account accessible to a wider public, a pamphlet was published at the price of one shilling.

Stylistically *Blincoe's Memoir* suffers from a kind of over-emphasis which defeats its own purpose, and the narrative lacks directness and a feeling of urgency. Brown may have drawn on several sources which he combined to create a story about the sufferings endured by a single parish apprentice in several cotton-mills, and he may have lacked the skill to convey an impression of immediate human experience. The final impression is one of extreme artificiality, while Brown's own comments anticipate the manner of the Evangelicals and Christian Socialists in the next few decades. Again we are made to realize that radical extremists and staunch conservatives shared the same religious vocabulary and that they possessed a similar mental attitude. Brown's passages of bitter lamentation strongly resemble the complaints voiced some ten years later by Charlotte Elizabeth Tonna, a conservative. Brown deplored the moral decadence of the industrial workers, attributing a "malific influence" to "a few great and unfeeling capitalists":

There never yet was such a crisis, when, in the commercial world, the march of avarice was so rapid, or its devastation so extensive upon the morals and well-being of society, as within the period embraced by this narrative; a march that seems to acquire celerity in proportion to the increasing spread of its malific *influence* and to derive *impunity* from the

prodigious wealth it accumulates in the hands of a few great and unfeeling capitalists, at the expense of the individual happiness, health,
and morals of the million.

(p. 187)

Brown maintains that thousands of weavers are treated with greater
cruelty than the slaves on a West India plantation; the factory
system throws odium upon the Crown at the same time that unscrupulous demagogues profit by the occasion to enlist support for
their manifold conspiracies. As a consequence "multitudes re-
nounce Christianity", a comment that the modern reader would
scarcely have expected from an ultra-radical paper.

One important difference can be observed between Brown's
story and the official reports on the condition of parish apprentices
in the cotton factories. The difference is one of emphasis. The
reports show that the children were subjected to a very strict discipline, and that they were exposed to overwork and consequent
fatigue and illness, and also to wanton cruelty. But as a rule cruelty
was seldom practised for the sake of sadistic pleasure or from
deliberate brutality; the motive would be the simple and basic
desire for greater profits, a desire induced by the very nature of the
factory system. It was the unregulated capitalist competition which
produced the miserable condition of the workers, adults as well as
children.

Brown's story of Blincoe's life is less persuasive than these
official reports because an overdose of horror blunts the effect, just
as the general character of the factory system is blurred by the many
detailed examples of sadistic practices. Thus it was one of the
diabolic "amusements" of the overseer to file the teeth of his
apprentices, or he would compel a boy to work "loaded with two
half hundred weights slung behind him hanging one at each
shoulder"; he would compel the children whom he wanted to
punish "to eat dirty pieces of candle, to lick up tobacco spittle, to
open their mouths for the filthy wretches to spit into". There is no
reason why these statements should be doubted, for it is unfortunately true that warped minds do enjoy tormenting the helpless –
but we also know that such behaviour is pathological and hence not
typical. Blincoe's memoir fails to describe the typical also because
it contains no realistic account of a normal working day, but such
as it is, it served as an important source for Frances Trollope's

novel *The Life and Adventures of Michael Armstrong, the Factory Boy* (1830-40).[24]

The political radicals were at one in demanding constitutional reform, but they were far from having the same attitude to the working classes, nor did they agree on the legislative measures required for their protection. The views of a man like Carlile with regard to child labour were directly contrary to those of his contemporary Harriet Martineau, who, although a political radical, subscribed to the economic principle of Free Trade. She discusses children at work often enough in her fiction, but she considers them as she might adults. Their presence is simply taken for granted. 'The Riot', published anonymously in 1827, concerns two young factory boys who help to destroy the machines, and are subsequently tried and sentenced to imprisonment. Harriet Martineau's only comment is that children should be protected from political agitators and taught sufficient political economy to make them realize the futility of strikes and riots. And in 'The Hill and the Valley' (*Illustrations of Political Economy*, 1832-4), the workers explode into violence on the death of a boy who is caught by an unfenced piece of machinery. One would have thought that the logical conclusion would be to fence the machines to prevent future accidents, but instead the author blames the boy for having been inattentive. She was nevertheless fond of children, and she is remembered today chiefly as the writer of popular children's books. Her attitude was conditioned by her dogmatic belief in Free Trade; she felt compelled to advocate a policy of non-interference in the relationship between the capitalists and the state.

3. The Human Engine

Stitch, stitch, stitch,
In poverty, hunger and dirt . . .
Work, work, work,
Like the Engine that works by Steam!
(Thomas Hood, 'The Song of the Shirt')

The Chartist attacks on the privileged classes had an unexpected effect – a new social sensibility began to manifest itself. Even the Romantic cult of sentiment had been incapable of turning the tide of public opinion in favour of the factory children and the many Parliamentary reports remained a largely unexplored source for imaginative literature. A change occurred during the late 1830s when working-class conditions, and particularly the plight of the children, finally attracted public notice. Large numbers of destitute children had been made to serve the needs not only of factories, but of agriculture, mining and the traditional crafts as well, and the workhouses, too, put their young wards to work. Most to be pitied were the ragged children who had neither home nor employment; in London alone these totalled 30,000 when Dickens began his campaign on their behalf.

With the controversy over the New Poor Law and the violent manifestations of working-class discontent in the years that followed, the prevalent lethargic indifference to these social problems was exchanged for a keen awareness of the grave danger which threatened the very foundations of society. Many members of the upper classes were appalled and confounded on being confronted with the condition of the industrial workers, and in the private letters, newspaper articles and public debates of this period we feel a profound anxiety for the future. This strong nervous tension became even more pronounced in the fourth decade of the century, which explains why the condition-of-England novel appeared at this particular time. A strong feeling of guilt on behalf of their social class compelled some authors to dwell with painful insistence on the subject, and the same feeling made the public accept and often acclaim the social fiction written in the 1830s and 1840s.

Charles Dickens was only one of many authors who transposed the experience of the oppressed child and the guilt complex of his generation into his fiction, but his artistic achievement was unique. True, on many occasions he would contrive happy endings for his miserable urchins, as in the case of Oliver Twist and David Copperfield, neither of whom is corrupted by his vicious environment. But Dickens would also describe how his little heroes and heroines suffer premature death, like Nell and Paul Dombey. It is symptomatic that readers on both sides of the Atlantic shed copious tears over their sad fate, possibly identifying Nell and Paul with all those miserable children who perished around them. Dickens's compassion was stirred not only by the spectacle of impoverished children, but also by their inadequate education. In *Hard Times* (1854) Dickens indignantly exposes the utter fallacy of the educational principle of the rationalistic utilitarians ('Facts, nothing but Facts'), and the utilitarian attitude towards child labour is strongly satirized in *The Old Curiosity Shop* (1841), as we see in the following speech by Miss Monflathers:

"Don't you feel how naughty it is of you", resumed Miss Monflathers, "to be a wax-work child, when you might have the proud consciousness of assisting, to the extent of your infant powers, the manufactures of your country; of improving your mind by the constant contemplation of the steam-engine; and of earning a comfortable and independent subsistence of from two-and-ninepence to three shillings per week? Don't you know that the harder you are at work, the happier you are?"

(chap. XXXI)

These two novels argue in favour of permitting free scope for the development of the imagination and a sense of moral values, at the same time that they illustrate Dickens's third favourite theme in relation to children – his idealization of the family circle. The happiness of a child is entirely dependent on its being part of such a closely-knit circle. The topicality of these themes did not hamper Dickens's narrative genius; his novels never degenerate into mere propaganda. I here emphasize the social content, but the symbolic import of his narratives is capable of a wide range of interpretations, and the literary critic may approach his child-heroes from different points of view.

One notices the absence of the factory child in Dickens's fiction; his boys and girls are Londoners, and among Londoners the chimney-sweep had attracted attention since the days of Jonas Hanway in the preceding century. Blake's well-known poem on the subject is, in a way, irrelevant because written primarily to illustrate the theme of lost innocence, the main point being that the child, despite its wretched existence, is capable of entertaining hope. The condition of these young toilers was only too obvious, since they performed their task under the very eyes of the public. This is no doubt why the chimney-sweep has figured so often in stories about children that he has achieved the status of a myth. One thinks, for example, of Charles Kingsley's *Water Babies* (1863), or again of Benjamin Britten's recent work *Let's Make an Opera* (1949) based on Blake's 'The Chimney Sweeper'. It is difficult to tell whose lot was the more pitiable – that of the child chimney-sweep or that of the child in the cotton mill. The former were apprenticed when they were between five and eight years old, and it took six months to learn how to climb a chimney so as to serve as a kind of human brush. Reluctant novices were compelled to climb to escape the heat of the fire lit to drive them up, and because it was often difficult to squeeze through angles in the chimney, death from suffocation was not uncommon. These unfortunate boys and girls – for even girls were apprenticed to the trade – remained in their blackened state throughout the week, the luxury of washing being reserved for Sundays. As they soiled whatever they touched, they could not be admitted into a home, and hence these little outcasts spent their nights in the cellar on beds of straw. Needless to say, they were completely illiterate.

Children apprenticed to one of the traditional crafts were in a very different position: they were placed in the workshops of their masters where they were taught a useful trade. The masters may have profited from the work of the children, but these in their turn were rewarded by learning the trade. A distinct change for the worse, however, occurred when the competition from machine-made products made itself felt. To meet this unequal competition, apprentices and master craftsmen had to prolong their working hours to the very limit of human endurance so that in the end children working for such masters came to suffer just as badly as children in the cotton mills, if not more so. But their plight, perhaps understandably, did not attract the same attention on the part of authors and the general public as the young 'operatives' in the textile industry, nor did that of children employed in other branches of industry. The attention paid to them by Charlotte Elizabeth Tonna is exceptional rather than typical. In her social novelette entitled 'The Forsaken Home' in *The Wrongs of Woman* (1843–4) she describes the tragedy of a family where the mother has to support husband and children because the owner of the local screw-factory prefers married women as machine operatives, since their wages are lower and their behaviour more docile. The woman's effort to support her family on nine shillings a week in the end proves futile; all of them degenerate. The husband becomes a drunkard, and the children are neglected. The author shows great concern for the babies of these women. When the central character enters the factory for the first time, she sees several infants "brought in by idle-looking, half-starved, or half-drunken men" or again "by children much too young for such a charge" to permit the babies to be "nourished at the breast" during the break. At first she cannot understand the unnatural stupor of these infants, until she is made to realize that they have been given a tranquillizing mixture of opium and boiled treacle water, the so-called 'Godfrey's cordial'. When a woman states that she has lost three children because of the "cordial", another remarks that it is much better that they should die. The retort – " 'Did I ever say it wasn't?' " – reveals the utter hopelessness of their position. Older children posed different problems. A heart-broken woman complains that her daughters, all of whom worked in the factory, had left their home in protest against having to keep their father. They "would not be dictated to by him." The story ends on a note of great sadness; a new-born baby dies, and the mother is finally compelled to send her children into the factory. (Their subsequent fate as factory workers is related in the novelette 'The Little Pin-Headers' reproduced in the Anthology.) The last story in the collection *The Wrongs of Woman* is entitled 'The Lace Runners', and in it is related the story of a family engaged in the manufacture of lace on machines in their own home. The whole family is compelled to work, even a three-year-old girl, and the baby is pacified with 'Godfrey's cordial'. Kate, a young country girl, joins the family to work as a lace-runner, but soon leaves in disgust to try her hand at the manufacture of stockings. But this kind of work proves equally unrewarding and Kate ends up in the streets as a common prostitute; she prefers this miserable fate to slow death by poorly paid and excessive hard work.

Charlotte Elizabeth Tonna took the details in her stories from the Blue Books and from other published documents, as she herself explains. These details, however, are subordinated to her imaginative presentation of clearly visualized scenes and episodes. She concludes her stories with a vehement denunciation of the privileged classes for their indifference to, or ignorance of, the suffering of the labouring class; the pillars of the English throne "rest on an awakening volcano".

Benjamin Disraeli's well-known novel *Sybil, or the Two Nations* (1845) touches on the problem of child labour in factories and mines. An episode takes place in an overgrown industrial village closely resembling the village of Willenhall as described in the report of the Children's Employment Commission. It has no local government, no school and no church, the rulers of the community being the master locksmiths. These are primitive and brutal men who employ boys and girls as apprentices. Four days in the week are devoted to hard labour, the remaining three to idleness and drink. A very young couple, both of whom are still apprentices, work for a master in whose brutality they seem to take a kind of perverse pride. The boy-husband boasts of a nasty scar on his forehead, caused by a piece of iron flung at him by his master.

The 1842 Report of the Commissions investigating the employment of children and young people in mines and collieries stirred public opinion to a lesser extent than the similar reports on the textile industries in 1833. This may have been because these industries were too far removed from urban life for writers to feel more than a general sympathy for a kind of existence that they were incapable of visualizing. But this did not deter a man like Disraeli, who simply paraphrased the more impressive passages in the Reports, as Cazamian has explained.[25]

Further references to the role of children in the mining industries can be found in Fanny Mayne's *Jane Rutherford, or the Miners' Strike*, serialized anonymously in the journal which she edited, *The True Briton* (1853), and published in book form in 1854. The sub-title indicates the author's chief interest. Although a Tory opponent of Trade Unions, Fanny Mayne freely criticizes the use (and abuse) of children as workers in collieries. This ambiguous attitude may seem illogical, but her compassion was clearly stirred by humanitarian rather than policial or social sentiments; her sincere feelings modify and mitigate her obvious class prejudice. Fanny Mayne adds no new items to the long catalogue of miseries endured by children working in the darkness of underground passages; she blames the adult miners, not the proprietors, for employing these children as 'drawers' of heavily loaded containers through corridors so narrow that they had to crawl. The loads were pulled by a chain fastened around the waist, or pushed by means of the head. Young children between six and eight years old were given the important task of securing the trap doors in the underground galleries to prevent draughts, since these often caused explosions in the days before the compulsory use of Davy's safety lamp. The task was tedious rather than difficult; the little 'trappers' were allowed no light and rats were their only company. No wonder, therefore, that they sometimes fell asleep despite their fear of severe punishment. Fanny Mayne learnt all these details from the Blue Books, but her mind was divided and her comments are non-committal. Another example of fiction describing the work of children in mines is 'The True Story of a Coal Fire' (1850) by Richard Hengist Horne reprinted in our Anthology.

Among the many kinds of work requiring the employment of older children none was more notorious than needle-work, an employment which had been important also in the pre-industrial period and which remained unaffected by the use of machines for a considerable time. The condition of the workers was nevertheless affected, and the trade developed what is usually referred to as the 'sweating system'. This vicious system inspired a poem and a novel which have become classics – Thomas Hood's 'Song of the Shirt' (1843) and Charles Kingsley's *Alton Locke, a Tailor Poet* (1850). Thomas Hood was a gifted journalist and poet, who was inspired to write the poem by an article in *Punch* referring to the case of a London needle-woman and her children. Hood's moving poem was an immediate success; it was printed in a number of papers and periodicals, at home and abroad, and translations into German and Russian inspired writers in these countries to turn to similar social subjects.

Charles Kingsley's sympathies with the working class found expression in two novels, *Yeast* (1848) and *Alton Locke* (1850). In the former he pities the children of farm labourers who come home "night after night, too tired to eat their supper, and tumble fasting to bed in the same foul shirt in which they've been working all the day, never changing their rag of calico from week's end to week's end, or washing the skin that is under it once in seven years" (chap. XIII). In *Alton Locke* the most impressive descriptions are found in the account of the hero's apprenticeship to a tailor and his visit to a girl who dies as a victim of the 'sweating trade'. Alton Locke is 14 when he becomes an apprentice, and on entering the premises of his master he is shocked by the stuffy atmosphere and the bad smells. Twelve workmen are seated bare-footed and crosslegged, busily stitching; they greet the newcomer with bitter jokes. Their work takes them directly to Heaven, they say, because they invariably die from tuberculosis. By the time that he visits the dying girl, Alton Locke has abandoned his craft and his master; the girl lives in a dilapidated house without furniture, and the two girls who are looking after her never stop stitching, since it is their work that supports the girl and their mother. The inadequacy of their wages compels them to serve as prostitutes as well, however much they hate it. As one of the girls puts it, her miserable existence will either drive her mad or make her court forgetfulness through drink (chap. VIII).

The heroine of Elizabeth Gaskell's *Mary Barton, a Tale of Manchester Life* (1848) is apprenticed to a seamstress, a fairly genteel occupation compared to factory work. At the height of the season Mary has to remain in the workshop day and night, and one of her friends ruins her eyesight with the incessant sewing of black mourning garments. The plight of the young seamstresses is presented in even starker colours in Elizabeth Gaskell's *Ruth* (1853), whose heroine spends most of the day and night sewing fashionable dresses for wealthy ladies. One of Ruth's friends is of delicate health, she cannot stand the strain, and dies after the rush of the season is over. Elizabeth Gaskell blames the ladies of fashion for their excessive vanity and their lack of consideration, and like Charlotte Elizabeth Tonna in her story 'Milliners and Dress-Makers' (the first story in the series *The Wrongs of Woman*, 1843), she pleads with the rich to respect the lives of those who depend upon their custom.

4. The Cruel Nation

"How long," they say, "how long, O cruel nation,
Will you stand, to move the world, on a child's heart –"
(Elizabeth Barrett Browning, 'The Cry of the Children')

Since the exploitation of child labour in textile factories stirred the conscience of the nation most profoundly, it is appropriate that this chapter should conclude with a survey of works where the main characters are children employed in cotton mills. Two of the most important of these are Frances Trollope's *The Life and Adventures of Michael Armstrong, the Factory Boy* (1839–40) and Charlotte Elizabeth Tonna's *Helen Fleetwood* (1839). These novels were published in serial form one year after Dickens's *Oliver Twist* (1837–1838), the great popularity of which had created a general interest in fictional accounts of the victimization of children.

Although the artistic merit of *Helen Fleetwood* is greater than that of *Michael Armstrong*, Frances Trollope is by far the better known of the two because of the reputation of her son, Anthony Trollope. She approached the task of writing her story in an eminently practical manner: when she had decided on an industrial setting, she went north to see for herself what the situation was like. To gain admission into the factories she secured a letter of introduction from the Tory champion of the cause of factory children, Lord Shaftesbury.[26] In addition she made the acquaintance of two particularly well-informed men, a minister who served as witness before the Royal Commission on the Employment of Children in Industry, and John Doherty, a Trade Union leader. It was Doherty who had published *Blincoe's Memoir*, and who drew the attention of Frances Trollope to this realistic account of child labour.

Michael Armstrong tells the story of a much-abused factory child, his lame brother and a little factory girl, and scenes from the life of child labourers are scattered through some thousand pages of a loosely constructed narrative. The children are depicted in general terms so that they represent types rather than individuals, and a mass of detailed information about the cotton industry is incorporated into the main stream of the narrative more or less at random. The author's good sense is shown by the introduction of comic scenes that provide enough variety and contrast to avoid the monotonous boredom of the solemn tone of voice so typical of novels dedicated to social problems.

The passages written on the basis of personal observation reveal a genuine sympathy with the young workers. According to Thomas Adolphus, his mother had witnessed "dreadful things" in the North, and we catch a glimpse of one such episode in the scene describing how the children gather at the gate of factory very early in the morning "while the lingering darkness of a winter's night had yet to last three hours . . . the ground was covered with deep snow, and a cutting wind blew whistling through the long line of old Scotch firs". Beneath them are hardly visible "the little figures of a multitude of Children . . . all huddled together on the ground, and seemingly half buried in the drift that was blown against them". The description conveys indignation as well as pity, and direct denunciation is expressed by one of the characters, who condemns the avarice of man for having conceived a system "so horribly destructive of every touch of human feelings". In order to "enable the giant engines of our factories to outspin all the world", factory owners callously exploit "the low-priced agony of labouring infants" (Book II, chap. 8).

The extent to which Frances Trollope depended on the *Memoir of Robert Blincoe* (1828) can be illustrated by means of a few parallel passages:

Robert Blincoe	Michael Armstrong
No soap was allowed: a small quantity of meal was given as a substitute; and this from the effect of keen hunger, was generally eaten. (p.183)	The coarse meal occasionally given out to supply its place [i.e. of soap] was invariably swallowed, being far too precious in the eyes of the hungry children to be applied to the purpose for which it was designed. (Book II, chap. 9)
The fatting pigs fared luxuriously compared with the apprentices . . . Blincoe and others, who worked in a part of the Mill, whence they could see the swine served . . . used to keep a sharp eye on the fatting pigs, and their meal-balls, and . . . used to slip downstairs, and stealing slyly towards the trough, . . . steal as many dumplings as he could grasp . . . Soon the pigs fought and grunted for their food, and a whip would dispel the children. (pp. 214f.)	Seven or eight boys had already made their way to the sort of rude farm-yard upon which this door opened, one and all of whom were intent upon purloining from a filthy trough just replenished for the morning meal of two stout hogs, a variety of morsels, which, as Michael's new acquaintance assured him, were 'dainty eating for the starving prentices of Deep Valley Mill'. 'Make haste, young 'un,' cried Charles good-naturedly, 'or they won't leave a turnip paring for us.' And on he rushed to the scuffle, leaving Michael gazing with disgust and horror at the contest between the fierce snouts of the angry pigs, and the active fingers of the wretched crew. (Book II, chap. 4)

The plot of this realistic social novel is patently absurd; the author wanted to write a popular book that might provide an income for her ailing family, and so she mixed incompatible ingredients. The three children are rescued by a benevolent rich heiress who later on marries Michael's brother despite the disparity in age, After having studied in a German university for two years, Michael. becomes a perfect young gentleman, and the young factory girl, too, is given education and is then married off to Michael.

Michael Armstrong was given a mixed reception by the public. Only a few reviews appeared, and these were largely negative. *The Athenæum* for 10 August 1839 (No. 615) printed a leading article deploring the fact that fiction was being written "for the purpose of scattering firebrands among the people". Novels like *Michael Armstrong* might in the long run cause "the burning of factories", "the plunder of property", "civil war, bankruptcy and national destruction". And in April 1840 (No. 649) the same periodical published a hostile review of the book. The two favourable reviews which appeared in the *New Monthly Magazine* (April 1839, p. 565, and October 1839, p. 286) reflect the fact that the editor, Henry Colburn, was Frances Trollope's publisher. Despite the scarcity of reviews, however, the book sold well; the publisher made no complaints, although he had paid a stiff price for the manuscript. The author herself registered her disappointment on discovering that her book was welcomed only by the Chartists, and the fact that she abandoned her project of writing a sequel may be an indication that she was frightened by the turn which the class-war took during the early 1840s.[27]

In one important respect the social criticism of *Michael Armstrong* was already dated: by 1839 establishments like the Deep Valley Mill were far from common, since factories were concentrated in the big industrial cities where the child labourers lived at home and so had totally different problems to cope with. The conditions at Deep Valley Mill, as described by Frances Trollope, therefore reflect an earlier period when factories were located in isolated valleys where rivers provided the source of power.

Charlotte Elizabeth Tonna was one of the severest critics of the factory system in general and in particular of the abuse of children in the textile industry. She wrote many articles about the evils of industrialization for the two Evangelical periodicals that she edited, and in one of them she serialized her novel *Helen Fleetwood*[28] (1839–40) – the first English novel completely devoted to the life of industrial proletarians. The story is very simple. An old and helpless woman is compelled by poverty to leave her native village and move to Manchester, where her grandchildren and an adopted grand-daughter (Helen Fleetwood) are put to work in textile factories. Some of the children die, others are corrupted by their evil environment, and the rest disperse so that the grandmother ends her days as a pauper in the workhouse. The cousins of these

children are brought into the story to illustrate the fatal consequences of introducing children into factories. The eldest, who is
dying from tuberculosis, has been crippled as the result of a factory
accident, and another has become deformed by the long hours of
work in a cramped and unnatural position. The younger cousin has
such a vacant and stupified expression that he "seemed to be under
the influence of a powerful narcotic". Their younger sister seems
like a mere "spectre of a very pretty girl"; she has narrow shoulders
and a livid complexion, while her "broad, unflinching stare" is said
to be "oppressive" (chap. 4). Suffering seldom ennobles, and these
unhappy children treat their parents and their relatives from the
country with impertinence and a complete lack of respect or
kindness.

The author reveals the interesting point that children were
occasionally sent into factories even when the parents did not need
the money, simply because this was an accepted practice. Thus one
of the workers in the novel comments bitterly on those adult mill
workers who profit from the labour of their children. He calls it "a
cannibal sort of life to be eating as one may say, the flesh off our
children's bones, and sucking the young blood out of their veins"
(2: 69). But this very man nevertheless has children at work in the
factories, an incident which reveals the subtle but compelling power
of social conformity in a manner which may have been beyond the
author's conscious intent. Mere recognition of evil practices is not
enough to enable an individual to resist them. Another character,
who voices the sentiments of the author, is a child of seven who
explains to a child of nine how his companions suffer:

My poor little companions are going on, on, on, in their weary slavery,
the whirling wheels always whirling, and not a pleasant sight, not a
cheerful sound to make a variety. Their bare feet hot on the boards and
to be pattering through the cold mud at night to their close, dirty homes,
where they won't be let sleep long enough to get refreshed for tomorrow's
toil.

(chap. 22)

Direct authorial comment was required to discuss topics incapable
of being conveyed through dialogue: health, education, or moral
issues, for example. The author's views are those of an ultra-
Protestant Evangelical who realizes the close connection between
moral and religious standards and general living conditions; as we

see from the short narratives that she published in religious periodicals from 1830 to 1850 under the name of Charlotte Elizabeth,
she was convinced that poverty caused moral decay and that there
was a very real danger that atheism would come to prevail in the
big industrial towns. *Helen Fleetwood* is a genuinely moving assault
upon the reader's conscience in its graphic description of what it is
actually like to be a young child compelled by poverty to work in a
factory. She pleads for an increase in the philanthropic efforts of
individuals, for better education and religious instruction, and for
legislation to be not only enacted but its provisions implemented.
Unlike so many Evangelical writers, Charlotte Elizabeth Tonna
was not primarily concerned with the pacification of the 'dangerous
class' but with the alleviation of their suffering. She argued that
hunger has two consequences: it degrades and it causes revolt, and
that the greatest sin of an industrial society is its complete indifference to the body, spirit, and human personality of its workers.

Although Benjamin Disraeli and Mrs Gaskell are sufficiently
well known, a few comments will serve to place them within the
context outlined here.

Disraeli's approach to the problem of child labour was that of a
Tory. While Frances Trollope and Charlotte Elizabeth Tonna
wrote in order to move the public to feel sympathy for the wretched,
Disraeli had a more immediate political purpose. His *Sybil, or the
Two Nations* (1845) criticizes the new industrial development and
attacks the principle of Free Trade. To this principle he opposed
the ideals of the New England movement and especially its semi-
feudal belief in class harmony. *Sybil* contains a number of realistic
scenes set in an industrial town or again in textile mills, metal
foundries, or mines, and it is obvious that Disraeli took much of his
information from the Blue Books, since some passages paraphrase
these books quite closely.

The most impressive of the factory children described by
Disraeli is Devilsdust, the illegitimate son of a young factory girl.
As a baby he was entrusted to the care of an old woman who makes
her living from nursing the infants of women workers, but when
his mother abandons him after two years, the old woman permits
the child to roam the streets in the hope that he may meet with a
fatal accident. He is fed, if at all, only irregularly and fights with
stray dogs over the remnants of food that he finds in the streets.
When he is five years old, a cholera epidemic kills off the old

woman and all her infant charges except the boy. On his aimless wanderings through the town he comes into the yard of a big factory, where the workers take an interest in him so that he is given the job of scavenger, and it is they who give the name of Devilsdust to this nameless boy of the streets. The name conveys a pun; the devil would certainly seem to have had a hand in the shaping of the career of this boy, but devilsdust is also the technical term for the 'flock made of old cloth by the machine called a devil'. Originally the term referred to the dust made in this process. The boy is possessed of a good mind and so manages to be admitted into a school, and later on he becomes a skilled workman and an enthusiastic partisan of the cause of the proletariat.

This concern for the fate of poor children was expressed by Disraeli at a time when the sensibility of the nation had been stirred and it is typical of the man that he never indulged in mere sentimental lamentations. Disraeli was a politician who considered the problem of child labour as part of the larger condition-of-England problem. The reason why his novel focusses so extensively on the condition of children is surely that a number of published reports provided him with the facts that he needed; in the case of adult workers no similar documentation was available. Disraeli had little or no personal knowledge of the issues he dealt with; his approach was purely intellectual, and his lack of empathy impaired his artistic powers. Whatever artistic merit the work possesses certainly cannot be attributed to the passages that describe the lives of children.

When Elizabeth Gaskell joined the ranks of the condition-of-England writers, many of the abuses suffered by children had become a thing of the past. During the four years when she wrote *Mary Barton, a Tale of Manchester Life* (1848), the Chartist movement was a much more urgent issue than child labour. By this time children had to be at least thirteen before they were admitted into factories; they were excluded from night shifts and some provision was made for their education. Although we know from reports submitted by factory inspectors that the regulations of the Factory Acts were transgressed by some master manufacturers, the majority of the children employed in the cotton industry enjoyed some measure of legal protection. And this was the major industry in the Manchester of Elizabeth Gaskell's generation. According to twentieth-century standards their condition left much to be desired, but it represented a distinct improvement when compared with the past. During the 1840s the problem of child labour engaged less public attention also because of the suffering experienced by the working class as a whole. When an entire family starves, their sole concern will be with food, everything being subordinated to the fight for mere physical survival. Mrs Gaskell dramatizes this situation in the episode concerned with the widow Davenport whose husband had died from a pestilent fever, leaving her with three hungry children. Because her son is too young to be permitted to work in a factory, she complains bitterly to a Chartist delegation, asking them to tell Parliament "what a sore trial it is, this law o' theirs, keeping childer fra' factory work" (Book I, chap. 8). And some years later, in *North and South* (1855), Mrs Gaskell has no reference at all to factory children; the time had definitely passed when they required – and finally obtained – the attention of the public.

But before we leave the subject of child labour, it will be of some interest to consider the frame of mind of the masters themselves as described by Elizabeth Stone[29] of Manchester in *William Langshaw, the Cotton Lord* (1842). This is a novel that may possibly have been written in order to refute Frances Trollope or Charlotte Elizabeth Tonna. Her fictional characters express the greatest impatience with outsiders who try to solve difficult problems without a proper grasp of the facts; thus it is much better for children to be prepared for the hard life they will have to experience as adults. When a lady argues that "the very fact of their being worked ten hours in the day is sufficiently lamentable", the callousness of the answer must be taken as typical. Life must be accepted on its own terms:

It is so; and to look at it theoretically every man with a humane heart would wish that children should be free and unfettered, and pass their early years in gaiety and liberty. But it is impossible. The children of the poor *must* work; and that being the case, the true philanthropist will bend his energies rather towards the amelioration of existing evils, than to the invention of a Utopian and unattainable system of freedom and happiness.

(Book I, chap. 13)

However much we may wish that children could be permitted to play and go to school, this "is impossible" and a mere Utopian vision!

It is strange to consider that this dismissal of the emancipation of children from work as a fanciful dream was expressed only some four generations ago by an average person endowed with common sense. This returns us to the question posed at the beginning of this chapter, the relationship between the technical development of a given society and the social sensibility of its members. It is a humiliating thought that the cruel exploitation of child labour began to stir general compassion only when the Industrial Revolution had been fully achieved and at a time when their contribution had become not only superfluous, but even something of an impediment to progress. It is equally painful to consider that the desire for the legal protection of children should be felt only when it became apparent that a number of social evils besetting the whole nation stemmed from the absence of such legislative measures. The development of a social sensibility, so it would seem, is less a matter of the reaction of individuals than of a change in the prevailing economic situation. The abuse of child labourers, however vicious, was tolerated with equanimity during the initial stages of the process of industrialization, and the public lost its sublime indifference only when the army of factory children became a pressing social problem. Finally one notices that this change of heart occurred when the fully mechanized industries had become so stable and prosperous that they no longer depended on the cheaply-paid, prolonged hours of a child's working day. One is led to conclude that feelings of social responsibility and reformist zeal could not manifest themselves until an economic basis had been created for Factory Acts restricting the use of child labour. Nevertheless, one must not underestimate the effect of reformist efforts, although one may admit that the timing of these efforts is important. But for such efforts society would remain crippled by archaic forms of organization and legislation utterly unsuited to its needs.

By way of summary we may conclude that social compassion is an expensive kind of sensibility requiring economic justification before it can be indulged. Technical progress coupled with a capitalistic system of free enterprise enslaved the child, but it also created the economic basis for its ultimate emancipation. And as we have seen, the story of this process is narrated in the literature surveyed in this study.

Notes

1. 'Review of the Eighteenth Century', *The Gentleman's Magazine* (1800), Supplement, 1273.
2. Defoe, *A Tour thro' the whole Island of Great Britain by a Gentleman* (1724), 101.
3. Josiah Tucker, *Instruction for Travellers*, 23.
4. Benjamin Fawcett, *The Religious Weaver or Pious Meditation on the Trade of Weaving* (1773), 105f.
5. Sarah Trimmer, *The Economy of Charity; or an Address to Ladies Concerning Sunday-Schools* (1787), 70.
6. [William Bray], *A Sketch of a Tour into Derbyshire and Yorkshire* (1778), 65.
7. [Sir Richard Joseph Sullivan], *Observation Made during a Tour through Parts of England, Scotland, and Wales* (1780), 141.
8. T. A. Wenderborn, *A View of England towards the Close of the Eighteenth Century* (1791), I, 226.
9. [Edward Clarke], *A Tour through the South of England, Wales, and part of Ireland, Made during the Summer of 1791* (1793).
10. *Op. cit.*, 87f.
11. James Boswell, *Life of Dr. Johnson* (Everyman edn), I, 369.
12. Hutchins and Harrison, *History of Factory Legislation* (1903), Appendix A, p. 304.
13. William Blake, *Vala, or the Four Zoas* (1795–1804), Night VII, 179–84.
14. Reproduced in the anthology.
15. England should bind herself "by statutes to secure / For all the children whom her soil maintains / The rudiments of letters . . ." (299–30).
16. "Essay IV. On the State of the Poor, the Principle of Mr. Malthus's Essay on Population, and the Manufacturing System 1812.", 114f.
17. *Correspondence of Crabb Robinson with the Wordsworth Circle* (1927), 626 (letter dated [20] May 1846).
18. Quoted from L. E. Watson, *Coleridge at Highgate* (1925), Appendix I, p. 177.
19. Coleridge, *Letters*, ed. E. L. Griggs (1959), No. 1127.
20. *The Lion* for 22 February, 256.
21. *Ibid.* 29 February, 276.
22. *Ibid.*, 14 March, 338.
23. *Ibid.*, 29 March, 401.
24. W. H. Chaloner, 'Mrs. Trollope and the Early Factory System', *Victorian Studies* IV (1961), 159.
25. Louis Cazamian, *Le Roman social en Angleterre* (Paris, 1903). Quoted from the edition of 1934 (vol. II, 93–9).

26. According to Thomas Adolphus Trollope, Lord Shaftesbury had written to his mother about the usefulness of an article she had written for the *Quarterly Review*, LVII (1836).
27. Lucy and Richard Poate Stebbins, *The Trollopes* (1936), 97f.
28. See I. Kovačević and Barbara Kanner, 'Blue Book into Novel: the Forgotten Industrial Fiction of Charlotte Elizabeth Tonna', *Nineteenth Century Fiction*, XXV (1970), 152–73. The novel was serialized in *The Christian Lady's Magazine* (1839–40), and published in 1841 by R. B. Seeley in one volume at 7 shillings – a sum representing a whole week's earnings for a factory girl.
29. Published by Richard Bentley and listed in *The English Catalogue of Books 1835–1862*. Elizabeth Stone, *née* Wheeler, lived for some time in Manchester where her father, John Wheeler, was the proprietor of the liberal *Manchester Chronicle*. See the unpublished M. Lit. dissertation on *Writers in Manchester 1831–1854* by A. S. Karminski (Cambridge, 1955), 182.

Chapter 4

The Ambivalence of a Generation

The more we study the early Victorians, the more we realize the ambivalence of their social philosophy, and its tentative and contradictory character. Overwhelmed as they were by the many problems created by the Industrial Revolution, the novelists groped their way among various ideologies, often combining basically irreconcilable concepts or ideas. This helps to explain the contradictory statements, the contrived characterization, the abrupt twisting of plot, the illogical and artificial devices so often encountered in condition-of-England novels. And since the subject-matter of these novels is so heterogeneous, the picture is the more confused. In order to clarify the issue, I propose to discuss the presentation of a single social problem – the conflict between capitalists and workers. It is true that few novelists had the courage to tackle this truly basic problem, but those who did committed blunders of a kind that are more revealing than the most cogent argument.

It will be useful to approach this problem by comparing the treatment given to it by two well-known authors, Charles Dickens and Harriet Martineau. These two novelists can not only be seen to represent opposite positions in their fiction, but they also conducted a public argument in defence of their social philosophy.[1] But despite the fact that each was a passionate champion of a consistently held system of ideology, neither managed to apply this system in a logical manner to the narratives invented to illustrate their views. This is seen most clearly in their treatment of the working class.

Harriet Martineau regarded fiction simply as a convenient means of conveying her social philosophy to a wide audience of readers not capable of abstract theorizing. Though not the first to grasp the usefulness of fictionalized propaganda, she was the first to concentrate on the conflict between capital and labour in industry;[2] whereas Dickens joined the ranks of the condition-of-England novelists when the path was already well trodden. Ten years older than Dickens, Harriet Martineau preceded him by a whole generation in her treatment of the industrial theme. Her first short story, 'The Rioters', appeared in 1827, 27 years before *Hard Times*, and her principal work, *Illustrations of Political Economy*, in 1832-4, before Dickens's first sketches. She started writing even before the Reform Bill of 1832, whereas he produced his industrial novel when the troubled 1830s and 1840s had been succeeded by the more stable 1850s. By then class relationships had undergone considerable modification, and so it may, perhaps, seem pointless to compare works so wide apart in time. And if in addition we consider the fundamental differences between the ideas of Dickens and Harriet Martineau on social problems, the comparison may seem strained. But as I shall show, a juxtaposition of these two writers reveals a significant similarity in their conscious and subconscious response to the heart of the problem, indicating that certain basic ideas were firmly held throughout their period; moreover, traces of these ideas are still apparent today, less in fiction perhaps than in party politics.

As a self-confessed 'emotionalist', Dickens rejected a rational approach to social problems in favour of intuitive perception. He agreed with Carlyle that the heart is closer to the truth than the mind; our efforts should be guided by our emotions and not by theories, which he dismissed as idle sophistry. Yet when Dickens concerns himself with the proletariat in his novels, he is repeatedly 'guilty' of rationalization. Not only does he argue instead of responding to the dictates of his heart, he also advances arguments that are contrary to the main trend of his reasoning. Thus when Dickens considers the relationship between masters and workers in factories, his views come fairly close to those of Harriet Martineau. Moreover, in his fictional treatment of the employer-employee controversy, Dickens departs from the facts which he recorded personally. The portrayal of the industrial workers and the fable of *Hard Times* are contrived to illustrate a social theory to which Dickens did not habitually subscribe, and which was unsupported by his personal observation.

Harriet Martineau, on the other hand, started from an opposite point of view. In her opinion reason and not feeling should determine one's social behaviour. She warned her readers that a sentimental approach to social matters could lead to a mistaken tolerance of working-class organization. Yet it appears that she herself was not immune to the contagion. Occasionally she surprises the reader by her intuitive grasp of the situation and by showing a better understanding of the psychology of the industrial worker than Dickens. In this manner the two can be said to change places in their duel over the working man.

Dickens revolted against the profiteering spirit of his age because it corrupts the individual and the civilization based on *laissez-faire* principles. Despite his clear stand on these issues, Dickens was capable of expressing contradictory views, as critics have often observed. *Hard Times, for These Times* (1854) contains inconsistencies in the treatment of the main theme as well as in plot and characterization. We shall first examine the inconsistencies in characterization, since Dickens insisted on the individuality, the 'otherness', of his proletarians. In *Hard Times* the relevant characters are the working-class hero and the woman he loves, and they are Dickens's only full-length portraits of industrial workers.

Stephen Blackpool is miserable because tied by marriage to a disreputable wife, a drunkard "disgracing herself in every way". Stephen wants to divorce his wife and marry Rachael, but he does not know if there is a law which will enable him to do so. He goes to his master Bounderby, of all people, to ask for advice. Bounderby is astounded and condemns Stephen for criticizing the Divorce Law, which allows divorce only at an exorbitant price. Presumably the dialogue between Bounderby and Stephen was intended to illustrate two points: the arrogance of the master and the dignity of the workman. In criticizing Bounderby, Dickens deplores the inability of the mill-owner to play the part of adviser and protector to his workers. This 'responsibility-of-the-superior' ideal was one of Carlyle's ideas to which Dickens subscribed. It aimed at reviving the feudal links between the governing class and the workers. Because it is founded on an obsolete concept, the scene between Bounderby and Stephen has a false ring. The industrial workers by no means resembled the agricultural labourers, who still preserved some of their servility towards the owners of the land they cultivated. Familiar as he was with the agricultural South, Dickens imagined that the same spirit existed among the factory workers. He believed that the workers really did turn to their masters for protection, but that the mill-owners were not equal to the task. Dickens was of course mistaken; the patriarchal relationship between social classes had disappeared in the large industrial cities by the time he wrote *Hard Times*. No factory worker, not even Stephen Blackpool, would have gone to the proprietor of the establishment in which he worked to consult him about his private problems.

The second point that Dickens wants to stress in this scene is Stephen's supposed independence of spirit. It is possible that our modern concept of human dignity prevents us from following Dickens's argument. Stephen is not servile, yet he stands by the door while his master continues eating, and is not invited to sit down. Bounderby's behaviour is consistently insolent; nevertheless, on leaving the house of his master Stephen gives the doorknob "a parting polish with the sleeve of his coat" when he notices that his hot hand has clouded it. This little detail reveals Stephen's character. He is neither "the oppressed man intensely miserable" nor "at the same time intensely attractive and important" as Chesterton would put it. Had Dickens strongly insisted on Stephen's degradation and at the same time on his dignity, the hero's character might have been saved from dullness. As it is, Stephen is without those characteristics which, according to Chesterton's penetrating analysis, create the contradictory tension of a successful social tale.[3] By emphasizing Stephen's individuality and placing him in exceptional circumstances, Dickens stresses those qualities in Stephen which make him different from his fellow workers, and a quarrel with the trade union makes him even more exceptional. Stephen places his loyalty to Rachael above the claims of his trade union; his personal commitment is more important than an abstract loyalty to a cause. The 'otherness' of Stephen contradicts Dickens's statement that *Hard Times* is "a story which has a direct purpose in reference to the working people all over England".[4] Dickens also contradicts his own theory of characterization. He first insists on the environmental factor in the formation of character, and then proceeds to present a character that refutes his theory. According to the environmental theory, Stephen, who grew up among the sordid slums of Coketown and the foetid atmosphere of its cotton-mills, should have emerged as a different man from the Stephen whom Dickens presents to us. From that point of view Stephen would fit any of Harriet Martineau's tales, because she is a staunch believer in absolute free will.

Dingle Foot has pointed out that it would be natural for Stephen to be an active member of the trade union instead of quarrelling with it,[5] and Stephen displays further odd traits. According to Dickens's explicit statement in chapter 5, Book I, the workers of Coketown were indifferent to religion, whereas Stephen is a pious man. It is known that the sexual relationships among the workers were fairly free, whereas Stephen insists on the chastity of his friendship with Rachael. Mrs Gaskell, who published her novel *North and South* in the following year, describes the factory workers as quick-witted, whereas Dickens's working-class hero is slow to the point of stupidity. Stephen admits that politics are beyond his grasp, and expects his 'betters' to wrestle with social problems. As far as he is concerned, these represent a big muddle which he and his class should not try to disentangle (Book II, chap. V).

Rachael, on her part, recalls the priggish working-class girls whose 'virtue' is praised in the stories published by the Tract Society. Her vigil beside the drunken wife of the man she loves provides Dickens with the opportunity of glorifying her self-assertive righteousness. It was Rachael's interference that caused Stephen's tragedy; it was she who stepped between him and the trade union because she was suspicious. A recent article by Sylvère Monod throws new light on Stephen's rupture with the union, but it does not indicate that he should be considered as possessed of a spirit of independence.[6] It is significant that the two working-class characters in *Hard Times* are opposed to the union because they lack a feeling of class solidarity. In this, of course, they are not typical, as Dickens clearly shows elsewhere.[7] On the other hand, if it were not dullness which kept Stephen and Rachael away from the union, their motives are difficult to account for. If they disapproved of the union's methods, they could have suggested alternatives. But they remain stubbornly silent about their objection to the union. Moreover, Dickens implicitly suggests that their behaviour is correct and that the other workers who join the strike are deluded. Consequently Stephen Blackpool and Rachael strongly resemble the 'deserving poor' of the tract-distributing philanthropists whom Dickens usually derided. This is not to say that people like Stephen and Rachael did not exist among the industrial workers in the North; but it is significant that Dickens as a declared friend of the people should have chosen a man of Blackpool's calibre to epitomize the English industrial worker. Like Ruskin, many later critics have found Stephen's character unsatisfying and unconvincing. One severe critic finds him "intellectually starved into premature senility", and concludes that his mind is "bovine".[8]

From the problem of characterization we may pass on to a consideration of ethical issues. Dickens represents his working-class protagonists as worthy of admiration, poor in material goods, but rich in virtue. Love is their source of power and the spring of their actions. Wealth is beyond their reach and they do not desire it; they are satisfied with the fate "assigned to them by Providence". But it is revealing to compare them with Bounderby, who began his life as a poor man. Bounderby had not been utterly destitute as he would boast in his inverted snobbishness; nevertheless, it appears that Bounderby became rich simply owing to his ability, while Stephen remained poor. Does Dickens mean that they had the same opportunities, but not the same capacity, and that able people would thrive under the existing system, while the less able would remain wage-earners? Are we finally to conclude that each gets what he deserves, that the poor remain destitute because they are impractical, or perhaps lazy? Is their lack of interest in the acquisition of material goods the real cause of their low position in society? All these questions arise from the situation presented in the novel, but arguments like these would plainly be contrary to Dickens's social philosophy as expressed elsewhere, both explicitly and more indirectly through his fiction. It would be preposterous to attribute such a purpose to *Hard Times* or any of Dickens's works. But the paradoxical question still remains whether the poor remain destitute and down-trodden *because* they possess the virtues praised by Dickens – simplicity and disinterestedness.

That Dickens did not associate moral excellence with poverty is shown by the generous distribution of wealth in the happy endings of his stories. And he contradicts the well-known principle that the poor should display a 'happy satisfaction' when he removes Sissy from the circus, thus enabling her to acquire a higher education and a higher standard of living than would normally have fallen to her share. Her adoption by the Gradgrinds is clearly presented as a beneficial event in her life, although Dickens of course primarily wanted to convey other points through the story of Sissy's life.

In *Hard Times* Dickens fails to provide a full description of the living conditions of a member of the working classes; he fails to bring to life the details of Blackpool's day-to-day existence inside the factory and out of it. *Household Words* and *All the Year Round* contain a number of articles by Dickens himself or his contributors presenting graphic descriptions of various abuses and scenes of appalling poverty, but all of this is absent from the pages of *Hard Times*. Fifteen years before he wrote this novel Dickens had stated in a letter from Manchester that what he had seen there had provoked his indignation, and he added that he would soon strike a blow against the abuses from which the Manchester operatives suffered. But when he finally decided to use the subject in a novel, the characteristic Dickensian detail is missing. Whether he had forgotten the details or deliberately dismissed them, must be a matter of conjecture. The fact remains that in *Hard Times* the descriptions of the districts where the poor live are given in a generalized way; we receive no adequate picture of the inside of a factory or an everyday scene in a working-class home. The hero's and heroine's plight is caused not by the circumstances of proletarian life, nor by the tyranny of the capitalist, but by the inadequacy of the Divorce Law and the tyranny of the union. Of all the condition-of-England novels familiar to me, *Hard Times* places the least emphasis on the effect upon the poor of their degrading living conditions.

The treatment of the class struggle in *Hard Times* betrays Dickens's preconceived ideas. He aimed at showing "the monstrous chains of domination made by a certain class of manufacturers, the extent to which the way is made easy for the working man to slide down into discontent."[9] The derogatory "slide down" reveals Dickens's disapproval. It is also significant that he was disappointed with what he saw of the great Preston Strike in February 1854.[10] But it is not clear exactly why he was disappointed since he found the conduct of the strikers peaceful and orderly on the whole, and the strikers themselves responsible and dignified. The competence of the chairman, a middle-aged weaver, and the purposefulness of the striker's committee, surprised Dickens. Not only men but women and girls as well joined in the strike, and the latter impressed him favourably: "A very large majority of these girls and women were comfortably dressed in all respects, clean, wholesome and pleasant-looking. There was a prevalent neatness and cheerfulness, and an almost ludicrous absence of anything like sullen discontent."[11] Dickens imagined that only "sullen discontent" would rouse a working-class community to strike. He found their good spirits "ludicrous" because the festive mood of well-organized strikers was unknown to him, as was the mood and mentality of the industrial workers in general. He mistakenly attributed to the trade union activity of the 1850s the revolutionary spirit which characterized the Chartism of the previous decade.

The main target of Dickens's attack is the politically active workers. In denouncing the trade union and its leaders he uses the same methods and arguments as the so-called 'friends of the people' in the penny-press financed by various anti-revolutionary societies. The physical appearance and behaviour of the agitator in Bounderby's factory is described in a manner intended to provoke dislike, and his address to the workers is recorded with sarcastic exaggeration.[12] He bullies the whole meeting into boycotting Stephen. Moreover Dickens gives his agitator the symbolic name of Slackbridge. Ignoring the fact that the agitator himself belonged to the 'lower orders', Dickens presents him as an impostor. The novelist forgets that his indignation was a natural enough reaction to the condition of his class; that before becoming a working-class leader he must have exposed himself to many inconveniences; that his trade union activity involved risk to him and his family – all this for an ephemeral notoriety and the short-lived gratitude of his followers.

Are we to believe that Dickens was ignorant of the moral fortitude which a man of Slackbridge's stamp possessed? His own writing refutes this supposition. In his article from Preston,

Dickens gives a favourable description of such a leader, just as he recognizes the moral strength of proletarians struggling against the overwhelming power of capital. The chairman of the meeting which Dickens attended was a local weaver, about 50 years of age, with a placid, attentive face and keen eyes. He conducted the meeting with composure. Moreover, the workers are not described as a gang of simple men, easily misled, like those in *Hard Times*. The Preston workers aroused the admiration of the novelist; he praised their "astonishing fortitude and perseverance; their high sense of honour among themselves; the extent to which they are impressed with the responsibility that is upon them of setting a careful example, and keeping their order out of any harm and loss of reputation; the noble readiness in them to help one another . . ."[13] Although Dickens had witnessed a famous strike, in *Hard Times* he 'refused to strike', as he wrote in a letter to Elizabeth Gaskell.[14] What he did was to record the preparations for a strike, in order to comment on strikes in general. He deplores them as a calamity, not only because they are a great waste of wealth, energy and time, but most of all because strikers undermine the solidarity of classes whose interests must be understood to be identical. Because he maintained that the classes should work together, and that the gulf between them should be bridged, Dickens contrived the fable of *Hard Times* in accordance with this conception. By so doing he comes nearest to Harriet Martineau's fictionalized propaganda in *Illustrations of Political Economy*. Although so bitterly outspoken against political economy and the Utilitarians, Dickens in this novel nevertheless stooped to preaching the dogma of 'identical interests'.

Since Dickens carefully avoided arousing class animosity, it remains to be seen how he presented the capital-labour problem. He did not try to reform either Bounderby or Bounderby's workers; not did he attempt a Scrooge-like reformation of Bounderby, or make the workers suddenly understand the principles of political economy. He gave up preaching tolerance to men inaccessible to argument and immune from feeling like Bounderby, "whose monstrous claims of domination" provoked understandable discontent. But he did preach to the workers, recommending submission to those same "monstrous" masters. This preaching of class harmony, however, was undermined by its inner contradiction. In the first place Dickens could present no pictures of class harmony because these would have been utterly implausible, and then, secondly, it was equally impossible to prove the beneficial effect of collaboration between the classes. His only choice was to show, instead, the vicious consequences of class struggle.

But if collaboration were pursued along the lines indicated by Dickens, its purpose would soon be defeated. When the capitalists possess wealth and power, and the workers have neither, collaboration must acquire the meaning which the masters give to it. The workers on their side can obtain a hearing only when they act against such 'collaboration'. Having neither capital nor influence, they are obliged to resort to their only weapon – combination. Unity of numbers is their strength and the wisdom of this was evident to the workers. That Dickens was blind to its simple logic has been attributed to his fear of revolution. Whatever its inspiration the moral lesson remains a very pessimistic one. It is preached with a heavy heart, as Dickens realized that it would never work in a modern world. In *Hard Times* no reconciliation is achieved, and the gulf between the classes remains. Shirking the portrayal of the inauspicious state of affairs in society, Dickens concentrates on individual cases, but in vain, for his solitary proletarian is tightly caught in the meshes of the social fabric. There is no way out for his hero, who dies a violent death.

The last but not the least important contradiction of *Hard Times* springs from Dickens's style, which is selfconscious because his feelings are out of harmony with his ideas. His sensibility, the main source of his creativeness, is repressed in this novel; he could not follow the dictates of his heart and delineate the plight of the working class fully. Logically, this would have involved a frontal attack on the social system; Dickens could not undertake such a task, and therefore had to stifle his emotions. Hence *Hard Times* is a tough book, an argumentative rather than imaginative narrative. Its symbolism is strained because he adopts a social philosophy contrary to the main stream of his thought, and in fact endorses the Utilitarian doctrine which he formerly denounced as rationalized inhumanity. It was the Manchester Utilitarians who urged the theory of identical class interests most strongly, and it is this very idea which constitutes the social message of *Hard Times*.

Hard Times pleased neither party, and attracted comparatively little attention. Although no favourite with the reading public, its didacticism has not escaped the notice of those who have endorsed it even up to the present century. Fearing the spread of the Bolshevik revolution, a contributor to *The Dickensian* wrote in 1919 that *Hard Times* shows "what might happen in England if thinking workers will insist on determining their own destinies, without the light of reason coming to their hearts". The writer ends with the words: "Yes, verily, I think *Hard Times* should be in the hands of every British worker".[15] A similar article appeared in the same periodical in 1928.[16]

These remarks provide a suitable link between *Hard Times* and Harriet Martineau's *Illustrations of Political Economy*. Her only aim in writing fiction was to introduce the workers to political economy (of the James Mill and Ricardo school). She realized that a number of readers who would not otherwise make the effort to grasp the dry doctrines of economics would digest them in fictional form.

Harriet Martineau was a wholehearted supporter of the Utilitarian social philosophy. She had a passion for truth derived from her Unitarian upbringing, and when she believed she had discovered the truth, she clung to it with militant zeal. "She was a singularly happy person", wrote Greg, "her unflinching belief in herself, her singular exemption from the sore torment of doubt or hesitation helped to make her so".[17] Consequently, she was relentless in imposing her ideas on others, and this was the source of her formidable series *Illustrations of Political Economy* (1832–4), the first and the most important popularization in fictional form of the economic doctrine of *laissez-faire*.

The seventh tale in the collection, entitled 'A Manchester Strike', is a long short-story, almost a novel by modern standards. It is of more than usual interest because it shows that even Harriet Martineau did not always write in harmony with her professed social theory. This story has been curiously neglected in surveys of condition-of-England fiction; Cazamian was the first to dismiss its value as creative writing,[18] and this has remained the attitude of critics ever since. Yet 'A Manchester Strike' has its undoubted literary merits. No dubious symbolism underlies the plot, no melodramatic incidents mar its composition, no mystification disfigures the proletarian characters. It is, nevertheless, characterized by all the defects of Harriet Martineau's style. The characters are only partially alive, their psychology is correct but superficial, the dialogue stilted, the bias of the author transparent. On the other hand it must be stressed that 'A Manchester Strike' provides a more complex and dynamic presentation of the class conflict in Robert Owen's day than any other work in English literature. Its main merits follow from the very contradictions, inconsistencies and illogicalities present in the story; in fact, it is these very errors which redeem 'A Manchester Strike' in the judgment of the modern reader. Had Harriet Martineau held consistently to her theories, the story would have been the poorer for it.

The strike in question begins because the masters refuse to equalize the wages in the factories of the town. It starts hopefully with bands playing music at the head of the strikers' parades. But the spirit of resistance begins to flag after three months when the assistance given by other workers' unions decreases. Reduced by want, the strikers are finally obliged to go back to work. But the strike does not end in defeat, as we would expect in a story by Harriet Martineau, who was violently opposed to strikes. The strikers partially succeed in their aims as the masters agree to equalize the wages, though at a lower level than originally suggested by the workers. Secondly, the workers legalize their union in the eyes of their masters. By allowing the strikers even this small degree of success, Harriet Martineau undermined the didactic effect of her story, which was to dissuade workers from striking. The neatly formulated summary appended to the story to the effect that strikes are bad because they harm the interests of the capital on which the workers depend, must have been partly lost upon the readers – if we assume that the tale was ever read by potential strikers, which remains to be proved.[19]

The third blow to Harriet Martineau's thesis is dealt by the hero of the story and the leader of the strike. Allan is portrayed as an intelligent, sensitive man of unquestionable integrity. He did not seek after power or notoriety. When asked to lead the strike, he agreed reluctantly because he was aware of the trouble that this would bring to his family. Nevertheless he made the sacrifice demanded of him because of his deep feeling of class solidarity. "We have our duty", says Allan, "as well as men of our make on the field of battle; and we must surrender ourselves, like them, to our duties." (chap. VIII). When the strike was over Allan's apprehensions were fulfilled, he was bewildered by the ingratitude of his fellow-workers and overwhelmed by the revenge of the Manchester employers. No master would give him work on account of the part he had played in the strike. But Allan bore his misfortune stoically without complaint or 'humility'. Though proud of being a factory worker, he had to stoop to becoming a street-sweeper. He "toiled with his water-cart in summer and his broom in winter; enduring to be pointed out to strangers as the leader of an unsuccessful strike" (chap. XII), concludes the author, almost with admiration. To the end of her narrative Harriet Martineau respects the integrity of her hero. She does not attempt to reform him, nor does she violate his character as Elizabeth Gaskell was to do in the case of John Barton, whom she transformed from a doughty Chartist into a lachrymose penitent. Harriet Martineau allows Allan to remain true to his class. In this respect one cannot agree with R. K. Webb when he remarks that "The idea of solidarity among working-men" was a subject "permanently closed to her imagination."[20]

Returning to the narrative, we find that it is not very persuasive in its attempt to defame the strikers, not only because the strike described ended with a partial victory, but also because its leader is represented as a tragic hero. The supposed working-class reader would have wished to identify himself with Allan and perhaps to emulate rather than to condemn him. An author intending to strengthen the moral fortitude of trade unions could not have chosen a better specimen than Allan, just as the blackleg, Hare, is despised by Harriet Martineau for his cowardice.

'A Manchester Strike' contains few examples of an idealization of the capitalists. Three of the four mill-owners are almost as bad as any of that class of men presented by Dickens. Although Harriet Martineau was to write that the manufacturers of Manchester were unsurpassed for their intelligence and public spirit,[21] they do not appear so in this story. One of them is stubbornly conservative, another a weakling, and a third abominably arrogant. The following passage describes his reception of the workers' delegation:

As they approached Mr. Elliott's house, they perceived that gentleman mounted on his favourite hunter, and in the act of leaving his own door. He was too much occupied with his own affairs to see them coming, for the most important part of his morning's business was setting off for his ride; and he had eyes for little else while he was admiring the polish of his boots, adjusting his collar, setting the skirts of his coat, and patting his horse's neck. Clack was not the man for ceremony; he came straight up before the horse, and laid his hand on the handsome rein, saying: "By your leave, sir".

"Hands off", cried Elliott, giving him a cut across the knuckles with his riding-whip. "How dare you stop me? How dare you handle my rein with your greasy fingers?"

(chap. III)

When the petition which the workers' delegation brought was handed to him, Elliott glanced at it "and then struck it contemptuously with his riding-whip into the mud."

Harriet Martineau did not glorify Manchester, as might have been expected; the seat of the cotton industry did not inspire her with pride. In its bleak atmosphere lives a race of people whose lives are devoid of happiness. The working-class districts are depicted as swarming with sickly children, and the scene showing how Allan's eight-year old daughter Martha works on during the long hours of the night is as painful to read as any Report on the Work of Children in the Cotton Factories of the United Kingdom. Martha was becoming lame as a result of overwork, and the local chemist advised rest. But the family could not spare her meagre wages, and "the little girl repaired to the factory, sighing at the thought of the long hours that must pass before she could sit down or breathe fresh air again". Meantime her mother bandaged her aching joints while she was at work. The night shifts were a great trial for the exhausted child. "About midnight, when Martha remembered that all at home were probably sound asleep, she could not resist the temptation to rest her aching limbs, and sat down".

She immediately fell asleep but awoke two minutes later. Winking and rubbing her eyes, she began to limp forward and use her trembling hands . . . When a bright sunbeam shone in through the window, thickened with the condensed breath of the work-people, and showed the oily steam rising through the heated room, the lamps were extinguished, to the great relief of those who found the place growing too like an oven to be much longer tolerable. The sunbeams rested now on the ceiling and Martha knew that they must travel down to the floor and be turned full on her frame and some way past it before she could be released; but it was a comfort that morning had come.

(chap. VI)

Harriet Martineau obviously read her Blue Books, a point confirmed in her *Autobiography*, but this cannot explain why she dwells on Martha's desperate conditions. This episode contradicts the non-interventionalist social policy that Harriet Martineau advocated. For who, after reading this passage, would not conclude that labour legislation was urgently needed? Consequently this part of the story is a failure as fictionalized propaganda because the author felt compelled to express an "uneconomical feeling of compassion". Although she repeatedly stressed that it was useless to arouse pity instead of giving practical advice, she could not have been more persuasive had it been her primary object to awaken compassion. It would seem that the logic of proved facts got the better of her and she overreached herself.

The plots of *Hard Times* and 'A Manchester Strike' contain two similar yet rather unusual situations in that the latter contains the nucleus of the circus episode in *Hard Times*. Dickens's group of circus artists – the Sleary family – was anticipated by two of the characters in 'A Manchester Strike', Martha's friend and her father, both of whom have been driven by poverty to abandon factory work and instead adopt the profession of public entertainers. The little girl now wears a silk dress with bright ribbons, and her rosy cheeks and round features form a strong contrast to Martha's sickly appearance. The reader is struck by the similarity of the contrasts. In the one, the bleakness of industrial Manchester is set against the jolly little dancer and her actor father; in the other, the circus group is contrasted to the drab life of Coketown. It is not improbable that Dickens, who must have been acquainted with *The Illustrations*, obtained his idea for the circus group from 'A Manchester Strike', and invested it with a symbolism which is absent from that story.

The ethics of Harriet Martineau are derived from the self-help social philosophy in its popular eclectic form. In it, different philosophical systems current among the radicals are mixed and diluted. It is based on Bentham's greatest-happiness-of-the-greatest-number theory, the principles of Malthus, the Puritan concept of self-discipline, and probably other ingredients as well. The ideal personal qualities in the opinion of Harriet Martineau are those which will harden the individual and make him fit for his career in the world of free enterprise. They must make the poor resistant to physical and moral temptation. Her ideal proletarian is industrious, thrifty and prudent; he performs his work with zeal, he saves from his small earnings against a rainy day, and he defers marriage till middle age to diminish his contribution to the population of the country. The epitome of these virtues is the worker Paul in the story 'The Hill and the Valley'. Paul, who is 30 and unmarried, is an exceptional specimen of the human race as regards sheer bodily endurance. He works full-time in a foundry and soon saves some money with which he buys the tools for further work in his leisure hours:

He purchased a tailor's and cobbler's implements, and he patched and cobbled for half the neighbourhood in his leisure hours. He still complained that he had not enough to do, and went to the next town to look for some employment which he might bring home. He brought a package of cork on his back, and a cork-cutter's knife in his pocket . . . He was up at four, summer and winter . . . and would sit from six to eleven in the evening cutting cork when he had nothing more profitable to do.

(chap. IV)

He was also a cattle dealer in a small way, "But he pinched himself with want and care as if he had still been a beggar". Paul's ambition is to accumulate capital with which to start business on his own. He is not a capitalist, yet he already shares the interests of his master. During a riot in the iron-works he distinguishes himself by pacifying the discontented. In the destruction of the machinery which nevertheless follows, he fights bravely to protect his master's property. When the destructive fury of the assailants is quelled by the soldiers, Paul points out those who carry most of the guilt. He does so without flinching, conscious of the fact that this is his duty. So far we recognize in Paul one of the family of the 'deserving poor'. But just as our admiration for Paul is awakened, Harriet Martineau begins to criticize him when she lets a minor character – a gentleman – in all seriousness advise him to turn to another and better mode of living:

As soon as you have enough to buy and furnish a cottage, and afford a small income, give up business, and occupy yourself with books, and politics, and works of benevolence [sic] and country sports and employments; with anything that may take off your attention from the bad pursuit which is ruining your health, and your mind, and your reputation.

(chap. XI)

This advice, offered quite seriously, defies interpretation in terms of propaganda for any social philosophy. Did the author begin by thinking about Paul as an admirable person, only to decide, in the end, that his devotion to his work was a "bad pursuit" ruining his reputation as well as his health ? The question, it would seem, must remain unanswered.

It is tempting to apply logic to Harriet Martineau's social philosophy. If all workers were to follow her advice and become small-scale capitalists, the whole system would be brought to a standstill for lack of workers. Harriet Martineau obviously cannot have intended that every worker should become a man of independent means concerned with books and politics and country sports. The solution suggested for workers who fail to 'better themselves', is that they must align their interests with those of their masters, because they are identical. But the action of several of Miss Martineau's stories plainly shows that they are not identical. Thus in 'The Rioters', 'The Turn-Out', 'A Manchester Strike', and 'The Hill and the Valley', the clash of capitalist and labour interests belies the theory of a 'common interest'. In these narratives the workers fight for clearly-defined aims which are quite contrary to those of their masters. It is true that Harriet Martineau puts the blame for those uprisings on leaders and agitators, but she shows that it is they who express the feelings of the whole body of workers. In other words, the condition-of-England tales of Harriet Martineau, founded as they are on a one-sided interpretation of Adam Smith's ideas, over-emphasize the question of production and dismiss the problems of the distribution of wealth which was the real cause of class disharmony.[22]

Another of Harriet Martineau's illogical premises arises in connection with combination. She absolutely refused to concede the workers' right to combine in order to defend their interests. Yet she did not blame the owners of the Manchester factories for combining when confronted with parliamentary intervention and the pressure of the trade union. In 1855 she even volunteered to write in favour of the Association of mill-owners of Manchester, and ultimately she did so. Yet when the workers combined, she reproved them most energetically. She blamed the workers for refusing to sell their only 'commodity' when its price in the market did not suit them. Had she consistently upheld the principle of Free Trade, she would have granted them the right of free bargaining.

In this she was quite explicit and more vociferous than Dickens.

On the other hand Harriet Martineau was more of a prophet; her vision of the future shows real insight into the long-term social trend initiated by the Industrial Revolution. She believed that Europe would be ravaged by a great war, after which a period of general chaos would follow; the existing property relationships would be fundamentally changed, and outdated systems of government reformed.[23] Although opposed to socialism, she recognized the importance of Owen's ideas. As regards property she observed that important modifications were taking place,

which have already altered the tone of leading economists and opened a prospect of further changes which will probably work out in time a totally new social state. If it should ever happen, it ought to be remembered that Robert Owen was the sole apostle of the principle in England at the beginning of our century.[24]

She realized that she must be prepared to see her favourite dogma abandoned even in the near future. Speaking of the Chartist movement and the social problems which gave rise to it, she wrote:

No thoughtful man can for a moment suppose that this question can be put aside. No man with a head and heart can suppose that any considerable class of a nation will submit for ever to toil incessantly for bare necessaries – without comfort, ease, or luxury, now – without prospect for their children, and without hope for their old age. A social idea or system which compels such a state of things as this must be, in so far, worn out. In ours, it is clear that some renovation is wanted and must be found.[25]

The illogical premisses of Charles Dickens and Harriet Martineau may be presented graphically as two symmetrical but reverse patterns. It remains to be seen how their inconsistencies affect the intrinsic value of their industrial fiction. When Dickens abandons the spontaneous emotional approach to his subject, he appears to lose the main inspiration for his creativeness. Not only is his social theory superficial, and hence unworkable, it also hampers the free play of his imagination. When he dresses his social philosophy in fictional garb in *Hard Times*, his empathy is so weak that the result can hardly be called successful. Moreover, it seems that even if he had adopted a social philosophy acceptable to the modern reader, the result would hardly have been better, for Dickens's characters become stilted as soon as he places a political argument in their mouths. Harriet Martineau's case is quite different. When she departs from her practical purpose of teaching political economy and takes flight into the world of fancy, we recognize her limitations. Imaginative creation was not her strong suit. Nevertheless, the reader is grateful for her occasional fanciful digressions; thanks to these she was able to bring to life a champion of the working-class movement on the eve of Chartism. As such characters were rare in fiction, it is her distinctive achievement to have created their prototype. Had Harriet Martineau written only 'A Manchester Strike', she would still deserve the appreciation of posterity as the first English writer to depict a militant proletarian.

Notes

1. See Harriet Martineau, *Autobiography*, III, 347–50; my doctoral dissertation, the second, revised edition entitled *Romanopisac i čartizam* (Beograd, 1968); also K. J. Fielding and Anne Smith, '*Hard Times* and the Factory Controversy', *Nineteenth Century Fiction* 24 No. 4 (March 1970), 404–27 or see p. 223, n. 26.
2. This is the conclusion drawn in chap. 4 of my dissertation and my subsequent research has confirmed its validity.
3. G. K. Chesterton, *Appreciation and Criticism of the Works of Charles Dickens* (1936), 194f.
4. Peter Cunningham, 'Friend of Dickens', *The Dickensian*, 53 (January 1957).
5. Dingle Foot, 'Introduction', *Hard Times* (Oxford U.P., 1955).
6. In the version printed today Blackpool refers to a promise he has made Rachael not to join the workers' union. This mysterious promise has been elucidated by Sylvère Monod on the basis of his study of the proofs. Here the promise is presented in an episode subsequently omitted from the text as first published in *Household Words*. See Sylvère Monod, 'Dickens at Work on the Text of *Hard Times*', *The Dickensian*, 64 (May 1968).
7. Notably in his report from Preston (see below, n. 11).
8. W. Kent, '*Hard Times* from a Socialist Standpoint', *The Dickensian*, 24 (September 1928).
9. Letter to John Forster, Preston, dated 29 January 1954 (*The Nonesuch Dickens*, II, 538).
10. *Ibid.*
11. 'On Strike,' *Household Words* (11 February 1854).
12. Book II, chap. 4.
13. 'On Strike'.

14. April 21 (*The Nonesuch Dickens*, II, 554).
15. W. J. Doran, *The Dickensian*, 15 (October 1919).
16. J. W. T. Ley, 'The Case of *Hard Times*', *The Dickensian*, 24 (September 1928).
17. W. R. Greg (ed.), *The Nineteenth Century* (1877), II, 97.
18. Louis Cazamian, *Le roman social en Angleterre* (Paris, 1903), I, chap. IV.
19. In her *Autobiography* Harriet Martineau refers to letters from workers who realized the usefulness of her teaching, but she does not quote any of her correspondents. No letters to this effect have been published so far.
20. R. K. Webb, *Harriet Martineau, a Radical Victorian* (1960), 349.
21. *The Factory Controversy, a Warning against Meddling Legislation* (Manchester, 1855).
22. Adam Smith wrote, in his *Wealth of Nations* (Book I, chap. VIII), that the interests of the capitalists and the workers "are by no means the same. The workmen desire to get as much, the masters to give as little as possible."
23. *Autobiography*, II, 455f.
24. *Ibid.*, I, 230–2.
25. *The History of the Thirty Years' Peace*; Book VI, chap. XVII, 446.

Part 2

Anthology

William Paley

1743-1805

A minister in the Church of England, and a great admirer of *belles lettres*, William Paley was far from considering himself as a man of letters. His many successful publications were devoted to theology and philosophy, but if the dramatization of an argument by means of dialogue can be said to constitute fiction, he crossed the line between propaganda-through-tracts and propaganda-through-fiction, and this justifies his inclusion in our Anthology.

William Paley was descended from a long-established family in the West Riding of Yorkshire. His father, a graduate of Christ's College, Cambridge, served first as vicar in the district of Craven, and then as headmaster of the local grammar school. This was also the school where William Paley acquired his education, and at 16 he went up to Christ's College, Cambridge, and in due course graduated as Senior Wrangler in 1763. His academic studies focussed on mathematics, Latin, and Greek, subjects which developed the young man's innate ability to think clearly and logically and to present his ideas in lucid prose. One of his contemporaries at Cambridge wrote that as a student Paley excelled in every subject, "so clear was his head and so retentive his memory". This confirms the truth of the father's observation when he wrote that William had "by far the clearest head I ever met with in my life."[1]

William Paley's first employment was as a teacher, but on becoming a Fellow of his college, he was ordained in 1767. The next ten years were spent in Cambridge as a lecturer in theology and philosophy, and in the course of this time he acquired a high reputation as a teacher. His students took copious notes that gained a wide circulation also outside Paley's own college. This promising career seemed at an end when Paley married in 1776 and moved to a village in Westmorland as a rural rector on an annual salary of £80. He was to remain in the same diocese for the next 20 years, pursuing an ecclesiastical career that slowly took him to the rank of archdeacon in Carlisle Cathedral. He obtained various preferments and absentee privileges, but none of these was at all considerable, so that his income was just barely sufficient to support a growing family. In his spare time therefore Paley turned to his Cambridge lecture notes, and on the basis of them wrote what was to become a standard textbook of ethics, *The Principles of Moral and Political Philosophy* (1785). The book was an immediate success; it ran through 15 editions in the author's lifetime, and by 1814 the sum total was 21.[2] His next book, *Horae Paulinae* (1790), although the most original of his works, was less popular. The greatest popularity was achieved by his *A View of the Evidences of Christianity* (1794), warmly acclaimed by all who considered religion the best safeguard against the flood of revolutionary ideas from France. This book ran into 20 editions in less than 20 years. Paley's last important work was his study of *Natural Theology* (1802), based on the familiar argument that the cleverness of the design of the created universe is evidence of the existence of a God. Paley's fame rests on these four books, but he also wrote a fairly large number of sermons and religious tracts.

Paley's success as a writer secured for him the offer of several remunerative livings in the east of England, which he accepted apparently without worrying about the moral issues involved in having a plurality of ecclesiastical appointments. He is reported to have taken his parish duties seriously and to have been an easy landowner who never pressed his tenants. Paley was by nature optimistic, hard-working, and thrifty, and at the same time pleased with his own life and achievements. This may explain why he never became a bishop despite his great reputation; he led a contented existence, enjoying to the full the pleasure of being a celebrity and the joys of a happy family life.

Two of Paley's works bear directly on the theme which is our concern here, his *Principles of Moral and Political Philosophy* (1785) and his *View of the Evidences of Christianity* (1794). The social and political views advanced in the former are typical of the age of enlightenment, and the fact that they are approached from a religious angle is in keeping with the English intellectual tradition, which never displayed the militant atheism so often encountered on the Continent. Paley's political philosophy posits that this is the best of all possible worlds, and actions, whether performed by the individual or society, are classified as 'good' or 'bad' insofar as they increase, or reduce, the 'general happiness' of all. This is the familiar argument of those philosophers who paved the way for nineteenth-century Utilitarianism, and Paley is generally seen as having played an important part, together with Jeremy Bentham, in popularizing this panacea for human ills. Paley's contemporary, Jeremy Bentham, was of course the leading apostle of the political and moral gospel of Utility, and Paley's chief disagreement with Bentham is found in his insistence that the wish for happiness is no mere human instinct, but the express volition of the Creator. Paley's view therefore provides divine sanction for the complacent belief that self-interest is identical with the interest of society. Paley believed in a perfect, and perfectly understandable, universe where everything was "intended for happiness and based on a design of utility" so that even the poor could be persuaded into contentment. Since God is the ultimate arbiter of the fate of each individual, it is to his will that the unequal division of rights and privileges must be attributed. Paley considered private property in the same manner: private property is established by the law of the land, and this law in its turn is supported by divine law. Consequently the justification of private property did not exist as an issue.

John Locke had advanced similar arguments and they had been repeated by his eighteenth-century followers. On one point, however, Paley, as well as the early Utilitarians, abandoned the cause of strict logic: he did not sanction the kind of property which consists in slaves. He was known as an active sympathizer with the Abolitionist movement, but the issue of Negro slaves was of minor importance on the eve of the French Revolution. The main problem which preoccupied philosophers on both sides of the Atlantic concerned public government, the theory of the 'civil contract' being partly abandoned as we may observe, for example, in Jefferson's *Declaration of Independence* (1776). Jefferson's concept of the inalienable right of all men to the pursuit of happiness had become well established in both hemispheres,[3] and Paley used it as his point of departure for a defence of the American War of Independence. He argued that Britain was violating this principle in her treatment of the American colonies. Logic compelled Paley to call for a revision of British laws whenever these could be seen to hinder the quest for happiness on the part of individuals or social groups. This was true, for example, of the Game Laws, the Poor Laws, and the laws limiting the rights of Catholics and Dissenters. If Paley had applied his logical mind consistently to political problems, he would have had to join the ranks of the reformers of his day. These argued that the House of Commons could not be said to represent the nation because the constituencies had not been re-distributed geographically when certain areas became depopulated or more densely populated, and because of the restricted suffrage. It was in the name of the happiness of the majority that the reformers advocated a change in the system of parliamentary representation.

Paley, far from joining the reformers, opposed them at every turn,

showing, in the process, how a logical mind may abuse the laws even
of logic when an end is sufficiently desirable. Thus he begins his
argument about constitutional reforms by stating a number of facts that
would seem decisive. The representation in both Houses is said to be
inadequate – 200 Members being elected by a body of voters totalling
a mere 7,000. This anomalous situation, however, elicits from Paley the
casuistic argument that it constitutes an advantage rather than a defect.
The voters are unimportant; what truly matters is the fact that those
who are elected belong to a class of people so closely linked with the
whole body of society that they must be considered eminently capable
of promoting general interests. Paley defended the prerogatives of the
Crown as well, and it is not surprising that the reformers were disappointed with his conclusion that the British constitution was perfectly
satisfactory. One of Paley's friends, G. W. Meadley, comments on his
failure to support the cause of reform in his *Memoirs*. "Many ardent
friends of civil and religious liberty have contended, that in pursuance
of the doctrines which he [Paley] had formerly advanced as a philosopher,
he ought to have taken a more decided part in favour of their cause."[4]

In order to reconcile Paley's deep-rooted conservative stand in
politics with his liberal ideas, we must remember the general political
atmosphere in England towards the end of the eighteenth century, and
the fact that Paley always opted for the moderate course, never for
extremes. Paley was by nature a practical man, intent on things as they
are and how they may be modified, rather than on more or less visionary
dreams of a future perfection; in other words, he thought in terms of a
more tolerable *status quo*. Consequently the contradictions that we find
in his philosophy are the result not so much of confused thinking
(unlikely to have occurred in a mind so devoted to mathematical
precision) as of a strong conviction that moderate measures would suffice:
via media, via aurea. He was a true representative of a generation
committed to a belief in the perfectibility of man and the inevitability of
progress. Ignorance, so he thought, was the real enemy; remove ignorance by providing adequate schooling for all, and a state of general
happiness would be the inevitable result.

During the second half of the eighteenth century only an exceptional
mind like William Blake's was capable of grasping the import of the
ideas stemming from France. Paley was no visionary. He was fully
convinced of the necessity of class distinctions; he knew no other
reality than the one he was brought up in as a member of the privileged
classes, nor did the contemporary writers who used phrases like 'social
superiors' and 'social inferiors' quite unselfconsciously. It seemed to
them in the very nature of things that there should be these distinctions.

To a man like William Paley it seemed far better to accept the shortcomings of the existing constitution than to permit its overthrow through violence, and he had no hesitation in joining Edmund Burke against Thomas Paine. A year after the events of 1789 Paley preached a sermon in a Cumberland village in refutation of the principles of the Friends of the French Revolution. He published this sermon in 1792 with the revealing title *Reasons for Contentment, addressed to the Labouring Part of the British Public,* and in it he supports his conservative argument with the authority of the Creator. God has so appointed things in this world that the majority must be satisfied to live in poverty, but the poor enjoy inestimable advantages compared to the rich whose privileges are a snare and a delusion. Their very pleasures are no such thing: "The rich who addict themselves to indulgences lose their relish. Their desires are dead . . . Hardly anything can amuse them, or rouse, or gratify them". Their leisure hours are "tiresome and insipid", while those of the poor are "sweet and soothing". It is these happy hours that constitute "the fortune of the poor". The luxurious environment of the rich – the grandeur of their houses, their fine apparel, their equipage and attendants – all this means "very little" to the rich for they regard it with "neglect and insensibility". The traditional religious argument about the rich and the poor is, of course, included. Paley admits – whether candidly or disingenuously, one wonders – that religion acts as a social sedative, preventing the fomentation of rebellious ideas, and promoting a spirit of reconciliation. "If in comparing the different conditions of social life," he writes, "we bring religion into the account, the argument is still easier. Religion smoothes all inequalities, because it unfolds a prospect which makes all earthly distinctions nothing." But Paley was no inflexible conservative; he saw hope for the poor in the future, not as a result of violent political action, but in "that gradual and progressive improvement of our circumstances which is the natural fruit of successful industry." Paley's tract therefore concludes by invoking the famous principle of self-help.

Paley's short tract entitled *Equality, as consistent with the British Constitution, in a Dialogue between a Master-Manufacturer, and one of his Workmen* was printed as an appendix to the second edition of *Reasons for Contentment* in 1793. The sub-title distinguishes this piece from similar parables because it mentions the relationship between an employer and a labourer engaged in industrial production. The writer displays a sense of humour and the dialogue is quite vigorous. The self-made Master reminds one a little of Dickens's Bounderby in his boastfulness and his attacks on the combination of workers. Moreover the Master is against the ideas of Tom Paine. Like Hannah More, Paley exploited the traditional English dislike of the French in an effort to discredit the political principles associated with France. The immediate butt of his attack was Thomas Paine's *Rights of Man* (1791–2), which was an answer to Burke's *Reflections on the Revolution in France* (1790). Nevertheless the success of Burke's pamphlet was such that it sparked off a multitude of similar works by English writers opposed to the Revolution.[5] A number of these were designed for people of some education, like the following items: A. Collins, *A Philosophical Inquirie on Human Liberty* (1790), John Courteney, *Reflections on the French Revolution* (1790), anon., *Thoughts on the French Revolution Influence in England* (1790), anon., *Liberty and Property Preserved against Republicans and Levellers* (1792), Vincent William, *A Discours* [upon levelling] (1792), Vincent William, *Short Hints upon Levelling* (no date), J. C. Somers, *On the Dreadful Tendency of Levelling* (1793), and Arthur Young, *The Example of France, a Warning* (1793). Writers who addressed the 'lower orders' in the manner of Paley and Hannah More, would try to lend greater persuasiveness to their arguments by using fictional characters. One is tempted to speak of an almost spontaneous generation, at this time, of semi- or pseudo-fiction, the nature of which is indicated in the following list of anonymous works: *A Dialogue between Mr. Worthy and Simple on some Matters relative to the Present State of Great Britain* (1782): Mr Worthy is a constable who persuades Simple, a rope-maker, to remain loyal; *Ten Minutes Caution from a Plain Man to His Fellow Citizens* (1792); *A Dialogue between an Associator and a well-informed Englishman on the grounds of the late Associations, and the Announcement of a war with France* (1793), a tract with a fairly liberal tendency touching on the Association for the Protection of Property; *Dialogues on the Rights of Britons between a Farmer, a Sailor and a Manufacturer* (1793): vehement attacks on Thomas Paine; *A Dialogue between a Gentleman and a Mechanic* (1798), which argues that inequality of fortune is salutary to society as a whole.

There is no need to tax the patience of readers by extending this list of works that may hardly be said to qualify as literature.[6] The point that should be stressed is that their appearance during the 1790s indicates that the time was ripe for the creation of a new literary genre capable of appealing to a reading public far below the social and intellectual level usually aimed at. For obvious reasons this new interest in what the common people would read coincided with the spread of liberal ideas that might conceivably upset the social *status quo*. The zeal of writers intent on stemming the tide of these ideas redoubled when Paine's *Rights of Man* reached such a wide circulation. The pamphlets that they wrote gradually established a tradition that was to form the point of departure for subsequent writers who were to make a deliberate, highly organized use of fiction for the purpose of disseminating political and social ideas.

Notes

1. Quoted by William Barker, 'Paley and His Political Philosophy', *Traditions of Civility* (1948), 198, n. 2.
2. *Ibid.*, 210.
3. On Jefferson's political thought, see Nelson Manfred Blake, *A History of American Life and Thought* (New York, 1963).
4. G. W. Meadley, *Memoirs of William Paley* [1809], 191.
5. The systematic expression, in print, of hostility to the French Revolution began with the publication of Edmund Burke's *Reflections on the Revolution in France* (1790), 30,000 copies being required to meet the demand. A treatise of this kind, however, was beyond the reach of a wider public, unlike Thomas Paine's *Rights of Man* (1791–2), whose argument could be grasped also by less well-educated readers. Mild as it may seem today, Paine's pamphlet caused serious concern in wide circles.
6. A comprehensive account of the anti-Jacobin action to provide an antidote to revolutionary ideas by means of disseminating cheap tracts is given in Richard Altick, *The English Common Reader, A Social History of the Mass Reading Public* (Chicago, 1957), chap. 3.

Bibliographical Details

Equality appeared in 1793 as an Appendix to the second edition of Paley's *Reasons for Contentment*. The text given here follows the first edition.

EQUALITY
as consistent with
The British Constitution

In a dialogue between a Master-Manufacturer, and one of his Workmen.

Workman. Good morning, master; I am come to tell you I cannot work to-day.

Master. Why, John, what is the matter, are you ill?

W. No, thank God! but I have made an engagement, which I want to go to.

M. Consider, John, you have a wife and four children, who entirely depend upon you for support; and, if you remain idle but one day in the week, you lose one sixth part of what is to subsist you and them, and you wrong your family!

W. Ah, master! what signifies a wife and children, when compared to liberty! it is to meet the friends of liberty that I am going; and, when I think of the rights of man, I never think of the wrongs of my family.

M. I find then, John, you are for the new system?

W. Yes, Master! and so would you had you read Tom Paine: he makes it quite clear that we are all born equal, and that we ought to have remained so; and that it is a shame to have kings and lords amongst a people, who ought to live like brethren.

M. Indeed, John, I seldom read except in my Bible and Ledger: it is sufficient for me to mind my shop, post my books, and take care of my affairs. On Sunday, which is a day of leisure, I go to church, and am content, without perplexing myself with different doctrines, to listen to the parson of my parish, who recommends me to live in peace, and to do as I would be done by. Yet, I own, Mr. Paine's book made so much noise, that, from curiosity, I have read it, and I find nothing in it to make me alter my conduct.

W. What, master! are you an enemy to the rights of man?

M. No, John! but I am a friend to the happiness of man; and I would prevent him from exercising rights which are injurious to himself. Mr. Paine has said, that every age and generation are free; but it is not the question, whether they *may*, but whether they *ought*, in prudence, to use that freedom; and whether by using it they will better themselves; and, that I may be able to judge, let me know, John, of what you and your party complain.

W. Lord, master! why you know well enough we complain that some are too rich, that others are too poor, that the people are taxed to support the expenses of the king, and that the money we labour for is taken from us, and squandered in places and pensions. We dislike lords: Why should a man be a lord because his father was? – We dislike kings: Why should one man be master of so many millions, who are as good as himself? – We dislike the mode of elections: Why should not every man be entitled to a vote? – In short, provisions are too high, liberty is too low, and we would be free and equal, as they are in France.

M. Ah! John, these are numerous complaints and great grievances to be sure; but, that we may perfectly understand them, let us examine them separately. Your first complaint is, that some are too rich, and others too poor.

W. Why, don't you think so, master?

M. Indeed, John, I do not: and, though there may be some exceptions, which under no government can be prevented, I believe people in general may choose whether they will be rich or poor.

W. Why, master, I choose to be rich.

M. How, John, you choose to be rich, when you are this very day going to make holiday! You earn, John, a guinea a week, which, excluding Sundays, is three shillings and sixpence a day: and, if in every week you lose a day, you lose nine pounds two shillings a year; this, in fourteen years, would make the sum of one hundred and ninety-two pounds. I believe you will confess, that, every day you make holiday, you spend on yourself as much as you miss getting; and thus, in fourteen years, you might have saved three hundred and eighty-four pounds.

W. Ah, Master! every body has not the same head for these reckonings that you have.

M. Every body, John, has nearly the same head, but every body has not the same inclinations to make use of it. The idle man, who prefers pleasure to gain, says, it is but one day, and but three shillings and sixpence lost. The frugal man, who prefers gain to pleasure, says, it is an hour, and that is three-pence farthing got.

The first clamours against government because he remains poor through his own indolence and extravagance; the last is contented with it because it secures to him the fruits of his industry and economy.

W. To be sure, master, there is some truth in that.

M. I came up to town, John, just as you did. I was the son of a small farmer, whose condition was little better than that of a common labourer. I had learned to read and write at a charity-school. I was first porter, then clerk, and afterwards partner in the house I entered into. I am now fifty years of age, and am worth thirty thousand pounds. The laws of my country secure me in the possession of it: the king dare not touch a farthing of it: I pay taxes, it is true, and they are considerable: but I pay them as a contribution for the protection of the rest of my property: heavy as they are, they are certainly not beyond the strength of the nation, since it flourishes under them; nor is my own situation singular, since the rise and condition of my neighbours have been and are nearly the same.

W. But certainly, master, you would pay less taxes if you were not to allow the king a million a year.

M. A great deal has been said about this million a year; but, though the sum sounds great, when examined it will not be found much: he pays out of it the judges, the foreign ambassadors, the secretaries of state, and other ministers. Without these no government ever attempted to stand, not even the new one of France; and, when these deductions are made, the sum will not be so enormous as you suppose.

Instead of a king, I will suppose a national assembly, as in France: the members I will fix at seven hundred and forty-five, as there; and the salaries of each at five hundred pounds per annum, a sum in proportion to what is allowed in France: Thus, John, when we had got rid of monarchy, we should still have near four hundred thousand pounds to pay, besides supporting our judges and our ministers.

W. But then, master, if you could strike off the pensions!

M. The pensions, John are chiefly paid out of the same million; and how far, John, do you think it would be justice or policy to reduce every man to want, who has served his country bravely and faithfully. You got drunk, I remember, John, when Rodney beat the French; you then thought he and his family deserved every thing; you now wish to make his children beggars.

W. However, master, taking away the titles would do no harm!

M. It might, John; and I am sure it would do no good. In this country, industry and frugality are the sources of every thing, and their rewards cannot be too numerous; and why should I be deprived of any distinction which accompanies those qualities?

W. You, master! why you are merry, surely: you do not expect to be made a lord?

M. Certainly I do not, John; but it is not at all improbable that my children should. I have four sons: my eldest I have bred up to my own business, and I bless God that he is diligent, sober, and frugal: my second is at the Temple, and studies the law: my third is in the army; and my fourth is in the navy. It is from such as these that lords are made: the first pursues trade, purchases lands, his son becomes an esquire, is returned to parliament, and, if he has abilities, may justly pretend to a peerage. The road of the others is more immediate: eloquence, skill, and valour, conduct them to eminence in their professions, and they are made lords by the same means that have promoted the whole house of peers: such has been the condition of all; and what has happened to them may happen to my children, and might to yours, if, instead of attending levelling meetings, you would work every day in the week.

W. Well, master; but, though your children may come to be lords, they can never come to be kings; and I do not see why a particular man, whether he is wise or foolish, should be made the master of so many millions?

M. I understand you, John: you do not see any reason why the crown should be hereditary. I have already told you I do not study politics much, and I fancy that is one of the reasons that I have succeeded so well in business; for two of my neighbours, who were thought to understand as much of the affairs of Europe as most men understood I find so little of their own, that they have become bankrupts, and I am told will not pay three shillings in the pound. Yet, though I do not study politics, those who do are so very industrious in communicating their knowledge, that I daily hear something: when any of these come to buy at my shop, they generally turn the discourse that way; and I have learned from them that there is but one crown in Europe elective, and that is the crown of Poland; and I find that the very people, who have appeared most zealous for abolishing hereditary distinctions here, have attempted to render the crown hereditary there. You see, John, how one part of their conduct contradicts another: and hence, I conclude, that their principal object is to talk themselves, or to hear others talk of them.

Nor is the king either your master or mine: he can neither make us go here or there, to do this or that: he cannot take from us a farthing: neither he nor his minister can encroach upon the liberty of the meanest Briton; and, if they do, they are subject to damages in a court of law.

W. All this, master, is very well; but why should I not vote for a member of parliament as well as you?

M. I have already told you, John, that industry and economy are in this country the source of every thing: it is by the first alone that a fortune can be made, and it is by the last alone that it can be kept. Instead of working only five days in the week, work six; and, in six years, you will have gained money enough to purchase a vote, if you please: this privilege the meanest man may soon acquire by persevering in his labours, and the richest will lose it, should he be idle and spend his property. I set out without any thing, and have got a vote; and, should my son be an idle fellow and a spendthrift, in selling what I leave him, he loses his vote.

W. Then, master, from all this, I suppose you do not approve of the French revolution?

M. How often, John, must I tell you, that I seldom trouble my head about these matters; yet, if you wish to know my sentiments, I will tell you them. In the first place, I do not think there is any comparison between France and England: there were certainly great grievances in France: the king could seize the property and person of every man; he could reduce him to beggary, could confine him in prison, and take away his life. Can the king of England do any such thing? I believe, John, that you would be glad that he were to take you up without your offending against the laws; it would be a good fortune to you.

W. Why, to be sure, master, I would make him pay sauce for it.

M. Then, John, if you would make him pay sauce for it, and he can do you no injury without your having the same redress against him as you could have against any of your fellow-subjects; are you not in the eye of the law equal to the king?

W. True, master, we are so in England; but you own it was not the case in France, and therefore they were certainly right in what they did.

M. That is a different thing, John: it does not follow, that, if government acted wrong, the people have acted right: I only know this, John, that it appears to me there never was a time when there was less right in France, and I will give you two instances of it in what has happened to myself. You remember that shopkeeper in Paris, who refused to pay me, about seven years ago, for a quantity of hardware that I sent out to him: I went to Paris, you also remember, applied to one of their courts of justice, and got my money.

W. To be sure, master, it would be very hard, if every man were not paid his own.

M. Yes, John, but what has happened since. – I sent out another parcel of hardware last year, to a person at Marseilles, who also refused to pay me: I went there to oblige him: I found there were no longer any courts of justice; I found that he was become a great patriot, a captain, John, in the national guards, and he only laughed at me, and told me, if I teized him about money, he would *denounce* me, as he called it, and have me put in prison.

W. What, put you in prison when he owed you money! Why, master, he must be a great rascal indeed!

M. This was not all, John – to appear a little smart, I had carried with me a new coat, with handsome steel buttons; in this I walked the streets, and was followed by some boys, who began to call out, Aristocrat, aristocrat! (a word which means an enemy to their constitution;) a mob immediately surrounded me, dragged me through the street, and would have hung me on one of the ropes on which they hang their lanterns, if, luckily, my banker had not come by, rescued me from their hands, by assuring them that I was in England a great patriot, or what he called a Jacobin.

W. Lord, master, were not you frightened terribly?

M. Certainly I was, John; and I'll take care how I venture there again.

W. But, master, the common people in France, such as myself, live surely better than they did.

M. How so, John! manufactures are at an end; and when the master can no longer sell his commodities, he can no longer pay the journeymen.

W. Why, what becomes of them?

M. They, John, as well as all of similar description, such as servants, labourers, and the lower class of manufacturers, are obliged to enter into the armies for bread; they are paid fifteen-pence a day, but they are paid in paper; that paper they are forced to exchange for little more than half of the commodities that could formerly be purchased with money of the same amount; they march without shoes or stockings, and their necessities oblige them to plunder, or exact contributions from every country they enter.

W. Why, I thought, master, they carried liberty every where?

M. It don't appear so, John, from the account that the inhabitants of Nice have presented to the national assembly, in which they complain that the French have ravished their wives and daughters, and stole their goods: – how should you like that, John?

W. Faith, master, not at all!

M. Nor is this the only thing to be dreaded; the farmer and labourer have left their ploughs to preach or fight for reform; the consequence is that the ground has been uncultivated, a famine begins to appear, and all provisions are double the price of what they were before the revolution: – how should you like this, John, who complain of the price of things, when bread is no dearer than it was ten or twenty years ago? In short, John, if the French and their doctrines come here, I shall shut up my shop, and have done with business; I shall place my money where I can most safely, and even bury it under ground, sooner than lend it to a constitution that subsists as their's does, by violence, and where every person, who is suspected or accused of being an aristocrat, is dragged to prison without any evidence, and is afterwards massacred by the populace. The French have always been our enemies; and, if they once enter England, they will not forget to revenge themselves for the many times we have beaten them by sea and by land: nor do I desire any of their equality, since, as this country now stands, I can become by industry and economy equally rich as a lord, and, while I behave myself with propriety, am equally independent as the king.

W. Right, master! and I thank you for explaining all this to me; and, instead of going to the liberty-club, I will begin my work; for, I should not like to see a Frenchman lie with my wife, or take the bread out of my children's mouths; and I now see, that, if I go on as you do, and mind my business, I may in time be as rich and as happy as you.

FINIS

Hannah More

1745-1833

Hannah More played a more important part in the creation of English public opinion than her literary reputation would lead one to expect. She is known today, if at all, as an amiable philanthropist and the author of very minor fiction and long-since outdated didactic treatises of a religious kind. But it is to Hannah More that we must turn to study the use of fiction for propagandist purposes; she it was who initiated this important literary trend, and such was her grasp on the psychology of her reading public that she could provide fiction as exactly suited to their tastes as to their pockets. She was a past master of the art of holding their attention while unobtrusively conveying her message.[1]

Hannah More was born near Bristol in 1745.[2] Her father was a scholar and pedagogue who provided an excellent education for his five daughters, and they in their turn came to establish one of the best-known schools for girls of their time. The father also passed on to his daughters his Tory sympathies and his High Church views. While in Bristol, Hannah More created something of a literary reputation for herself by writing plays and poems with a moralizing bias, and on visiting London for the first time in 1773, she was received into high society on the strength of letters of introduction written by her Bristol friends. Although greatly admired for her wit and her good looks, she never married, nor did any of her sisters. The provincial celebrity caught the limelight of the capital virtually overnight: her poems were praised and her plays performed at Covent Garden.[3] The famous actor David Garrick and his wife were among her best London friends, and she was befriended and admired by Dr Johnson, Edmund Burke, Sir Joshua Reynolds, and the ladies of the Blue Stocking coterie. Politicians and church dignitaries found her equally attractive, but in the midst of her social activities she nevertheless found time for assiduous reading of theological treatises.

In the 1780s Hannah More's ardent nature was fired by the enthusiasm of Abolitionist friends who were launching one of the earliest propaganda campaigns of modern society – the campaign against the slave trade. Among the most active Abolitionists were members of the Evangelical movement, and these impressed her profoundly by the fervour of their religious sentiments. Her close association with men like William Wilberforce and Zachary Macaulay influenced her to the extent that she came to consider the stage as sinful, but she did not distance herself from the fashionable world. It was her duty, she thought, to try to reform society by reforming "the manners of the great". She did this by publishing edifying tracts like her *Estimate of the Religion of the Fashionable World* (1790). This pamphlet addressed to the lukewarm Christians of her day had a wide circulation, and it is no exaggeration to state that her publications designed for the upper levels of society contributed substantially to that revival of interest in religion which was to become such a marked feature of the Victorian period.

Hannah More usually spent the summer months in Somerset where she found ample scope for the practice of philanthropy. Thus she discovered that the mining district of the Mendip Hills was a very backward area, and she was shocked to discover the distress and general ignorance of the inhabitants. Not a single resident clergyman was to be found in 13 villages; the country-side was "almost pagan" and the farmers themselves no better than ignorant "savages". She decided to open a Sunday school in Cheddar, and in 1791 she and a sister saw to it that a cottage was hired and a teacher appointed so that a proper school could be established. Despite strong opposition several schools were subsequently opened in the neighbouring districts. The sisters were indomitable; they visited villages in all weathers to persuade parents to send their children to school, they fought the stubborn resistance of farmers and refuted accusations levelled against them by a jealous clergy. Their triumph was great. At the end of the first year no less than 500 children were attending school.

Apart from these Sunday schools the sisters also ran schools where girls could attend one day a week to learn reading and sewing. For adults they instituted evening readings of sermons, common prayers and singing of hymns. The sisters encouraged attendance by distributing prizes for good behaviour and by organizing annual school feasts which were attended by large numbers.

Meanwhile the pen of Hannah More did not remain idle; she continued to produce edifying tracts for a large circle of approving readers. In the years following the French Revolution she was petitioned by admiring friends to turn from religion to politics to counter the influence of Thomas Paine, whose radical ideas were becoming popular. She hesitated for some time, but finally acceded to their request. The result was her pamphlet on *Village Politics* (1793), written in the semi-fictional form of a dialogue. The dialogue is sufficiently brisk and witty to entertain, as one would expect from an author who had written for the stage, and the message sufficiently simple to be understood even by uneducated readers. In writing her pamphlet she drew on Edmund Burke's famous attack on Thomas Paine, and one must admire the art with which she transposed his arguments into humorous dialogue. Jack Anvil the blacksmith meets Tom Hod the mason, who looks so dismal that Jack asks what is the matter:

> *Tom.* Matter? Why, I want liberty.
> *Jack.* Liberty! That's bad, indeed! What! has any one fetched a warrant for thee? Come, man, cheer up, I'll be bound for thee. Thou art an honest fellow in the main, tho' thou dost tipple and prate a little too much at the Rose and Crown.
> *Tom.* No, no, I want a new constitution.
> *Jack.* Indeed! Why, I thought thou hadst been a desperate healthy fellow. Send for the doctor directly.
> *Tom.* I'm not sick; I want liberty and equality, and the rights of man.
> *Jack.* Oh, now I understand thee. What! thou art a leveller and a republican, I warrant?

We have Hannah More's own account of how this pamphlet was written. Apparently it came into being in "an evil hour, against my will and judgement, on one sick day", and she adds that it is "as vulgar as heart could wish; but it is only destined for the most vulgar class of readers".[4] However, such was the success of this "vulgar" piece of writing that it encouraged her to begin her famous series of *Cheap Repository Tracts*.[5] Her output was truly remarkable: between 1795 and 1798 she prepared three tracts for publication every month, and of the 114 tracts constituting the series, it is surmised that she was the author of at least fifty. The remaining tracts were written by her sisters and some of their friends.

The tremendous success of this publishing venture can be seen from the sales statistics. In the course of the first six weeks about 300,000 copies were sold, and by July the same year no less than 700,000. During the first year alone more than 2,000,000 tracts found their way into almost every labourer's home, and some of them were still being read as late as the middle of the next century, and by large numbers of readers.[6]

The Cheap Repository Tracts had been backed by private donors, but since it proved such a profitable venture, the publisher carried on with the enterprise even after Hannah More ceased her association with it in

1798. The *Tracts* were popular in Ireland as well, and in Scotland an Edinburgh publisher issued a large reprint edition. William Cobbett, then still an anti-Jacobin, was delighted by them and promoted their circulation in the United States. Later on, when Cobbett had become a Jacobin, his own publication, *Twopenny Trash*, ironically enough caused a brief revival of the *Cheap Repository Tracts* when Hannah More was invited from official quarters to re-commence writing in order to counteract the effect of Cobbett's publications. The series was revived for a few months only, as Cobbett was obliged to flee from England in April 1817. It is uncertain which of the tracts in this second series were written by Hannah More, but none shows any sign of improvement on the level represented by the first series.

In 1808 Hannah More delighted her educated readers with a didactic novel, *Coelebs in Search of a Wife*. Together with other publications this book secured for her a considerable fortune, enabling her to spend her old age in comfort and surrounded by admirers. Philanthropists made pilgrimages to her village to meet the formidable Miss More, whom Cobbett had dubbed the "Bishop in petticoats". Since her death in 1833 she has never been completely neglected, although never much esteemed by literary critics. But as this biographical sketch will have indicated, Hannah More's impact on her own generation was sufficiently strong for a serious consideration of her influence to be called for.

The message which Hannah More brought to so many readers is the simple and straightforward one of fearing God and the king, of working hard and always remaining submissive. One of her most popular tales, 'The Shepherd of Salisbury Plain', illustrates her favourite theme of hardship stoically endured in complete reliance on God and his dispensation. The distress of the shepherd and his family is caused by an economic crisis in the village during the early phase of industrial capitalism. He lives in a dilapidated cabin with his wife and eight children, and they are short of food as well as fuel. The family, nevertheless, are contented because consoled by a fervent faith in God. All of them work at all times: the boys knit stockings while minding their flocks, and the "Little maidens, before they are six years old, can first get a halfpenny, and then a penny a day by knitting." For the political agitators the shepherd has nothing but contempt:

"When these men who are now disturbing the peace of the world, and trying to destroy the confidence of God's children in their Maker and their Saviour, when those men, I say, come to my poor hovel with their doctrines and their new books, I would never look into one of them; for I remember it was the first sin of the first pair to lose their innocence for the sake of a little wicked knowledge;

besides my own Book told me 'to fear God and honour the King –
to meddle not with them who are given to change – not to speak evil
of dignitaries – to remember to whom honour is due'."

This story enjoyed a wide circulation: there were two French translations
and one into Russian. A sequel appeared in 1817 entitled 'The Delegate'.
In this tale the shepherd is visited by political agitators who distribute
tracts written by Thomas Paine and William Cobbett, and the reaction
of the family is indicated by Sarah, the shepherd's wife, quietly taking
up her Bible, pressing it to her heart, and dropping on it "a silent tear
of love and reverence".

Humble submission is the theme also of the 'The Riot; or Half a
Loaf is Better than no Bread, in a Dialogue between Jack Anvil and Tom
Hod, Written during the Scarcity of 1795.' Jack the blacksmith again
serves as the author's mouthpiece: trials must be endured in patience
because imposed by Providence for our own good. The lesson is conveyed in lilting rhythms to increase the effect:

> Besides I must share in the wants of the times,
> Because I have had my full share in its crimes;
> And I am apt to believe the distress which is sent,
> Is to punish and cure us of all discontent.
>
> . . .
>
> So I'll work the whole day, and on Sundays I'll seek
> At church how to bear all the wants of the week.
> The Gentlefolks too will afford us supplies,
> They'll subscribe – and they'll give us their puddings and pies.

Readers dazed by so much humility will find some relief in the un-
intentional comic note struck by the reference to the "puddings and
pies" of the genteel. And 'Patient Joe: or the Newcastle Collier' is made
to express the same belief in a *laissez-faire* philosophy in a couplet
which could serve as an epigraph for the whole series of *Cheap Repository
Tracts*:

> When rich or when poor, he alike understood
> That all things together were working for good.

'The Lancashire Collier Girl' is of unusual interest because it is one
of the few tracts to include descriptions of an industrial environment.
Originally published in 1795, it sold for a penny. Although included in
Hannah More's works published in 1800, this story was excluded from
the editions of 1830, 1831, 1834, and 1847. It is possible that she may
have felt that it was lacking in originality. As I accidentally discovered,
Hannah More borrowed her material from an anonymous contribution

to *The Gentleman's Magazine*, the very title being identical.[7] The author, who signed himself 'The Rambler', tells a simple and pathetic story. A father, unable to find work above ground for his family, takes two of his six children into the coal pit with him. There the nine-year-old girl and the seven-year old boy work diligently as 'drawers', pulling basketsful of coal through the underground passages. "It is with pride that we make known to little children that Betty and her brother, at this early age, cleared their parents seven shillings a week." Tragedy intervenes, however, when the father is killed in an accident. The mother becomes "instantly deranged, and never afterwards recovered her senses", and the parish has to take care of the destitute family, except for Betty. Betty, then between 11 and 12 years old, goes on working in the mine "in preference to throwing herself upon the parish, as she was then capable by her own labour of earning a shilling a day." She earns more as she grows older, so that she can take her mother out of the work-house to be nursed at home. When two brothers are ill, she nurses them as well, but to no avail. All three die, and to pay for the burials Betty works in double shifts. No wonder that she suffers hallucinations "such as are known to be brought on by grief, poor food and excessive fatigue." Unable to carry on in the mine, Betty applies for the post of under-servant in the neighbouring Hall. The owner at first hesitates to take a collier-girl into his household, but is persuaded by the recommendation of Betty's master in the mines. This is the gist of the story told by 'The Rambler'. In a follow-up story published in *The Gentleman's Magazine* three years later, under the title 'Promotion of the Lancashire Collier-Girl',[8] Betty succeeds in becoming a cook. But praise and publicity cannot spoil the character of this humble girl, who crowns her career by persuading her only remaining brother to enlist in the army to fight the French, and by donating all her savings to support the war.

On the publication of the first part in *The Gentleman's Magazine* for 1795, the letters sent to the editor by interested readers afford a signifi-cant indication of a change in attitude to the problems of the poor. One socially-minded reader requests the name of the gentleman who took Betty into his household, thus proving his benevolence to the poor.[9] This praise of active social benevolence points forward to the Cheeryble brothers in Charles Dickens's *Nicholas Nickleby*, or again to Mr and Mrs Garland in *The Old Curiosity Shop*. While 'The Rambler' had stressed Betty's humility and self-reliance, this letter from a reader reveals a strong concern for the condition of the girl, and a desire that she should improve her lot in life. This new interest in the improvement of the position of common labourers indicates the growth of a new sensibility, and as this sentiment increased in strength, it came to inspire the reformist movement of the next generation.

When Hannah More adapted this material, she failed to indicate her indebtedness, but it is quite possible that she had the permission of the author, since we know that they had met. This is indicated in a letter written by 'The Rambler' to *The Gentleman's Magazine*, where reference is made to a conversation with Hannah More prior to the publication of the story. And in the story itself the anonymous author maintains that his little heroine would have become an even finer character if she could have enjoyed the "advantage of Sterne, or of Hannah More, who takes the poor under her protection". 'The Rambler' never protested publicly against Hannah More's obvious plagiarism, but he did object to her changing some of the details in Betty's story.[10] Since Hannah More was familiar with the mining population in her part of the country, she could easily have written a story of a local collier-girl; the fact that she borrowed an apparently true story from Lancashire may, perhaps, be attributed to haste; also she seems to have attached but little importance to the artistic or literary merits of her tracts. Like 'The Rambler', she viewed her work as a philanthropic contribution to a worthy cause; authorship as such did not matter. And as for Hannah More, had she not written, somewhat ironically, about one of her tracts that it is "as vulgar as heart could wish"?

Hannah More's revised version of the story of the Lancashire collier-girl was an effective piece of fictionalized propaganda. Some 20 years later it inspired a vicar by the name of James Plumbtre to revive the case in a story dedicated to Hannah More and entitled *Kendrew, or the Coal Mine* [Cambridge, 1818]. Although the collier girl is no longer the central character, she is clearly a great favourite with the author who includes a number of episodes illustrating the hardships she endured.

'The Lancashire Collier Girl' is characteristic in its insistence on the 'contentment' of the poor. Society was not quite safe enough if the poor were merely *reconciled* to their condition, they had to be *satisfied*. Hannah More, like the source she drew on, will have it that the families of the colliers lead 'cheerful' and 'contented' lives. The heroines of both – in Hannah More's story her name is Mary – refuse to depend upon the parish, and this is a point often underlined in *The Cheap Repository Tracts*. One sees, of course, why the class who had to pay Poor Rates wanted to recommend the great virtue of being self-reliant, like Mary. The reluctance of the benevolent master to engage the services of a collier-girl is a reflection of the immoral conditions under which such girls were working. We know from Parliamentary reports that sexual promiscuity was common among both sexes, but as a pious Evangelical Hannah More could not even hint at such depravity. It is quite likely, nevertheless, that her unspoken thoughts are reflected in this particular detail of her story, for she could not but know how people would react to a girl who had been exposed to such a polluted environment.

The strong insistence on the spirit of self-help in this story anticipates themes and attitudes that were to prevail later on. It is a typical specimen of the kind of story that we find in *The Cheap Repository Tracts*, and one of its virtues is that it shows the social changes caused by the process of industrialisation, and that it is one of the first fictionalized accounts to record this change.

A twentieth-century reader is tempted to observe the faults of Hannah More rather than her merits. The calmness with which she relates how an entire family perishes seems callous; her doctrine of subordination nauseates, and the bluntness with which she declares her class partisanship is bound to shock in an age when no political party dare proclaim a programme of inequality. And atheists and believers alike are equally repelled by the way in which she uses religion to trap people into mental and spiritual captivity. Consequently it is hardly surprising that her works have not been reprinted since the middle of the nineteenth century. By then she had become totally "out of fashion", to quote Sir Leslie Stephen, who objected to what he called "her strong desire to keep the poor in their place."[11] Nevertheless, when all has been said about the stark hypocrisy of Hannah More's concern for the common people, her redeeming qualities remain and must be remembered. In an age marked by rampant self-interest she joined the group of those who devoted themselves to the good of *all* members of society – or so at least they believed. Besides, from a purely practical point of view she performed a most useful service when she brought education to a district like the Mendip Hills.

In matters of religion she was remarkably clear-headed. Regardless of her preoccupation with the sacraments, when she addressed the common reader she was merely practical. Whatever she taught, she did so with a view to its usefulness, and she considered Christianity as a power which tended to preserve society in the form that she was familiar with. The purpose of all her work for the poor may best be summarized in her own words:

My plan of instruction is extremely simple and limited. They learn, on week-days, such coarse work as may fit them for servants. I allow of no writing for the poor. My object is not to make fanatics, but to train up the lower classes in habits of industry and piety. I know of no way of teaching morals but by teaching principles; or of inculcating Christian principles without imparting a good knowledge of Scripture. I own I have laboured these points diligently.[12]

Not such a poor epitaph, after all, perhaps, for a "Bishop in petticoats".

Notes

1. Charlotte Elizabeth Tonna, a worthy disciple of Hannah More, wrote about her in the 1840s, reminding the public of Miss More's great merit in creating a new method of approach to the uneducated in order to counteract "the inflammatory harangues of seditious traitors", *Recollections* (1849), 210.
2. William Roberts, *Memoirs of the Life and Correspondence of Mrs. Hannah More* (1834); Henry Thompson, *The Life of Hannah More* (1838); *Mendip Annals, or, A Narrative of the Charitable Labours of Hannah and Martha More; being the Journal of Martha More*, ed. Arthur Roberts (1859); Anna Buckland, *The Life of Hannah More* (1882); Charlotte Yonge, *Eminent Women* (1888); Marion Harland, *Hannah More* (New York, 1900); Annette Meakin, *Hannah More* (1911); James Silvester, *Hannah More* (1934); Harry Weiss, *Hannah More's 'Cheap Repository Tracts' in America* (New York, 1946); M. G. Jones, *Hannah More 1745–1833* (1952).
3. The bibliography of Hannah More's works includes: pastoral drama, sacred drama, tragedy, legendary tales, stories for the middle rank of society, tales for the common people, sketches, tracts, essays on various subjects (mostly religious), poems, etc. The collections of her works range from six volumes (1833–4) to 19 volumes (1818–19).
4. Letter to Mrs Boscawen, 1793, quoted by Annette Meakin, *op.cit.*, 311.
5. Jones, *op.cit.*, chap. VI, section 3.
6. M. M. Maison, *Search your Soul, Eustace: Victorian Religious Novels* (1961), 89.
7. 'The Lancashire Collier Girl, A True Story', *The Gentleman's Magazine* (March 1795), 197f.
8. December 1798, 1030.
9. November 1795, 922.
10. December 1795, 993.
11. Article in the *Dictionary of National Biography*.
12. Letter to the Bishop of Bath and Wells [Cowslip Green], 1801, *The Letters of Hannah More*, ed. R. Brimley Johnson (1925), 183.

Bibliographical Details

Village Politics first appeared as a pamphlet in 1793. In 1795 it was reprinted as one of the *Cheap Repository Tracts*, and the text given here follows that edition. 'The Lancashire Collier Girl' appeared in 1795, also as a *Cheap Repository Tract*, and the text given here follows the first edition.

VILLAGE POLITICS

Addressed to all Mechanics,
Journeymen, and Labourers in Great Britain.
By Will Chip, a Country Carpenter.*

It is a privilege to be prescribed to in things about which our minds would otherwise be tost with various apprehensions. And for pleasure, I shall profess myself so far from doating on that popular idol, Liberty, that I hardly think it possible for any kind of obedience to be more painful than an unrestrained liberty. Were there not true bounds, of magistrates, of laws, of piety, of reason in the heart, every man would have a fool, nay, a mad tyrant to his master, that would multiply him more sorrows than the briars and thorns did to Adam, when he was freed from the bliss at once, and the restraint, of paradise, and became a greater slave in the wilderness than in the inclosure.—*Dr. Hammond's Sermons.*

A dialogue between Jack Anvil, the Blacksmith – and Tom Hod, the Mason.

Jack. What's the matter, Tom? Why dost look so dismal?

Tom. Dismal indeed! Well enough I may.

Jack. What! is the old mare dead? or work scarce?

Tom. No, no, work's plenty enough, if a man had but the heart to go to it.

Jack. What book art reading? Why dost look so like a hang-dog?

Tom (looking on his book). Cause enough. Why, I find here that I am very unhappy, and very miserable; which I should never have known, if I had not had the good luck to meet with this book. Oh! 'tis a precious book!

* This piece, as a pamphlet, was published, and most extensively circulated, in 1793, to counteract the pernicious doctrines which, owing to the French revolution, were then become seriously alarming to the friends of religion and government in every part of Europe.—Ed.

Jack. A good sign, tho' – that you can't find out you're unhappy, without looking into a book for it! What is the matter?

Tom. Matter? Why, I want liberty.

Jack. Liberty! That's bad, indeed! What! has any one fetched a warrant for thee? Come, man, cheer up, I'll be bound for thee. Thou art an honest fellow in the main, tho' thou dost tipple and prate a little too much at the Rose and Crown.

Tom. No, no, I want a new constitution.

Jack. Indeed! Why, I thought thou hadst been a desperate healthy fellow. Send for the doctor directly.

Tom. I'm not sick: I want liberty and equality, and the rights of man.

Jack. Oh, now I understand thee. What! thou art a leveller and a republican, I warrant?

Tom. I'm a friend of the people. I want a reform.

Jack. Then the shortest way is to mend thyself.

Tom. But I want a *general* reform.

Jack. Then let every one mend one.

Tom. Pooh! I want freedom and happiness, the same as they have got in France.

Jack. What, Tom, we imitate them! We follow the French! Why, they only began all this mischief at first, in order to be just what *we* are already; and what a blessed land must this be, to be in actual possession of all they ever hoped to gain by all their hurly-burly. Imitate them, indeed! Why, I'd sooner go to the Negroes to get learning, or to the Turks to get religion, than to the French for freedom and happiness.

Tom. What do you mean by that? ar'n't the French free?

Jack. Free, Tom! ay, free with a witness. They are all so free, that there's nobody safe. They make free to rob whom they will, and kill whom they will. If they don't like a man's looks, they make free to hang him without judge or jury, and the next lamp-post serves for the gallows; so then they call themselves free, because you see they have no law left to condemn them, and no king to take them up and hang them for it.

Tom. Ah, but, Jack, didn't their king formerly hang people for nothing, too? and besides, were not they all papists before the revolution?

Jack. Why, true enough, they had but a poor sort of religion; but bad is better than none, Tom. And so was the government bad enough too; for they could clap an innocent man into prison, and keep him there too, as long as they would, and never say, with your leave, or by your leave, gentlemen of the jury. But what's all that to us?

Tom. To us! Why, don't our governors put many of our poor folks in prison against their will? What are all the jails for? Down with the jails, I say! all men should be free.

Jack. Harkee, Tom, a few rogues in prison keep the rest in order, and then honest men go about their business in safety, afraid of nobody; that's the way to be free. And let me tell thee, Tom, thou and I are tried by our peers as much as a lord is. Why, the *king* can't send me to prison, if I do no harm; and if I do, there's reason good why I should go there. I may go to law with Sir John at the great castle yonder; and he no more dares lift his little finger against me than if I were his equal. A lord is hanged for hanging matter, as thou or I should be; and if it be any comfort to thee, I myself remember a peer of the realm being hanged for killing his man, just the same as the man would have been for killing *him*.*

Tom. A lord! Well, that is some comfort, to be sure. – But have you read the Rights of Man?

Jack. No, not I; I had rather by half read the "Whole Duty of Man." I have but little time for reading, and such as I should therefore only read a bit of the best.

Tom. Don't tell me of those old-fashioned notions. Why should not we have the same fine things they have got in France? I'm for a constitution – and organization – and equalization – and fraternization.

Jack. Do be quiet. Now, Tom, only suppose this nonsensical equality was to take place; why, it would not last while one could say Jack Robinson; or suppose it cou'd – suppose, in the general division, our new rulers were to give us half an acre of ground apiece; we cou'd, to be sure, raise potatoes on it for the use of our families; but as every other man would be equally busy in raising potatoes for his family, why then, you see, if thou wast to break thy spade, I, whose trade it is, should no longer be able to mend it. Neighbour Snip would have no time to make us a suit of clothes, nor the clothier to weave the cloth; for all the world would be gone a digging. And as to boots and shoes, the want of some one to make them for us, would be a still greater grievance than the tax on leather. If we should be sick, there would be no doctor's stuff for us; for doctor would be digging too. And if necessity did not compel, and if no inequality subsisted, we cou'd not get a chimney swept, or a load of coal from pit, for love of money.

Tom. But still I should have no one over my head.

---

* Lord Ferrers, hanged, in 1760, for killing his steward.

Jack. That's a mistake: I'm stronger than thou; and Standish, the exciseman, is a better scholar; so that we should not remain equal a minute. I shou'd out-*fight* thee, and he'd out-*wit* thee. And if such a sturdy fellow as I am, was to come and break down thy hedge for a little firing, or take away the crop from thy ground, I'm not so sure that these new-fangled laws wou'd see thee righted. I tell thee, Tom, we have a fine constitution already, and our fore-fathers thought so.

Tom. They were a pack of fools, and had never read the Rights of Man.

Jack. I'll tell thee a story. When sir John married, my lady, who is a little fantastical, and likes to do every thing like the French, begged him to pull down yonder fine old castle, and build it up in her frippery way. No, says sir John, what! shall I pull down this noble building, raised by the wisdom of my brave ancestors; which outstood the civil wars, and only underwent a little needful repair at the Revolution; a castle which all my neighbours come to take a pattern by – shall I pull it all down, I say, only because there may be a dark closet, or an awkward passage, or an inconvenient room or two in it? Our ancestors took time for what they did. They understood foundation work; no running up your little slight lath-and-plaster buildings, which are up in a day, and down in a night. My lady mumpt and grumbled; but the castle was let stand, and a glorious building it is; tho' there may be a trifling fault or two, and tho' a few decays want stopping; so now and then they mend a little thing, and they'll go on mending, I dare say, as they have leisure, to the end of the chapter, if they are let alone. But no pull-me-down works. What is it you are crying out for, Tom?

Tom. Why, for a perfect government!

Jack. You might as well cry for the moon. There's nothing perfect in this world, take my word for it: tho' sir John says, we come nearer to it than any country in the world ever did.

Tom. I don't see why we are to work like slaves, while others roll about in their coaches, feed on the fat of the land, and do nothing.

Jack. My little maid brought home a little storybook from the charity-school to'other day, in which was a bit of a fable about the belly and the limbs. The hands said, I won't work any longer to feed this lazy belly, who sits in state like a lord, and does nothing. Said the feet, I won't walk and tire myself to carry him about, let him shift for himself; so said all the members; just as your levellers and republicans do now. And what was the consequence? Why, the belly was pinched, to be sure, and grew thin upon it; but the hands and the feet, and the rest of the members, suffered so much for want of their old nourishment, which the belly had been all the time administering, while they accused him of sitting in idle state, that they all fell sick, pined away, and would have died, if they had not come to their senses just in time to save their lives, as I hope all you will do.

Tom. But the times – but the taxes! Jack.

Jack. Things are dear, to be sure: but riot and murder is not the way to make them cheap. And taxes are high; but I'm told there's a deal of old scores paying off, and paying off by them who did not contract the debt neither, Tom. Besides, things are mending, I hope; and what little is done, is for us poor people; our candles are somewhat cheaper, and, I dare say, if the honest gentleman who has the management of things is not disturbed by you levellers, things will mend every day. But bear one thing in mind; the more we riot, the more we shall have to pay; the more mischief is done, the more will the repairs cost; the more time we waste in meeting to redress public wrongs, the more we shall increase our private wants. And mind, too, that 'tis working, and not murmuring, which puts bread in our children's mouths, and a new coat on our own backs. Mind another thing, too: we have not the same ground of complaint; in France the poor paid all the taxes, as I have heard 'em say, and the quality paid nothing.

Tom. Well, I know what's what, as well as another; and I'm as fit to govern –

Jack. No, Tom, no. You are indeed as good as another man, seeing you have hands to work, and a soul to be saved. But are all men fit for all kinds of things? Solomon says, "How can he be wise, whose talk is of oxen?" Every one in his way. I am a better judge of a horse-shoe than sir John; but he has a deal better notion of state affairs than I; and I can no more do without his employ than he can do without my farriery. Besides, few are so poor, but they may get a vote for a parliamentman; and so you see the poor have as much share in the government as they well know how to manage.

Tom. But I say all men are equal. Why should one be above another?

Jack. If that's thy talk, Tom, thou dost quarrel with Providence, and not with Government. For the woman is below her husband, and the children are below their mother, and the servant is below his master.

Tom. But the subject is not below the king: all kings are "crowned ruffians;" and all governments are wicked. For my part, I'm resolved I'll pay no more taxes to any of them.

Jack. Tom, Tom, if thou didst go oftener to church, thou wou'dst know where it is said, "Render unto Cæsar the things that are Cæsar's;" and also, "Fear God, honour the king." *Your* book tells you that we need obey no government but that of the people; and that we may fashion and alter the government according to our whimsies: but *mine* tells me, "Let every one be subject to the higher powers, for all power is of God, the powers that be are ordained of God; whosoever therefore resisteth the power, resisteth the ordinance of God." Thou say'st, thou wilt pay no taxes to any of them. Dost thou know who it was that worked a miracle, that he might have money to pay tribute with, rather than set you and me an example of disobedience to government? an example, let me tell thee, worth an hundred precepts, and of which all the wit of man can never lessen the value. Then there's another thing worth minding; when Saint Paul was giving all those directions, in the epistle to the Romans, for obedience and submission; what sort of a king, now, dost think they had? Dost think 'twas a *saint* which he ordered them to obey?

Tom. Why, it was a kind, merciful, charitable king, to be sure; one who put nobody to death or in prison.

Jack. You was never more out in your life. Our parson says he was a monster – that he robbed the rich, and murdered the poor – set fire to his own town, as fine a place as London – fiddled to the flames, and then hanged and burnt the Christians, who were all poor, as if *they* had burnt the town.* Yet there's not a word about rising. Duties are fixed, Tom – laws are settled; a Christian can't pick and choose, whether he will obey or let it alone. But we have no such trials. We have a king the very reverse.

Tom. I say we shall never be happy, till we do as the French have done.

Jack. The French and we contending for liberty, Tom, is just as if thou and I were to pretend to run a race; thou to set out from the starting-post when I am in already; thou to have all the ground to travel, when I have reached the end. Why, we've got it, man! we've no race to run! we're there already! Our constitution is no more like what the French one was, than a mug of our Taunton beer is like a platter of their soup-maigre.

Tom. I know we shall be undone, if we don't get a new *constitution* – that's all.

Jack. And I know we shall be undone if we *do*. I don't know much about politics, but I can see by a little what a great deal

* The Emperor NERO.

means. Now, only to shew thee the state of public credit, as I think Tim Standish calls it. There's Farmer Furrow – a few years ago he had an odd £50 by him; so, to keep it out of harm's way, he put it out to use, on government security, I think he calls it; well, t'other day he married one of his daughters, so he thought he'd give her that fifty pounds for a bit of a portion. Tom, as I'm a living man, when he went to take it out, if his fifty pounds was not almost grown to a hundred! and wou'd have been a full hundred, they say, by this time, if the gentleman had been let alone.*

Tom. Well, still, as the old saying is – I shou'd like to do as they do in France.

Jack. What, shou'dst like to be murdered with as little ceremony as Hackabout, the butcher, knocks down a calf? or, shou'dst like to get rid of thy wife for every little bit of tiff? And as to liberty of conscience, which they brag so much about, why, they have driven away their parsons, (ay, and murdered many of 'em,) because they would not swear as they would have them. And then they talk of liberty of the press; why, Tom, only t'other day they hang'd a man for printing a book against this pretty government of theirs.

Tom. But you said, yourself, it was sad times in France, before they pull'd down the old government.

Jack. Well, and suppose the French were as much in the right as I know them to be in the wrong; what does that argue for *us?* Because my neighbour Furrow t'other day pull'd down a crazy old barn, is that a reason why I must set fire to my tight cottage?

Tom. I don't see, for all that, why one man is to ride in his coach-and-six, while another mends the highway for him.

Jack. I don't see why the man in the coach is to drive over the man on foot, or hurt a hair of his head, any more than you. And as to our great folks, that you levellers have such a spite against; I don't pretend to say they are a bit better than they should be: but that's no affair of mine; let them look to that; they'll answer for that in another place. To be sure, I wish they'd set us a better example about going to church, and those things; but still *hoarding's* not the sin of the age; they don't lock up their *money* – away it goes, and every body's the better for it. They do spend too much, to be sure, in feastings and fandangoes; and so far from commending them for it, if I was a parson, I'd go to work with 'em, but it should be in another kind of way; but as I am only a poor tradesman, why 'tis but bringing more grist to my mill. It all comes among the people. Their very extravagance, for which, as I said before, their

* This was written before the war, when the funds were at the highest.

parsons should be at them, is a fault by which, as poor men, we are benefited; so you cry out just in the wrong place. Their coaches, and their furniture, and their buildings, and their planting, employ a power of tradesmen and labourers. Now, in this village, what should we do without the castle? Tho' my lady is too rantipolish, and flies about all summer to hot water and cold water, and fresh water and salt water, when she ought to stay at home with sir John; yet when she does come down, she brings such a deal of gentry, that I have more horses than I can shoe, and my wife more linen than she can wash. Then all our grown children are servants in the family, and rare wages they have got. Our little boys get something every day by weeding their gardens, and the girls learn to sew and knit at sir John's expense; who sends them all to school of a Sunday besides.

Tom. Ay, but there's not sir John's in every village.

Jack. The more's the pity. But there's other help. 'Twas but last year you broke your leg, and was nine weeks in the Bristol infirmary, where you was taken as much care of as a lord, and your family was maintained all the while by the parish. No poor-rates in France, Tom; and here there's a matter of two million and a half paid for the poor every year, if 'twas but a little better managed.

Tom. Two million and a half!

Jack. Ay, indeed. Not translated into tenpences, as your French millions are, but twenty good shillings to the pound. But, when this levelling comes about, there will be no infirmaries, no hospitals, no charity-schools, no Sunday-schools, where so many hundred thousand poor souls learn to read the word of God for nothing. For who is to pay for them? *Equality* can't afford it; and those that may be willing won't be able.

Tom. But we shall be one as good as another, for all that.

Jack. Ay, and bad will be the best. But we must work as we do now, and with this difference, that no one will be able to pay us. Tom! I have got the use of my limbs, of my liberty, of the laws, and of my bible. The two first I take to be my *natural* rights; the two last my *civil* and *religious* rights: these, I take it, are the *true rights of man*, and all the rest is nothing but nonsense, and madness, and wickedness. My cottage is my castle; I sit down in it at night in peace and thankfulness, and "no man maketh me afraid." Instead of indulging discontent because another is richer than I in this world, (for envy is at the bottom of your equality works,) I read my bible, go to church, and look forward to a treasure in heaven.

Tom. Ay, but the French have got it in *this* world.

Jack. 'Tis all a lie, Tom. Sir John's butler says his master gets letters which *say* 'tis all a lie. 'Tis all murder, and nakedness, and hunger; many of the poor soldiers fight without victuals, and march without clothes. These are your *democrats!* Tom.

Tom. What, then, dost think all the men on our side wicked?

Jack. No – not so, neither: – if some of the leaders are knaves, more of the followers are fools. Sir John, who is wiser than I, says the whole system is the operation of fraud upon folly. They've made fools of most of you, as I believe. I judge no man, Tom; I hate no man. Even republicans and levellers, I hope, will always enjoy the protection of our laws; though I hope they will never be our law-*makers*. There are many true dissenters, and there are some hollow churchmen; and a good man is a good man, whether his church has got a steeple to it or not. The new-fashioned way of proving one's religion is to *hate* somebody. Now, though some folks pretend that a man's hating a papist, or a presbyterian, proves him to be a good *churchman*, it don't prove him to be a good *christian*, Tom. As much as I hate republican works, I'd scorn to *live* in a country where there was not liberty of conscience, and where every man might not worship God in his own way. Now, that liberty they had not in France; the bible was shut up in an unknown, heathenish tongue. While here, thou and I can make as free use of our's as a bishop; can no more be sent to prison unjustly, than the judge who tries us; and are as much taken care of by the laws as the parliament-man who makes them. Then, as to your thinking that the new scheme will make you happy, look among your own set, and see if any thing can be so dismal and discontented as a leveller. – Look at France. These poor French fellows used to be the merriest dogs in the world; but since equality came in, I don't believe a Frenchman has ever laughed.

Tom. What then dost thou take French *liberty* to be?

Jack. To murder more men in one night, than ever their poor king did in his whole life.

Tom. And what dost thou take a *Democrat* to be?

Jack. One who likes to be governed by a thousand tyrants, and yet can't bear a king.

Tom. What is *Equality?*

Jack. For every man to pull down every one that is above him; while, instead of raising those below him to his own level, he only makes use of them as steps to raise himself to the place of those he has tumbled down.

Tom. What is *the new rights of man?*

Jack. Battle, murder, and sudden death.

Tom. What is it to be an *enlightened people?*

Jack. To put out the light of the gospel, confound right and wrong, and grope about in pitch darkness.

Tom. What is *Philosophy*, that Tim Standish talks so much about?

Jack. To believe that there's neither God, nor devil, nor heaven, nor hell; to dig up a wicked old fellow's* rotten bones, whose books, sir John says, have been the ruin of thousands; and to set his figure up in a church and worship him.

Tom. And what is a *Patriot* according to the new school?

Jack. A man who loves every other country better than his own, and France best of all.

Tom. And what is *benevolence*?

Jack. Why, in the new-fangled language, it means contempt of religion, aversion to justice, overturning of law, doting on all mankind in general, and hating every body in particular.

Tom. And what mean the other hard words that Tim talks about – *organization*, and *function*, and *civism*, and *incivism*, and *equalization*, and *inviolability*, and *imprescriptible*, and *fraternization*?

Jack. Nonsense, gibberish, downright hocus-pocus. I know 'tis not English; sir John says 'tis not Latin; and his valet de sham says 'tis not French neither.

Tom. And yet Tim says he never shall be happy till all these fine things are brought over to England.

Jack. What! into this Christian country, Tom? Why, dost know they have no *Sabbath* in France? Their mob parliament meets on a Sunday to do their wicked work, as naturally as we do to go to church,† They have renounced God's word and God's day, and they don't even date in the year of our Lord. Why dost turn pale, man? And the rogues are always making such a noise, Tom, in the midst of their parliament-house, that their speaker rings a bell, like our penny-postman, because he can't keep them in order.

Tom. And dost thou believe they are as cruel as some folks pretend?

* Voltaire.

† Since this they have crammed ten days into the week, in order to throw Sunday out of it. – One of the first and most capital strokes against Christianity was the alteration of the calendar, and the division of time into *decades*, instead of weeks of seven days. But though the French convention had such very able mathematicians and astronomers among them, as Bailly and Lalande, their blundering scheme of atheism only served to expose the folly of the inventors. The proscribed calendar was restored, for the sake of convenience; but the Christian Sabbath in France is still desecrated.—ED.

Jack. I am sure they are, and I think I know the reason. We Christians set a high value on life, because we know that every fellow-creature has an immortal soul: a soul to be saved or lost, Tom – Whoever believes that, is a little cautious how he sends a soul unprepared to his grand account. But he who believes a man is no better than a dog, will make no more scruple of killing one than the other.

Tom. And dost thou think our rights of man will lead to all this wickedness?

Jack. As sure as eggs are eggs.

Tom. I begin to think we are better off as we are.

Jack. I'm sure on't. This is only a scheme to make us go back in every thing. 'Tis making ourselves poor when we are getting rich, and discontented when we are comfortable.

Tom. I begin to think I'm not so very unhappy as I had got to fancy.

Jack. Tom, I don't care for drink myself, but thou dost; and I'll argue with thee, not in the way of principle, but in thy own way: when there's all equality, there will be no superfluity; when there's no wages, there'll be no drink; and levelling will rob thee of thy ale more than the malt-tax does.

Tom. But Standish says, if we had a good government, there'd be no want of any thing.

Jack. He is like many others, who take the king's money and betray him: let him give up the profits of his place before he kicks at the hand that feeds him. Tho' I'm no scholar, I know that a good government is a good thing. But don't go to make me believe that *any* government can make a bad man good, or a discontented man happy. What art musing upon, man?

Tom. Let me sum up the evidence, as they say at 'sizes – Hem! To cut every man's throat who does not think as I do, or hang him up at a lamp-post! – Pretend liberty of conscience, and then banish the parsons only for being conscientious! – Cry out liberty of the press, and hang up the first man who writes his mind! – Lose our poor laws! – Lose one's wife perhaps upon every little tiff! – March without clothes, and fight without victuals! – No trade! – No bible! – No Sabbath, nor day of rest! – No safety, no comfort, no peace in this world – and no world to come! – Jack, I never knew thee tell a lie in my life.

Jack. Nor wou'd I now, not even against the French.

Tom. And thou art very sure we are not ruined?

Jack. I'll tell thee how we are ruined. We have a king, so loving, that he wou'd not hurt the people if he cou'd; and so kept in, that he cou'd not hurt the people if he wou'd. We have as much liberty as can make us happy, and more trade and riches than allows us to be good. We have the best laws in the world, if they were more strictly enforced; and the best religion in the world, if it was but better followed. While Old England is safe, I'll glory in her, and pray for her; and when she is in danger, I'll fight for her, and die for her.

Tom. And so will I too, Jack, that's what I will. (*sings*) "*O the roast beef of Old England!*"

Jack. Thou art an honest fellow, Tom.

Tom. This is Rose and Crown night, and Tim Standish is now at his mischief; but we'll go and put an end to that fellow's work, or he'll corrupt the whole club.

Jack. Come along.

Tom. No; first I'll stay to burn my book, and then I'll go and make a bonfire, and –

Jack. Hold, Tom. There is but one thing worse than a bitter enemy; and that is an imprudent friend. If thou wou'dst shew thy love to thy king and country, let's have no drinking, no riot, no bonfires, but put in practice this text, which our parson preached on last Sunday, "Study to be quiet, work with your own hands, and mind your own business."

Tom. And so I will, Jack – Come on.

THE
LANCASHIRE COLLIER GIRL
A true story

In a small village in Lancashire there lived, a few years ago, an industrious man and his wife, who had six children. The man himself used to work in a neighbouring colliery, while the wife took care of the family, attended also to their little farm, and minded the dairy, and when all her other work was done, she used constantly to sit down to spin. It will naturally be supposed that the children of such a mother, even when very young, were not suffered to be idle. The eldest daughter worked with the mother at the spinning-wheel, which she learnt to think a very pleasant employment, and she sometimes accompanied her work with a chearful hymn, or a good moral song, which her parents had taken care to teach her.

But the second daughter, of the name of Mary, is the chief subject of the present story; when this girl was nine years old, the honest collier finding that he had but little employment for her above ground, took her to work with him down in the coal-pit, together with one of his boys, who was then no more than seven years of age. These two children readily put their strength to the basket, dragging the coals from the workmen to the mouth of the pit; and by their joint labours they did the duty of one of those men who are commonly called "the drawers," clearing thereby no less than seven shilling a week for their parents. It must be owned to be not impossible, that they may have sometimes exerted themselves even beyond their strength, which is now and then the case with little children, through the fault of those who exact the work from them; but since in this case the father had an eye to them during the hours of labour, while they had a prudent and tender mother also, to look after them at home, there is no particular reason to suppose, that the time of which we are now speaking, they were ever much over-worked.

Here, then, let us stop to remark how different was the case of this numerous family from that of many others, in the same humble situation of life. Mary and her brother, so far from being a burden, were bringing a little fortune to their parents, even when they were eight or ten years old; all the family were getting forward by the help of these little creatures, and their worldly comforts were now encreasing on every side.

But, alas! in the midst of this cheerful and contented diligence, on one fatal day, while the good man was in the act of fixing a basket, in order to its being wound up, the children standing near him in the coal-pit, some stones fell from the top of the pit, one of which fell on the father's head, and killed him on the spot. What a melancholy event was this! some dismal circumstances also remain to be told, which were the consequences of it; but in order to relieve the pain of my reader, I will here remark, that the most grievous afflictions are often appointed by Providence, to be the means, in one way or other, of calling some extraordinary virtue into exercise: and accordingly we shall see that the calamity which is now spoken of will introduce Mary, the young collier girl, to the further good opinion of the reader.

The mother, on hearing the news of her husband's death, together with the description of the sad accident which gave occasion to it, received such a shock, that her mind was not able to bear up under it; she became disordered in her understanding, nor did she to the end of her life recover her senses. Being now rendered extremely helpless, she was separated from her children by the parish officers, who continued to take the charge of her for the space of five years. A short time after the father's death, the eldest daughter (the spinner) married, and went from home; two of the brothers (of the ages of nine and seven) were bound apprentices by the parish, which also took the charge of two others (one three years old, the other an infant) until they should be sufficiently grown up to be bound out also.

In this place I cannot avoid observing, what a blessing it is to poor people in this country, that parish officers are obliged, in all such cases of necessity as that of which I am now speaking, to give maintenance to those who apply to them, and what a pity it is that this wise and merciful provision of our laws should ever be abused. Mary, the girl of whom we are giving the history, having been already trained to industry, was by no means disposed to seek an unnecessary help from the parish, and being now between eleven and twelve years old, she determined to maintain herself, like a little independant woman, by her usual work in the coal-pit, where she was generally able after this time to earn at least a shilling a day; in three or four years afterwards earning no less than two shillings. And now I would ask my young female readers what they think was the manner in which she employed all this fruit of her industry? Do you imagine that she laid it out in vanity of dress, in nice eating and drinking, or other needless expence? or do you suppose that she would now indulge herself in idleness on one or two days in the week, because she had got enough for herself to live upon during the four or five working days? no: I trust you will have formed no such expectation: I hope you will be well aware what Mary did with her money, by having already reflected what you would have done with it in the like case. She in the first place released the parish from the burden of maintaining her mother, which she did as soon as she was arrived at the age of sixteen, being extremely anxious to take this poor disordered helpless parent home to live with herself: she then relieved the parish officers from the charge of one of her brothers, and she continued to provide for him until he died. Having been taught never to consider her duty as done, while any part of it seemed to be left undone she afterwards undertook the maintenance of one of her other brothers, who remained with her during sixteen weeks' illness, at the end of which period she followed him to the grave, burying him at her own expence. After about seven years the mother died also, and was buried in like manner by this dutiful child, without any assistance from the parish.

If any of my readers should here inquire how it could be possible for so young a child to support all these relations, many of them being also occasionally very burthensome through their sickness? the answer is, that in the case of these extraordinary calls upon her, she used to betake herself to extraordinary labour, sometimes earning no less than three shillings and sixpence in the four and twenty hours, by taking what is called "a double turn" in the coal-pits.

The ready submission of Mary to her parents when she was in early life, is so pleasing a part of her character, that it may be proper in this place again to make a remark upon it. Let my young readers recollect that in submission to the command of her father, or rather to that law of God which enjoins parental obedience, she cheerfully followed him down into the coal-pit, burying herself in the bowels of the earth, and there at a tender age, without excusing herself on account of her sex, she joined in the same work with the miners, a race of men rough indeed, but highly useful to the community, of whom I am also happy to say that they have the character of being honest and faithful, as well as remarkably courageous, and that they have given moreover some striking instances of their readiness to receive religious instruction, when offered to them. Among these men, to their honour be it spoken, Mary's virtue was safe, and after the death of her father, she is even said to have received protection as well as assistance from them, her fatigue having been sometimes lessened, through their lending her a helping hand, with great feeling and kindness.

But though Mary's mind was naturally strong, and her constitution of body was very stout also, yet towards the end of the period which has been spoken of, she began to be bowed down in some measure, by the afflictions and labours which she had endured. It was evident that she had now been led to exert herself beyond her strength. How lamentable is it, that while so many people in the world are idle, and are contracting diseases both of body and mind, from the abundance of their riches, and from the want of some wholesome and useful exercise, there should be any bending like Mary, under their work, hidden in coal-pits, or from some cause or other removed from observation! what a pity it is, I say, that the former should not employ a little of their time and money, in endeavouring to find these distressed objects! And I may also add, how lamentable a thing is it, that while so many poor people are seen, who are apt to complain too soon, there should be any, who do not tell their distresses to those who can help them (which I trust however does not often happen) till it is almost too late!

I was observing that Mary began about this time evidently to lose her strength, and her head was also troubled by some of those strange and unpleasant imaginations, which are known by persons conversant with the diseases of the poor, to be no unusual consequence of bad food, and great bodily fatigue, joined with excessive grief. At first she was not aware that she laboured under any disorder, for she had seldom experienced ill health, while her relations were alive; and it seems probable that the comfort which she derived from the reflection of affording them support, and the pleasing sensation which arose during the exercise of her attention to them, had served both to keep up her spirits, and to prevent her constitution from breaking down.

I trust it is not superstitious to suppose that when sincere Christians come, as Mary now did, into very trying circumstances, they may hope, notwithstanding any appearances to the contrary, to experience still, in one way or other, the peculiar blessing of

Heaven; I do not expect that such persons will be free from pain, poverty, or sickness, or other worldly evils, for it is often quite the contrary, but then I believe that these very afflictions will be made the means of encreasing their trust in God, and prove in the end, (I mean either here or hereafter) to have been entirely designed for their good. The calamities of Mary were now risen to such a height, that those who are not accustomed to view things in this religious and most comforting light, might be ready to imagine that the Almighty had forsaken her, and that there is little use in serving him. Let us here number up her afflictions. She had seen with her own eyes the dreadful death of her father, she had for a long time witnessed the affecting condition of her mother, who used to follow her about the house without knowing the hand by which she was supported; Mary, besides this, had attended the long and drooping sickness of her two brothers; and now, having fallen sick herself, being both weak in body, and sadly enfeebled in her mind, she was dwelling all alone in a little comfortless habitation; having been deprived by death of every one of those dear relatives, the sight of whom had many a time cheered her spirits, while the idea of supplying them with a comfortable subsistence, had been used to sweeten her employment, and lighten the severity of her toil.

It was at this period of her extremity that it pleased God to raise up for her some kind friends, in the manner which I shall now describe.

A lady of the same village heard that a servant's place was vacant in a neighbouring family, and advised Mary, feeble as she was, to present herself there as a candidate to fill this comparatively easy and comfortable situation. Accordingly the poor girl, with anxious heart, went to offer her services; she mentioned, with her usual honesty, what had been the habits of her former life, and what was the state of her health also: it seemed undoubtedly much against her interest to do so, but it was perfectly right; and how can any of us hope for the blessing of God, or expect any true comfort in our minds when we fall into affliction, if we fly to unfair means of rescuing ourselves out of it; and instead of trusting in God, trust to our own little frauds and crooked contrivances.

The answer made to Mary's application was unfavourable, for it was thought, and indeed it was gently hinted, that a young woman, hitherto so much exposed as she had been, was not likely to prove a very fit inmate in a sober private family.

Mary felt very keenly this unhappy suspicion against her character, but what could she do? she walked very quietly away, with a down-cast look, and with a mind quite broken down by this fresh affliction and disaster. The owners of the mansion happened however to observe her countenance, and the peculiar modesty of her manner, as she was taking her departure, for her patient and silent grief touched them far more sensibly than any loud complaints could have done, and they therefore determined to make some enquiries concerning her. The gentleman went himself on the same day to the colliery, where the master of the pit replied to his questions, nearly in the following terms. "Sir," said he, "she is a poor girl that has over-worked herself, for she has undertaken what we call taskwork, which is very hard labour; she is one of the best girls that ever I knew, and is respected by all the colliers, and though (added he) I cannot deny that now and then my men take a cup too much, which is apt to make them sometimes quarrelsome, yet they never suffer a bad word to be spoken, or an affront to be offered to a girl in the pit, without punishing the fellow who may be guilty, and making him heartily ashamed of himself."

This rule of decency and propriety towards young women, established by a set of coarse miners, is here recorded for the benefit of some of those persons, who are pleased to call themselves their betters.

The gentleman, after a very minute and full examination, was so well satisfied of the good character of Mary, that she was received into his service, in which she has now been living comfortably for the space of six years. Her health is recovered, her habits of diligence are still very great, and she is said to be of a very remarkable modest, humble and contented spirit. It may not be improper to mention, that the master of the house in which she is, has furnished all the materials of this story.

I will now take leave of my readers, by remarking, that the little tale which I have been reciting, seems to me to hold out the following useful lessons:

In the first place, I think it may teach the poor that they can seldom be in any condition of life so low as to prevent their rising to some degree of independance, if they chuse to exert themselves, and that there can be no situation whatever so mean, as to forbid the practice of many noble virtues. It may instruct the rich not to turn the poor from their doors, merely on account of first appearances, but rather to examine into their character, expecting sometimes to find peculiar modesty and merit, even in the most exposed situations. This story also may encourage the afflicted to serve and trust God in every extremity: and finally, it may teach all descriptions of persons, who may have to pass through dangerous and trying circumstances, that they may expect the divine protection and blessing, provided they are not needlessly throwing themselves in the way of temptation, but are endeavouring, like Mary, "to learn and labour truly to get their own living, and to do their duty in that state of life, into which it hath pleased God to call them."

THE END

William Godwin

1756-1836

As he is such a major figure in the history of his period, William Godwin requires only a brief general introduction so that my main concern here will be with his novel *Fleetwood, or the New Man of Feeling* (1805), or rather with that particular part of it which bears directly on our subject. The episode narrated in chapters 11–14 is of unusual historical importance as it represents the first occurrence in prose fiction of social criticism directed against the factory system. This part of the book was obviously written to denounce the exploitation of child labour in textile factories and to accuse the factory system itself of having a dehumanizing effect on the workers. The significance of this passage, however, has been unrecognized by critics both of his own period and of later times.

The son of a Dissenting minister, William Godwin first became a minister himself. But as his Noncomformist background had debarred him from the university and predisposed him in favour of liberal principles, he was soon captured by the ideas of the Encyclopedists and his faith in the main dogmas of Christianity was shaken. He therefore resigned his ministry and decided to settle in London and earn his living by his pen. He soon acquired a considerable reputation in left-wing circles and became a regular contributor to political reviews, and in the course of his long career as a writer he produced a great variety of works such as essays, pamphlets, novels, plays, text-books, and books for children.[1]

In 1797 Godwin married Mary Wollstonecraft, who died in the same year after giving birth to a daughter, Mary, who was to become the second wife of the poet Shelley. Godwin's wife was a rebel against the established order, but in private life she was known as "a generous, impulsive woman, always affectionate and kind". Her *A Vindication of the Rights of Woman* (1792) was a resolute attack on the convention which made women subservient to the male sex. Her ideas seemed very bold to her contemporaries, but being generally accepted today they no longer appear so remarkable. Both husband and wife were visionaries dreaming of a new, reformed world. When he became a widower with two children to bring up (Mary and her half-sister Fanny, Mary Wollstonecraft's daughter by Imlay), Godwin decided to remarry, and the necessity of supporting a growing family forced him into hack-work and a humiliating dependence on rich patrons. Though he exercised a great influence on a generation of free-thinkers, Godwin's hold on public opinion diminished as he grew older. He died in 1836 at the age of 80.

Under the impact of the French Revolution Godwin was inspired to write *An Inquiry Concerning the Principles of Political Justice and Its Influence on General Virtue and Happiness* (1793), which brought him into sudden prominence. The influence which this pamphlet exercised on public opinion was great, but it never reached a wide reading public as it was sold at the exorbitant price of three guineas a copy. The ideas put forward are those of a man who believes in the power of reason and in the possibility of human improvement. Godwin advocates a theory already advanced by Locke, according to which politics, as well as morals, could be made a demonstrative science. If only man were governed by reason, he would be compelled by logic to adopt a line of action in keeping with his conclusions. The ultimate social ideal, according to Godwin, must be "the greatest general good", and to achieve this, justice must be strictly observed in all public relationships. But Godwin doubted that political justice could ever be achieved under any kind of government – he actually hoped to see the State wither away – and for this reason he is considered to have influenced the anarchists of the nineteenth century. Nonetheless, Godwin was resolutely against the use of violence for the achievement of political goals. His seminal influence is reflected not only in the doctrines of the anarchists, but in those of other nineteenth-century ideologists as well.

The tenets of *Political Justice* may be traced in the pages of Godwin's novels, written not so much to provide entertainment as to persuade his readers to adopt his views. The brief episode from *Fleetwood* included in the Anthology cannot reflect the breadth of Godwin's social philosophy, but it is a fine example of his humanitarianism. This episode constitutes a tale within the tale in that it relates a minor character's memories of hardships endured as a child labourer. Since it has only the most tenuous connection with the rest of the novel, the narrative would hardly have suffered from an aesthetic point of view if these particular chapters had remained unwritten. To a student of literature, however, this section is of unusual interest as the first fictional record of sentiments that were to be strongly stressed later on, when novelists were profoundly perturbed by the serious social problems besetting industrial England.

The Ruffigny episode poses a number of interesting questions. What could have induced Godwin to reveal such obvious social concern, and where did he obtain the necessary information concerning the work of factory children? What has been the critical response to the story? And, last but not least, is it possible to trace a connection between Godwin's pathetic narrative and the similar story told by Dickens in *David Copperfield*? But our first concern will be with the genesis of Godwin's story.

Godwin wrote his novel three years after the passing of the First Factory Act in 1802, and the Ruffigny episode testifies to his whole-hearted approval of the new legislative measures for the protection of child labourers. Godwin, however, presents his exposure of the cruel abuse of children in a highly oblique manner by locating his story in France during the reign of Louis XIV. He may have wanted to protect himself against attack by distancing himself from the issues involved, or again he may have wanted to discredit the whole system of child labour by associating it with pre-revolutionary social abuses in France. What is quite certain is that the chapters contain much material familiar to us from committee reports on the state of children employed in the manufactures of the United Kingdom, but the fact that such reports were available cannot explain why Godwin should have decided to present a fictionalized account of the social problems that they investigate. These reports were accessible to all, yet Godwin alone saw fit to use the art of fiction as a vehicle for the presentation of their contents. Some 30 years were to elapse before the limelight of publicity was to fall on this particular social problem, and this is why Godwin's presentation of it in 1805 is of considerable historical significance.

Godwin had other sources to draw on besides the Parliamentary Papers. His interest in factory children may have been stirred by reading the self-taught poet Thelwall, by the various activities of his friend Horne Tooke, or again by the memoirs of William Hutton. Some importance must also be attached to Godwin's personal contact with the Wedgwood family, the well-known magnates of the Potteries.

The point that the Ruffigny episode is the first fictionalized account of the victimization of children has already been made by B. R. Pollin in his excellent study of *Education and Enlightenment in the Works of William Godwin* (1962). Pollin rightly argues that the compassionate attitude is entirely in keeping with the ideas expressed in Godwin's *Political Justice* (1793), just as he draws attention to the fact that a similar account already existed in a poem by John Thelwall – 'On Leaving the Bottoms of Glostershire; where the Author had been entertained by several families with great hospitality, August 12, 1797.'[3]

Two points, however, must be added to this observation: that descriptions of child labour, in prose and verse, had appeared long before Thelwall turned to this subject, and, secondly, that all of them express an attitude of approval and hence contain no social criticism of the kind which is such a marked feature of the Ruffigny episode.

The history of Thelwall's association with Godwin is a curious one. The memoirs written by Thelwall's second wife[4] underline the poet's keen interest in the social issues of the day, which was not surprising since he had had a hard childhood and youth. While working as an assistant in his mother's shop he nevertheless found time to read assiduously, and he was an enthusiastic amateur actor as well. During his apprenticeship to a London tailor, he developed asthma and gave up tailoring for art and literature. At the age of 22 he managed to earn £50 per annum, and from then on he worked incessantly as pedagogue, labour leader, and publisher. He owned and edited *The Tribune* (1796), a periodical inspired by the ideas of the French Revolution; the same ideas prompted the formation of the Society of the Friends of the People in Southwark, of which Thelwall became a member. Thelwall was indicted in the famous treason trial of 1794, and on that occasion Godwin wrote two pamphlets in his defence addressed to the Lord Chief Justice. The group was acquitted after a trial lasting several days, and so one may suppose that Godwin's eloquence was not entirely wasted. Although persecuted for his revolutionary ideas and pestered by government spies, Thelwall was a man of peace strongly opposed to what, in a pamphlet dated 26 October 1795,[5] he called "tumultuary violence". But a man like Godwin could not accept even the most moderate of public demonstrations as he was against mass meetings of any kind. For this reason the three Friends of the People – Thelwall, Horne Tooke, and Holcroft – offended Godwin by calling meetings and speaking at them. Godwin dissociated himself from their company, and distanced himself from his former friend to such an extent that he refused to visit him during his subsequent imprisonment in the Tower.[6] B. R. Pollin, who is usually so well informed about Godwin's life and career, is at a loss to account for a malignant public attack on Thelwall by Godwin in the pamphlet entitled *Consideration*.[7] Thelwall on his side nevertheless retained a dispassionate attitude and refrained from engaging in public debate; and as John Colmer informs us, he even defended Godwin against S. T. Coleridge.[8] Thelwall's wife was undoubtedly justified in stressing her husband's integrity and his firmness of character.

Although Godwin cut himself off from Thelwall, he seems to have been familiar with his poem 'On Leaving the Bottoms of Glostershire', some lines of which are perhaps echoed in the Ruffigny episode. The first 40 lines reflect the poet's feelings on parting from a scene the beauty of which is such that it wakes the beholder to "social rapture". By way of contrast he conjures up a vision of over-grown factories dominating the landscape: with "unwieldy pride",

> where Opulence,
> Dispeopling the neat cottage, crowds his walls
> (Made pestilent by congregated lungs,
> And lewd association) with a race
> Of infant slaves, brok'n timely to the yoke
> Of unremitting Drudgery – no more
> By relative endearment, or the voice
> Of matronly instruction, interspers'd –
> Cheering or sage; nor by the sports relax'd
> (To such how needful!) of their unknit prime
> Once deem'd the lawful charter.

II. 47–61

It is fortunate, the poet adds, that "Little here / Intrude . . . pompous mansions – better miss'd." This almost casual social criticism is an isolated occurrence in Thelwall's poetry, and it may have caught Godwin's attention, if he read Thelwall's *Poems Chiefly Written in Retirement* (1801). This obscure volume may, of course, have escaped Godwin's attention at the time, but it is likely that he had read it since the publisher, R. Phillips, also had a hand in the publication of Godwin's *Fleetwood*.

After the famous Spitalfield riots of 1768 Godwin's radical friend Horne Tooke undertook to investigate the disorder among the silk-weavers, so that he became familiar with the conditions under which they worked; many years later, in 1801 when the first Factory Act was being considered in the House of Commons, Horne Tooke finally succeeded in becoming a Member of Parliament. Although his friendship with Godwin had cooled off by then, he remains a likely channel through which Godwin could have obtained relevant information.[9] Occasional articles on the silk trade had appeared in popular periodicals like *The European Magazine*,[10] but these accounts failed to satisfy Godwin, who wrote two letters in November 1804 inquiring about the Silk Throwing Machine and its use in southern France.

For various reasons it is difficult to ascertain whether Godwin himself ever saw the "little victims of human avarice". His biographers do not mention the cities visited by Godwin on his various tours, and his letters are still scattered among a number of collections on both sides of the Atlantic. Godwin's diaries for the crucial year 1804 have been said to reveal "no fact of general or social interest, except the usual intercourse with the literary world of London,"[11] but more specific information is bound to become available with the appearance of the new

critical edition of Godwin's journals now being prepared by Professor
Lewis Patton.[12] What we do know is that Godwin visited Etruria as a
guest of the Wedgwoods in the summer of 1797, and that his host provided a visit to the potteries.[13] The condition of the many children at
work in these factories was just as deplorable as in the textile mills, but
we have no information concerning the possible impressions that Godwin may have received.

By far the most likely source for Godwin's Ruffigny story is the autobiography of an obscure contemporary by the name of William Hutton.[14]
Such is the similarity between Hutton's childhood memories and those
of Ruffigny that there must be a connection. Hutton was put to work in
Lombe's Silk Mill in Derby in 1730 at the age of seven, and his account
of his early years must be the first of all English testimonies concerning
factory children. This must be so for the simple reason that this was the
first English factory, built in 1726 by the brothers Lombe on an island
in the River Derwent. Hutton's father was a very poor wool comber
with a large family, and the seven-year old William had to be sent to
work in the neighbouring silk-mill. At this time a child had just been
born, and as Hutton records the event he adds the dry comment that
he "soon left us, by which he escaped that distress which awaited me."
Another child died soon afterwards, and the only word of comfort given
to a weeping brother was that he ought to stop crying, as he would be
sure to go next. Death, in other words, was a hoped-for merciful release.
It is only when we realize that to these people life itself was worse than
death, that we can understand how they could send such small children
into factories; whether they died inside a factory or outside was a mere
side-issue. William Hutton served as apprentice for seven years, but he
learnt no trade. His task, although tiring, was so simple that it taught
him nothing, and this was true of all the factory children that the First
Factory Act was supposed to protect. Hutton fared much worse in
actual life than the young Ruffigny in Godwin's novel. "My situation at
the mill was very unfavourable," says he, and goes on to explain why.
"Richard Potter, my master, had made a wound in my back with his
cane. It grew worse. In a succeeding punishment, the point of his cane
stirred the wound, which brought it into such a state that a mortification was apprehended. My father was advised to bathe me in Keddle-
stone water. A cure was effected, and I yet carry the scar." Because he
was too short to reach the machine he was appointed to tend, "a pair of
high pattens were therefore fabricated and tied fast about my feet, to
make them steady companions." This is a unique detail which, as far as
I have been able to ascertain, is not to be found in the many testimonies
given before the Parliamentary select committees, yet Godwin was
familiar with it. He relates how Ruffigny, on entering a mill for the first

time as a child, is shocked to see children made to walk on stilts to enable them to reach the machines. Godwin's fictional child labourer even entertains the same thoughts as Hutton in real life: both feel morally and socially degraded. Hutton explains how he was compelled "to be the constant companion of the most rude and vulgar of the human race, never taught by nature, nor ever wishing to be taught. A lad, let his mind be in what state it would, must be as impudent as they, or be hunted down. I could not consider this place in any other light than that of a complete bear garden."[15]

This basic similarity makes the difference in attitude between Hutton and Godwin the more striking. Like the vast majority of his contempararies, Hutton can see no harm in child labour as such. Although he still carries the marks of the overseer's cane, he never once accuses a social system which permitted children to be abused in this manner. Indeed, the whole point of this part of his life story is to stress his own achievement in overcoming the handicap of absolute poverty until, as the result of his own efforts, he finally became a rich man. He boasts of his career in a manner which recalls Bounderby in Charles Dickens's *Hard Times*. Like Bounderby of Coketown, Hutton of Birmingham started life at the very bottom of the social ladder, and his purpose in recalling his years of early suffering is equally boastful. Godwin's purpose, however, was to stir the conscience of the public by playing on their feelings of compassion. This is why he included so many factual details that could serve as powerful arguments for the abolition of child labour – details that often bear a strong resemblance to what we read in Hutton's autobiography: the tender years and the frailty of the workers, the hard factory discipline, the merciless overseers, the long working hours, and the complete neglect of anything even resembling education. The facts are similar, but they differ widely in the impact they make upon the reader. The actual suffering of Hutton is more painful than that of the Ruffigny boy, but the plight of the latter appeals much more strongly to the reader's sensibility. The sub-title explains the paradox: it is Godwin himself who is the "new man of feeling". His compassion contrasts strongly with Hutton's matter-of-fact attitude and with the general indifference of his generation to the suffering of the child worker. Godwin therefore must be said to foreshadow the growth of a new sensibility exercised on behalf of the victims of social injustice. Godwin's more modern sensibility is shown in his description of the singing of these children. While the poet John Dyer had envisaged them as "a choir of larks" (*The Fleece*, 1757), Godwin makes the point that it is no expression of joy but a kind of monotonous incantation to make the rhythm of the work a little easier to sustain.

Godwin's firm stand against the use of children in industry was prompted by two considerations: his strong humanitarian feelings, and his attitude to education. Godwin was far ahead of his contemporaries as an educationalist, but since his ideas are universally prevalent today, they do not strike us as being at all exceptional. But in his own day they were indeed radical. Godwin was unique in insisting on respect for the child as "an individual being", as he puts it in a pamphlet of 1797. "The most fundamental of all principles of morality is the consideration and the deference that man owes to man; nor is the helplessness of childhood by any means unentitled to the benefit of this principle."[16] When Godwin stressed "the helplessness of childhood" in the Ruffigny episode, he wrote as an educationalist intent on securing for all children, as 'individual beings', the possibility of physical and intellectual development. Godwin's strongest indignation is felt when he denounces the factory system for its degrading effect on the emotions and the intelligence of the child; he is much less eloquent when his concern is with physical suffering. The detrimental psychological effect of mechanized work poses a problem that still awaits solution, and by underlining the potential danger Godwin made his argument relevant even to twentieth-century readers, at a time when the process of mechanization has been taken far beyond the wildest dreams of Godwin's generation.

Godwin shows little psychological insight in the narrower sense of this word; his empathy is strictly limited, and as a boy of eight years old Ruffigny is made to speak like a newspaper reporter. It is in keeping with the period of Louis XIV that the mill which he describes is of the oldest type worked by horse power, but Godwin may have wanted to avoid the impression of seeming to blame the new technical inventions that had led to more modern machinery.

The traditional praise of England's commercial and industrial prosperity is conspicuous for its absence in *Fleetwood*. While Arthur Young viewed the capitalists as men of exceptional merit, Godwin distrusted the honesty of the self-made man, as we may see from a passage in his *Political Justice*: "He who from beggary ascends to opulence is usually known not to have effected the transition by methods very creditable to his honesty or his usefulness."[17] One of the characters exposed to ridicule is a factory-owner of precisely this stamp, who is made to boast that he and his friends contributed to the welfare of society by relieving parents and the municipality of the burden of supporting the children. Instead of being an encumbrance, children of three and four years of age are taught to be useful and industrious, which makes this worthy gentleman conclude that his factory is a blessing comparable to Paradise itself. Although this satirical portrait is obviously prompted by strong feelings, the author's recommendation for the solution of this social problem seems curiously half-hearted; he proposes, very cautiously, that children should not be set to work when they are clearly much too young, and he adds a general reflection on the fact that suffering is man's universal predicament.

Ruffigny's escape from his bondage is reminiscent of David Copperfield's flight from his menial employment. I have pointed to the similarities of the fates of these two boys in a previously published article.[18] It seems to me significant that both Godwin and Dickens had recourse to the same fictional device for rescuing their heroes. The two boys are so to speak taken by the hand by their respective authors and led away from the terrible world where they had suffered a temporary exile. The other children are left to their unrelieved misery; the veil which had been lifted for a moment, is dropped, and an unpleasant social problem is left to the care of Providence. So completely does Godwin forget the young sufferers in the Lyons silk-mill that he never so much as refers to them in the rest of his story.

Fleetwood proved less popular with the public than Godwin's earlier novels, as we see from B. R. Pollin's *Synoptic Bibliography* (1967), which contains only a short list of contemporary reviews. Few of these touch on the Ruffigny episode. There is no mention of it in the *Anti-Jacobin Review* or *The British Critic*, and only the briefest of references in *The Annual Review* and *The European Magazine and London Review*.[19] The *Imperial Review*, however, expressed complete approval; Godwin is praised for this story of a silk-mill where "a kind of activity is pursued which deserves censure."[20] *The Monthly Review* goes so far as to consider the Ruffigny story "the best episode in the novel."[21] *The Literary Journal*, on the other hand, argued that this episode "affects the hero more than the reader",[22] while *The Monthly Anthology and Boston Review* found that the author "lingers too long in the Lyons silk-mill."[23]

Modern critics have bestowed even less attention upon *Fleetwood*; specific references to, or discussions of, the book are few. It was completely ignored by Sir Leslie Stephen when he wrote an article on Godwin's novels in 1902, and equally by Henri Roussin in his French doctoral dissertation on Godwin (1913.) The mid-century critics P. N. Furbank and D. H. Monro at least discuss the novel as a whole, but they ignore the Ruffigny story. A more positive attitude, however, makes itself felt after the Second World War; George Woodcock and David Fleisher stress its importance, and two recent studies fully recognize its significance. K. N. Cameron considers the story of Ruffigny's childhood "one of the best-written sections of the novel", and B. R. Pollin draws attention to the description of child labourers which he characterizes as "another of Godwin's extraordinary innovations".[24]

Notes

1. His novels include, *Things as they are, or the Adventures of Caleb Williams* (1794); *St. Leon, A Tale of the Sixteenth Century* (1799); *Fleetwood, or the New Man of Feeling* (1805); *Mandeville, a Tale of the Times of Cromwell* (1817), etc. His plays are *Antonio, or the Soldier's Return* (1800); *Faulkner* (1807), etc. His principal pamphlet is *An Inquiry Concerning Political Justice etc.* (1793); among his historical books are *A History of the Commonwealth of England*, 4 vols (1824–8); and *The Life of Geoffrey Chaucer* (1803). His other writings are works of a varied nature, ranging from philosophical treatises to stories for the young.

2. The manuscript of *Fleetwood* is in the Carl Pforzheimer Library in New York. Godwin's method of composition was casual, as we learn from K. N. Cameron's valuable study *Shelley and his Circle* (1961). Godwin prepared one draft only, which he then sent off to the printer. He used the proofs for revision, which he continued even after the book had been set up. The Ruffigny episode is found in the original manuscript, and no important insertions or revisions were made in the process of proof-reading. *Fleetwood* was published by Richard Phillips of Bridge Street, Blackfriars.

3. *Poems Chiefly Written in Retirement* (1801) by John Thelwall. The quotation that follows is from the edition of 1802.

4. *Thelwall John. His Life by his Widow* (1837).

5. *General Pamphlets* I (1859), in the Bodleian Library.

6. Charles Cestre, *John Thelwall* (1906), original in French.

7. B. R. Pollin, *Godwin Criticism: a Synoptic Bibliography* (Toronto, 1967), 180.

8. John Colmer, *Coleridge, Critic of Society* (1959), 385. For an account of the friendship between Thelwall and Coleridge see C. B. R. Kent, *The English Radicals* (1899), 153.

9. Minnie Clare Yarborrough, *John Horne Tooke* (Columbia, 1926), see also entry in *Dictionary of National Biography*.

10. 'An Address to the Ladies in the Behalf of the Weavers and Others Concerned in the Silk Manufacture in the Parishes of Spital Fields, Bethnal Green and c.', *European Magazine*, XL, (1801), 268 and 466; 'Observations on the Silk Trade', XLII (1802), 349 and 449.

11. C. Kegan Paul, *William Godwin, his Friends and Contemporaries* (1876), quotation from the Boston edition of the same year, vol. II, 122.

12. Microfilm in the Duke University Library, Durham.

13. R. G. Grylls, *William Godwin and his World* (1953), 122.

14. *Life of Hutton* (1898); quotations are from the second edition of 1817.

15. *Ibid.*, 82 to 92 *passim.*
16. *The Enquiry*, quoted by Jean de Palicio, 'Encore du nouveau sur Godwin', *Etudes anglaises* (Paris, Janv.–Mars, 1969).
17. Edition 1793, III, 212.
18. Ivanka Kovačević, 'William Godwin, The Factory Children and Dickens' David Copperfield', *Filološki pregled*, III–IV (Beograd, 1970), 29–43.
19. *Anti-Jacobin Review* (Aug. 1805), 337–58; *The British Critic* (Aug. 1805), 189–94; *The Annual Review*, 4 (1806), 649–50; *The European Magazine etc.*, 49 (April 1806), 259–61.
20. May 1805, 576–86.
21. Jan. 1806, 102.
22. March 1805, 238–49.
23. March 1806, 159–60.
24. Leslie Stephen, 'William Godwin's Novels', *National Review* (Feb. 1902), 908–23; Henri Roussin, *William Godwin* (Paris, 1913); P. N. Furbank, 'Godwin's Novels', *Essays in Criticism*, v (July 1955), 214–28; D. H. Monro, *Godwin's Moral Philosophy* (1953); George Woodcock, *William Godwin, a Biographical Study* (1949); D. Fleisher, *William Godwin, a Study of Liberalism* (1951); K. N. Cameron, *Shelley and his Circle* (1961), 339; B. R. Pollin, *Education and Enlightenment in the Works of William Godwin* (New York, 1962), 179.

    For further study see: William Angus, 'The Novels of William Godwin', *The World Review* (June 1951), 37–40; H. N. Brailsford, *Shelley, Godwin and their Circle* (1913); Ford K. Brown, *The Life of William Godwin* (1926); N. I. Kareyev, 'Godwin and his *Political Justice*', *Uchenye Zapiski* (Moscow, 1929) 3; A. E. Rodway, *Godwin and the Age of Transition* (1952).

Bibliographical Details

Fleetwood appeared in 1805; the text of chapters 11–14 given here follows the first edition.

Orphaned at an early age, Ruffigny had the misfortune to become the ward of an unscrupulous uncle who schemed to seize his property. From Switzerland, where they lived, his uncle took him to Lyons in France and placed him under the care of a Monsieur Vaublanc. At first Ruffigny was sent to school, but he was soon to learn that a different future was in store for him.

FLEETWOOD,
or The New Man of Feeling

Chapter XI

I had for about three months frequented the lessons of my instructors, when one morning the elder of Vaublanc's sons came to my bed-side at about six o'clock, and bade me rise immediately, for his father wanted to speak to me. I obeyed.

My little lad, said Vaublanc, you are not to go to school to-day.

No, sir? What, is it a red-letter day?

Your uncle has written to me to put you into a different berth.

Ah, I am very sorry! Ours is a sweet school, and I like the masters and every body that belongs to it.

William Mouchard, said my host, I know very little of you or your uncle either. But that is nothing to me. While he requires of me nothing that it is contrary to my notions, or out of my way, to do, I intend to be his fair and punctual correspondent. All that he said to me while he was at Lyons, was like an honest man. He said, he had a numerous family of his own, and that he could not do much for you, an orphan cast upon his charity.

I stared. I remembered the severe injunctions of my guardian, and was silent.

It appears that he has had repeated misfortunes in the world, and that he can just make shift to bring up his children in a humble way. It cannot therefore be expected that he should do much for you. I can make his case my own, and I am sure I should look to my own flesh and blood. He has resolved to keep you from starving, and that is very generous of him. There is only one thing I cannot understand: Why he sent you to this school at all. I think he was out in his judgment there.

This was the first time in my life, that the ideas of subsistence and property had been plainly stated to me. My notions, like a child's, were very confused on the subject. But, I suppose, proceeding by a sort of implicit conclusion from the visible circumstances of my father, I had always considered myself as entitled to a full participation of those benefits and blessings which a child can enjoy. What Vaublanc said however, convinced me that my uncle was deceiving him. I understood little of the descent of property, and whether, upon my father's death, it ought to devolve to his son or his brother; but I understood still less of the equity of just preserving from death by hunger the only son of a man, who had possessed every luxury and indulgence that were in use in his country. In a word, the views now stated to me, enlightened my understanding at once; and, when I found myself thus thrown upon the world, I apprehended, as it were by necessity, the laws and constitutions of human life.

What is to be done with me, sir? said I.

You must do as I do, replied Vaublanc. People who have nobody else to maintain them, maintain themselves. You have seen shoemakers, and smiths, and joiners at their work?

They get money by their work, and with that money they buy meat and drink? Does my uncle wish me to learn to be a smith or a joiner?

No, no. Any body that taught you to be these trades would require to be paid for the trouble of teaching you, and you would get nothing by it these seven years. We have a trade in Lyons that we teach to younkers for nothing.

And shall I get money by my work immediately?

No, not for a month.

What shall I get then?

Twelve sous a week*.

Will that be enough to save every body else the trouble of paying any thing for my food, and my lodging, and my clothes?

That it will not. A sprig, like you, cannot do that; he must do what he can.

And my uncle will pay the rest?

He cannot help himself. – You are willing then to do what I have been telling you?

I must not say much about my willingness, M. Vaublanc. I never did any work in my life.

The more is the pity! In Lyons we find work for children from four years old: sometimes sooner.

_____
* Five-pence English.

And in——in——the country I come from, the children never do any work, till they are almost as tall as their fathers. They do little offices indeed to be useful sometimes, but nothing like what you call working for their living. I do not know which way is right; but I know which is agreeable. I should not so much matter a little hardship; but you say, I must go no more to school. – I cannot think why, M. Vaublanc, you asked any thing about my willingness!

And, saying this, a flood of tears burst from my eyes.

When a school-boy, continued I, is to be punished, the master never asks him whether he chooses it. – M. Vaublanc, I cannot help myself. I am in a strange country, and have neither father, nor mother, nor any body to care for me. Take me, and dispose of me, as you please, and as you tell me my uncle directs. I dare say, you are a just man, and will do me no harm. Wherever you put me, I will endeavour to be a good boy, and that nobody shall be angry with me. I will be attentive, and learn as well as I can, and work as hard as I can. But, pray, pray, M. Vaublanc, do not ask me another time, whether I am willing?

That will do, boy, said he, nodding his head. You will get better satisfied with your situation, as you grow used to it.

Saying this, he put on his hat, and bid me follow him. As we passed along:

You know, I believe, what I am?

I have heard: a manufacturer of silk.

One part of this business is to prepare the silk, as it comes from the worm, for the sempstress and the weaver. This is done by means of mills: I have two or three large ones, and employ a great number of work-people in them. – You had rather work for me, than for a master you did not know?

That I had! The thing is frightful to me because it is a thing I never thought of. But I should fear it more, if it placed me altogether among strangers.

You cannot think, pursued M. Vaublanc, what an advantage these mills are to the city of Lyons. In other places children are a burthen to their poor parents; they have to support them, till they are twelve or fourteen years of age, before they can do the least thing for their own maintenance: here the case is entirely otherwise. In other places they run ragged and wild about the streets: no such thing is to be seen at Lyons. In short, our town is a perfect paradise. We are able to take them at four years of age, and in some cases sooner. Their little fingers, as soon as they have well learned the use of them, are employed for the relief of their parents, who have brought them up from the breast. They learn no bad habits; but are quiet, and orderly, and attentive, and industrious. What a prospect for their future lives! God himself must approve and bless a race who are thus early prepared to be of use to themselves and others. Among us it is scarcely possible there should be such a thing as poverty. We have no such thing as idleness, or lewdness, or riot, or drunkenness, or debauchery of any sort. Let the day of judgment come when it will, it will never surprise us in a situation in which we should be ashamed to be found.

I never heard M. Vaublanc so eloquent. Eloquence was not his characteristic; but he was now on his favourite topic, a topic intimately connected with his fame, his country, and the patriotic services which he rendered her. He did not completely recollect, while he talked on so interesting a subject, that he was addressing himself to a child, scarcely more than eight years of age. Some things that he said, were not exactly in accord with the vivacity of my temper, and the present state of my feelings. But on the whole I was fixed and penetrated by the warm colouring he bestowed on his picture; I checked the rebelliousness of my heart, and said, Probably it is better for me that I should be admitted into so pure and exemplary a society; I longed to set my foot upon the threshold of the terrestrial paradise he described.

My impatience was speedily gratified. We entered a very spacious building, which was divided however no otherwise than into four rooms, floor above floor. The lower or under-ground apartment was occupied by the horse that gave motion to the mill, and that was relieved every hour. Two horses were the stock to each mill. Above-stairs the walls were lined on three sides, with the reels, or, as the English manufacturers call them, swifts, which received the silk, as it was devolved from certain bobbins. Of these there were about eleven hundred in the first floor, as many in the second, and as many in the third; in all between three and four thousand. It was curious to recollect that all these, by means of wheels and other contrivances in the machine, were kept in perpetual motion by a single quadruped. In each apartment I saw several men, more women, and a greater number of children, busily employed. M. Vaublanc was so obliging as to take me over the whole, before he assigned me my task.

You will not suppose there was any thing very cheerful or exhilarating in the paradise we had entered. The idea of a mill is the antipathy of this. One perpetual, dull, flagging sound pervaded the whole. The walls were bare; the inhabitants were poor. The children in general earned little more than twelve sous in a week; most of the women, and even several of the men, but about one

French crown*. We must correct our ideas, and imagine a very sober paradise, before we can think of applying the name to this mansion.

I was most attentive to the employment of the children, who were a pretty equal number of both sexes. There were about twenty on each floor, sixty in all. Their chief business was to attend to the swifts; the usual number being fifty-six which was assigned to the care of each child. The threads, while the operation of winding was going on, were of course liable to break; and, the moment a thread was broken, the benefit of the swift to which it belonged was at a stand. The affair of the child was, by turning round the swift, to find the end, and then to join it to the corresponding end attached to the bobbin. The child was to superintend the progress of these fifty-six threads, to move backward and forward in his little tether of about ten feet, and, the moment any accident happened, to repair it. I need not tell you that I saw no great expressions of cheerfulness in either the elder or the younger inhabitants of these walls: their occupations were too anxious and monotonous – the poor should not be too much elevated, and incited to forget themselves. There was a kind of stupid and hopeless vacancy in every face: this proceeded from the same causes.

Not one of the persons before me exhibited any signs of vigour and robust health. They were all sallow; their muscles flaccid, and their form emaciated. Several of the children appeared to me, judging from their size, to be under four years of age – I never saw such children. Some were not tall enough with their little arms to reach the swift; these had stools, which they carried in their hands, and mounted as occasion offered. A few, I observed, had a sort of iron buskins on which they were elevated; and, as the iron was worked thin, they were not extremely unwieldly. Children, before they had learned that firm step with the sole of the natural foot, without which it is impossible ever to be a man, were thus disciplined to totter upon stilts. But this was a new invention, and not yet fully established.

This, or nearly all this, I observed upon my first survey of M. Vaublanc's manufactory. In addition to this I afterward found, what you will easily conceive, that it was not without much severity that the children were trained to the regularity I saw. Figure to yourself a child of three or four years of age. The mind of a child is essentially independent; he does not, till he has been formed to it by hard experience, frame to himself the ideas of authority and

* Two and sixpence English.

subjection. When he is rated by his nurse, he expresses his mutinous spirit by piercing cries; when he is first struck by her in anger, he is ready to fall into convulsions of rage: it almost never happens otherwise. It is a long while (unless he is unmercifully treated indeed) before a rebuke or a blow produces in him immediate symptoms of submission. Whether with the philosopher we chuse to regard this as an evidence of our high destination, or with the theologian cite it as an indication of our universal depravity, and a brand we bear of Adam's transgression, the fact is indisputable. Almost all that any parent requires of a child of three or four years of age consists in negatives: stand still: do not go there: do not touch that. He scarcely expects or desires to obtain from him any mechanical attention. Contrast this with the situation of the children I saw: brought to the mill at six in the morning: detained till six at night; and, with the exception of half-an-hour for break-fast, and an hour at dinner, kept incessantly watchful over the safety and regularity of fifty-six threads continually turning. By my soul, I am ashamed to tell you by what expedients they are brought to this unintermitted vigilance, this dead life, this inactive and torpid industry!

Consider the subject in another light. Liberty is the school of understanding. This is not enough adverted to. Every boy learns more in his hours of play, than in his hours of labour. In school he lays in the materials of thinking; but in his sports he actually thinks: he whets his faculties, and he opens his eyes. The child from the moment of his birth is an experimental philosopher: he essays his organs and his limbs, and learns the use of his muscles. Every one who will attentively observe him, will find that this is his perpetual employment. But the whole process depends upon liberty. Put him into a mill, and his understanding will improve no more than that of the horse which turns it. I know that it is said that the lower orders of the people have nothing to do with the cultivation of the understanding; though for my part I cannot see how they would be the worse for that growth of practical intellect, which should enable them to plan and provide, each one for himself, the increase of his conveniences and competence. But be it so! I know that the earth is the great Bridewel of the universe, where spirits, descended from heaven, are committed to drudgery and hard labour. Yet I should be glad that our children, up to a certain age, were exempt; sufficient is the hardship and subjection of their whole future life; methinks, even Egyptian taskmasters would consent that they should grow up in peace, till they had acquired the strength necessary for substantial service.

Liberty is the parent of strength. Nature teaches the child, by the play of the muscles, and pushing out his limbs in every direction, to give them scope to develop themselves. Hence it is that he is so fond of sports and tricks in the open air, and that these sports and tricks are so beneficial to him. He runs, he vaults, he climbs, he practises exactness of eye, and sureness of aim. His limbs grow straight and taper, and his joints well-knit and flexible. The mind of a child is no less vagrant that his steps; it pursues the gossamer, and flies from object to object, lawless and unconfined: and it is equally necessary to the development of his frame, that his thoughts and his body should be free from fetters. But then he cannot earn twelve sous a week. These children were uncouth and ill-grown in every limb, and were stiff and decrepit in their carriage, so as to seem like old men. At four years of age they could earn salt to their bread; but at forty, if it were possible they should live so long, they could not earn bread to their salt. They were made sacrifices, while yet tender; and, like the kid, spoken of by Moses, were seethed and prepared for the destroyer in their mother's milk. This is the case in no state of society, but in manufacturing towns. The children of gipsies and savages have ruddy cheeks and a sturdy form, can run like lapwings, and climb trees with the squirrel.

Chapter XII

You will readily imagine what a thunder-stroke it was to me, to be entered as one of the members in this vast machine. Up to the period of eight years of age I had been accustomed to walk upon the level plain of human society; I had submitted to my parents and instructors; but I had no idea that there was any class or cast of my fellow-creatures, superior to that in which I was destined to move. This persuasion inspires into the heart, particularly the heart of the young, such gaiety of temper, and graceful confidence in action! Now I was cast down at once, to be the associate of the lowest class of mechanics, paupers, brutified in intellect, and squalid in attire.

I had however the courage to make up my resolution at once to the calamities of my station. I saw what it was to which it would be necessary for me to submit; and I felt too proud, to allow myself to be driven by blows and hard usage to that from which I could not escape. I discharged with diligence the task assigned me, and wasted in torpid and melancholy labour the hours of the day.

What may appear strange, this terrible reverse of fate by no means operated to stupefy my intellect. I was like those victims of Circe that we read of in Homer, who, though they had lost the external symbols of a superior nature, retained the recollection of what they had been, and disgust at what they were. You will perhaps scarcely suppose that my age was ripe enough for this. If I removed to a pleasing scene, if I had continued a pupil in the schools of liberal education, the impressions of my early years would probably have faded by degrees from my mind. But in the dreary situation in which I was now placed, they were my favourite contemplation; I thought of them for ever. It was by remembering them only, that I felt the difference between myself and the squalid beings around me. When Adam and Eve were driven out of Paradise, and turned loose upon the dreary and inhospitable plains, how fondly did they recollect the bowers and lawns they had quitted, the luxuriant flowers and blushing fruits, and the light and soothing employments which had there been their pursuit!

It was naturally to have been expected, that I should look back to my native country, and, finding myself thus cruelly and iniquitously treated, should seek among the scenes and the acquaintances of my infant years the redress of my grievances. If I had returned to the vale of Urseren and the foot of the St. Gothard, nay, if I had whispered the particulars of my story in the ears of one man of eminence and respect within the circuit of Switzerland, it cannot be but that I should have found a friend, a protector and a champion. But I dared not do this. The mysterious threatenings of my uncle still sounded in my ears. He had given me a new name; he had left me among new faces; he had entered me upon a new species of existence. He had expressly prohibited all reference and connection between my former and my present state. What did this mean? I had too little knowledge of the modes of human life to be able to appreciate his menaces. This was the second revolution in my fortune. By the death of my father I found myself placed in absolute dependence upon an uncle, who had before had no power over me. A child has no standard within himself for these things; he is sensible of his own weakness; he watches the carriage and demeanour of the persons about him, and from thence judges what he is, and what he can be.

The injustice practised toward me by my uncle rendered me from the period of my removal to Lyons a creature of soliloquy and reverie. Children at the early age at which I then was, are usually all frankness and communication; they tell to their companions and playmates every thing they know, and every thing they conjecture.

I had a secret that must never be uttered. Once or twice in the few months in which I frequented the school I have mentioned (for afterward my temptations grew less), I was on the point of disclosing my history to a youthful favourite. But, when I had half resolved to unload my bosom, such apprehension suddenly seized me, that my tongue faltered, and my heart beat with violence, as if it would choke me. At one time, walking with my youngster-friend on a narrow bank, just as I had prepared myself to speak, my foot slipped, and I sprained my ancle, so as to occasion a considerable swelling. At another, by a strange coincidence, a terrible clap of thunder burst upon me, succeeded by uncommon lightning and rain, which of necessity forced the thoughts both of my companion and myself into a new channel. These accidents took a superstitious hold of my fancy, and made me more reluctant than before to break the injunctions which had been laid upon me.

Had I dared to attempt to deliver myself from the cruel bondage into which I had been kidnapped, it would have been a very arduous task for a child of little more than eight years of age. I might have chosen for my confident and preserver some creature of my uncle, and have thus rendered my situation more desperate. No indifferent man would have undertaken my cause and my rescue; he would have looked on my distress with a sense of momentary compassion, and then, like the Levite in the parable, have passed by on the other side. It could be only a man of warm humanity, animated with a strong love of justice and hatred of oppression, that, for the sake of me, a friendless outcast and an exile, would have strung himself to the encounter of prosperous and successful vice. It would naturally have required on my part, that I should have digested a resolute plan, and have persisted in the execution in spite of every obstacle that might arise.

But I had by no means the courage adequate to such an exploit. I felt like one of those unhappy beings we read of in books of supernatural adventures, who are placed in the hands of some powerful genius invisible to mortal sight, who dare not move lest they should meet with his hand, nor speak lest they should offend an unknown and never-absent auditor. It was thus I feared the ascendancy of my uncle. If men of powerful and vigorous minds, a Rousseau and others, have surrendered themselves up to the chimeras of a disturbed imagination, and have believed that they were every where at the disposal of some formidable and secret confederacy, what wonder that I, a boy of eight years old, should be subject to a similar alarm? Childhood is the age of superstition. The more I indulged this fear, the more my terror grew; and, in a short time, I believe I could sooner have died, than have brought myself to divulge a secret, the publication of which so obviously led to my benefit. Thus, by the machinations of my cruel guardian, I was involved in a state of slavery, body and soul, such as has seldom been the lot of a human creature.

I remained for a considerable time an inmate of my prison-house. M. Vaublanc found that a person, so mean in his destination as I was, was not entitled to the luxuries and refinements of his mansion and board, and placed me as a lodger with one of the labourers in his mill. At the same time he took from me the clothes which I had hitherto worn, and assigned me a garb similar to that of my fellow-slaves. Thus I became in all external respects like the companions with whom I was now associated; and, whatever I might feel within, could in no point be distinguished by the common observer from the miserable beings around me. I became familiar with objects of distress. The sort of training and drilling, necessary at first to preserve an infant during twelve hours together from the guilt of a distracted attention, was continually before my sight. The supervisor of the machine contracted from necessity a part of the rugged and ferocious character, which belongs to a slave-driver in the West Indies. There was one phenomenon among us that might have surprised and misled an ordinary spectator. Our house of confinement often echoed with songs, and frequently an hundred voices from different parts of the machine joined in the same tune. Was not this a clear indication of gaiety and tranquillity of heart? I remember one day when I was in England, I had occasion to spend two hours in your prison of Newgate. The window of the apartment where I sat overlooked the press-yard, where a number of convicts were assembled, waiting the occasion of being transported to the other side of the globe. They were employed in the manner I have mentioned, singing out in chorus some of the popular songs of their country. But, alas! there, as in the silk-mills of Lyons, it was a melancholy ditty. The tone was heavy, monotonous and flat. There was the key and the note of gaiety, but the heart was wanting. It was like the spectacle of a fresh and well-grown human body placed erect against a wall, satisfactory in other respects, – but it was dead. They sung, bold and audacious in the face of despair, just as the fear-struck peasant sings along the church-yard at midnight, expecting every moment to see a ghost start up at his feet.

On each returning Sunday the chains which confined my footsteps were suspended. This day I regularly devoted to solitude and reverie. It is not to be described what pleasure I derived from this resource. It was a new being that descended upon me. In the room of dead, naked and discoloured walls, I beheld the canopy of heaven. In the room of the ever-turning swifts, which in multitudes surrounded me on every side, I beheld the trees and the fields, the fruits of rural industry, and the grand features of all powerful nature. Oh, Switzerland! I would have said, if I had dared trust my lips even in soliloquy with the enchanting sound, – nurse of my cheerful infancy, in these beauteous retreats, methinks I see thee still! I scented the fragrant air, and I exchanged the flagging songs of my brother-slaves, for the joyous warbling of the vocal woods. The poorest slave that lives, when withdrawn into a solitude like this, is upon a level with the greatest lord. If he does not tread upon floors of porphyry, and is not canopied with roofs of granite, he however possesses himself in the midst of a palace more glorious than human fingers ever formed.

You may think perhaps that my Sunday enjoyments, such as I describe, were of too grave and contemplative a character, to belong to such early years. I assure you however I do not describe them up to the height of what I then felt, and now remember them. In answer to your objection I can only remark, that adversity, or rather the contrast between present adversity and past good fortune, tends beyond all other things to sharpen the apprehension. These scenes would have produced no such effect upon the other boys of the mill, because they had known no such contrast. They would not have afforded me the delight I describe, had I not been so much restrained from them, and restrained in so hateful a confinement. My heart felt no less unchained and free at these periods, than is the river, which had been locked up in frost, and at length by the influence of genial zephyrs is restored to her beloved murmurings and meanders.

I firmly believe that, if there had been no Sundays and holidays, I should have remained many years the prisoner of M. Vaublanc. My days of labour were days of oblivion. It is impossible to describe to you the state of mind of a human creature, whose incessant office it is from morning to night to watch the evolution of fifty-six threads. The sensorium in man has in it something of the nature of a mill, but it is moved by very different laws from those of a mill contrived for the manufacture of silk-threads. The wheels move in swifter rotation than those I was appointed to watch, and to keep this rotation constantly up to a certain pace is one of the great desiderata of human happiness. When the succession of ideas flags, or is violently restrained in its circumvolutions, this produces by degrees weariness, *ennui*, imbecility and idiotism. Conceive how this progress is impeded by the task of continually watching fifty-six threads! The quantity of thought required in this office is nothing, and yet it shuts out, and embroils, and snaps in pieces all other thoughts.

Another law which governs the sensorium in man is the law of association. In contemplation and reverie, one thought introduces another perpetually, and it is by similarity, or the hooking of one upon the other, that the process of thinking is carried on. In books and in living discourse the case is the same; there is a constant connection and transition, leading on the chain of the argument. Try the experiment of reading for half an hour a parcel of words thrown together at random, which reflect no light on each other, and produce no combined meaning; and you will have some, though an inadequate, image of the sort of industry to which I was condemned. Numbness and vacancy of mind are the fruits of such an employment. It ultimately transforms the being who is subjected to it, into quite a different class or species of animal.

My Sundays, as I have said, restored me to the sort of creature I had been. At first, the feeling of this was enough for me; I was too happy to be capable of much reflection. I leaped, and skipped, and ran, and played a thousand ridiculous antics, that I might convince myself that I was not wholly an automaton. In a few weeks however, when the novelty of these periodical seasons of rest was somewhat worn off, I began to feel my pleasure tarnished by the recollection that, when Sunday was gone, Monday, and after that five other mortal days, would inevitably follow. The day of rest was so short!

Chapter XIII

By degrees I became more serious and meditating. I said to myself, "What am I, and wherefore am I here?" The years of nonage in the human creature are many, partly because he is surrounded with parents and kindred and acquaintances, whose habit it is to take care of him, and to direct his steps. Perhaps the majority of human beings never think of standing by themselves, and chusing their own employments, till the sentence has been regularly promulgated to them, It is time for you to take care of yourself. For my part, I found myself cast upon a new world, without relations, acquaintances or friends, and this urged me on prematurely to acts of discretion. I could scarcely persuade myself that the life to which

I was devoted, deserved the name of taking care of me, and there-fore began to cast about in my own thoughts what I should do.

I need not tell you that I detested the condition in which I found myself placed, and longed to escape from it, and seek my fortune. But whither direct my steps? I dared not think of Switzer-land. There resided my uncle, that malignant demon, the recollec-tion of whom haunted my thoughts, waking and sleeping. In all the rest of the world I knew not even the private and proper name of a human creature. I had listened however to the old songs of Switzerland, and had some acquaintance with the romances of the middle ages. Mine were the years of romance. Without knowledge enough of what was actually passing in the scenes of the universe, yet with a restless imagination, and a powerful motive urging me to consult it, I patched up as I could, from narratives of humble life, and tales of chivalry, what it was that I should have to en-counter. I knew I must have bread, and that bread did not grow in every hedge. I concluded that I must find or make a friend, by whose assistance to support life, and, if possible, attain to some-thing beyond bare subsistence.

At first I was somewhat terrified with the project I had con-ceived. Again and again I sat down in despair, and said, I am too young; I must wait yet some years, before I can launch upon so great an undertaking. But my tasks would not wait: they beset me from morning till night, and, when I had once conceived the idea of flight, became continually more insupportable. From the extreme of despair I passed to the extreme of sanguine expectation. I brooded over my plans, till all difficulties seemed to vanish before me; the scenes I anticipated at length became as familiar to me, as any thing which had absolutely passed in any former period of my life.

You will smile when I tell you that my favourite scheme was to go to Versailles, and throw myself at the feet of the king of France. It was the project of a child, and will show you how ripe and unripe at once was the state of my intellect. The Gallic sovereign is of all kings the favourite of the people of Switzerland. I had listened to the songs and popular tales concerning Francis I and Henry IV; and a king of France appeared in my eyes the most gallant and generous of mortals. I did not know exactly how much I proposed to tell the king; I scrupled the secret my uncle had so severely enjoined me to preserve; yet, if he should insist upon knowing the whole, surely he was able to protect me against the resentment of a burgher of Uri! However this point might be disposed of, I felt in myself a destination superior to that of a handicraft in the silk-mills of Lyons; I believed that I was capable of extraordinary things; what boy from the swifts but myself, would have had the boldness to think of applying for redress to the king of France? I was persuaded that I could interest his majesty in my case, that I could induce him to judge me deserving of his protection. I would say to him, Sire, dispose of me as you please; make me one of your pages; you shall find me the most zealous and faithful of your servants!

Louis XIV was at this time in the height of his glory. Among the little topics, by my excellence in which I had distinguished myself in the halcyon days of my childhood, was history. It will easily be supposed that my knowledge amounted to scarcely more than a few names and dates. But I had heard certain familiar anecdotes of Henry IV, pleasing to my boyish imagination, and had long since made him my hero; I was told that Louis XIV was the worthy grandson of this free-hearted prince. In one of my Sundays' excursions I fell in with an old French soldier; the military private is usually of a loquacious and communicative temper. I was eager to be acquainted with the character of his master; he was no less prompt to tell me all he knew. He spoke of the beauty of his figure, and the affability of his demeanour. He related the victories he had won, and described the palaces and public edifices which he had founded or adorned. He swore that he was the most generous, condescending and tender-hearted of mankind; and he happened to have two or three instances, which he affirmed to have occurred under his own eye, not unhappily illustrative of this character. Every thing, as I thought, seemed to concur for the success of my design. The magnificence of Louis XIV fascinated my imagination; the examples of his gentleness and humanity were so many omens assuring my good fortune. I bought a portrait of this monarch; it was almost the only extravagance of which I had been guilty, since my last degradation. I carried it in my pocket: on Sundays, when I had wandered into the most obscure retreat I could find, I held it in my hand, I set it before me, I talked to it, and endeavoured to win the goodwill of the king. Sometimes I worked myself into such a degree of fervour and enthusiasm, that I could scarcely believe but that the portrait smiled upon me, and with a look of peculiar benignity seemed to say, Come to Versailles, and I will make your fortune!

While I attended the lessons of the regents of the free-school of Lyons, I received the weekly stipend usually allotted to boys of my age. I had before, as I have mentioned, received a louis d'or and a three livres piece from my uncle and cousin at parting, Like a boy,

I sometimes spent my money upon toys and *confitures*; but for the most part I reserved it, and suffered it to grow into a little stock. Young as I was, from the moment of parting with my uncle I could not conceal from myself that I was in an extraordinary situation. The secrecy that had been enjoined me weighed upon my mind. Compelled to deny my family, my friends and my country, and suddenly dropped in a city where I was unacquainted with a single creature, I incessantly said, "What is next to befal me? It is necessary for me to provide myself, and not to be wholly un-prepared for events which it is not in my power to foresee." Youth is in some respects the age of suspicion; at least it was so with me. Whenever a child of the age at which I was arrived, feels that he is thwarted and rigorously used, he half-suspects some motive, obscure and unavowed, in the individual from whom his mortification is derived.

The period I ultimately fixed for my flight was the week of Easter. At this time we were allowed at the mill two holidays in addition to that of Sunday. I was perhaps partly influenced in chusing this season by the idea that when I was not wanted at work, my presence or absence would be little taken notice of. The people with whom I lived were too wretched, and too anxious about their own children, to feel much kindness for me; and I should not be reported to the overseer till Wednesday. But the principal consideration that guided me was the cheerfulness of the season; liberty was to the whole lower class of the people the order of the day; I had three days of freedom, why should I not make this the starting-post of my eternal liberty?

I will not trouble you with a detail of my smaller adventures on the road. Full of the anticipation of my grand undertaking, I had repeatedly turned my steps on my days of relaxation toward Paris, and made many enquiries respecting the way. I had learned the names of the principal towns. I set out with a beating heart, and, having walked gravely till I was out of the city, I then began to run. I did not however run far; my thoughts were too full of agita-tion to admit any regularity of motion. Sometimes I slackened my pace, because I feared I should be taken for a fugitive, and some-times, because I said to myself, I must manage my strength, if I expect it to carry me far.

Two hundred and fifty miles was a great undertaking for a boy under nine years of age. One advantage I possessed; I had money, more than I could prudently spend on the passage. My mind was too intently fixed upon the end of my journey, to be capable of much calculation respecting the obstacles I had to encounter. One resolution however I fixed, firm as the basis of my native mountains, "No consideration on earth, no difficulties, no discouragements shall ever carry me back!" A mechanic becomes a sort of machine; his limbs and articulations are converted, as it were, into wood and wires. Tamed, lowered, torpified into this character, he may be said perhaps to be content. It is well! it seems necessary that there should be such a class of animated natures in the world! It is probable, if I had continued much longer in the silkmills of Lyons, I should have become such a being myself. But, with the conceptions and recollections which continually beset my imagination, it appeared the most horrible of all destinies. I, that dared at nine years of age, launch myself in the world, that dared to a certain degree to revolve the various chances of human affairs, and defy the the worst, that purposed to challenge the attention, the equity and the compassion of the king of France, should I be thus neutralised! – Why did I feel thus? Because my early education had not prepared me for my present lot. I understood why my companions of my own age were put into the silk-mill: their parents were engaged in employments equally deadening; their parents were unable by their labour to obtain bread for themselves and their offspring: but I did not understand why I was there. I felt such a loathing at this moment to the occupation which had engrossed me for months, that, if I could have been assured that such should be my occupation for as many months to come, I believe, child as I was, I should sooner have taken a knife, and thrust it into my heart, than submit to it.

In thinking over my situation as I passed along, I felt that the thing most immediately pressing upon me was to avoid exciting the curiosity and suspicion of the persons whose assistance might be necessary to me on the road. The production of a louis d'or for example might be fatal to a boy of my childish appearance and coarseness of attire. In my journey from Urseren to Lyons I had learned something of the nature of inns, and I retained all these things as perfectly as if they had occurred only yesterday. I resolved to go only to the meanest inns, and ask for the plainest accommodations. On the second day I joined a waggoner who was conducting his commodities to Dijon, and this considerably facilitated the first part of my journey. I began with asking him of my road to Macon, the first considerable place through which I was to pass. He was going through Macon. How much further? To Dijon. The meanness of my attire encouraged him to question me in his turn: What had I to do at Macon? I was going to see the world, I replied.

I perceive, my spark, cried the waggoner, what you are. You belong to the silk-mills; you are a runaway, and I have a great mind to take you up, and send you back to your master.

I was surprised at his so instantly fixing on my true character; though, on reflection, it was by no means extraordinary that a person just come from Lyons should have made the conjecture; the costume was sufficiently peculiar.

I will never stay at the silk-mill, said I; nobody has a right to confine me there.

Nobody has a right, youngster? Not your parents? Your wildness, I dare say, will break their hearts.

I have no parents – I confessed to him that I was determined to go to Paris.

And what will you do at Paris? You will be starved to death.

Better be starved, than undergo such misery as I have suffered. But I will not starve!

The waggoner began to reflect, that, if I had no parents or kindred, nobody would be greatly injured by my elopement. He contented himself therefore with seriously expostulating with me on the folly of my project, and advising me to return. Finding his remonstrances of no avail, he agreed to take me under his protection, as far as he was going on my way. Thus I conquered more than one-third of the road.

Chapter XIV

Dijon was so capital a city, that I thought I might venture here to change my piece of gold, the parting present of my treacherous uncle. But I was mistaken. I hated the clothes I wore, since they had led the waggoner to discover the situation to which I belonged. I went into a clothier's shop with a determination to change them. them. Unfortunately I plunged headlong into the house of man of rugged temper and a hard-favoured countenance. The moment I looked at him, I trembled. But it was too late to draw back.

What is your pleasure, my lad? said he.

I want some clothes.

Where do you live? Who is to pay for them? Where shall I send them?

I am a stranger in Dijon.

Why does not your father or somebody come with you? How can such a child as you chuse a suit of clothes?

I am all alone.

Alone! And how are you to pay for clothes?

Perhaps you would allow me something for the clothes I have got on. And I have a louis d'or, – showing it.

A louis d'or! said he, coming from the other side of the counter. Tell me, sirrah, where you got that louis d'or?

My uncle gave it me.

Who is your uncle? I shall send for him immediately, and find out the truth of this.

I tell you, sir, he does not live here; I am a stranger in Dijon, never saw the city till last night. But you need not frighten me; if you do not chuse to sell me any clothes, I will go away without them. I assure you, I am an honest boy, and my money is my own.

We shall see that presently. You do not like to be frightened! But I shall frighten you, and most confoundedly too, before I have done with you. You must go with me to the mayor.

I will go with you, where you please, said I; believing it was impossible that any body should be more frightful to me, than the honest slopman before me. But I had rather go back to my inn.

The trader conducted me to the magistrate. I found myself right in my conjecture, that I should be better off in his hands, than in those of the Argus who had first seized me. The mayor was a sober, creditable man, middle-aged, and inclined to corpulence, who made a point of faithfully discharging his duty, but who took no particular pleasure in frightening little boys. He was too much accustomed to office, to feel any high gratification in its swagger and insolence. His passions were dead; he could scarcely be said to love or hate, to be gentle or furious; he was the law, and nothing but the law.

As I and my conductor passed along the streets to this man's house, I fixed the plan of action that I would observe. I determined to take refuge in silence and reserve. I said to myself. They cannot find out that I have stolen my money, because I have not stolen it; and therefore, after having examined and tried me as much as they please, they must dismiss me. I will not betray my family-story, and I will not furnish them with a clue by which they may send me back to Lyons.

The slopman led me into the justice-room and told his story. The magistrate listened, and made his observations. My adversary endeavoured in vain to inspire his own passions into the mayor; the clothier was earnest, abusive and eloquent; the mayor was considerate and inquisitive. He asked me who I was, and I refused to tell.

Did I know what it was to be brought before a magistrate?

Not very well, I replied.

It would be worse for me, if I did not give a proper account of myself.

I answered that I could not satisfy his curiosity. I had been ill-used by cruel relations, but did not dare to complain. I had had a father, who was kind and rich; but my father was dead, and I was driven out from my country and friends.

The magistrate employed every artifice to extort my story from me. He said, My secret should be safe with him, and my cruel relations should never know that I had disclosed it. He said, He would take me under his protection, and oblige them by the interposition of the law to do me justice. He then changed his tone, put on an angry brow, and told me, that he perceived that all I had related was a fiction, but that he would send me to prison, and have me punished, till I told the truth. He put a variety of subtle and artfully contrived questions to wrest my secret from me. I stuck to the same point, made two or three answers which I hoped would move him to favour me, and repeated them again and again in return to every interrogatory he uttered. He sent for the people of the inn, where I confessed to have slept the night before: luckily it was not the same inn the waggoner used, and they could discover nothing.

The magistrate was as good as his word, and sent me to prison. At entering, it struck me, that the scene was not new to me, but that it was very like a silk-mill; the same meanness in the building, the same squalidness in the inhabitants, the same dejection in every countenance. Presently however I perceived a difference; the people there were employed, and here were idle; there were vacant and incurious, and here eagerly crowded about a new tenant of their wretched mansion.

Thus I had twice in one day been introduced into situations calculated to impress a youthful mind with inexpressible horror. To be taken before a magistrate, to be thrust into a jail, would to most children of my tender years have appeared no less terrible than death itself. But I had entered upon an extraordinary undertaking, and had worked myself up to an uncommon pitch of resolution. I knew that for such an urchin as I was, to undertake his own establishment in life was no holiday project. I knew that no small degree of courage and perseverance would be necessary to introduce me to the presence and speech of Louis XIV. It is inconceivable, at least judging from my own instance, of what an extent of exaltation and enthusiasm nine years of age are capable. Enthusiasm is often indebted for much of its fervour to a complete ignorance, and want of practice, in the ways of the world; and, as far as that constitutes a qualification, this immature period of life is of course admirably endowed. In this state of mind, I felt a contempt of difficulties, under which at any other time I should have sunk. I seemed to myself as if I were made of iron, and nothing hostile appeared to make any impression upon me. It was my business to proceed upon my high destination and my choice of life, and to suffer none of these things to interrupt me.

The prisoners crowded about me, and were eager to learn for what crime such a child as I was, was brought into their society. It was presently rumoured, that it was upon suspicion of having stolen some money, that I had obstinately refused to tell the mayor how I came by it, and that I was committed for re-examination. The moment the word money was mentioned, two or three came about me at once, and told me that it was the universal practice, for every new-comer to pay a certain sum by way of entrance-money, at the same time vociferously demanding from me the established fee. It fortunately happened that the magistrate had taken from me my whole stock, to be returned the next day, if no discoveries were made; otherwise it is highly probable these obliging comrades of mine would have stripped me of all that I had. After the first bustle of my introduction was over, a very grave-looking man of the set drew me into a corner, and told me I was the most promising boy of my age he ever saw. He said, he had conceived a particular liking to me; and greatly commended my firmness in refusing to tell the magistrate how I came by my money. That showed I was true game! He observed that he would, if I pleased, put me into a way by which I might make a man of myself for ever, and offered to become my instructor. He swore, that it would be a thousand pities that such talents as I had showed, should be lost for want of encouragement.

I made little answer to these compliments, though the person from whom they flowed certainly succeeded in exciting my curiosity, and I was desirous of hearing to what so extraordinary a preface would lead. Having intimated this, he entered into a very animated and earnest dissertation upon the different modes of committing theft without danger of detection. Observing however that I did not exactly enter into his feelings, he stopped short, and complained of my timidity. He soothed me in the gentlest, and, as he believed, the most flattering manner, and employed a hundred arts of rhetoric, worthy of a better cause. I told him, that he had mistaken my character, that I had stolen no money, and that what

I had was honestly my own. On this he assumed a smile, expressive of grave and gentle derision, and replied, that that was all very well, but that it was not worth while to persist in declarations of innocence among friends. – My mind was full of other projects, and therefore the representations of my sage Mentor had no effect upon me. This however was the sort of exhortation to which I was exposed; and, if I had been the kind of person the magistrate conceived me to be, this night's lodging would too probably have completed my character for ever.

The next day I was brought again before the mayor, and persisted in my resolution to discover nothing. The interval which had passed during the silence of the night, enabled me to collect more firmness, and to express myself with greater coherence. I said, Sir, I am a friendless little boy, and you may do with me whatever you please. But I am not so much afraid of any body, as of my hardhearted uncle. I am afraid, if I tell you who I am, you would send me back to him, or write a letter to him about me. You tell me you would not; but rich men think it a good action to deceive little boys, I am sure I have reason to know that. Oh, sir, do you think it was a small thing that determined me to run away, and go among strangers? I would sooner die than return!

You will easily imagine that what I said, did not in the smallest degree move the man to whom it was addressed, to compassion; the magistrate, who could consign such a child as I was, for one night to the horrors and dangers of a prison; could be little accessible to the relentings of nature. This reflection is obvious enough to me now; but it was not so then. The actions of their elders are always mysteries to children; they do not see the springs of the machine; they wait with a sort of superstitious anticipation, to observe how their seniors will act upon every new event, and are surprised at nothing.

But, though the magistrate was guilty of no meltings of compassion toward me, he was not inflexible. He saw not what he could do further with me; he had exhausted upon me every expedient he could devise to render me frank and communicative. At length he calculated within himself, as I suppose, the fruitlessness of detaining me: perhaps he was inclined to think me innocent, and to believe the story I told. If he detained me longer, it might be a trouble to him, and ultimately produce a burthen to the corporation in which he presided. He dismissed me with a moderate portion of good advice, recommended to me not to become a vagrant, in consequence of which I should finally be made a scoundrel and a thief, if I was not so already, and, above all, warned me of the

stubbornness of my temper. He had never seen so stiff-necked a
little villain, and he augured an untimely and a shameful death
from such beginnings. I listened to his advice with passive attention; but, what I prized much beyond his advice, before he sent
me from his presence he returned to me my money.

I left Dijon with a beating heart. I was full of exultation at the
thought of my liberty, once more restored to me. I foresaw every
thing that was fortunate from the issue of my first adventures.
The discovery of my class of life by the waggoner had been productive of no mischievous effects to me. The adventure of the slopman
and the louis d'or had seemed to threaten the greatest dangers; but
by my prudence and perseverance (for I was willing to take the
whole praise to myself) I had been extricated from them all. All
difficulties would vanish before my courage and abilities. I should
infallibly become a page to the king of France. – From this goal
my impetuous imagination took its flight. The marshal's truncheon
and the ducal coronet danced before my charmed sight: I sighed
for princesses, and the blood-royal was mixed in my offspring.
Alnaschar in the Arabian Nights was but a driveller to me.

Harriet Martineau

1802-1876

Harriet Martineau's position within the world of Victorian letters may be inferred from the formidable size of the bibliographies concerned with her work.[1] The lady herself was undoubtedly an equally formidable phenomenon: her achievement as a writer may seem slight when compared to major figures like Dickens but she helped to create a strong public opinion, as any study of her life, however brief, will show. The following survey of her career focusses primarily on those aspects that have a direct bearing on her presentation of the industrial theme.

The *Norfolk Antiquarian Miscellany* (Norwich, 1877) informs us that one Gaston Martineau arrived from France in 1695, and that he became the founder of a well-known family in Norwich,[2] and it seems to me probable that Harriet Martineau's family descended from this French immigrant. Her father was a textile manufacturer and merchant, and her maternal grandfather a wholesale grocer and sugar refiner. The Martineaus were prosperous, and an excellent education was provided for the girls as well as the boys. Harriet was a precocious child and a great reader; the atmosphere in her home was marked by an austere intellectualism and among the visitors to the house were quite a few eminent persons. The family were Protestants of the Unitarian persuasion and their political views were fairly liberal, as we may learn from the pages of Miss Martineau's *Autobiography*. We may read, too, about the little girl of seven who read Milton's *Paradise Lost*, and about the hypersensitive adolescent girl who lost her hearing when she was sixteen. But since the self-centred Harriet of the *Autobiography* reveals little interest in the city where she lived, one must look elsewhere for sources that may reveal the roots of that allegiance to the capitalist class that was to become such a marked aspect of her personality in later years. Her social background alone cannot explain this development; one must also consider the fact that although she was born into this class she had experienced what it meant to lose the privileges bestowed by wealth when her father suffered great financial losses during the depression of 1825. On his death the following year he left six children for whom no proper provision had been made, and complete financial collapse occurred in 1829. Two of Harriet's sisters had to support themselves as governesses, while she did her best to earn her living at home by needle-work and her efforts as a writer. Unlike Charles Dickens she was not moved by her experience of economic hardship to embrace the cause of the underprivileged; she was totally committed to the principles of a youthfully vigorous industrial bourgeoisie, and her commitment was a matter not only of political persuasion. She was so to speak born to it – it was her heritage which no purely personal experience could invalidate.

The depression of 1825 must be connected with the fact that after centuries of prosperity the centre of the textile industry had moved away from the southern and eastern areas, which meant that the periodical economic depressions would be more strongly felt in Norfolk than for example in Lancashire. The situation was especially difficult in Norwich in 1826, just before Harriet Martineau wrote her two first industrial tales, and it is recorded that "several disgraceful riots took place".[3] Even during a century of alleged prosperity we come across grim chronicles of riots in a work like *The Norfolk Tour*, published by R. Beatniffe in 1795. An artillery company had to be called in to disperse a rioting populace in 1720; in 1752 a disturbance was caused by a dispute between master-combers and their journeymen, and rioting was occasioned in 1766 "by the high price of provisions".[4] These eighteenth-century riots, however, were not followed by public executions as in the preceding century.

This sustained conflict between social classes with opposed interests must have resulted in an equally sustained feeling of distrust and animosity. The very air of Norwich breathed class hostility and this was especially true of the circles where Harriet Martineau moved. Already as a young girl she took her stand with the 'masters' against the 'operatives', but without being at all aware of the existence of class prejudice. What seems odder still, perhaps, is the fact that her radical political views concerning the reform of Parliament made her proclaim herself a friend of the working classes. She certainly had every intention of being their friend, but her acts may be said merely to confirm the truth of the cynical prayer for protection against friends, since enemies are more easily disposed of.

Harriet Martineau wrote her first pieces before she was 20, and as she was a devout Protestant she sent them to religious periodicals. After some time she became a regular contributor to the pages of *The Monthly Repository*, a radical paper whose editor, W. J. Fox, paid her the meagre sum of £15 per annum for a considerable number of articles, reviews, short stories and poems. W. J. Fox of Craven Hill had been a weaver in Norwich as a boy, and later on became a Unitarian minister and a radical journalist who turned *The Monthly Repository* into a vehicle for philosophical radicals of a utilitarian bent, convinced of the perfectibility of man and society. They advocated popular education, social reform and, above all, the new political economy, but had no confidence in trade unions and little concern with the issue of child labour. After years of close association with *The Monthly Repository* Harriet Martineau became estranged from its editor Fox and from the Unitarians,[5] and in later years she made her breach with confessional religion final by professing herself an unbeliever.

It is after the depression of 1826 that we first encounter the industrial theme in Harriet Martineau's work. Her first short story, 'The Rioters' (1827), tries to show the futility of strikes and their negative effect. While this story may have been inspired by a newspaper report, her second tale of industrial life, 'The Turn-out' (1829), was written at the request of a group of factory owners in Nottingham and Derby who had noticed the useful way in which 'The Rioters' had conveyed its political message. Hence they asked her in urgent terms to write a story showing how completely useless all disputes over wages were between masters and men.[6] Both stories were subsequently published by Houston of Wellington in Shropshire.

We have Harriet Martineau's own words about her original purpose in writing these stories. Her social message, she maintains, should not be seen as an attempt to champion a certain ideology or political system of economy; her only concern had been to urge the folly of riots:

> A county bookseller asked me to compose for him some little work of fiction; I thought that I might join the useful to the agreeable, as I had the choice of the subject, if I could show the folly of the populace of Manchester, who had just been destroying the machinery, to the great detriment of the manufactures, on which their bread depended. I produced a little story, entitled "The Rioters", and the following year another, on wages, called the "Turn-out". I was far from suspecting while I wrote them, that wages and machinery had anything to do with political economy; I do not even know whether I had ever heard the name of that science.[7]

A summary of 'The Rioters' (104 duodecimo pages) will indicate its tenor. A commercial traveller who has come to Manchester while a riot is in progress relates how by the glare of torches he could see the "haggard and infuriated countenances of the mob, which were, indeed, terrible enough to strike fear into any heart." He is unable to procure a single order or, indeed, a single shilling, while the machines are being broken despite the efforts of the soldiers called out to quell the riot, and so he merely watches the fight as the workers cry out that "cut-throats" have been called in "to trample us down." The efforts of the commanding officer to reason with the angry crowd are fruitless: "he might as well have spoken to the raging sea; not a syllable was heard and, brickbats flew in all directions." That evening the traveller meets a group of rioters consisting of women and factory children; their attack on their master's factory has been easily repelled, and the traveller undertakes to act as adviser to those whose attention he has obtained by offering charity to their families. When he recommends moderation and patience in the interest of the workers themselves, he quite obviously voices the opinion of the author.[8] Trade, so he argues, is bound to revive when the glutted market becomes decongested, but his most telling argument is fetched, not from political economy, but from the Bible. After having quoted the famous passage on the necessity of subordination, the author concludes with laconic brevity: "Fear God; honour the King."

The historical importance of this story is considerable. The plot is more elaborate than we should expect from a popular tract, and life in an industrial environment was an unfamiliar subject in fiction. Its moral message, however, is not of a kind usually associated with the term 'social fiction'; Harriet Martineau introduces the industrial worker, not to plead his cause, but to convince him of the wisdom of a policy of *laissez-faire*. The 'Turn-out' (1829) is even more outspoken in its advocacy of this policy, and in this case the authority of the Bible is not invoked. The story is set in a town where cloth-manufacture is carried on, and where the workers combine to demand a rise in wages at a time when business is slack, and the request is refused. A long discussion takes place between the owner of the biggest factory and Henry Gilbert, the leader of the workers. Since no agreement is reached, a strike follows which is continued for several months on the strength of financial support from trade union organizations in neighbouring areas. But with the onset of winter the spirit of resistance flags and the strike is called off without the achievement of increased wages. The author rounds off her story with a few comments on the harmful effects of strikes for masters and men alike.

Both stories show that Harriet Martineau knew the mentality of industrial workers far better than the well-known condition-of-England novelists in later decades. Gilbert is probably drawn from life; he is no mere puppet but an intensely class-conscious proletarian typical of the powerful trade union movement of the 1830s. If he were to see his whole family "in the workhouse, or dying of starvation, he would still insist upon it that he is in the right, and that the next generation will think so, if we don't." The author is quite fair in her description of the way in which the striking workers proceed through the centre of the town; they do so in orderly ranks preceded by a band and carrying flags and posters. She makes the point that the observers are moved by the contrast between the liveliness of the music and the gloom painted on the faces of the workers, so that "money flowed in on every side" despite the remonstrances of the masters against such "misplaced" charity. The reason for the turn-out is made clear by the man elected as spokesman: "They say that a spirit has been roused among the operatives all over the kingdom, and that they begin to understand their right: and that if they now make a vigorous struggle, they will set themselves on an equal footing." This insistence on an equal footing is altogether a new purpose, quite distinct from that of the radical movement, and apparently independent of it. It is interesting to observe that a similar trend was beginning to manifest itself at this time within the ranks of the radical philosophers also; thus the left-wing radical, Thomas Hodskin, had published a pamphlet on *Labour against the Claims of Capital* in 1825, and in 1827 he presented this argument in more elaborate form in a treatise entitled *Popular Political Economy*. Hodskin's main tenet is that the labourer is entitled to receive the full value of what he produces – a view so unacceptable to his radical associates that an enstrangement followed. Among those who denounced Hodskin's theories was the American Professor Thomas Cooper who published a course of lectures given at Oxford in a book entitled *Lectures on the Elements of Political Economy* (1826). Miss Martineau reviewed the London edition published in 1831 in an article 'On the Duty of Studying Political Economy', and such was the fervour with which she herself embraced this duty – characterized as "a positive obligation on every member of society who studies and reflects at all"[9] – that her former enthusiastic advocacy of Unitarianism was exchanged for the truths of political economy. Harriet Martineau describes how she came to be introduced to the great school of English political economy by Mrs Jane Marcet:

> I took up the book [*Conversations On Political Economy*] chiefly to see what Political Economy precisely was; and great was my surprise to find that I had been teaching it unawares, in my stories about Machinery and Wages. It struck me at once that the principles of the whole science might be advantageously conveyed in the same way.[10]

It was precisely to prepare readers for her *Illustrations of Political Economy* (1832–4) that she recommended Professor Cooper's book and insisted on the necessity of studying and disseminating the doctrines of political economy. Cooper's own theories, however, were more reserved than her own belief in the principle of *laissez-faire*; like his great teacher, Adam Smith, Cooper was not insensitive to the injustice with which the workers were treated, especially with regard to what he calls "the laws against combinations of journeymen to raise wages". In his comment on the repeal of these laws Cooper states that it was "assuredly anything but evenhanded justice, which made it an offence for journeymen to combine to raise their wages, while masters might combine with impunity for the purpose of lowering wages."[11] Such considerations were alien to Harriet Martineau, whose vision of the industrial scene failed to include and to honour the rights of labour. No wonder, therefore, that she turned not to Cooper but to James Mill's *Elements of Political Economy* for inspiration as she wrote the stories contained in her *Illustrations of Political Economy*. As R. K. Webb has shown,[12] these stories not only incorporate material from Mill's work, but do so in the same sequence, so that the structure is virtually identical.

Once she had taken the decision to use fiction to convey the science of political economy to a wider audience, she imposed upon herself a rigid daily schedule. When she sat down to write in the morning, she kept at it until she had finished the twelve pages she had decided on as her daily output. She set about her task in such a methodical manner that her manuscripts required very little revision, and hence she produced her impressive series of stories within the span of two years. Her perseverance came in very useful in her dealings with various publishers. She had approached several firms before Charles Fox finally undertook to print her manuscript,[13] a risk he had no occasion to repent, as each monthly issue sold more than 10,000 copies. Harriet Martineau was perfectly right to insist that a book of this kind was badly needed; her tales were widely read and she herself became a celebrity almost overnight. When she moved to London she changed her daily schedule to permit social engagements: after having spent some six or seven hours at work, she would meet people to discuss topics of current interest. She is said to have been a most lively conversationalist, not in the least embarrassed by having to use an ear-trumpet, and among her friends or acquaintances she listed people like Thomas Malthus, Robert Owen, James and John Stuart Mill, Florence Nightingale, Charles Knight, and Sidney Smith. She was on friendly terms with many writers of her day, among them Charles Dickens, William Makepeace Thackeray, Mrs Gaskell, Charlotte Brontë, Douglas Jerrold, and Thomas Carlyle.

Reviewers were upon the whole favourable,[14] although some of them objected to her social philosophy. While *The Monthly Repository* at first had responded favourably, an anonymous review printed after the series had been concluded takes issue with her "attempt to construct a permanent fabric out of transitory materials". The stories "take for granted the immutability" of social structures, and discuss them as if they represented "universal and absolute truths". All these errors are attributed by the reviewer to the "irresistible tendency of the human mind to become the slave of its own hypothesis."[15] *The Edinburgh Review* similarly criticized her principles, but praised the tales, in contrast to the reviewer who stated in *Frazer's Magazine* that her work was "a long tirade against all charity, and an elaborate defence of the closest selfishness". *The Quarterly Review*, a journal associated with the interests of Tory landowners, was severely critical, and *Cobbett's Magazine* condemned her advocacy of Malthus' theory. They found her argument in favour of late marriages "too repugnant to nature for us to believe that it was ever put on paper by one of her sex."[16]

The many reviews, whether positive or negative, helped to create something of a sensation; people constantly discussed Harriet Martineau's stories, siding with the author or firmly opposing her. Queen Victoria read them and so did the trade union leader John Doherty, who remarked, *à propos* of 'A Manchester Strike', that "Anyone familiar with the great turnout of 1829 could place several of the characters."[17] And Lord Brougham, who was patron of the Society for the Diffusion of Useful Knowledge, was annoyed to discover that the contributors to the Library of Useful Knowledge knew less about what was wanted than the deaf Norwich girl.[18]

Her strong desire to be of use to society made Harriet Martineau offer her services to the Whig Cabinet, and she was invited to study their proposal for new financial measures before these were introduced to Parliament. This inspired her next series of tales in five instalments, the *Illustrations of Taxation* (1834), and to these were added *Poor Laws and Paupers Illustrated* (1833-4),[19] three instalments written at the time when the controversy over the Poor Laws was at its most intense. These two series, however, never achieved the popularity of her *Illustrations of Political Economy*.

Harriet Martineau spent the better part of 1836 in America, where she supported the Abolitionists in their work to liberate the Negro slaves. On her return to England she became a prolific contributor to *The Westminster Review*, *The Edinburgh Review*, and *Household Words* at the same time that she wrote leading articles for *The Daily News*.[20] She wrote on an extraordinary range of subjects: the national political scene, British rule in India, the Muslim faith in Egypt, the condition of Ireland, Negro slavery, problems of sanitation in the army, philosophy, Mesmerism, health, education and topography. It is truly surprising that, obliged as she was to live in the country for reasons of health, she nevertheless managed to keep abreast of recent developments in so many diverse areas, and to write so frequently and so persuasively about them that she came to exert a very real influence on public opinion.

Much of what she wrote bears directly on the subject of industry and the working classes. Urged by a feeling of social responsibility she kept on trying to re-create the industrial worker in the image of the class to which she herself belonged, and she did this not only in her propagandist fiction, but also in her work as a journalist and a popularizer of useful information. She wrote many pieces addressed directly to working-class readers, like the pamphlet on *The Tendency of Strikes and Sticks to Produce Low Wages and of Union between Masters and Men to Ensure Good Wages*, published in 1834. In it she describes the great Bedford strike of 1825–6, and she does so with the greatest fairness to its leader, John Tester, who was as intelligent as he was honest – so much so, indeed, that he may have served as a model for William Allen in 'A Manchester Strike'. As far as John Tester is concerned, the author expresses the hope that his experience will make honest workers think twice before they decide in favour of strikes; those who advocate strikes do so for the most despicable of selfish reasons:

> It makes one's blood boil to think of four or six unprincipled fellows flattering so many thousands about their interests and their liberties, while they are making slaves of them, and bringing them down to starvation that they themselves may fatten on the substance they never tried to earn.

No wonder that *The Monthly Repository*, although friendly to Miss Martineau, found her pamphlet unfair to the strikers, who ought to be "encouraged in their exertions for the improvement of their condition." One must expect workers to be swayed by those whose hearts are with them, and though this is no doubt true also of Miss Martineau, the reviewer feels that "the fact will not be evident to them in her present publication."[21] More than 20 years later these powerful attacks on strikes signed by her name were still being printed in the *Daily News*.[22]

While it is fairly easy to understand her bias against strikes, modern readers will find her arguments against labour legislation incomprehensible. Such was her commitment to the sacred name of liberty, that she opposed all efforts to secure some degree of legal protection for women and children employed in factories and mines. Since she held that the freedom of the individual to enter into any agreement about labour should be absolute, it was possible for her to write about the Factory Acts that those who deprived the workers "of the free disposal of their own labour would steal from them their only possession."[23] And in 1855 she wrote with grim satisfaction that the effect of the Factory

Acts proved the vicious character of "meddling legislation".[24] She devoted a great deal of her energy to attacking people like Leonard Horner, an inspector of factories, and those who contributed articles to *Household Words* in favour of legislation to protect workers from accidents by fencing the machines. In the end this conflict between the humanitarian reformers and those who believed in a policy of *laissez-faire* caused a complete break between Harriet Martineau and Charles Dickens, so that she ceased writing for his *Household Words*. I have discussed their relationship in an earlier publication,[25] and a detailed account may also be found in the *Dickens Centennial Essays* (1971) in an essay written by K. J. Fielding and Anne Smith.[26]

This ideological antithesis between conflicting approaches to the same social problem had aesthetic ramifications. Dickens's well-known antipathy to industrial scenes stimulated him to a kind of writing which points forward to twentieth-century expressionistic techniques, while Harriet Martineau makes one remember the many eighteenth-century prose paeons on the subject of industrial prosperity. One example will illustrate the similarity. 'The Hill and the Valley' (the second tale in *Illustrations of Political Economy*) contains a discussion between an advocate of industry and one of its enemies, Mr Armstrong, who deplores the sad effect on his valley of the building of a foundry and houses for the workers. He deplores the loss of natural beauty, and the change in the people employed in the foundry, who have become mere slaves to capital. Harriet Martineau's refutation of these charges is given by one of the proprietors of the metal-works, Mr Wallace, who sees beauty of a different kind in the industrial scene – in the busy throng of workers, for example, as they hurry to and fro among warehouses and furnaces. His praise, given in an elevated prose style, is genuine enough, and it is clearly the sincerity of the author that manifests itself in this passage. Men of Mr Wallace's calibre felt dedicated to higher pursuits than the mere accumulation of wealth; they considered themselves as pioneer creators of a new social order. Hence they saw everything pertaining to this new order in a favourable light – including, so it would seem, the many chimney stacks belching smoke and the slums where the workers lived. In her articles for the daily press Harriet Martineau might refer to such unpleasant phenomena in passing, but preferred to focus her attention on descriptions of technological processes and viewed the entire scene as 'picturesque'. And while on a visit to Birmingham in 1851 she wrote that it struck her that "a full but picturesque account of manufacturies and other productive processes might be valuable both for instruction and entertainment".[27] Picturesque is the key word here as it emphasizes the aesthetic principle of Harriet Martineau in relation to the industrial scenery. And as far as the traditional fusion between the instructive and the entertaining is concerned, absolute priority was certainly given to the principle of usefulness.

In view of this professed preference for the useful, it is scarcely surprising that Harriet Martineau's literary achievement was a very modest one,[28] her greatest success being in the field of books for children. The measure of this success should not be underestimated, since her stories for the young are still being read in the present century – a discovery that came as something of a surprise when I first made it. 'Feats on the Fiord', for example, originally published in *The Playfellow* for 1841, was reprinted in 1906, 1909, 1910, 1915, 1928, and 1947. The most readable of her works, and also the ones of greatest value to the student of the early Victorian period, are her *Autobiography* and her *History of England during the Thirty Years Peace 1816–1846*. Her contemporaries recognized her influence and her genuine importance, and the government expressed its appreciation by offering her a State Pension on three occasions, in 1837, 1841, and 1873. It was entirely in keeping with her belief in private enterprise that she refused, while she accepted the sum of £1,400 raised by private subscription.

Harriet Martineau died in the summer of 1876, and two days later, on 29 June, *The Daily News* published an obituary written by herself. Her estimate of her own achievement is almost startlingly dispassionate:

> None of her novels or tales have, or ever had, in the eyes of good judges or in her own, any character of permanence . . . Her original power was nothing more than was due to earnestness and intellectual clearness within a range. With small imaginative and suggestive powers, and therefore nothing approaching genius, she could see clearly what she did see, and give a clear expression to what she had to say. In short she could popularize, while she could neither discover nor invent.

Despite the severity of this assessment, an anonymous critic, writing for *Blackwood's Edinburgh Journal* (April 1877), complained that "Almost before the echo of the living voice is over, we are startled by a postscriptal harangue from the tomb." He queries her supposed eminence and the impact of her writing; he has "read with amazement of the commotion of society – the agitation in the highest circles . . . all on account of these little Sunday-school stories", and he concludes that "we cannot but think she has been very much overrated as a writer". Pool's Index of the periodical press lists 20 articles written in commemoration of Harriet Martineau, and those I have been able to read tend in the same direction. They doubt the validity of her high reputation as a writer, a reaction which is partly explained by considering the extent to which her intransigent spirit must have annoyed the liberal-minded generation of the last quarter of the nineteenth century. But although her fame has been threatened by oblivion, the time has come for her to be restored to her proper place in the history of English fiction as the first writer whose plots were entirely based on social relationships within an industrialized society.

Notes

1. A bibliography of separately printed books (45 titles in 130 editions) compiled by Joseph B. Rivlin was published in 1947 for the New York Public Library. The following monographs may be listed here: Mrs Fenwick Miller, *Harriet Martineau* (1884); Theodora Bosanquet, *Harriet Martineau, an Essay in Comprehension* (1927); J. C. Nevill, *Harriet Martineau* (1943); Vera Wheatley, *The Life and Works of Harriet Martineau* (1957), and – by far the best and most scholarly study – R. K. Webb, *Harriet Martineau, a Radical Victorian* (1960). Two doctoral dissertations were written in the early 1930s: Nerola Elizabeth Rivenburg, *Harriet Martineau, an Example of Victorian Conflict* (Columbia University, 1932), and Mary Anderson, *Harriet Martineau, a Representative of the Nineteenth Century* (University of Pittsburg, 1933).
2. Walter Rye (ed.), *Norfolk Antiquarian Miscellany* (1887), 100 and 147f.
3. *A General History of the County of Norfolk* (1839), printed by and for John Stacy, I, 94f.
4. *The Norfolk Tour* (1795; 2nd edn 1808), printed and sold by R. Beatniffe.
5. Francis E. Mineka, *The Dissidence of Dissent. The Monthly Repository 1806–1838* (Chapel Hill, N.C., 1944).
6. If not otherwise stated, this and other details are taken from the *Autobiography*, with Memorials by Maria Weston Chapman (1877).
7. 'Some Autobiographical Particulars of Miss Harriet Martineau', in a letter to M. B. Maurice dated London, 3 June 1833. Printed in *The Monthly Repository*, VII (1833), 612f.
8. Her own compassionate attitude makes itself felt in the following realistic description of acts of violence taken from her *History of England during the Thirty Years' Peace 1816–1846* (1849–50), Book II, chap. 9: "There was such fearful suffering among the poor of the manufacturing districts, that one could not wonder much at the spirit of violence which broke out in Lancashire . . . the mob going from town to town, from factory to factory; snatching their food from bakers' shops and public houses, throwing stones at the

soldiers, and being shot down . . . leaping from two-story windows to escape the soldiery after having cut up every web, and hewn
down every beam and stick within; striking at their pursuers with
table-knives made into pikes; with scythes and sledgehammers;
swimming canals, hiding in woods, parading the streets of towns, in
the number of 10,000 at a time, frightening the night with cries of
hunger and yells of rage – all this was terrible; but it came at the
end of many months of such sore distress as rouses the fiercest
passions of men. On the first day three persons were killed by the
soldiers; on another day nine."

9. *The Monthly Repository*, New Series, VI (Jan. 1832), 24–34.
10. *Autobiography*, III, 138. Mrs Jane Marcet (1769–1858) was the
daughter of a wealthy Swiss merchant who wrote handbooks on
scientific subjects for children. She was also the first to attempt a
popularization of political economy. Her *Conversations on Political
Economy; in which the elements of that science are familiarly explained*
(1816) was sufficiently popular to warrant new editions in 1817, 1821
and 1824. The fictional framework is a mere sketch and not fully
realized as in Harriet Martineau's stories.
11. Thomas Cooper, *Lectures on the Elements of Political Economy*
(Columbia, 1826), 91. The London edition appeared in 1831.
12. R. K. Webb, *Harriet Martineau, a Radical Victorian* (1960), 116.
13. Several London firms turned her down, but Charles Fox finally
agreed to publish the 23 tales in 25 parts, on condition that 1,000
copies were sold within a fortnight after the publication of the
second instalment. She collected 300 subscribers. Charles Fox was
the brother of her friend James Fox. See Webb, *op. cit.*, 114.
14. The following reviews may be listed here: *The Atheneum*, no. 224
(2 Feb. 1832), 95; no. 238 (19 May 1832), 319; no. 254 (8 Sept.
1832), 58; *The New Monthly Magazine*, VI no. 37 (Feb. 1833),
58; *The New Monthly Magazine*, VI no. 37 (Feb. 1833), 146–51; *The
Monthly Repository*, New Series, LXII (Feb. 1832), 136; VI no. 63
(March 1832), 211, and VI no. 66 (March 1832), 429.
15. *The Monthly Repository*, VIII: 25 (1834), 319.
16. *The Edinburgh Review*, LVII (April 1933), 1–39; *Frazer's Magazine*,
VI (Nov. 1832), 403; *The Quarterly Review*, XLIX (April 1833), 136;
Cobbett's Magazine, no. 3 (1833), 215.
17. Quoted by Webb, *op. cit.*, 122, from *The Poor Man's Advocate* for
29 September 1832.
18. Mrs Fenwick Miller, *Harriet Martineau* (1884), 101f.
19. The Lord Chancellor gave her access to a wealth of documents
compiled by assistant commissioners before these were published.
See Webb, *op. cit.*, 129f.

20. She also contributed to *Macmillan's Magazine, Cornhill Magazine, The Atlantic Monthly, Once a Week, The Spectator*, and *The National Anti-Slavery Standard* of New York.
21. 'Strikes and Sticks', *The Monthly Repository*, VII (1834), 308f.
22. See *The Daily News* for 8 August 1859 and 29 November, 1859, and *The Anti-Slavery Standard* for 1 October 1859 as quoted by Webb, *op. cit.*, 348.
23. *Autobiography*, IV, 7, p. 514.
24. See *The Factory Controversy: a Warning against Meddling Legislation* (1855), published by The National Association of Factory Occupiers.
25. *Romanopisac i čartisam* (Beograd, 1968), 20–2. The book has a summary in English.
26. 'Hard Times and the Factory Controvery: Dickens vs. Harriet Martineau', in *Dickens Centennial Essays*, ed. Ada Nisbet and Blake Nevius (Berkeley, Cal., 1971), 22–45 or see p. 127, n.1.
27. When the proprietors of *Household Words* asked her to write stories for them, she refused. She was no longer in the mood for that kind of writing, and instead she submitted a number of feature articles on various factories beginning with several in the Birmingham area. See Section VII of the *Autobiography*, p. 69f.
28. She published a novel, *Deerbrook*, in 1839 and another novel, *The Hour and the Man*, in 1841.

Bibliographical Details

'A Manchester Strike' appeared in 1832; the text given here is of the first edition.

A
MANCHESTER
STRIKE

Chapter I

THE WEEK'S END

One fine Saturday evening in May, 18 – , several hundred work-
people, men, girls, and boys, poured out from the gates of a factory
which stood on the banks of the Medlock, near Manchester. The
children dispersed in troops, some to play, but the greater number
to reach home with all speed, as if they were afraid of the sunshine
that checquered the street and reddened the gables and chimnies.
The men seemed in no such haste; they lingered about the
factory, one large group standing before the gates, and smaller
knots occupying the street for some distance, while a few proceeded
slowly on their way home, chatting with one or another party as
they went. One only appeared to have nothing to say to his companions, and to wish to get away quietly, if they would have let
him. He was one of the most respectable looking among them,
decent in his dress, and intelligent though somewhat melancholy in
countenance. He was making his way without speaking to anybody,
when first one and then another caught him by the button and
detained him in consultation. All seemed anxious to know what
Allen had to relate or to advise; and Allen had some difficulty in
getting leave to go home, much as he knew he was wanted there.
When he had at length escaped, he walked so rapidly as presently
to overtake his little daughter, Martha, who had left the factory
somewhat earlier. He saw her before him for some distance, and
observed how she limped, and how feebly she made her way along
the street, (if such it might be called,) which led to their abode. It

was far from easy walking to the strongest. There were heaps of rubbish, pools of muddy water, stones and brickbats lying about, and cabbage-leaves on which the unwary might slip, and bones over which pigs were grunting and curs snarling and fighting. Little Martha, a delicate child of eight years old, tried to avoid all these obstacles; but she nearly slipped down several times, and started when the dogs came near her, and shivered every time the mild spring breeze blew in her face.

"Martha, how lame you are to-day!" said Allen, taking her round the waist to help her onward.

"O father, my knees have been aching so all day. I thought I should have dropped every moment."

"And one would think it was Christmas by your looks, child, instead of a bright May day."

"It is very chill after the factory," said the little girl, her teeth still chattering. "Sure the weather must have changed, father."

No; the wind was south, and the sky cloudless. It was only that the thermometer had stood at 75° within the factory.

"I suppose your wages are lowered as well as mine," said Allen; "how much do you bring home this week?"

"Only three shillings, father; and some say it will be less before long. I am afraid mother—"

The weak-spirited child could not say what it was that she feared, being choked by her tears.

"Come Martha, cheer up," said her father. "Mother knows that you get sometimes more and sometimes less; and, after all, you earn as much as a piecer as some do at the hand-loom. There is Field, our neighbour; he and his wife together do not earn more than seven shillings a week, you know, and think how much older and stronger they are than you! We must make you stronger, Martha. I will go with you to Mr. Dawson, and he will find out what is the matter with your knees."

By this time they had reached the foot of the stairs which led up to their two rooms in the third story of a large dwelling which was occupied by many poor families. Barefooted children were scampering up and down these stairs at play; girls nursing babies sat at various elevations, and seemed in danger of being kicked down as often as a drunken man or an angry woman should want to pass; a thing which frequently happened. Little Martha looked up the steep stairs and sighed. Her father lifted and carried her. The noises would have stunned a stranger, and they seemed louder than usual to accustomed ears. Martha's little dog come barking and jumping up as soon as he saw her, and this set several babies crying; the shrill piping of a bulfinch was heard in the din, and over all, the voice of a scolding woman.

"That is Sally Field's voice if it is anybody's," said Allen. "It is enough to make one shift one's quarters to have that woman within hearing."

"She is in our rooms, father. I am sure the noise is there; and see, her door is open and her room empty."

"She need not fear leaving her door open," observed a neighbour in passing. "There is nothing there that anybody would wish to carry away."

Allen did not answer, but made haste to restore peace in his own dwelling, knowing that his wife was far from being a match for Sally Field. As he flung open the door, the weaker party seemed to resign the contest to him; his wife sank into a chair, trembling all over. Her four or five little ones had hidden themselves where they could, some under the table, some behind the bed, having all been slapped or pushed or buffeted by Sally for staring at her with their thumbs in their mouths. She was not aware that Sally Field in a passion was a sight to make any one stare.

Allen carried Martha to a seat in preparation for turning out Sally Field and locking the door upon her, which he meant to do by main force if gentler means should fail. Her surprise at seeing him, however, and perhaps some degree of awe of his determined countenance, made her pause for a moment.

"What is all this, wife?" inquired Allen.

"I am sure I don't know. Sally has been rating me and the children this hour past, and heaven knows what for."

Sally proceeded upon this to declare a long list of offences of which Allen's family had been guilty towards her, and Allen suffered her to go on till she had exhausted her breath. When at length she lost her voice – a catastrophe which happens sooner or later to all scolds, – he took up the word.

"I'll tell you what, Sally," said he; "I am very sorry for you, and very much ashamed of you, and I should be more angry on my wife's account than you ever saw me if I did not know you well, and understand what is at the bottom of all this. Remember, Sally, I have known you and your husband since you were this high, as well as if you had been children of my own. Don't put me in mind how young you are. Don't make me treat you like a child when you have taken upon you so early to be a woman. Don't make me call your husband to take care of you as if you could not take care of yourself."

"Call him! call him and welcome, if you can find him," cried

Sally. "Show me where he is, and I'll find a better use for my tongue than in scolding your mean-spirited wife there that looks as if she were going to die whenever one speaks. Go, pray, call my husband."

"Aye, aye; that's the grievance, I see," said Allen. "We all have our grievances, Sally, and it is great folly to make them worse of our own accord. Do you expect to tempt your husband to stay at home with you by scolding as you were doing just now?"

"Do you leave your wife for the twenty-four hours together?" cried Sally. "Do you make yourself drunk with your last shilling? – and yet any man had rather see his wife in a passion now and then than have her such a poor, puny, crying creature as your wife is."

"Hush, hush, mistress!" interrupted Allen. "I will lock the door upon you this moment, and would have done it before but that you would raise a mob in the street if I turned you out. Sally, you know you have not a friend in the world if you quarrel with us, and what will you do with your sore heart then?"

The poor creature's passion now dissolved in tears. She threw herself on the bed and sobbed bitterly. She was left to herself for some time. Allen produced his week's wages, and settled with his wife how they should be disposed of, and persuaded her to go out herself and make the necessary purchases, saying that he would search for Field and try to get him home. Allen's wife sighed.

"You are not afraid to trust me in an ale-house?" said he smiling.

"Bless your heart, no; that I never was nor ever shall be: but I was thinking of what you said, that we all have our grievances. Here is three shillings less wages this week."

"Yes, and another sixpence off Martha's too: but don't fret, wife; we must do as others do, and be glad if nothing worse happens. See to poor Martha's knees before you go out; she is more lame than ever to-day. – And now, Sally, if you will promise me to go to your own room, and stay there till I bring your husband back, and if you will give me your word to keep the peace with him whatever he may have been doing, I will go and search him out, and see what I can do to make him behave better to you."

Sally promised to keep the peace, but begged to stay and take care of the children till their mother should return. Seeing however that Martha looked up beseechingly in her father's face, and that the little ones clung to their mother's apron, she cursed herself for having deserved that they should be afraid of her, and ran down to bolt herself into her own room and recover her composure as she might.

As there was no fire, and as Martha was very discreet for her years, the parents promised the children to lock them up, that no scold might come and terrify them while they had to take care of themselves. Martha was advised to sit still, and her bulfinch was taken down from the window and placed beside her to be fed and watered; the other little things promised to be good, and their father and mother went, the one to the Spread-Eagle and the other to the market.

It required no great sagacity to prophesy that Field would be found at the Spread-Eagle. He varied his excursions a little, according to times and seasons; but those who knew his ways could easily guess at which of his haunts he might be expected when missing from home. When he stole out before getting to his loom in the morning, or after leaving it late at night, he generally stepped only to the dram-shop, for a glass of gin to warm him for his work, or to settle him to his sleep, as his pretence was; but when he had finished his piece and got his pay, he felt himself at liberty to go to the Spread-Eagle and have a carouse, from which he returned in the dark, sometimes reeling on his own legs, sometimes carried on other men's shoulders. This habit of drinking had grown upon him with frightful rapidity. He had a year before, been described by his employers as a steady, well-behaved lad. He had fallen in love with Sally and married her in a hurry, found her temper disagreeable and his home uncomfortable, tried in vain to keep her in order, and then, giving up all hope, took to drinking, and would not tolerate a word of remonstrance from any one but his old friend Allen.

There were more customers this evening at the Spread-Eagle than was usual even on Saturdays. Allen was warmly welcomed as he entered, for it was supposed he came to keep company with his companions from the same factory. Almost all present were spinners and power-loom weavers under the firm of Mortimer and Rowe; and the occasion of their assembling in greater numbers than usual, was the reduction of wages which had that day taken place. Room was made for Allen as soon as he appeared, a pipe and pot of porter called for, and he was welcomed to their consultation. But Allen looked round instead of taking his seat, and inquired for Field. The landlord pointed to a corner where Field lay in a drunken sleep under a bench.

"Let him lie," said one. "He is too far gone to be roused."

"What concern is it of yours?" cried another. "Come and listen to what Clack was saying."

"You shirked us in the street," said a third: "now we have caught you, we shall not let you go."

The landlord being really of opinion that Field had better lie where he was for an hour or two, Allen sat down to hear what was going on.

Clack turned to him to know what their masters deserved for lowering their wages.

"That depends upon circumstances," replied Allen. "Be they much to blame or little, something must be done to prevent a further reduction, or many of us will be ruined."

"Shake hands, my fine fellow!" cried Clack. "That was just what we had agreed. It is time such tyranny was put down, and we can put it down, and we will."

"Gently, gently," said Allen. "How do you think of putting it down?"

"Why should not we root out the one who is the most of a tyrant, and then the others may take warning before it is too late? We have nothing to do but to agree."

"No easy matter sometimes, friend."

"Stuff! we have agreed before upon a less occasion, and when there was danger in it. Had not we our combinations, when combination was against the law? and shall not we have them again now that the law lets us alone? Shall we be bold in the day of danger and shrink when that day is over?"

"Well, well, neighbour: I said nothing about being afraid. What would you have us agree to do?"

"To root out Messrs. Mortimer and Rowe. Every man in our union must be sworn not to enter their gates; and if this does not frighten the masters and make them more reasonable, I don't know what will."

"And if, instead of being frightened, the masters unite to refuse us work till we give up our stand against Mortimer and Rowe, what are we to do then?"

"To measure our strength against theirs, to be sure. You know they can't do without us."

"Nor we without them; and where both parties are so necessary to each other, it is a pity they should fall out."

"A pity! To be sure it is a pity; but if the masters drive us to it, the blame rests with them."

"I hope," said a timid-looking man, Hare by name, who had a habit of twirling his hat when silent, and of scratching his head when he spoke, "I hope, neighbour, you will think what you are about before you mention a strike. I've seen enough of strikes. I had rather see my children on the parish than strike."

Clack looked disdainfully at him, and said it was well that some dove-like folks had not to manage a fight against the eagle. For his part, he thought any man ought to be proud of the honour of making a stand against any oppression; and that he had rather, for his own share, have the thanks of the Union Committee than wear Wellington's star. Would not his friend Allen say the same?

No. Allen agreed with Hare so far as thinking that there could be few worse evils than a strike; but at the same time it was an evil which might become necessary in certain cases. When convinced that it was necessary in defence of the rights of the working-man, he would join in it heart and hand; but never out of spite or revenge, – never to root out any master breathing. – So many agreed in this opinion, that Clack grew more eager than ever in defending himself and blaming the masters in question.

"Dare any one say," he cried, "that the Dey of Algiers himself is a greater tyrant than Mortimer would be if he dared? Does not he look as if he would trample us under foot if he could? Does not he smile with contempt at whatever is said by a working-man? Does not he spurn every complaint, and laugh at every threat? and if he takes it into his lofty head to do a kindness, does not he make it bitter with his pride?"

"All true, Clack, as everybody knows that works for Mortimer; but – "

"And as for Rowe," interrupted the talker, "he is worse, if possible, in his way."

"I don't know," said Hare, doubtfully. "Mr. Rowe came once and talked very kindly with me."

"Aye, when he had some purpose to answer. We are all, except you, Hare, wise enough to know what Rowe's pretty speeches mean. You should follow him to the next masters' meeting, man, and hear how he alters his tone with his company. The mean-spirited, shuffling knave!"

"Well, well, Clack; granting that Mortimer is tyrannical and Rowe not to be trusted – that does not alter the case about rooting them out. To make the attempt is to acknowledge at the outset that the object of our union is a bad one: it will fill the minds of the operatives with foul passions and provoke a war between masters and men which will end in the destruction of both. Whenever we do strike, let it be in defence of our own rights, and not out of enmity to individuals among our employers."

Clack muttered something about there being shufflers among the men as well as the masters; to which Allen replied that the way to make shufflers was to use intimidation. The more wisdom and moderation there was in the proceedings of any body of men, the better chance there was of unanimity and determination. He repeated that, as long as the Union of which he was a member kept in view the interests of the body of operatives, he would be found ready to do and to sacrifice his share; but as soon as it should set to work on other objects, he should withdraw at all risks.

Before he had done speaking, the attention of his companions was called off by an unexpected addition to their company. Music had been heard gradually approaching for some minutes, and now the musician stood darkening the door and almost deafening the people within with the extraordinary variety of sounds he produced. An enormous drum was strapped across his body; a Pan's pipe employed his mouth, and his hat, with a pointed crown and a broad brim, was garnished with bells. A little girl, fantastically dressed, performed on the triangle, and danced, and collected half-pence from the bystanders. While the musician played a jig, jerking his head incessantly from side to side, nobody thought of looking particularly at him: but when he turned to the company within doors and set his little companion to sing to his playing

"Should auld acquaintance be forgot,"

several of the debaters began to fancy that they knew the face and figure of the musician. "It is – yes, it certainly is Bray!" said one to another; and many a hand was held out to him.

"I thought you were not likely to forget old acquaintance, even if they come in a new dress," said Bray, laughing heartily,and proceeding to deposit his decorations with one or another of his former companions. He put his hat on Allen's head, slipped the strap of his drum over Clack's shoulders, and gave the triangle to Hare.

"Come," said he, "let us have a concert. It is my turn to see spinners turn strollers. Come, Allen, shake your head, man, and let us hear what comes out of it."

"How we have wondered," exclaimed Allen, "what had become of you and yours! Is that poor little Hannah that used to be so delicate?"

"The same that your good wife nursed through the measles. She would hardly know her now."

Allen shook his head.

"Ah, I see what you mean," said Bray. "You had rather see her covered with white cotton flakes than with yellow ribands; but remember it is no fault of mine that she is not still a piecer in yonder factory; and I don't know that I need call it my misfortune any more than my fault. Look how strong and plump she is! so much for living in the open air, instead of being mewed up in a place like an oven. Now, don't take off the hat on purpose to shake your head. What can a man do – " and looking round, he appealed to the company, "what can a proscribed man do but get his living, so as not to have to ask for work?"

A loud clapping and shuffling of feet was the answer to his question. The noise half roused the drunken man in the corner, who rolled himself over to the terror of little Hannah, who had got as far as she could out of the way of the smokers, among whom her father had been so well received. Allen rose to go, having some hope that Field might be safely set on his legs again by this time. He asked Bray whether he meant to stay in the neighbourhood, and where he would lodge.

"You must stay," cried one, "and play a tune before your old masters' gates."

"You must stay," said another, "and see how we manage a strike now-a-days."

"A strike! Are you going to try your strength again? You will make me wish I was one of you still; but I can head the march. Stay? Yes, I'll stay and lead you on to victory. Hurra! I'll go recruiting with my drum. I'll manage to meet Mortimer, when I have a procession a mile long at my heels!"

"You lay by your drum on Sundays, I suppose?" said Allen.

"Yes, yes. We keep within and take our rest on Sundays. It is as great a treat to us to sit within doors all day once a week, as it is to some other folks to get into the green meadows. If the landlord can give us lodging, you will find us here in the morning, Allen."

"Let Hannah go home with me, Bray. I know my wife will be glad to see her and to hear her story, and this is no place for a child. If I can rouse yon sleeper, I will go now, and send my wife with a cloak or something to hide the child's frippery, and then she will spend tomorrow in a fitter place than a public-house."

Bray sat gravely looking at his child for a few moments, and then started up, saying that he would undertake to rouse the sleeper. Blowing the Pan's pipe close by his ear made him start, and a rub-a-dub on the drum woke him up effectually: so that he was able, cross and miserable, to crawl homewards with the help of Allen's arm, and to be put to bed by his wife with the indistinct dread in his mind of a terrible lecture as soon as he should be in a condition to listen to it.

Chapter II

CHILD'S GOSSIP

Much business was transacted at the Spread-Eagle on the Sunday by the Committee of the Union. It was the general opinion that a great struggle between masters and men was on the eve of taking place, and measures were adopted for finding out what was the disposition of the operative spinners respecting a general strike, if an equalization of wages was not to be obtained by other means. It had been agreed on the Saturday night that twenty-five members of the Union should employ the Sunday in obtaining the names of as many as were willing to turn out, or to subscribe for the assistance of those who should turn out, in case of opposition from the masters. These twenty-five men were to bring in their reports on Sunday night; after which, if the affair should look promising, a petition was to be addressed to the masters, for a public meeting, at which an equalization of wages was to be agreed on.

Clack was somewhat at a loss how to apportion his own business, and that of other people, on this occasion. Having a very high opinion of his own powers of persuasion, and being confident of his knowledge of law, he wanted to be everywhere at once, and to guide all the movements of the people he employed. As this was impossible, however, he thought it best to remain in some known place of appeal where parties might come to him for direction and information. He therefore sat at the Spread-Eagle all day big with importance, and dissatisfied only because his underlings could not be about their business abroad, and listening to him at the same time.

The Allens knew nothing of what was going forward. Mrs. Allen was so full of interest and curiosity about little Hannah Bray, that she had no thoughts to bestow on public affairs, as the transactions of the Union were commonly called. Her husband had gone early into the country with Bray this day dressed like other people, to visit some relations of the latter, who did not know what had become of him after he had been refused employment in Manchester, and obliged to betake himself to some new mode of obtaining a livelihood.

Little Hannah slept till the sun was high on the Sunday morning, and might have slept longer if Mrs. Allen had not feared she would not get breakfast over in time for church. Hannah jumped up with the excuse that the place was so quiet, there was nothing to wake her.

"Indeed!" said Mrs. Allen. "We think the children and the

neighbours make a great deal of noise; but I suppose you sleep in public-houses for the most part."

Hannah observed that people call so loud for what they want in public-houses, and they care so little for hours, that there is no knowing when you may sleep quietly.

"Have you no other frock than that, my dear?" asked Mrs. Allen. "I suppose you go to church on Sundays, and you cannot possibly go in all those gay ribands."

"O no," said Hannah. "I have a dark frock for Sundays, and a straw bonnet; but they are in father's pack, and I suppose that is at the Spread-Eagle."

"And he is gone into the country for the day. Well, you must change with Martha when church time comes. Poor Martha has but one tidy frock; but she is too lame to go out to-day, even as far as the apothecary's; and I am sure she will lend you her frock and tippet to go to church in."

Martha was willing to lend but had rather put on her factory dress than Hannah's red frock with yellow trimmings. Hannah hinted that she should like to stay within with Martha all day; and the indulgent mother, seeing Martha's pleasure at the prospect of a companion and nurse of her own age, left the little girls to amuse themselves, while she took the younger children to church with her as usual.

"Father says he heard you sing last night," said Martha when they were left alone. "Will you sing to me?"

"I am so tired of singing!" pleaded Hannah. "I don't know many songs, and I sing them so very often! Won't that bird do as well? Let me get down the cage, may I?"

"Yes, do, and we will give him some water, poor fellow! He is my bird and I feed him every day. Somebody that could not afford to keep him sold him to father, and father gave him to me. Had you ever a bird?"

"No, but I had a monkey once. When we went away, father got a monkey, and I used to lead him about with a string; but I was glad when we had done with him, he was so mischievous. Look here how he tore my arm one day, when somebody had put him in a passion with giving him empty nutshells."

"What a terrible place!" said Martha. "Was it long in getting well?"

"No; father got an apothecary to tie it up, and it soon got well."

"My father is going to show my knees to Mr. Dawson, the apothecary. Do look how they are swelled; and they ache so, you can't think."

"O, but I can think, for mine used to ache terribly when I walked and stood before the wheels all day."

"But yours were never so bad as mine, or I am sure you could not dance about as you do."

"Not so bad, to be sure, and my arms were never so shrunk away as yours. Look, my arm is twice as big as yours."

"I wonder what's the reason," sighed Martha. "Mother says I get thinner and thinner."

"You should have meat for dinner every day as I have," said Hannah, "and then you would grow fat like me. Father gets such good dinners for us to what we used to have. He says 'tis that, and being in the air so much that prevents my being sickly, as I used to be. I don't think I could do the work that I used to do with all that noise, and the smell of oil and the heat."

"And I am sure I could not sing and dance as you do."

"No, how should you dance when you are so lame?"

"And I don't think I can sing at all."

"Come, try, and I will sing with you. Try 'God save the king.' "

"It is Sunday," said Martha gravely.

"Well, I thought people might sing 'God save the king' on Sundays. I have heard father play it on the drum, just before the Old Hundred. You know the Old Hundred."

Martha had heard this hymn-tune at church, and she tried to sing it; but Hannah burst out a laughing.

"Lord! Martha, your voice is like a little twittering bird's. Can't you open your mouth and sing this way?"

"No, I can't," said Martha, quite out of breath; "and besides, Hannah, you should not say 'Lord!' Father and mother never let us say those sort of words."

"Nor my father either. He is more angry with me for that, than for anything; but it slips out somehow, and you would not wonder if you knew how often I hear people say that, and many worse things."

"Worse things?" said Martha, looking curious.

"Yes; much worse things; but I am not going to tell you what they are, because father made me promise not to tell you about any of the bad people that I have heard swear and seen tipsy. Was your father ever tipsy?"

"Not that I know of; but our neighbour Field is often tipsy. I am afraid every day that he will topple down stairs."

"My father was tipsy once," said Hannah, "and he beat me so, you can't think."

"When? Lately?"

"No, just after we began to stroll. Though it is so long ago, I remember it very well, for I was never so frightened in my life. I did not know where to go to get away from him; and the people pushed him about and laughed at me the more the more I cried. I asked him afterwards not to get tipsy any more, and he said he never would, and he never has. It was only because we had got more money that day than we ever got in a day before: but it soon went away, for when father woke the next morning, his pocket was quite empty."

"And did you soon get some more money?"

"O yes; we get some every day except Sundays. I carry the hat round every time we stop to play, and I always get some halfpence and sometimes a silver sixpence."

"Ah! then, you get a great deal more than I do, Hannah. I brought home only three shillings this week."

"I take much more than that, to be sure; but then it is my father's earning more than mine. His great drum sounds farther and brings more people to listen than my triangle."

"Is your triangle here? I wish you would teach me to play," said Martha. "Now do. If you will, I will ask mother to show us the pictures in grandfather's bible when she comes home."

Hannah had been very fond of these pictures when she was recovering from the measles; and this bribe and her goodnature together overcame her disgust at the instrument she had to play every day and almost all day long. She indulged herself with a prodigious yawn, and then began her lesson. When Mrs. Allen came back, she found the bulfinch piping at his loudest pitch to the accompaniment of the triangle, Hannah screaming her instructions to her new pupil, and poor palefaced little Martha flushed with flattery and with the grand idea of earning a great many silver sixpences every day if her father would let her make music in the streets instead of going to the factory.

Chapter III

NO UNION OF MASTERS

The achievements of the twenty-five who canvassed for support during Sunday were such as to put Clack into high spirits. The list of names with signatures or marks annexed, amounted to several thousands; and if the orator had been allowed to have his own way, he would have proclaimed war against the masters at once, and the turn-out would have begun on the Monday morning: but there were a few soberer folks than himself engaged in the consultation; and these smiled at his brag of the many thousand pounds that would pour in from Leeds, Coventry, Liverpool, Glasgow, and other places, and insisted upon offering the masters the option of a peaceable agreement before any measures of opposition were taken.

Clack retorted that these men were afraid of their wives, and declared that they might wait long for a strike if it was necessary to refrain till the women voted for it, since there was never a woman yet who did not hate a turn-out as she would the plague.

This observation called forth some joke at his expense, for Clack was known to be engaged to be married, and it was thought he spoke from awkward experience. In the eagerness of defence he went a step too far. He asked if it was likely, knowing the disposition of the women on this subject, that he should consult any woman breathing as to the part he should take, or provoke opposition from any female tongue, or care for it if he should happen to meet with it. These words were, as he might have expected, carried to the ears which should never have heard them, and prevented his next meeting with his betrothed from being the pleasantest in the world. While a storm was brewing at a distance in consequence of his indiscreet boast, Clack made himself very merry with those who were less bold than himself.

"Where is Hare to-day? Henpecked, I warrant. Did not he promise faithfully to be one of the twenty-five?"

"Yes, and he is no where to be found," said a neighbour.

"But I wonder, Clack, you troubled yourself to take a promise from such a shilly-shally fellow as Hare. His being married has nothing to do with it: he was never in the same mind for an hour together from his youth up."

"How did he get married then?"

"O there was another and a steadier mind concerned in that matter, you know: not that I mean any harm against his wife: she is as mild as she is sensible. I only mean that her judgment strengthens his when they have to act together."

"Then I suppose she does not like the idea of a strike any better than the other women, and persuades him not to come?"

"More likely she knows nothing of it. If there is one thing rather than another that Hare is afraid of, it is combination. That imprisonment of his father under the old combination laws made him a coward for life; and there is no use in telling him that the law leaves us to manage our own business now as long as we keep the peace."

"He does, indeed, make a pitiful figure between his dread of belonging to the Union and his horror of being left out. But why do we waste our breath upon him? Who has seen Allen to-day, and why does he not come? We shall count his modesty for backwardness if he does not take care."

"Don't be in a hurry to blame a better man than yourself," said a neighbour. "Allen has been in the country all day."

There was no offence in such a comparison; for Allen was generally looked up to as the first man in that branch of the Union, though he was so little aware of his own merits that he did not come forward so much as he should have done, except on urgent occasions; and then he never failed to do all that was expected of him.

When the petition to the masters to hold a public meeting was prepared, and when Clack had appointed himself and two others to carry it round the next day, the Committee terminated their present sitting.

The first firm to which the deputies addressed their petition was that of Mortimer and Rowe.

"Are the partners at home?" they inquired.

"I don't know whether Mr. Mortimer is here yet, but there is Mr. Rowe. Sir! Mr. Rowe!" called the clerk, as he saw the junior partner making his escape, "these men wish to speak with you, sir, if you please."

Mr. Rowe, perceiving that he had been seen, came forward to be spoken with.

"A public meeting, – equalization of wages, – aye, very fair: hum! very well, my good fellows. Well: what do you want me to do?"

"To give your voice in favour of this public meeting."

"Why, you know you have a good friend in me. You surely cannot anticipate any difficulty with me. I am a friend of peace, you know, No man more so."

"Aye, sir: but there is more than one sort of peace. The masters have called it peace when they had all their own way, and their men were cowed by the law and dared not openly resist. The men call it peace when the two parties have confidence in each other, and make a cordial agreement, and keep to it. This is what we want at the present time."

So said Gibson, whose turn it was to be spokesman; but Clack could not help putting in his word.

"And if either party refuses peace, you know, sir, the next thing is war."

"O, no war!" said Mr. Rowe. "A cordial agreement, as you say, is the right thing. So, for this purpose you wish for a public meeting. Well; I shall be happy to attend a public meeting, if – "

"We are happy to find you so agreeable, sir. Will you just sign for self and partner, if you please."

"Sign! I see no signatures."

"Because you happen to be the first person we have applied to, sir; that is all. We hope for signatures plenty before the day is over. Will you please to sign, as you approve of the meeting?"

Mr. Rowe suddenly recollected that he must consult his partner who sat in a back room. The men had not to wait long. The junior partner, indeed, did not appear again, but Mr. Mortimer issued forth, looking not a whit less haughty than usual. He begged the deputies would make the best of their way off his premises, as he had nothing to say to them.

What were his sentiments respecting the meeting, if they might inquire?

His sentiments were, that the masters had been far too tolerant already of the complaints of the men; and that it was time the lower orders were taught their proper place. He had neither leisure nor inclination to argue with any of them, either there or elsewhere; so the sooner they took themselves off the better.

"You may live to change your sentiments, sir," observed Gibson.

"Beware of threats!" said Mr. Mortimer. "There is law yet for the punishment of threats, remember."

"I have neither forgotten the law, Mr. Mortimer, nor used threats. I said, and I say again, you may live to change your sentiments; and, for your own sake, it is to be hoped you will. Good morning, sir."

"He is too busy even to wish us good morning," observed Clack. "How coolly he looked over the letter he took from his clerk, as if we were not worth attending to for a moment!"

"Haughty as he is," said Gibson, "I would sooner bear with his pride than Rowe's behaviour or Elliot's."

"They are young men, Gibson, and Mortimer is old, and we would sooner bear with an old man's mistakes than a young man's, be they what they may! Where next? To Elliot's?"

"Yes, we are sure of being ill-treated there; so the sooner it is over the better."

As they approached Mr. Elliot's house, they perceived that gentleman mounted on his favourite hunter, and in the act of leaving his own door. He was too much occupied with his own affairs to see them coming, for the most important part of his morning's business was setting off for his ride; and he had eyes for little else while he was admiring the polish of his boots, adjusting his collar, settling the skirts of his coat, and patting his horse's neck. Clack was not the man for ceremony; he came straight up before the horse, and laid his hand on the handsome new rein, saying, "By your leave, sir – "

"Hands off," cried Elliott, giving him a cut across the knuckles with his riding whip. "How dare you stop me? How dare you handle my rein with your greasy fingers?"

"How would you get such a rein, I wonder, sir, if we did not grease our fingers in your service?" said Clack, indignantly.

"I'm in a hurry," said Elliott; "you can speak to the people within, if you want any thing."

"We will not detain you, sir," said Taylor, who was now spokesman, "but nobody but yourself can answer our question." And he told the story in a few words, and put the petition into the gentleman's hands.

Elliott glanced his eye over it as well as the restlessness of his horse would permit, and then struck it contemptuously with his riding-whip into the mud, swore that that was the proper place for such a piece of insolence, rode up against the men, and pranced down the street without bestowing another look or word upon them.

"Pride comes before a fall; let the gentleman take care of himself," said Gibson, quietly picking up the petition and wiping off the mud with his handkerchief.

Clack talked about using his greasy fingers to cram the soiled petition down the gentleman's throat, and seemed disposed to harangue the laughing bystanders; but his more prudent companions took him by the arm and led him away. Mr. Elliott's clerk, who had seen the whole proceeding from an upper window, and was ashamed of his master's conduct, came after them, out of breath, to ask them in while he copied the petition, which was not, as he observed, fit to show to any other gentleman. Gibson thanked him for his civility, but observed that the soiled paper would tell part of their story better than they could tell it themselves. The clerk, therefore, slowly returned, saying to himself that it is a pity when young men, coming to a large fortune obtained in trade, forget by whose means their wealth was acquired, and by what tenure it is held.

After visiting several manufacturers, some of whom were more and others less favourable to their claims than they expected, the deputies requested an interview with Mr. Wentworth. Mr. Wentworth had been rich as a young man, had failed through unavoidable misfortunes, and had worked his way up again to a competence, after having paid every shilling he owed. He was now an elderly man, homely in his person, somewhat slovenly in his dress, not much given to talk, and, when he did speak, causing some surprise and weariness to strangers by the drawling twang of his speech. Those who knew him well, however, had rather hear his voice than any music; and such of his men as belonged to the Union agreed that ten words from him were worth a speech of an hour long from Clack. There was, to be sure, no need for so many words from him, as from other people, for he practised a great variety of inarticulate sounds, the meaning of which was well understood by those accustomed to converse with him, and served all the purposes of a reply.

Mr. Wentworth was sitting at his desk when the deputies were introduced. As they uncovered their heads and made their bow, some murmurings and clutterings reached them which they understood as a welcome. He looked steadily at them from under his shaggy eyebrows while they explained their business, and then took the petition to look over.

"You can hardly have any paper-makers in your Union," said he, chuckling as he unfolded the sheet; "or are you saving your pence against a strike, that you can't afford paper as fair as your writing?"

"Aye, aye; wait a while and you will see him grow wiser," was his observation on hearing the story of Elliott's insolence. "We were all boys before we were men. – Hum: – equalization – Who will avouch that this equalization is all that you want?"

"I, sir," said the ever-ready Clack – "I drew it up, and so I ought to know."

Gibson observed, that though no further object was expressly contemplated by the Union, he would not answer for their not increasing their demands as they proceeded. If there was any attempt to equalize the wages by reducing all to the lowest now given, the Union would demand an advance.

"Who gives the lowest?" inquired Mr. Wentworth.

"Except some upstarts whom we can easily manage, Mortimer and Rowe give the lowest, and you, sir, the next lowest, and Elliott the highest."

"Who was lamenting lately that the combination laws were repealed, so that the masters cannot be prosecuted for oppression? Who proposed to burn them in effigy, tied to one another's necks?"

The deputies looked at one another, and then answered that all this was only private talk of one of their meetings; it was never meant for earnest.

"Well, I only let you know that you may look about your Committee-room and find where the little bird builds that carries the matter; and if you can't find her, take care that she has nothing to carry that you would be ashamed to own. Did you learn from her that the masters combine against you?"

"We learn it from our own eyes, and ears, and senses," said Clack. "Have not masters oppressed their men from the beginning of the world?"

"Indeed I don't know," said Mr. Wentworth. "If Adam had a gardener under him in Paradise, they might have tried to turn one another out, but I never heard of it."

"Stuff and nonsense, sir, begging your pardon. Don't we know that masters always have lorded it over the poor? They were born with a silver spoon in their mouths, and – "

"I wonder where mine is," observed Mr. Wentworth; "I will look in my mother's plate chest for it."

The orator went on, –

"They openly treat us like slaves as long as they can, and when we will bear it no longer, they plot in secret against us. They steal to one another's houses when they think we are asleep; they bolt their doors and fill their glasses to their own prosperity, and every bumper that goes down their throats is paid for with the poor man's crust."

"They must have made the little bird tipsy, Clack, before she carried you such a strange story as that."

"Don't tell me, sir, that it is not true! Don't tell me!"

"I am not telling you anything; for the plain reason, that I have nothing to tell. I only want to ask you one or two things, as you seem to know so much more than we do. Pray what have the masters combined for just now?"

"To lower our wages, to be sure."

"And yet Mortimer pays one rate, and I another, and Elliott another. Why don't I ask as much labour for my money as Mortimer?"

"You dare not," cried Clack.

"You know it's not fair," said Taylor.

"You are not the man to grind the poor," said Gibson.

"You have not hit it, any of you. You all seem to think it is a matter of pure choice with us, what wages we give."

"To be sure," said Clack, "and that is the reason we want parliament to settle the matter at once and for ever."

"Parliament has no more choice in the matter than we masters," drily observed Mr. Wentworth. "If ever Parliament passes a Bill to regulate wages, we must have a rider put to it to decree how much rain must fall before harvest."

Clack muttered something about not standing any longer to be trifled with; but his companions thought it possible that Mr. Wentworth might have something to say that was worth hearing, and persuaded the orator to be quiet. Gibson inquired, –

"Where then does the choice rest, sir, if neither with the government nor the masters?"

"Such power as there is rests with those who take, not with those who give wages. Not such power as tips our friend's tongue there," nodding at Clack, "not such power as you gain by the most successful strike, not such power as combination gives you, be it peaceable or threatening; but a much more lasting power which cannot be taken from you. The power of the masters is considerable, for they hold the administration of capital; but it is not on this that the rate of wages depends. It depends on the administration of labour; and this much greater power is in your hands."

The deputies thought that they who pay wages must always have power over those who receive.

"That is as much as saying that wages are a gift. I thought you had supposed them your right."

All were eager to urge the rights of industry.

"Aye, all very true; no right can be clearer when we see what wages are. Come, Clack, tell us, (for who knows if you don't?) tell us what wages Adam gave his under gardeners. You can't say? Why, I thought you knew all that the masters did at the beginning of the world. Well, when Adam was some hundred years old, (you may trust me, for I am descended from him in a straight line,) he said to Eve, 'Stay you here and spin with the women, while I go yonder and set my men to delve; and don't expect us back in a hurry, for tillage is tough work here to what it was in Eden, and we must gather our crops before we can bring them to market. Come, my good fellows, work hard and you shall have your shares.' 'And pray, sir,' said the men, 'what are we to live upon while our fruit and vegetables are growing?' 'Why,' says Adam, 'instead of my sharing the fruit with you when it is grown, suppose you take your portion in advance. It may be a convenience to you, and it is all the same thing to me.' So the men looked at the ground, and calculated how much digging and other work there would be, and then named their demand; not in silver money with king George's head upon it, but food and clothing, and tools."

"Then at harvest time," observed Gibson, "the whole produce belonged to Adam?"

"Of course. The commodity was made up, like all commodities, of capital and labour; Adam's capital and the men's labour."

"And of a deal besides," cried Clack. "If it was grain, there was the root, and the stalk, and the ear; and if it was fruit, there was the rind, and the pulp, and the juice."

"Begging your pardon, friend, there was nothing but capital and labour. Without labour, and the soil and the tools which made the capital, there would have been neither grain nor fruit; and if grain and fruit grew wild, they could be no commodity without labour, any more than the diamond in the mine, and the pearl in the sea, are a commodity before the one is dug, and the other fished up. Well, Adam and his men expected to get as much by their crop as would pay for their subsistence and their toil; and this much the men asked, and Adam was willing to give, and a fair surplus remained over for himself. So they made their bargain, and he bought their share of the commodity, and had to himself all the flax and other things that his produce exchanged for in the market. And so that season passed off, and all were contented."

"And what happened next season, sir?"

"Next season, twice the number of men came to ask work in the same plot of ground. Adam told them that he had very little more wages to pay away than he had the year before, so that if they all wanted to work under him they must be content with little more than half what each had formerly earned. They agreed, and submitted to be rather pinched; but they hoped it would be only for a time, as it was a very fine harvest indeed, so much labour having been spent upon it, and there being a fine profit into Adam's pocket."

"Did they wear pockets then, sir?"

"No doubt; for the women were improving their tailoring, as much as the men their gardening, and expecting, like them, to increase their gains in consequence; and so they would have done, but that four times the number of labourers appeared next year, so that, notwithstanding the increase of capital, each had not so much as one-third the original wages; and the men grew very cross, and their wives very melancholy. But how could Adam help it?"

"Why did not the men carry their labour elsewhere?" asked Clack contemptuously.

"Why do you go on spinning for Mortimer and Rowe, when Elliot pays higher wages?"

"Because nobody is taking on new hands. I can't get work."

"Well, nobody was taking on new hands in Adam's neighbour-hood; all the capital was already employed."

"But I don't mean to go on so," said Clack. "I shall strike with all the rest of Mortimer's men, if we don't get better paid."

"Aye, it is as I thought, Clack. Adam's head labourer was your grandfather, for he said just the same thing you are saying; and what is more, he did it. They all turned out, every man of them, and let the field take care of itself."

"And what happened?"

"Only half a harvest came up; so that, of course, wages were lower than ever next year. The worst folly of all was that they went on to blame Adam, though he showed them that the harvest would not even pay its own expenses; much less leave anything to divide between him and them. 'You talk to me,' says he, 'as if I could get capital down from the clouds as fast as I please: whereas you might have seen from the beginning, that I have a certain quantity and no more. If you choose to bring a thousand labourers to live upon the capital which was once divided among a hundred, it is your fault and not mine that you are badly off.' "

"If the thousand men agreed to live for so little, it was their own affair, to be sure."

"And if they did not agree, their bidding against each other could not shift the blame upon Adam. If there was such competition among the men as to enable him to obtain more labour for the same wages, he was not to blame, was he, for employing three men for what he had at first paid to one?"

"Nor were the men to blame, sir, for bargaining for such wages as were to be had."

"Certainly. Where then was the evil?"

"Clearly in there being too many hands for the work to be done", replied Gibson. "But who could help that, sir?"

"Nobody could relieve the immediate pressure, Gibson, unless some had the means of taking themselves off, or of applying their labour to some employment which was less overstocked; but all had it in their power to prevent the evil returning. By foresight and care, labour may be proportioned to capital as accurately as my machinery to the power of my steam-engine."

"What has all this to do with our petition?" asked the orator, who was impatient of remaining so long in the background.

"A great deal," replied Gibson. "Mr. Wentworth means to point out how much rests with the masters, and how much with the men, and to warn us against a strike. But, sir, about equalization of wages: you think that fair enough, I suppose. In the very same market, and under the very same circumstances, labour ought to be paid at the same rate, surely?"

"One circumstance, you know, is the extent of the master's capital, which is seldom the same in any two cases, and on which his power of waiting for his returns depends. But I agree with you that a man cannot safely lower his rate of wages much and permanently below that of his competitors, and that an equalization of wages is desirable for all parties; so I will sign my agreement to your wish for a public meeting. Coming, Charles, coming."

Gibson had observed Mr. Wentworth's old gray pony in the yard for some time, and he now saw that Charles looked tired of leading it backwards and forwards while the animal turned its head one way and another, as if looking for its usually punctual master. While helping the gentleman on with the heavy great-coat, which he wore winter and summer, the deputy apologized for having kept the rider and his steed so long asunder.

"Never mind," drawled Mr. Wentworth. "Dobbin and I have two rounds, a long, and a short; and I dare say he has made up his mind already which it will be to-day. If I have helped you to a short cut to your business, you will not think your time wasted any more than I." Then as he buttoned the last button, and pulled his hat over his brows, "That's well: all tight. Hey ho, Dobbin! Good day to ye all."

The shaggy pony pricked up his ears, quickened his pace, and well nigh nodded to his master at the sound of his voice. When Mr. Wentworth scrambled up into the saddle and left the yard at a funeral pace, the deputies looked with much more respect on him and his equipage, than on the brilliant spectacle they had met at Elliott's door.

Chapter IV

UNION OF MEN

As soon as it was ascertained that, though many of the masters declined committing themselves by signing their names, most or all of them would attend the desired meeting. Clack took upon himself to issue a placard, whose large red and black letters attracted the eyes of all who could read. It made known the intention of the masters to meet at the York Hotel, on the Wednesday afternoon, and of the Committee of the men to hold a previous meeting at the

Spread Eagle, in the morning, in order to prepare resolutions to be laid before the masters. The Committee was to be escorted to and fro by a circuitous route by a procession; and the place appointed where those were to meet who wished to make a part of the show, was St. George's Fields. The placard began and ended by an appeal to the people to guard their rights against oppression. Many were surprised at the anxiety of the leading men among the spinners to disown this placard. It seemed to the crowd very spirited and eloquent, and they began to look out their decorations for the procession.

Bray was one of the first on the spot, piping, drumming, and shaking his bells at the appearance of every new group. Other musicians joined the train, flags were displayed, the women gathered to look on, the children cheered and brought green boughs, and all had the appearance of rejoicing, though it would have been difficult for any one to say what there was to rejoice about. Many had no clear idea of what was doing or going to be done: some had no idea at all, and those who knew best thought it a pity that such a display should have been made as might bear the appearance of being intended to intimidate the masters. The Committee were so generally of this opinion, that they did not attend, but went quietly, one by one, to the Spread Eagle; so that, in fact, the procession was formed to escort Clack, and nobody else. This was all the more glorious for him, he thought; and he walked proudly just behind the chief musician, Bray, now shaking hands from side to side, now bowing with his head on his heart, now bidding all halt and giving the signal for groans or cheers. There were three groans at Mortimer and Rowe's, and three cheers at Elliott's, which were received with infinite disdain by that gentleman as he sat at his breakfast table, balancing his egg-spoon and glancing at the newspaper. The procession next overtook Mr. Wentworth in Chancery Lane, pacing to business on his gray pony. All eyes were turned to Clack for a signal whether to groan or cheer. There was, in the meanwhile, a faint beginning of each, at which the pony looked more astonished than his master, who only chuckled and murmured in his usual manner as he looked upon the assemblage with a quiet smile.

"What do you expect to get by this fine show?" said he to a youth near him.

"Cheap bread! Hurrah!" cried the lad waving his bludgeon, and wishing there was a loaf on the top of it.

"And you, and you, and you?" said Mr. Wentworth to one and another as they passed.

"No potato peelings! Reform and good wages! Liberty and cheap bread!" cried they, according to their various notions. The children's only idea was (and it was the wisest) that it was a holiday, with a procession and a band of music.

When Clack had got a little a-head of the slow-moving pony and its rider, he decided to halt and hold a short parley. Advancing with a bow, he said,

"You call yourself the poor man's friend, I believe, sir?"

"No man's enemy, I hope," replied Mr. Wentworth.

"Then allow us the honour of giving you three cheers on your pledge to support our interests this evening. Hats off!"

"Better wait awhile," said Mr. Wentworth. "Cheers will keep, and I dislike unnecessary pledges."

Clack looked suspicious, and nods and winks went round.

"We might differ, you know, as to what your interests are, and then I might seem to break my word when I did not mean it."

"Let him go free," said a bystander. "He knows the consequences if he opposes us."

"That is rather a strange way of letting me go free," observed the gentleman, smiling. "However, friend, threats are empty air to a man who knows his own mind; and my mind is made up to consider the interests of all, come groans, come cheers."

"It is not everybody, sir, who would speak so independently, – to our faces too."

"True, friend. All the masters and all the men have not my years, and have not learned to look steadily in honest faces; and that is why I am sorry to see this parade, which looks too much like intimidation. Come now, be persuaded. I will give you house-room for your flags, and my old friend Bray there shall not lose his job; he shall make it a holiday to the children in my factory."

It was too much to ask of Clack. He could not give up his procession, and so made haste to march on. As Mr. Wentworth turned in at his factory gate in Ancoats Street, every man in the long train bowed respectfully. In his case, the regard of his neighbours was not measured by the rate of wages he paid.

The procession, having deposited Clack at the Spread-Eagle, was by no means so ready to depart as to arrive. They insisted that it should be an open meeting, and that they should have a voice in the demands to be offered to the masters. They rushed through the house to the skittle-ground behind, caused a table with paper and ink to be placed in an arbour, and, setting the Committee entirely aside on the plea that this was a special occasion, began to call aloud for Allen to take the chair. Allen was nowhere to be found on the premises, for the good reason that he was at his work, and knew little of what was going on. Being sent for, he presently appeared and asked what he was wanted for.

"To take the chair."

But Allen was too modest to accept the honour at a word; he drew back, and urged his being totally unused to come forward at public meetings, and named several who understood the management of that kind of business better than himself. Those that he named were all single men; for he bore in mind, – and this certainly added to his reluctance, – that the sin of taking a prominent part in a combination of workmen, is apt to be remembered against the sinner when the days of trouble are over; and he felt that a family man was not the one who ought to be made to incur the risk. – When further pressed, he did not scruple to declare this to be one of his objections; but the people were in the humour to overcome objections, and they promised faithfully that he and his family should not be injured; that if discharged from the factory, they should be maintained by the Union; and that as no one knew so much of their affairs as Allen, as he could express himself with moderation in speech, and with ease on paper, he was the man to be at the head of their affairs, and that it was his bounden duty to accept the office.

Allen could not deny this, and did not, therefore, dally with his duty; but it cost him a bitter pang. While Clack listened and looked on with a feeling of jealousy, and thought it a moment of triumph such as he would fain have enjoyed himself, he little knew how little Allen was to be envied. He could not guess what feelings rushed on Allen's mind at the moment that he took the decisive step into the arbour and seated himself at the table, and received the pen into his hand. Thoughts of the dismay of his timid wife, of the hardships to which he might expose his children, of the difficulties of his office, and the ill-will which its discharge must sometimes bring upon him, – thoughts of the quarrels in which he must mediate, and of the distress which, in case of a turn-out, he must witness, without much power to relieve, – might have overcome a man of firmer nerve than Allen; but though they distressed, they did not conquer him, convinced as he was that he ought not to evade the choice of the people. His fellow-labourers allowed him a few minutes to collect his thoughts before addressing them, and while he was seemingly arranging the papers before him, they packed themselves and one another closely, in order to leave room for new comers, without creating a noise and bustle. Those who stood nearest the arbour hung the flags so as to make a sort of canopy over it, and a few of the most efficient of the standing Committee took their places on each side of Allen. – His address was in natural accordance with the feelings which had just passed through his mind:–

"Combinations are necessary, my fellow-labourers, when one set of men is opposed to another, as we are to our masters. The law could not prevent combinations, even when severe punishments visited those who were engaged in them; which was a clear proof that men must combine, that the law was of no use, and ought therefore to be done away. Let me congratulate you that these severe laws are done away; that a man cannot now be shut up in prison for many months together for agreeing with his companions to withhold their labour in order to increase its price. Let me congratulate you that when a man cannot be caught in the trap of the combination laws, he can no longer be punished under a law against conspiracy, which was made long before such a thing as combinations of workmen were thought of. We can now meet in the face of day, and conduct our bargains with our masters either by agreement or opposition, without any one having a right to interfere, as long as we keep the peace. Evils there are, indeed, still; and such a thing is still heard of as persecution in consequence of a combination; but such evils as are inflicted by the crushing hand of power light on a few, and the devotion of those few secures the exemption of the rest. It is certainly an evil to a peaceably disposed man to see himself regarded with a fierce eye by those to whom he no longer dares touch his hat lest he should be accused of suing for mercy. It is certainly an evil to a man of independent mind to be placed under the feet of any former enemy, to receive his weekly subsistence from the hands of his equals, and to fancy that the whisper is going round – 'This is he who lives upon our gathered pence.' – Such evils await, as you know, him who comes forward to lead a combination; but they belong to the state of affairs; and since they can neither be helped, nor be allowed to weigh against the advantages of union, they should be, not only patiently, but silently borne. Well is it for the victim if he can say to himself that now is the time for him to practise the heroism which in grander scenes has often made his bosom throb. He may even esteem himself honoured in his lot being somewhat of the same cast, – though his own consciousness alone may perceive the resemblance, – something of the same cast, I say, with that of venerated statesmen who have returned to the plough to be forgotten in their own age, and remembered in another, – with that of generals who have held out the decrepit hand with a petition to the gay passers

by to give a halfpenny to the deliverer of their country. – Nay, no
cheers yet! Your cheers only recall me with shame to that which I
was going to say when my personal feelings led me away, – led me
to compare that which is universally allowed to be moving because,
it is noble, with that which, if moving at all, is so only because it is
piteous. As I was saying, combinations are ordered by laws more
powerful than those which, till lately, forbade them; and this
shows the wisdom of the repeal of the latter. If it had been wished
to prevent our meeting for caprice or sport, laws might have
availed. If their object had been to hinder the idle from meeting to
dissipate their tediousness, or the gamesome from pursuing that
on which no more valuable thing was staked than their present
pleasure, these laws might have been successfully, though somewhat tyrannically, enforced. But such are not they who form
combinations; but rather such as have their frames bowed with over-
toil, and their brows knit with care, such as meet because the lives
and health of their families, their personal respectability, and the
bare honesty of not stealing a loaf from another man's counter, are
the tremendous stake which they feel to be put to hazard. Sound
and wise laws can restrain the fiercest passions of the few, because,
being sound and wise, they are supported by the many; and it is
therefore clear that when laws give way like cobwebs before the
impulse of a body of men too united to be brought together by
caprice, those laws are neither wise nor sound. Such were the combination laws, and therefore were they repealed. Never again will it
be attempted to set up the prohibition of parliament against the
commands of nature, – a threat of imprisonment against the
cravings of hunger. Security of person and property being provided
for, (as, indeed, they were already by former laws,) we are left free
to make the best agreement we can for the sale of our labour, and
to arrange our terms by whatever peaceable methods we choose.

"Combination on our part is necessary from power being lodged
unequally in the hands of individuals, and it is necessary for
labourers to husband their strength by union, if it is ever to be
balanced against the influence and wealth of capitalists. A master
can do as he pleases with his hundred or five hundred workmen,
unless they are combined. One word of his mouth, one stroke of his
pen, can send them home on the Saturday night with a blank
prospect of destitution before them; while these hundred or five
hundred men must make their many wills into one before his can
even be threatened with opposition. One may tremble, another may
mourn, a third may utter deep down in his heart the curses he
dares not proclaim; but all this is of no avail. The only way is to

bring opposition to bear upon the interests of the master; and this can only be done by union. The best of the masters say, and probably with truth, that their interests demand the reductions under which we groan. Be it so: we have interests too, and we must bring them up as an opposing force, and see which are the strongest. This may be, – allow me to say, must be – done without ill-will in any party towards any other party. There may be some method yet unknown by which the interests of all may be reconciled; if so, by union we must discover it. But if, indeed, interests must continue to be opposed, if bread must be fought for, and the discord of men must for ever be contrasted with the harmony of nature, let the battle be as fair as circumstances will allow. Let the host of pigmies try if they cannot win a chance against the regiment of giants by organizing their numbers, and knitting them into a phalanx. The odds against them are fearful, it is true; but more desperate battles have been sustained and won. I have not indeed, as the friend at my elbow reminds me, represented our case so favourably as I might have done. Many here think that the power is in our own hands; some that the chances are equal, and the least sanguine, that the chance is fair. – I have spoken of the general necessity of union, and not with any intention of taking for granted that we are on the eve of an express struggle. This depends on circumstances yet to be disclosed. Some change, and that a speedy one, there ought to be in the condition of the working classes; they cannot go on long labouring their lives away for a less recompense than good habitations, clothing, and food. These form the very least sum of the just rewards of industry; whereas a multitude are pinched with the frosts of winter, live amidst the stench of unwholesome dwellings in summer, have nearly forgotten the taste of animal food, and even sigh for bread as for a luxury. The question to be debated, and to be put to the trial if necessary, – and I wish every master in Manchester was here to take down my words for his further consideration, is whether a social being has not a right to comfortable subsistence in return for his full and efficient labour." – Allen's pause was interrupted by a voice from behind the crowd, declaring, –

"No doubt, no doubt, my good fellows: a clear right, and I wish with all my heart you may win your right."

It was Rowe, who had entered as if for the purpose of convincing the men that he was on their side. An opening was made from the table to the outskirts of the crowd; but Rowe slunk back in opposition to all attempts to push him forward. The fact was, he saw another person present whom he little expected to meet, and before whom he was sorry to have committed himself. Mr. Wentworth advanced through the opening, with his memorandum book in his hand: –

"I am willing to put down your question, Allen, for further discussion, provided you add a clause to it: – 'Whether a member of society has not a right to a comfortable subsistence in return for full and efficient labour, *provided he does not, by his own act, put that subsistence beyond his reach?*'"

Allen smiled, and all within hearing stared at Mr. Wentworth's simplicity in adding this clause which nobody could dispute.

"We have certainly nothing to object to your addition, sir," said Allen. "Only I cannot think it necessary."

"Let it stand, however, for my satisfaction; and now go on with what you have to say."

A seat was offered to Mr. Wentworth, and proclamation was made of one for Mr. Rowe, who, however, had disappeared. Allen proceeded: –

"I have only a few words to add respecting the terms on which I will consent to resume my present office on any future occasion, or to accept of any power you may wish to put into my hands. I must be supported by you in all measures taken to preserve our own peace and that of the masters; and to this end, there must be the utmost strictness in the full performance of all contracts. Whether the present dispute be amicably settled this very evening, or whether it be protracted, or a partial or a general strike should take place, – none of these things can set aside a contract previously entered into. Integrity must be our rule as much as liberty is our warrant and justice our end. The first man who deserts the work he has pledged himself to perform, puts the weapon of the law into the hands of our opponents; the first who is legally convicted of a breach of contract, brands our cause with indelible disgrace. We want no truants here, and we will own none but honest labourers to be of our company; and unless I am aided in preserving the reputation of our cause, I declare, – whatever may be thought of the importance of the threat, – that from that moment I withdraw my countenance and my help. If at the period of any strike, and part of my contract with my employers is undischarged, I shall hold it to be my duty to work for them during the stated number of hours, even if I should repair from their factory to preside over a meeting like the present; and the same is expected of every man who enrols himself in our bands. Honour towards our masters is as necessary as fidelity to each other."

The meeting having signified an unanimous assent to what Allen had said, he proceeded to draw up a statement of wages to be presented to the masters. A great number of men pushed and jostled one another in order to get near the table and state their grievances; for some under every firm supposed their wages to be the lowest. It was found to be as the deputies had stated, that Mortimer and Rowe paid the lowest wages, and Elliott the highest. – Mortimer and Rowe were therefore to be requested to answer this evening, yes or no, whether they would give Elliott's rate of wages. Allen, Clack, and Gibson were deputed to wait on the masters with the written demand.

The meeting broke up for a while, and the quietest and most industrious of the men went home, while the rest prepared to parade again through the streets.

Allen withdrew one of the last, as he wished to see the place quiet before he left his post. As he turned from the door of the public-house, his hands in his pockets and his eyes bent on the ground in deep thought, he was startled by some one taking his arm. It was his wife, who had been watching and lingering in the neighbourhood till she was tired and frightened.

"Why, Mary," said her husband, smiling, "you will make me lose my good name. This is the way wives haunt the public-house when their husbands are given to drink."

Mary could trust her husband for soberness if ever woman could; but she feared his being drawn in to join against the masters, and bring ruin on his family.

Allen answered that he was not the man to be *drawn in* to do what his wife knew he disliked as much as she could do; but he might of his own free choice determine to do what she feared; and, in that case, he trusted the discharge of his public duty would not be embittered by domestic opposition and discontent. His prospect was not a very cheering one, however, in this respect. When fairly seated in his own home, his wife seemed prodigiously inclined to lock the door and pocket the key; and she cried so piteously at the bare idea of a strike and its distresses, that Allen longed to go to sleep, and forget all that had been done, and all that was in prospect.

Chapter V

NO PROGRESS MADE

The masters' meeting was a tedious affair to all parties. The chairman and the three deputies held such long disputes, as to whether

wages were really much lower than formerly, that the people who
waited in anxious expectation at the Spread-Eagle, began to
wonder whether the deputies had lain down to take a nap, or found
their business a different kind of affair from what they had expected. If they had known what point was in dispute, they would
have wondered what room there was for argument, as any man
among them could have told what he was paid two years before,
and what now. They all knew that they were now paid by Mortimer
and Rowe, only three and fourpence per one thousand hanks,
while some time before, they had had upwards of four shillings.
How, they would have asked, could there be any doubt as to
whether wages were lowered?

Clack was profuse in his expressions of astonishment at the
stupidity of those who made a question of so plain a matter; but his
wonder did no more towards settling the point than the shuffling of
the chairman, who did not understand the true state of the case,
and could therefore render no service in throwing light upon it.

If it had not been for Mr. Wentworth, and one or two more who
held his views, nothing at all would have been done.

"Nobody doubts," observed Wentworth, "that you now take so
many shillings less than you took five years ago; but that matters
nothing to you or to us."

The chairman and Clack stared in about an equal degree.

"My dear sir, that is the very point," said the one.

"I always thought you had had a heart to feel for the poor,"
cried the other.

"I beg your pardon," said the gentleman quietly, "it is not, sir,
the point in dispute, and I trust, Clack, my observation does not carry
any great cruelty in it. If a penny a week would enable a man to buy
all necessaries for himself and his family, and if a pound would do
no more, would it signify to any man whether his wages were a
penny or a pound?"

"Certainly not; but who ever heard of such wonderful pennies?"

"I have heard of shillings which you might think nearly as
wonderful as such pennies: shillings which would buy more than
twice as much at one time as at another."

"To be sure," said Clack, laughing contemptuously, "every
child knows that the price of bread and other things rises and falls."

"Very well. Your concern is about how much of bread and other
things you get in return for your labour, and not how many shillings. Shillings are of no value to you but for what they buy. If half
the money in the kingdom were to be carried off by fairies this night,
so that you could have only half your present nominal wages, you

would be no worse off than at present. The same quantity of food and clothing would be in the market, and you would get as much for sixpence as you now get for a shilling. This is why I said the nominal amount of your wages mattered little. I said nothing about the real amount."

"But you do not deny, sir," said Allen, "that our real wages are less than they were?"

"I am afraid it is as true as that our profits are less. There is less surplus remaining over our manufacture for us to divide. If this division were made in kind, instead of your being paid in money in advance, you would see the real state of the case, – that we cannot afford higher wages."

"In kind! Lord, sir," cried Clack, "what should we do with a bundle of yarns on a Saturday night? what baker or grocer would take them?"

"None, I dare say; and therefore, for the convenience of the parties, payment for labour is made in money; but it is not the less true that your wages consist of the proportion you receive of the return brought by the article you manufacture. You know how the value of this return varies; how, when an article is scarce, it brings in a large return, and how, when it is plentiful, our customers give less for it; and you must therefore see how your wages vary independently of our will."

"But whose doing is it, sir, that the return varies so much?"

"It is partly your doing; I mean that of those who bring labour to market. We masters have nothing to do with the quantity of labour brought to sale any further than to purchase it. If you bring so much as to reduce its price too far, whose fault is that?"

"To be sure we cannot expect you to pay high, when you can purchase labour cheap," said Allen, "any more than we would give sixpence for a loaf, if we could get as good a one for fivepence."

"If," observed one of the masters, "you brought only half the present quantity of labour to us, we must, whether we liked it or no, pay double for it. If you choose to bring up large families who will in turn rear large families to the same occupation, it is a necessary consequence that wages will fall to the very lowest point."

"What do you call the lowest point?"

"That at which the labourer can barely subsist. If he cannot subsist, he cannot labour, of course. If he can do more than merely subsist, his wages are not at the lowest point."

"Ours are so now," said Gibson, despondingly.

"Not exactly so," replied the manufacturer. "Don't fancy that I wish them lower, or would not make them higher if I could; but I cannot allow that they are at the lowest. Do you know no Irish hand-loom weavers who make only four shillings a week?"

"Poor creatures! yes; but how do they live? Crowded together on straw, with mere rags to cover them, and only half as much food as they could eat. It is dreadful!"

"It is; and God forbid we should see many more sinking down into such a state! I only mentioned their case to show you that your wages may still fall, if the labourers' proportion of the returns to capital is still further divided among a number. Upon the proportion of your labour to our capital depends the rise and fall of wages through the whole scale of payment."

"What would you call the highest rate?" inquired Allen.

"The greatest possible proportion of the return that the capitalist can spare, so as to leave it worth his while to manufacture; and this highest rate is, of course, paid only when labour is difficult to be had."

"We cannot wait till that time," said Clack. "If we waited till a war or a fever carried off part of our numbers, it would do little good; for there are plenty of young ones growing up. We must bestir ourselves and see if a strike will not do as well. The plague would no doubt be more acceptable to gentlemen, as long as it did not stop their manufacture, like a strike; but the poor must raise themselves by such means as are in their own hands, and not wait for a judgment of Providence."

"I quite agree with you," said Mr. Wentworth. "Providence would have men guide themselves by its usual course, and not by uncommon accidents. But I doubt whether a strike is one of the means which will gain your point. It will leave your case worse than in the beginning, depend upon it. A strike works the wrong way for your interest. It does not decrease your numbers, and it does decrease the capital which is to maintain you."

Clack would hear nothing against a strike. Let the masters all give the same wages as Elliott, or prepare for a strike. Rather to silence the orator than with hope of much benefit from the observation, Gibson said that a pernicious multiplication of hands took place from the big piecers being allowed to spin. The masters for the most part liked that they should, because they soon got to employ them to spin at less wages; and too many of the men liked it, also, because it saved them trouble: and some would even sit down to read, while their piecers were looking after the wheels; but it seemed to him very hard that good spinners should be sometimes out of work, while piecers were practising their business.

The masters thought that any regulation of the kind Gibson

wished for, would only have a slight effect for a short time; it could not permanently keep down the spinning population to the number required to ensure sufficient wages.

Clack would not be diverted any longer from the plain answer to his plain question, would Messrs. Mortimer and Rowe raise their wages to Elliott's rate? Rowe took a long pinch of snuff to avoid answering. Mortimer sat bolt upright with his arms folded, and replied, "Certainly not." Not a word more could be got out of him. Others of the masters tried to mediate, proposing that Elliott and Mortimer should meet half-way, that is, at Mr. Wentworth's rate: but this proposal was rejected by all parties. Elliott said he left these things to the people under him; but he believed his clerk was popular with the operatives and wished for no change any more than himself; so that he should not reduce. Mortimer would not be dictated to by a mob; and the representatives of this 'mob' declared their intention of calling Wentworth to account, when they had done with Mortimer, and that his rate must not therefore be proposed for adoption. And thus the matter was no nearer being settled than before.

"Pray is it true," inquired Mortimer, "that you have talked of rooting me out?"

"Such a thing has been mentioned in private, sir," replied Allen, "but immediately scouted. It was never proposed at any public meeting, and will not be mentioned again I dare say."

"So! you have more prudence than I gave you credit for. I almost wish you had made the trial, that you might end by learning your own place. You would soon have known what comes of dictating to us."

This was a signal for Clack to renew his oratory. The peacemakers on both sides found it was time to separate, as there seemed no chance of coming to any agreement. The three men made their bow and withdrew, – Allen with a heavy heart, leaving the masters to agree that the affair must be gone through with firmness and temper; that is, some were for firmness, and some for temper. Mortimer was annoyed at being exposed to annoyance from people so much beneath him; and Wentworth and others thought that the shortest way to a good issue was to regard the claims of the people with respect, their mistakes with gentleness, and their distresses with compassion.

Before Allen could speak a word in reply to the inquiries of his eager companions, Clack began in a strain of indignation to pronounce him a trimmer, for having answered Mortimer as he did about the proposal to root him out. The men being disposed at the moment to listen to everything that regarded the punishment of Mortimer, were hard upon Allen, though not so abusive as Clack. Allen kept his temper, stood the brunt of that to which his rectitude of principle exposed him, stayed till the business of the evening was finished, and then pondered, on his way home, the hard chance by which he was exposed to the displeasure of the masters, the un-reasonableness of his comrades, and the timid complaints of his wife. Allen was not made for ambition.

Before the operatives separated, it was agreed that all employed at a lower rate of wages than Elliott's should turn out the next morning, except the children, whose maintenance would cost so much that it was desirable they should earn as long as allowed to do so. Meetings were to be held from day to day, first to appoint a fresh committee, and afterwards to take measures for securing assistance from fellow-labourers at a distance.

Bray, who had taken care that the meeting should not want for harmony of one kind at least during its sitting, betook himself at its close to the York Hotel, just when the masters were dispersing, and with some degree of impudence stated his desire to be impartial, and his readiness to drum the gentlemen home, if they would please to marshal themselves, as he had played in front of the men in the morning. Elliott called for a waiter to turn the fellow away, and Wentworth observed that he feared his travels had not improved the quality of his wit.

Chapter VI

NIGHT AND MORNING

"How is Martha?" was Allen's first inquiry on meeting his wife at the head of the stairs. Martha had been asleep when he had returned in the middle of the day; for it was now her turn for night-work at the factory, and what rest she had must be taken in the day. Her mother said that her lameness was much the same; that she had seen Mr. Dawson, the apothecary, who pronounced that rest was what her weak limbs most required; and that as perfect rest was out of the question, her mother must bandage the joints while the child was at her work, and keep her laid on her bed at home. Here was the difficulty, her mother said, especially while Hannah was with her, for they were both fond of play when poor Martha was not too tired to stir. She was now gone to her work for the night.

The little girl repaired to the factory, sighing at the thought of the long hours that must pass before she could sit down or breathe the fresh air again. She had been as willing a child at her work as could be till lately: but since she had grown sickly, a sense of hardship had come over her, and she was seldom happy. She was very industrious, and disposed to be silent at her occupation; so that she was liked by her employers, and had nothing more to complain of than the necessary fatigue and disagreeableness of the work. She would not have minded it for a few hours of the day; but to be shut up all day, or else all night, without any time to nurse the baby or play with her companions, was too much for a little girl of eight years old. She had never been so sensible of this as since her renewed acquaintance with Hannah. This night, when the dust from the cotton made her cough, when the smell and the heat brought on sickness and faintness, and the incessant whizzing and whirling of the wheels gave her the feeling of being in a dream, she remembered that a part of Hannah's business was to walk on broad roads or through green fields by her father's side, listening to the stories he amused her with, and to sit on a stile or under a tree to practice a new tune, or get a better dinner than poor Martha often saw. She forgot that Hannah was sometimes wet through, or scorched by the sun, as her complexion, brown as a gipsy's, showed; and that Hannah had no home and no mother, and very hard and unpleasant work to do at fairs, and on particular occasions. About midnight, when Martha remembered that all at home were probably sound asleep, she could not resist the temptation of resting her aching limbs, and sat down, trusting to make up afterwards for lost time, and taking care to be on her feet when the overlooker passed, or when any one else was likely to watch her. It is a dangerous thing, however, to take rest with the intention of rousing oneself from time to time; and so Martha found. She fairly fell asleep after a time, and dreamed that she was attending very diligently to her work; and so many things besides passed through her mind during the two minutes that she slept, that when the overlooker laid his hand upon her shoulder, she started and was afraid she was going to be scolded for a long fit of idleness. But she was not harshly spoken to.

"Come, come, child; how long have you been asleep?"

"I don't know. I thought I was awake all the time." And Martha began to cry.

"Well, don't cry. I was past just now, and you were busy enough; but don't sit down; better not, for fear you should drop asleep again."

Martha thought she had escaped very well; and winking and

rubbing her eyes, she began to limp forward and use her trembling hands. The overlooker watched her for a few moments, and told her she was so industrious in general that he should be sorry to be hard upon her; but she knew that if she was seen flagging over her work, the idle ones would make it an excuse to do so too. Martha curtsied, and put new vigour into her work at this praise. Before he went on in his rounds, the overlooker pointed to the window and told her morning was come.

It was a strange scene that the dawn shone upon. As the grey light from the east mingled with the flickering, yellow glare of the lamps, it gave a mottled dirty appearance to everything; to the pale-faced children, to the unshaved overlooker, to the loaded atmosphere, and even to the produce of the wheels.

When a bright sunbeam shone in through the window, thickened with the condensed breath of the work-people, and showed the oily steam rising through the heated room, the lamps were extinguished, to the great relief of those who found the place growing too like an oven to be much longer tolerable. The sunbeams rested now on the ceiling, and Martha knew that they must travel down to the floor and be turned full on her frame and some way past it, before she could be released; but still it was a comfort that morning was come.

She observed that the overlooker frequently went out and came back again, and that there was a great deal of consultation among her betters as the hours drew on. A breath of fresh air came in now and then from below, and news went round that the gates were already open, two hours earlier than usual. Presently the tramp of heavy feet was heard, like that of the weavers and spinners coming to their daily work. Martha looked up eagerly to the clock, supposing that the time had passed quicker than she had been aware of; but it was only four o'clock. What could bring the people to their work so early? They could scarcely have mistaken the hour from the brightness of the morning, for it had now clouded over, and was raining a soaking shower. More news went round. Those who had arrived had barely escaped being waylaid and punished for coming to work after a strike had been proclaimed. They had been pursued to the gates and very nearly caught, and must now stay where they were till nightfall, as they could not safely appear in broad daylight, going to and returning from their dinners. Many wondered that they had ventured at all, and all prophecied that they must give up to the will of the Union if they wished to be safe. The overlooker, finding much excitement prevailing on the circulation of the news, commanded silence, observing that it was no concern of any of the children present. There was no strike of the children, and they would be permitted to go and come without hinderance. Martha determined to get away the first moment she could, and to meet her father, if possible, that he might not encounter any troublesome people for her sake.

Allen was watching the moment of release as anxiously for his little daughter as she could have done for herself, and he was to the full as weary as she. On the previous evening he had carried home paper and pens, preferring to write the necessary letters at his own dwelling to spending the night at the Spread-Eagle. He got his wife to clear and wipe down the deal table, when she had put all the children to bed; and then he sat down to compose a pattern letter, stating the circumstances which had led to a strike, and urging an appeal to their fellow-workmen in distant places for aid in the struggle which might be deemed a peculiarly important one. Having tolerably well satisfied himself that the letter was the proper thing, he read it to his admiring wife, who by turns smiled because she was proud of her husband, and sighed to think how perilous an office he had undertaken. She then went to bed and was soothed to sleep by the scratching of his nicely-mended pen. From this time all was silence in the apartment, except the occasional crackle when Allen folded his paper, or the cautious taking up and laying down of the snuffers when the long candle-wick craved snuffing, or the passing squalls of the baby, who, however, allowed himself to be so quickly hushed as not materially to disturb the scribe.

When nearly twenty copies of his letter had been written, each varying a little from the original, according to the differing circumstances of those to whom it was addressed, Allen was so weary that he could write no longer without some refreshment. He put out his light, and opened the window for a minute to breathe the fresh air. The pattering of the rain wakened his wife, who roused herself to fret over the weather and wonder how Martha was to get home. Her husband told her he meant to go for the child, and would carry a shawl to wrap her up in. If Mary had known what lions were in her husband's path, she would not have let him go.

There was but one man visible when Allen went forth, and he was walking rapidly at some distance. It was Hare, – who, having never been well disposed towards a turn-out, and being supported in his dislike of it by his wife, hoped to avoid mischief and continue his earnings by going to the factory before people should be looking for him, and doing his work as usual, without talking about wages to anybody. Such devices did not suit the purposes of the Union, and were guarded against, as in all similar cases. Hare thought it just possible that he might meet with opposition, and looked as far before him as his eyes could reach; but he did not suspect an ambush on either hand. When he continued in the same direction, however, so as to render it certain that he was making for the factory, six men issued, one by one, from opposite alleys, and formed a line across the street. Hare's name was shouted to some one still concealed, coupled with a question whether he was under contract.

Having received their answer, they coolly told their trembling fellow-workman that as he had not the pretence of any contract, and was nevertheless going to work at an unfair price, he must be ducked. They had a rope ready, and would deliver him up to be dragged through the river.

Hare turned from one to another with as large a variety of excuses as he could invent at the moment. Among the rest, he vowed that he came to watch who would be wicked enough to go to work at this same factory after having sworn to strike. He was laughed at, let off with a roll in the kennel and with being hunted part of the way home, whether he ran to seek refuge with his wife in panting terror, and presenting a woeful spectacle of disgrace. He perhaps owed it to his known cowardice that he fared no worse; as his companions were well assured he was sufficiently daunted not to attempt to cheat them a second time.

Allen proceeded at his best pace while this judgment was being inflicted on Hare, never supposing that he could be suspected of taking work unfairly; but, like all eminent men, he had his enemies, and these chose to take for granted that he could not be going to the factory with any honest design. He was seized, girded with the dreadful rope, and hauled towards the river, though he produced the shawl, demanded time to call witnesses, and used all the eloquence he could command. His last resource was to explain that the supplies from a distance must be delayed if any harm happened to him. This occasioned a short pause, during which the night-children came forth from the factory. One of the ambush, who had some sense of justice, and wished to find out the truth about Allen, ran up to Martha, as soon as she appeared, and before she could know what had happened, and asked her whether her father was not late in coming to work this morning?

"He is not coming to work at all," said the child; "but he said he would come for me. Perhaps the rain made him stay at home."

This testimony released Allen, and disappointed some of the lads who stood round of a frolic, which they had desired to fill up the time till they could proceed to a frolic of a different kind. They looked up at the clouds, and hoped the rain would not make the parson cheat them. They were going to be married. Several had begun to think of this some time before (as lads and lasses that work together in factories are wont to do); and this seemed the very time, when they had a holiday they did not know what to do with, and were sure, they believed, of ten shillings a week as long as the turn-out should last. So, amid the warning looks of elderly friends, and the remonstrances of parents who justly thought this the worst possible time to take new burdens upon them, several thoughtless young couples went laughing through the rain to the altar, and snapped their fingers at the clergyman behind his back because his careful enquiries brought to light no cause why the solemnization of matrimony should not proceed.

Chapter VII

A COMMITTEE

This was an eventful day. The masters published a placard, (not, however, signed by all,) threatening to turn off every man in their employ who should continue, after a certain day, to belong to the Union. The effect was exactly what the wisest of them expected; the turn-out became general; and the workmen, being exasperated, put new vigour into all their proceedings. Their Committee was enlarged and instructed to sit daily. Delegates were despatched on tours to distant places, with authority to tell the tale, and collect supplies; and the people at home consented to receive, for their weekly maintenance, no more than half what the young bridegrooms had settled as the probable allowance. Five shillings a week was to be allowed as long as the children remained at work; and in case of their employment failing, the sum was to be increased in proportion to the capability of the fund. Weekly meetings were ordered to be held in St. George's Fields, at which any one should be welcome to attend; and it was agreed that it would be worth while going to some expense to have the proceedings of the body made public through the newspapers.

Allen was strongly in favour of having only three members of the Committee sit daily for the dispatch of common business; viz., the treasurer, secretary, and one of the other members, in rotation, for the sake of a casting vote. He knew enough of such Committees to believe that ill-natured tittle-tattle was particularly apt to find its way into them, and that quarrels between masters and men were often kept up by these means long after they would naturally have died out; and that a weekly sitting, at which the three members should be accountable for all they had done, would be sufficient for the interests of the association. The proposal gave offence, however; some supposing that he wanted to keep the power in few hands, others being unwilling to enjoy the pomp and privilege of their office no oftener than once or twice a week, and some honestly thinking that the voices of all were wanted for the decision of questions daily arising. Allen would have cared little for his motion being rejected; but, in spite of all the allowance he strove to make, it vexed him to the heart to hear evil motives assigned for every proposition which did not please the people. He often said to himself that it must be a very different thing to sit in a committee of gentlemen where opinions are treated as opinions, (*i. e.*, as having no moral qualities, and to be accepted or rejected according to their expediency,) and in a committee of persons who expose their deficiencies of education by calling all unkind or foolish who differ from themselves. Such remarks appeared to Allen to proceed from the same spirit which tortured martyrs in former days, and proscribed the leaders of a combination in the present.

Any one committee-meeting afforded a pretty fair specimen of all. Sometimes there were more letters than at others, sometimes larger, sometimes smaller remittances than had been expected, and occasionally none at all. Sometimes there was a dearth of gossip about the sayings and doings of the masters, and then again an abundance of news of spiteful devices and wilful misrepresentations and scornful sayings, for which there should be a sure retribution. But the same features distinguished all; and one sketch will therefore describe the whole.

A little before ten, the committee-men might be seen tending towards St. George's road. They could win their way but slowly, for they were continually waylaid by one or another who had some very important suggestion to make, or question to answer; or a piece of news to tell which would sound well in committee. Allen was the most sore beset.

"Lord! Allen, what work yours must be with such a many letters to write! Why, it must cost a mint of money to pay postage."

"All for the cause, you know. Let me go, will you? I am rather late."

"Not a clock has struck yet, man, and I want to know whether it's true about the large order that's gone to Glasgow because Elliott can't execute it?"

"All true, perfectly true. Good bye."

"Well, but have you seen Elliott since? Lord! I should love to see him look chap-fallen when he finds the power is with us."

" 'Tis for us to look chap-fallen, I think," said Allen, trying to disengage his button; "where's the power if more such orders go the same way?"

"Stop, Allen, one thing more. Do you know, several of us are of a mind that it is a disgrace to the Union that Wooller, with his large family, has no more on a pay-day than Briggs."

"Briggs has a sick wife, and his children are too young to work."

"Wooller must have more, however, and that you'll find to your cost, if you don't take care. Pretty encouragement to turn out, indeed, if such a man as he is to be sacrificed to worse men than himself!"

"Let him carry his complaint to the proper place, if he is discontented. The committee ordered his allowance, and it is they must alter it, not I."

Allen now thought he had made his escape; but his gossip called after him that he had something to tell him on which the whole fate of the strike depended. Allen was all ear in a moment. It was said, and on very good authority, that the masters would never employ a Manchester man again. They had sent to Glasgow and to Belfast, and all over England, and if they could not get workmen enough by these means, they would bring them in troops from abroad.

"Who told you this?" said Allen, laughing.

"That's between him and me," replied the gossip mysteriously; "but you may rely upon it, it is true."

"Aye, we have been told so twice a day since we turned out," said Allen; "but that is no reason why we should believe it. You might as well tell me they mean to take their mills on their backs and march over the sea to America."

"You may laugh, sir, but I'm far from as sure as you that we are not going to ruin."

"I am sure of no such thing," replied Allen. "I wish I were; but if we are ruined, it will not be by French people spinning in Chorlton Row."

A knot of smokers, each with as much to say, stood or lolled about the door of the Spread-Eagle. Allen looked at the window of the committee-room, and wished he could have got in that way; but there was no escape from the file of questioners. Several of his companions were ready to tell him that he was late, when he at length took his seat at the end of the table, and began to arrange his papers.

"I know it; but I left home half an hour since. I have been stopped by the way."

"And so you always will be. You're so soft, man, you're not fit for office if you can't say 'no.' "

Dooley, the representative of the Irish hand-loom weavers, here took up Allen's defence, urging that it would be too hard if the people out of office might not make their remarks to those who were in; and that a secretary must be as stony-hearted as the last speaker to refuse them a hearing.

"Come, come; to business," cried Allen, to stop the dispute. "But first shut the door, Brown, and make every one knock that wants to come in. If they won't obey at once, slip the bolt. We must preserve the dignity and quiet of the Committee."

"O, by all manner of means," said the Irishman, sitting down demurely at the board, and twirling his thumbs; "it puts me in mind of the way his honour set us to play when we were children –"

"I have here a letter from number three," Allen began, as if all had been silence, "who has prosecuted his journey successfully as far as Halifax, from whence he hopes to transmit, in a post or two, a sum nearly as large as was contributed by that place to the Bradford strike. It will gratify you, I am sure, to know with how much friendly anxiety our fellow-labourers watch the result of our present noble struggle; and I trust you will agree with me that their suggestions are entitled to our respectful attention. Dooley, be so good as read the letter to the Committee, while I look what must be brought forward next."

"With real pleasure, Mr. Secretary; but first I'll take leave to wet my throat with a little ale or spirits. It's dry work reading and advising, and a clear sin to keep so many men shut up on a summer's day with not a drop to help their wits."

"Whatever is ordered is at your own cost, remember," said Allen; "and I would recommend your going elsewhere to refresh yourself. Meanwhile, will some one else have the goodness to read the letter now under consideration?"

After much complaint and discussion, Dooley was prevailed on to be quiet and let the business go forward. Having first loaded Allen with abuse and then with praise, he tried to behave well, much in the same way as if his priest had put him under penance.

The letter in question and some others having been discussed and dismissed with due decorum, a member brought before the notice of his fellow-workmen a calumny which he believed had been widely circulated, and which was likely to impair the credit of the association, and thus to deprive them of the countenance of their distant friends and of all chance of reconciliation with the masters. It was said and believed –

A push at the door. "Who is there?"

"Only Tom Hammond."

"Learn what he wants."

Tom Hammond only thought he would look in and see whether it was a full committee-day, and how they got on: which thought only occasioned the door to be shut in his face, and the delivery of an admonition to go about his own business and leave other people to manage theirs in quiet.

"Well; what was this libel?"

It was said that the Committee had taken upon themselves to go round as inspectors, and to examine the work done by all members of the Union, and determine whether the price given for it was fair or not. Allen thought it incredible that any of the masters could have given heed to so absurd a report; but if one instance could be brought of its having been actually believed, he would be the first to propose some measure of effectual contradiction.

Clack would wish that the secretary was somewhat less inclined to make light of the information brought to the committee by some who were as likely to know what was going forward as himself. The association was not to lose its character because its secretary chose to laugh at the foul calumnies circulated against it, and which seemed anything but laughable to those who had the honour of the Union really at heart. And so forth.

The secretary begged to explain that nothing was further from his intention than to risk the good name of the association; and he must further assert that no man breathing had its honour more at heart than himself. He need but appeal to those who had heard him say but just now – And so forth.

The result was a resolution that a paper should be drawn up and presented to the masters, containing an explanation of what the office of this committee consisted in; *viz:* – not in determining the value of work and the rate of wages, but in managing the affairs of the turn-out after the strike had been actually made; in collecting and distributing money, and conducting the correspondence and accounts.

While Allen was consulting his companions about the wording of this letter, the rub-a-dub of a drum, accompanying shrill piping, was heard approaching from a distance, and presently the sounds of merriment from without told that Bray was among the smokers on the outside. Sometimes a rumble and screech seemed to show that the unskilful were trying his instruments, and then it appeared from the heavy tread and shuffling of feet that some were dancing horn-pipes under his instructions. Dooley soon started up.

"Let us have Bray in here. He'll put a little life in us, for all this is as dull as sitting at a loom all day. We make it a point of honour, you know, not to trample on a fallen man. We let Bray come and go as if he was still one of us, poor cratur."

"Wait till he comes," said Allen. "He is thinking no more of us at this moment than we need think of him."

Dooley returned to his seat with the mock face of a chidden child, and walking as softly as if he trod on eggs, twirling his thumbs as before. He had not long to wait for his diversion. Bray suddenly made a lodgment in the window, sitting astride on the sill with his drum balanced before him and playing with all his might, so as almost to deafen those within. When he saw the vexed countenances of two or three of the men of business, he ceased, dropped into the room, rolled his drum into a corner, flung his belled cap behind it, and said, –

"Don't scold me, pray. I'll make it all up to you. I'll have bars put up at the windows at my own cost to prevent any more idle fellows dropping in upon you when you have made all safe at the door. Moreover, I will give you the benefit of my best wisdom at this present time. What's the matter in hand?"

The Committee found their advantage in the consideration which made them admit Bray to their councils, though he had no longer any connexion with their affairs. His natural shrewdness and travelled wisdom were valuable helps upon occasion. When the terms of the disclaimer were agreed upon, Bray told them he had something of importance to say, and he should say it out as plainly as he had heard it, since he hoped they were all men, all possessed of resolution enough to bear what might be said of them, and to surrender their own gratification for the public good.

Clack was the first to give a vehement assent. With his hand on his heart, he protested that he would take his heart in his hand and give it to be toasted at the hangman's fire, if it would do the cause any good. All with different degrees of warmth declared their readiness to sacrifice or to be sacrificed. Allen's assent was given the last and the least confidently, though without hesitation. He had inwardly flinched on first hearing Bray's portentous words, but the recollection that he had already devoted himself, restored his firmness and prepared him for whatever might be coming. He would have flinched no more, even had Bray's story concerned himself instead of another.

"I have been a pretty long round this morning," said Bray, "and among other places to Middleton, and there some good fellows and I had a pot of ale. Who should come in there but a traveller who deals, I am told, with several firms in this place. Well; he heard us talking about the strike, and not liking, seemingly, to overhear without speaking, like a spy, he joined in with us, and talked like a very sensible man, – more so than I should have expected, considering how much he has clearly been with the masters."

"You never miss a stroke at your old enemies, Bray."

"As long as they are enemies to me and such as me, I shall give them a hit at every turn. Well; this gentleman told us that he could speak to the dispositions of the masters, if any one could; and he was positive that if the men would take one step, they would soon have overtures from the masters. 'If,' said he, 'they will prevent Clack from having anything to do with their strike, the masters will begin to come round from that moment.'"

"Turn *me* out!" exclaimed Clack. "Prevent *my* having anything to do –"

Bray pursued as if Clack were a hundred miles off. " 'They think that fellow,' says he, 'a vulgar speechifier that knows nothing about the matter in dispute, and is only fit to delude the more ignorant among the spinners and to libel the masters. Send him back into the crowd where his proper place is, and then you will see what the masters have to say to the Committee.' "

Allen endeavoured to stop remarks which it must be painful enough to Clack to hear under any form, and which were made needlessly offensive by Bray, who was rather glad of the opportunity of giving a set down to the mischief maker. Clack was necessarily soon stopped also by general consent. He raged and vowed revenge in such a style that it was plainly right to dismiss him now if it had not been so before. He could no longer be trusted with any degree of power against the masters, if the Committee wished to preserve their character for impartiality. As soon as he could be persuaded to leave the room to have his case considered, it was agreed to recommend him to resign, if he wished to avoid being regularly deposed at the next public meeting. He preferred the appeal to the public; and his companions could only hope that the masters would hear of what had passed, and would take the will for the deed.

It was next proposed by a member of the Committee that a sum of money should be presented to Allen in consideration of his services; and he had the pain of hearing himself lauded at the expense of Clack, according to what seemed the general rule, to admire one man in proportion to the contempt with which another was treated. If Rowe was railed at, Wentworth was praised; if

Clack was complained of, Allen was immediately extolled. Being aware of this, Allen would have declined the gift, if for no other reason than that a fit of generosity might be transient; but he had other reasons for refusing to listen to all mention of a gift. He chose to keep his disinterestedness beyond all question; and he feared that the funds were about to decline on the whole, though liberal contributions were looked for from particular places.

To stop further argument, which he intended should be unavailing, he returned brief thanks to his companions and broke up the Committee.

Chapter VIII

A TETE-A-TETE

It was the policy of the Committee to hold the public meetings of the workmen on pay-days, in order that they might appear on the green refreshed and in good spirits, and thus give the masters the most favourable impression possible of their resources and of the vigour with which they meant to maintain the strike. This arrangement had not the effect of raising the spirits of the leaders. Pay-day was an anxious and painful day to them. In addition to all the sad stories of distress which they must hear, and the discontent which they must witness, there was a perpetual dread of the fund appearing to decline, and of the confidence of the people being therefore shaken. It was frequently necessary to borrow money, – sometimes as much as a hundred pounds at a time, – on the security of what was to come in during the next week; and even those least disposed to foresight could not help asking themselves and each other what was to be done next time, if the remittances of the week should not superabound.

Allen was turning these things over in his mind as he proceeded to the Spread-Eagle on the morning of the day when Clack was expected to be dismissed from the Committee by the public voice. News was afloat which did not tend to cheer his spirits, though he thought he discerned in it a sign that the measures already taken concerning Clack were prudent. Ann Howlett, Clack's betrothed, had been taken up on a charge of breach of contract, and had been committed to prison by the magistrate. This woman having been singled out as an example seemed to indicate enmity against Clack; and if it was indeed necessary to propitiate the masters by sacrificing him, it was well that the sacrifice was offered by the Committee before the arrest of the woman instead of in consequence of it. A more painful piece of intelligence followed. Immediately after this arrest, a carrier, who was conveying work into the country for Mortimer and Rowe, was attacked on his way out of the town, his cart ransacked, himself beaten, and the work carried off in triumph. Ten or twelve men had been concerned in the outrage; and it was acknowledged that they belonged to the Union; but Allen in vain attempted to learn who they were. His integrity was so well known, that it was understood that he would deliver the offenders up to justice, be they who they might; and therefore, though many knew no one would tell. Mute signs and obscure hints conveyed that Clack headed the enterprise; but nothing in the shape of evidence was offered.

Mr. Rowe was standing at his window when Allen's gossips left him to pursue his way. The gentleman threw up the sash, looked cautiously up and down the street, to ascertain whether he was observed, and then mysteriously beckoned to Allen to come into the house.

"What do you want with me, sir?"

"I want a little conversation with you, that's all. Can't you come in for a quarter of an hour?"

"If I could find any one to take my place at the board," replied Allen, who thought that some overture might be coming. "If you will let me step to the Spread-Eagle or write a note, I am at your service."

The plan of writing a note was preferred, on condition that Allen should not say whence or why he wrote. He saw that the gentleman glanced over his shoulder, to see whether he kept his word, and turning sharp round, held up the paper in Rowe's face, saying,

"There is honour on the part of us men, I assure you, sir, whatever suspicion there is on the part of you gentlemen. Read the note, if you please."

Rowe did as he was desired, disclaiming suspicion, of course, and getting entangled in a complimentary speech which Allen listened to very quietly, waiting, with his arms by his side, for the end of it.

As an ending did not come readily, however, the gentleman broke off in order to send the note. He gave a penny to a child in the street to carry the note to the Spread-Eagle, and run away directly without saying where he came from; and then returning, made Allen sit down and take a glass of ale, – particularly fine ale, – such capital ale that the gentleman often indulged himself in a draught with a friend.

When nothing more remained to be said about ale, Mr. Rowe sighed, and observed what a pity it was that people should fall out to their mutual injury, and that those who had power to reconcile differences should not endeavour to do so.

Allen asked what party was meant by this description.

"You," replied Rowe, shaking him warmly by the hand. "You must know, Allen, that you can do what you please in the Union; and I only wish you knew how the masters look up to you, and respect your manly, moderate conduct. Any proposition from you would meet with attention from both parties; if you would –"

"I beg pardon, sir; but you forget that my propositions are before the masters already, and do not meet with attention. My propositions are those adopted by the Union –"

"Yes, yes; I know well enough what they are; but you must bring forward something new. Is there nothing else you can propose that we can support without going from our word?"

"Just tell me plainly," said Allen, "since you seem to like plain speaking: will you yourself make a concession about raising the wages to a middle point, if we yield some of our demands of equal importance?"

"Why, you see," replied Rowe, edging his chair closer, and filling Allen's glass, "I don't want to come forward the first in this kind of thing. Indeed, as a junior partner, I ought not so to commit myself. I can't be the first, you see; but I have no objection to be the second. Yes, you may, between you and me, depend upon my being the second."

"Between you and me!" exclaimed Allen, laughing. "That leaves me nothing to propose to the meeting. See now how they would laugh at me! – 'My fellow-workmen, I propose that we should lower our demands because a person (I am not at liberty to say who) offers, between himself and me, to yield in part after others have yielded.' Why, sir, they would jeer me off the stand, or bid me say to their concealed opponent, 'Thank you for nothing. If others have yielded first, we shall owe nothing to you.'"

"Well but, Allen, you don't seem to me to know the difficulty I am in, if you use my name. You don't know how unpleasant –"

"Pardon me, sir, I do know. You and I are neither of us men of nerve, Mr. Rowe, and so far, you have chosen your listener well. Clack would have laughed in your face, by this time, and been half way to the Spread-Eagle to tell the people there all that you have been saying; but I have so far a sympathy with you that I know the misery of looking round and seeing entanglement with one party or another on every side – blame from one or another sure to come. I know the longing to be somehow out of the scrape, the shrinking back with the hope of keeping out of sight, the dread of every one that comes near lest some new difficulty should be arising. I can pity you, sir, for all these feelings, for I have felt them myself."

"Have you? have you indeed?" replied Rowe, grasping his hand again. "What a sad thing it is for you, then, to be a leader of a turnout."

"I am of a different opinion, sir. Because these feelings are natural to some persons, it does not follow that they should be indulged. It will not do to indulge them, sir, believe me. We have our duties as well as men of our make on the field of battle; and we must surrender ourselves, like them, to our duties, or be disgraced in our own eyes. Happen what will within us or without us, it is for you and me to speak out, to act openly, and bear the consequences. You will excuse my freedom."

Another grasp of the hand, with a speech about the secretary's integrity; upon which Allen rose, saying, –

"Then as we are of one mind, sir, suppose we go together to the meeting, and say what we have to say there, instead of shut up in this parlour. I believe I can promise you a courteous hearing."

"O no, no; that is quite out of the question. I have no offer, you know, to make on behalf of the masters, – nothing to say that I should think of occupying the meeting with."

"Then you can have nothing to say to me, sir, since, as an individual, I have no power to negotiate. Good morning, Mr. Rowe."

"Stay a moment, Allen. You understand that the men are not to know of this interview; and it is of more importance still that the masters should not. Promise me, Allen."

"I can promise no such thing," said Allen, returning from the door. "I regard your consent to be the second to raise wages as a concession, and I was going to report it to Mr. Wentworth."

"For God's sake don't!"

"I must," said Allen, firmly; and all entreaty, all reproach, was in vain.

"At least, don't give up the name. The fact will do just as well without the name. Give me your word to conceal the name till you see me again."

Out of pure compassion, Allen yielded thus far. Mr. Rowe accompanied him to the house-door, harping upon "the name, the name," till Allen turned round to say gravely.

"A promise once given is enough, sir, between honest men. I have given you my word."

"True, true, my good friend. It is only a trick I have got of repeating my sentences."

And the gentleman shut the door behind his guest, feeling very like a child who has persuaded her maid not to tell her governess who broke the china cup; knowing all the time that the mishap must come to light, and trembling every time any one goes near the cupboard.

Chapter IX

A PUBLIC MEETING

"How much did you fall short to-day?" inquired Allen, as he joined in with a group of committee-men going to the meeting.

"Sixty pounds; but we shall make it up before three days are over, depend upon it; and, besides, the masters will yield as soon as Clack is done for, you'll see. Wentworth is before us, going to the meeting. But what have you been about, Allen, playing truant on pay-day?"

"Preaching fortitude and giving a fillip to the faint-hearted."

"As Christian a duty as feeding the hungry and easing the poor," observed a companion. "If Allen is absent from a good deed, you may be sure he is doing a better."

There was no part of Allen's duty that he disliked more than opening the weekly meetings. The applause discomposed him. He could not, like Clack, make a deprecating flourish of the hands, or shake his head modestly, or look round with a proud smile. He was very apt to fidget and swing his hat, and make a short, ungraceful bow. As soon as he found this out, he adopted one posture, from which he determined not to move till the thing was over. He folded his arms and dropped his head upon his breast, and so stood as if facing a gust of wind, till the clapping had sunk into silence. – This day, the clapping on his appearance was twice as long and twice as vehement as usual, Clack's former popularity being transferred to himself. Mr. Wentworth appeared in time to share his honours, and to relieve him from applause, which seemed as if it would never end. Clack would fain have appropriated both series of cheers; but he could not manage it. As soon as he began to bow and look flattered, there arose cries of "Off, off!" which strengthened into groans when he attempted to brave them. With a nervous sneer, the orator observed to those within hearing that his time would soon come, when he would carry off more cheers than any of them.

"Better put yourself under Allen's wing, if you want to be clapped," observed Mr. Wentworth. "I conclude it was because I stood next to him that they cheered me to-day, instead of groaning, as they did a week ago. We must submit to be beholden to Allen – hey, Clack?"

With a look of ineffable contempt, the orator withdrew as far as he could from Allen, without going out of sight, while Mr. Wentworth sat down to take a pinch of snuff on the edge of the waggon in which the speakers were stationed.

The object of the meeting was to obtain the opinions of the people on certain questions to be proposed; and, in order to put Clack out of the pain of suspense, his affair was the first brought on. Allen expressed himself in the most moderate terms he could devise, saying that it sometimes happened that the usefulness of an individual was not in proportion to his zeal in the cause he had espoused, or to his desire to fulfil its duties, especially where the likings of two opposite parties had to be consulted; that it so happened, in the present case, that the individual in question did not possess the confidence of the masters, and that his remaining a member of the Committee might therefore prove an obstacle in the way of an amicable agreement. It was for the meeting to declare whether they were willing to take the chance of an accommodation by naming some substitute for Clack, who might be equally energetic in their service, and more agreeable to their employers. After a pause, and with evident effort, he added, that if the conduct of the person in question had been, in all respects, such as the Union could approve, it would have gone hard with the committee before they would have sanctioned his removal from office; but, as it seemed too evident that the cause had received injury by his means in ways which he might be spared the pain of pointing out, they might consider themselves relieved from the perplexity of reconciling consideration for the individual with a regard to the interests of the body.

A hubbub ensued; a strong party of Clack's friends raising shouts on his behalf, while opposing cries rose on all sides of "Down with the blusterer!" "Who waylaid the carrier?" "He is none of us. The Union keeps the laws." "Law and concord! No Clack!"

Quiet was restored on Mr. Wentworth's rising to explain that his being present was not to be considered as a sign that the masters would yield on Clack's dismissal. He had no authority to confirm any such belief.

Applause, – and Clack doomed by an overwhelming majority; whereupon his supporters made their way to the waggon, agreed with him that the meeting was not worth addressing, even if he *had* been allowed to speak; and carried him off on their shoulders to fish for popularity in the streets of Manchester, while the meeting conducted its affairs as well as it could without him. So ended that matter, except that somehow Clack and his party were forestalled in their return into the town, and the walls everywhere presented, conspicuous in white chalk, the phrase which still rang in their ears, "Law and Concord! No Clack!" An extraordinary number of little boys too seemed to have taken the fancy to mimick the action of weaving, with arm and foot, crying at the same time

> "Clickity, clickity, clack,
> Lay him on his back!
> Clickity, clickity, clack,
> Away let him pack!"

Far more decorous was the meeting in their rear, while the queries were dismissed, each in its turn.

"The case of Ann Howlett being admitted by all parties to be a hard one, (her contract being for wages which would not support her,) was her breach of contract sanctioned by the Union?"

Shouts of "No; we would have helped her to perform it!"

"If this breach of contract had been sanctioned by the Union, was it thought lawful revenge for the committal of Ann Howlett to waylay the carrier and strip his cart?"

Groans, and shouts of "No revenge!"

Some one near the cart having spoken to Allen, he put the question, –

"Supposing this attack to have no connexion with Ann Howlett's affair, does the Union sanction forcible attempts to prevent work being carried into the country?"

Answer, "No. Law and Concord for ever!"

"If the men abide by the law, and the masters are found disposed to concord, will the Union be disposed to concession?"

Mixed cries, the most distinguishable of which was, "Stick by the Union! The Union for ever!"

Mr. Wentworth and Allen exchanged nods, as much as to say, "You see" – "Yes, I see."

"Supposing the Union to be preserved entire, are its members disposed to any concession in respect of wages?"

Cries of "Equalization!"

"An equalization is, as the Committee knows, indispensable;

but the point on which the Committee has not yet received your instructions is whether that equalization may be fixed below the highest rate, *viz.*, that which Elliott is now giving?"

The answers were at first hesitating, then confused, so that no one prevailed.

"Don't press for an answer yet," said Mr. Wentworth. "I may tell them something which may help their judgments."

Way was made for Mr. Wentworth, and he presented himself to speak.

"Before you put this question to the vote, let me just mention a circumstance or two that you may not be aware of, from your having been lately out of communication with the factories. There are few things that we hear more of than of the changes that all mortal things are liable to; and these changes affect the affair we have in hand, like all other affairs. We are told that every one rises from sleep in the morning a different man from him who lay down at night; there having been a waste and repair of the substance of which the bodily man is composed. In the same manner, you may find that your strike is a different thing to-day from what it was at its beginning. Some of its parts have fallen off, and others have been added. Whether your body, having undergone this change, be the more vigorous, like a man refreshed with sleep, you know better than I. But further, whenever you return to your work, you may find a factory a very different place on re-entering from what it was on your leaving it. There has been much waste, I fear, without any repair. You know what kind of waste I refer to. You have heard of large orders, which we have been unable to execute, having been sent to Scotland and elsewhere. You know that much of our capital, which ought by this time to be returning to us again, has been for many weeks locked up in our stocks of raw material. You know that the expense of keeping on our establishments has not been repaid by the production of goods for the market; or the cost of maintaining ourselves and our families, by the profitable employment of our time and our wits. We have been consuming idly, and so have you; and thus there must needs have been great waste. – And what is it which has been thus wasted? The fund which is to maintain you; the fund out of which your wages are paid. Your strike has already lasted long enough to change our ground of dispute. You will find that the question with the masters now is, whether fewer of you than before shall be employed at the same wages, or fewer still at higher wages, or as many as before at lower wages than you have yet received. Keep on your strike a little longer, and the question will be, how many less shall be employed, at how much less. Keep it on long enough, and the question will be entirely settled; there will be no wages for anybody. Do you understand me?"

The speaker took snuff while the murmur of disapprobation went round, and then continued.

"I do not suppose, any more than you, that we shall come to this pass, because your capital must be exhausted sooner than ours, and then you must have bread, and will come to us for work before our fund for wages is all wasted away; but the nearer you drive us to this point, the more injury you do yourselves. Let me hear your objection, friend," he continued to a man in the crowd who looked eager to speak. "Where do you think me wrong? You acknowledge that a strike is a bad thing, but sometimes necessary to obtain a good one. Refusing wages altogether for a time, is to be the means of securing better afterwards. Do I understand you right? Why, that would be very true if you had the power or were in the habit of keeping workmen and wages in proportion to each other. If the masters had more capital than was necessary to pay you all at the rate you have hitherto received, you might gain your point by a strike, not as you sometimes do now, just for a little time till the masters can shake themselves free of their engagement, –but permanently. But this is not the case. The masters' capital does not return enough to pay you all at the rate you desire. If they are to keep their capital entire, you must either take less wages, or fewer of you must take wages at all. If you will all have the wages you desire, the capital which pays them wastes away, and ruin approaches. This is the worst event that could happen, as I am sure we shall all agree. Your alternative, therefore, is to withdraw a portion of your people from taking wages, or all to take less than you are striking for. You are not satisfied yet? (speaking to the same man.) Well, let me hear. There are places where there are no strikes, because the workmen get as high wages as they wish for? Very true; there are such places, and London is one; concerning which I heard, the other day, a case in point.

"The money wages of skilled labour in London were higher from 1771 to 1793 than was ever known. They had been raised because prices were high. They were afterwards somewhat lowered; but as prices fell in a greater proportion after the war, the real wages of skilled labour are at present higher than they had ever been. They cannot be lowered while, as at present, there is an occasional deficiency of labour, since the men would strike when most wanted by the masters, and the loss thus caused would be greater than the gain of giving lower wages. In London there are two seasons in every year; a slack season in which many workmen remain unemployed; and a busy season in which they work overhours, because there are not hands enough. Now, here, you see, lies their advantage; in the supply of labour being limited. If it was the case with them, as with you, that some of their class always remained unemployed, the unemployed would undersell the busy, and wages would fall. Then, as here, there would be strikes; and then, as here, strikes would be of no avail. Where there are permanently fewer workmen than are wanted the men hold the power. Where there is the exact number that is wanted, the power is equal, and the contest fair. Where there are more than are wanted, even to the extent of three unemployed to a hundred, the power is in the masters' hands, and strikes must fail. Must there not be a larger surplus of unemployed labour than this in our neighbourhood, and elsewhere, since wages are fallen too low to enable the labourer to do more than barely exist? Allen, is there a silk small-ware weaver present, do you suppose? They have just struck, I find."

Proclamation was made for a silk small-ware weaver, and several held up their hands. In answer to questions, they stated that within two years their wages had been reduced forty-five per cent. Two years before, common galloon weaving was paid at the rate of 1*s* 10*d*. per gross; it was now reduced to 1*s*. 4*d*. per gross; and it was for an addition of 2*d*. per gross that the men struck: little enough when it is considered that, in the winter season, a weaver cannot average more than twelve gross per week. As he has to pay for the hire of his loom, for winding, for candle-light, and other expenses belonging to his work, he left only about 8*s*. a week for himself and his family.

"Could so dreadful a reduction have ever taken place," continued Mr. Wentworth, "if you had not undersold one another? And how are the masters to help you if you go on increasing your numbers and underselling one another, as if your employers could find occupation for any number of millions of you, or could coin the stones under your feet into wages, or knead the dust of the earth into bread? They do what they can for you in increasing the capital on which you are to subsist; and you must do the rest by proportioning your numbers to the means of subsistence. But see how the masters are met! In Huddersfield the masters are doing their utmost to extend their trade; but the multitudes who are to subsist by it increase much faster. There are now thirteen thousand workpeople in that place who toil for twopence half-penny a day. At Todmorden, the most skilful work fourteen hours a day for the pittance of one shilling. In the fair county of Kent there are thirty thousand who earn no more than sixpence a day. Compare this state of things with the condition of skilled labour wages in London, and see how much depends on the due proportion of labourers, and the capital by which they are to be fed. Would you could be convinced that your strike, besides occasioning vexation and ill-will between the two parties, besides inflicting distress upon your-selves, and inconvenience upon your employers, cannot but be worse than in vain!"

During the last few sentences, several persons had been engaged in conference with Bray, who leaned over a corner of the waggon to hear what they had to say. He now came forward and placed himself beside Mr. Wentworth, observing that all that had fallen from the gentleman seemed pretty true and reasonable as far as it went, but that it did not at all explain what course the people had now to pursue. It was poor comfort to tell the people that wages could not be any higher on account of their numbers, since it was not in their power to lessen those numbers.

"It is not with the view of giving present comfort," replied Mr. Wentworth, "that I represent what appears to me to be the truth: for alas! there is but little comfort in the case any way. My object is to prevent your making a bad case worse; and if it were possible, to persuade you not to prepare for your descendants a repetition of the evils under which you are yourselves suffering. All that you can now do, is to live as you best may upon such wages as the masters can give, keeping up your sense of respectability and your ambition to improve your state when better times shall come. You must watch every opportunity of making some little provision against the fluctuations of our trade, contributing your money rather for your mutual relief in hard times, than for the support of strikes. You must place your children out to different occupations, choosing those which are least likely to be overstocked; and, above all, you must discourage in them the imprudent, early marriages to which are mainly owing the distresses which afflict yourselves and those which will for some time, I fear, oppress your children. You ask me what you must do. These things are all that I can suggest."

"But these things, sir, will not guard our children any more than ourselves from the fluctuations in trade you speak of."

"But they will prevent those fluctuations from being so in-jurious as they now are. The lower wages are, the more are such fluctuations felt. In India, where an average day's wages are only three-pence, the people live in the poorest possible manner, – such as the poorest of you have no idea of. Any decrease of wages, therefore, makes the more weakly of the labourers lie down and die. In Ireland, where the average is five-pence a day, there is less positive starvation than in India, but more distress on a fall of wages, than in England. In England, such fluctuations are less felt than in old days, when the people knew nothing of many things which you now call necessaries. The better the state of the people, the better able are they to stand against the changes to which all trades are liable; but the worst of it is that we are all too little inclined to foresee the effects of these changes, and to provide for them; and when we experience the necessary consequences of a change which took place twenty years before, we are apt to suppose these consequences arise from something amiss at the present time. When a demand for any article of manufacture makes labour unusually profitable, labourers provide for a great decline of wages in future years, by bringing up large families to the same employment. During many years, that is, while their children are growing up, they feel no ill effects, and suppose that all is going on right. When a decline of wages comes, they suppose it happens from some new circumstance, and not from their own deed in overstocking the labour market. Again; it must be some time before the effects of a decline in lessening the supply of labour are felt. A part of the population perishes slowly from want and misery, and others are made prudent in respect of marriage; but by the time these checks are seen to operate, a new period of prosperity has arrived, which is ascribed by the people to accident. It is this impossibility of making the supply of labour suit the demand at a moment's notice, which makes fluctuations in trade so sensibly felt, for good or for evil, by the labourer. Since he cannot, as you say, Mr. Bray, diminish the number of workmen when trade is slack, and if he wishes his descendants not to be plunged into degradation by extreme poverty, he will do what in him lies to prevent population from increasing faster than the capital which is to support it."

Mr. Wentworth was encouraged to pursue his argumentative manner of speaking by the attention of the people near the waggon. Some of them had become a little tired of the weekly meetings at which their orators had said the same things over and over again, and were pleased to be reasoned with by one whom they esteemed, and to obtain, by these means, a better insight into their affairs than was given them by leaders who were all of one party. The more the present meeting assumed the character of a conference, the more eagerly the most thinking men in the crowd pressed towards the waggon, and cheered the questions and replies. Those on the outskirts, who were more fond of noise and display, were at liberty to come and go as they pleased; to listen to Mr. Wentworth, or to follow Clack.

Bray now observed that population must increase rapidly indeed, as it had outstripped the increase of capital in the cotton manufacture. He believed so rapid an increase of capital had never been known before. To this Mr. Wentworth replied by asking of the crowd whether there was any one among them who had known James Hargraves. An old man stept forwards and said that he was a native of Blackburn, and had been accustomed, as a boy, to frequent Hargraves' workshop; that he remembered seeing the carpenter busy about his invention, and his own delight at having the design of the spinning-jenny explained to him by the inventor; he saw directly how eight threads could be spun instead of one, and thought it a very fine thing, and had little notion how soon it would be so much improved upon as that a little girl might work one hundred, or one hundred and twenty spindles. When was this? Why, a few years after the old king George began to reign; in 1767, he believed.

"When that king came to the throne," observed Mr. Wentworth, "the whole value of the cotton goods manufactured in this country was only 200,000*l.* a year."

"There were very few people employed in it then," interrupted the old man. "We had no factories and no towns full of cotton-spinners and weavers. My father used to take his work home to his own cottage, and grow the flax that was then used for warp in his own garden, and set my mother to card and spin the raw cotton for the weft. This, and getting the warp from Ireland, was the way till Arkwright's spinning frame came into use."

"Then was the time", said Mr. Wentworth, "that the people in China and in India had no rivals in the market for whatever was made of cotton. We owe it to these machines, and the mule-jenny, and the power-loom that came in afterwards, that though we have to bring our cotton from thousands of miles off, and though the wages in India are, as I said, only 3*d.* a day, we have beaten them in the competition, and can carry back their cotton five thousand miles, made into a cheaper fabric than they can afford. Such powers as these must make our capital grow; and the fact is that the cotton manufacture is the chief business carried on in the country, and that it has enabled us to sustain burdens which would have crushed any other people. Instead of 200,000*l.*, the annual produce of the manufacture is now more than 36,000,000*l.* We have no means of knowing how few persons were employed sixty years ago; but it is reckoned that the manufacture now affords subsistence to more than 1,400,000 persons. This enormous population has arisen naturally enough from the rise of the manufacture; but your present condition shows that it has already gone too far; and it rests with yourselves to determine whether the evil shall be found to have increased fifty years hence. And now, Allen, you know the reason of the clause I added to your query in the arbour."

"Will our trade go on increasing?" was the next question asked.

"I hope and trust that it will, as we have got the start of our competitors abroad; but it will probably increase at a slower rate; and a succession of strikes may prove its destruction."

Here the speaker abruptly ceased, and nothing could induce him to say more. He let himself down from the waggon, and quietly made his way through the crowd, thinking perhaps that the people would draw their inferences from what he had said more freely in his absence.

The substance of Mr. Wentworth's argument, and especially the last words he spoke, left Allen and others thoughtful. They would not, on the impulse of the moment, advise a compromise with the masters; but appointed another general meeting for the next day, to take into consideration some matters of important concern.

One matter of important concern was taken into immediate consideration, however. As soon as Allen had turned his back, some members of the committee recalled the crowd for a few minutes, related how Allen had, from time to time, refused money in compensation for his services, and moved that a suit of clothes should be voted to him. This was a present which he could not refuse, if given under colour of enabling him to appear more respectably as their advocate before the masters, and would serve to make a proper distinction between such a sound friend to their cause as Allen, and such a frothy fellow as Clack. The motion was carried by acclamation; and as all Allen's scruples were so forestalled as that he could not decline the gift, he was, before nightfall, clothed in a suit which must mark him out at the meetings as leader of the Union proceedings.

Chapter X

HOPE DECLINING

Alas! what is so fleeting as popularity! Allen's was in great part gone before morning. Some mischievously disposed persons, who had marked what impression had been made on the mind of the secretary by Mr. Wentworth's speech, and who had afterwards ascertained that he wished to propose a compromise with the masters, took upon themselves to make known that the favourite secretary had turned tail and meant to betray the cause. A general gathering about the waggon of all who scorned to be betrayed was advised, in order to keep his friends at a distance and to raise a hiss with the more effect. When, confident of his reception, Allen advanced with a smiling countenance, in order to express his gratification at the mark of esteem he had received, he was startled by a burst of groans and hisses. For a moment he looked about him to see if Clack or any other unpopular person was standing near; but signs not to be mistaken convinced him too soon that he was the object of the people's dislike. He coloured scarlet, and was about to cover his face with his hands, but checked himself, and, by a strong effort, stood it out. Those who were near him saw how the papers in his hand shook; but his countenance was fixed and his attitude firm. After many vain attempts to make himself heard, he stripped off his new coat, folded it up and placed it in the hands of the committee-men near, and sent a messenger home for his working dress. This he communicated to the meeting the first moment that they would let him speak. He would not accept any gift from those to whom his services were no longer acceptable. He was ready to resign his office, – an arduous office, which they no doubt remembered had been forced upon him, – as soon as they should direct him into whose hands he should deliver his papers. In the meanwhile, he would proceed with their business, forgetful of all personal considerations.

All propositions, whether made by himself or others, tending to a compromise, were rejected, and the meeting, after a stormy discussion, in which no point was settled, broke up. The whole affair put Clack and his friends in glee, and filled wiser people with grief and apprehension of the consequences.

The first consequence was that all the children were turned off. The masters were bent on bringing the affair to a close as speedily as possible; and, being disappointed in the hope that the men would propose a compromise, endeavoured to drive them to it.

This was thought by some parents far from being the worst thing that had happened. While the Committee shook their heads over this weighty additional item of weekly charge, many tender mothers stroked their children's heads and smiled when they wished them joy of their holiday, and bade them sleep on in the mornings without thinking of the factory bell. – It was some days before the little things got used to so strange a difference from their usual mode of life. Some would start up from sound sleep with the question, "Father, is it time?" Some talked in their sleep of being too late, and went on to devour their meals hastily, as if their time was not their own. – It would have amused some people and made others melancholy to watch the sports of these town-bred children. One little girl was seen making a garden; – that is, boring a hole between two flints in a yard with a rusty pair of scissors and inserting therein a daisy which by some rare chance had reached her hands. Others collected the fragments of broken plates and teacups from the kennels, and spread them out for a mock feast where there was nothing to eat. The favourite game was playing at being cotton-spinners, a big boy frowning and strutting and personating the master, another with a switch in his hand being the overlooker, and the rest spinners or piecers, each trying which could be the naughtiest and get the most threats and scolding. Many were satisfied with lolling on the stairs of their dwellings and looking into the streets all day long; and many nursed their baby brothers and sisters, sitting on the steps or leaning against the walls of the street. Hannah Bray, when not abroad with her father, took pains to stir up her little neighbours to what she called play. She coaxed her father into giving them a ball, and tried to teach the children in the next yard to play hide and seek; but she often said she never before saw such helpless and awkward people. They could not throw a ball five feet from them, or flung it in one another's faces so as to cause complaints and crying-fits. In hiding, they always showed themselves, or came out too soon or not soon enough, or jostled and threw one another down; and they were the worst runners that could be conceived. Any one of them trying to catch Hannah looked like a duck running after a greyhound. Hannah began with laughing at them all round; but observing that her father watched their play with tears in his eyes, she afterwards contented herself with wondering in silence why some children were so unlike others.

The affairs of all concerned in the strike looked more and more dismal every day. There were more brawls in the streets; there was less peace at home; for none are so prone to quarrel as those who have nothing else to do, and whose tempers are at the same time fretted by want. All the men who were prone to drink now spent hour after hour at the alehouse, and many a woman now for the first time took to her "drop of comfort" at home. Many a man who had hitherto been a helper to his wife and tender to his children, began to slam the door behind him, after having beaten or shaken the little ones all round, and spoken rough words to their trembling

mother. While she, dashing away her tears, looked for something
to do, and found one thing that she would wash if she had fuel and
soap, and another that she would mend if she had material and
cotton. – Now was the time to see the young woman, with the babe
in her arms, pushing at the curtained door of the dram-shop, while
her husband held it against her, – he saying, – "Well, I tell you
I'm coming in five minutes; I shan't be five minutes," – and she
plaintively replying, "Ah, I know, you always say so." – Now was
the time to see the good son pacing slowly to the pawnbroker's to
pledge his aged mother's last blanket to buy her bread. These were
the days when the important men under the three balls civilly
declared, or insolently swore, that they could and would take no
more goods in pawn, as their houses were full from top to bottom,
and there was no sale for what they had encumbered themselves
with. Never before had they been so humbly petitioned for loans, –
a mother shewing that her winter shawl or her child's frock would
take very little room, – or a young girl urging that if a pawnbroker
did not want her grandmother's old bible he could get more for it
at a book-stall than she could. These were the times for poor landlords to look after their rents, and for hard landlords to press for
them. These were the days for close scrutiny to be made by the
Union Committee whether men's wives were really lying-in, and
whether each really had the number of children he swore to; and,
therefore, these were the times when knaves tried to cheat and
when honest men were wounded at having their word questioned.
Now was the time when weak-minded men thought themselves
each worse off than his neighbour. Many landlords were pronounced
the hardest that ever owned two paltry rooms; many an applicant
was certain the committee had been set against him by some
sneaking enemy. In the abstract it was allowed, however, that the
sneakers had the most to bear. Hare, for one, was in the depth of
distress. Opposition was made, week after week, to his having any
relief from the committee because he was not a hearty member of
the Union; and on one occasion, when he had with the utmost
difficulty obtained an extra shilling for his lying-in wife, and had
failed in his plea that he was dunned for rent, he found on returning
home that his landlord had sent in the officers during his absence,
who had taken away all the little he possessed, but the mattress on
which his wife lay. It was laid on the floor, the bedstead being
gone; and the children and their mother were left crying within
four bare walls. – Allen, to whose knowledge this hard case was
brought, could do little to relieve it; but he almost succeeded in
convincing his nervous wife that their own sufferings were light in

comparison. Yet they had many painful sacrifices to make, – the more painful to Allen because his wife was not convinced that they were necessary. She urged that he might now ask for some of the money the Committee had formerly offered him, since his services had not been repaid even in empty good-will, to the degree that he deserved. It was his duty, she thought, to demand more than the common weekly allowance; and the least he could do for his children was to take the suit of clothes back again which he had thrown away in a pet. Failing in her arguments, she had recourse to two measures, – one of action and the other of persuasion. She went secretly to the Committee, and asked in her husband's name for the clothes, which she sold on her way home, trying to persuade herself that she was only doing a mother's duty in providing her children with bread; and then she assailed her husband on the subject of taking work at the master's prices. She knew that he now wished for a compromise and thought the strike had been continued too long, and she would not see why he was bound to wait till the Union viewed the matter as he did. She thought it very cruel to talk of honour, and very absurd to plead duty when he knew that his family were in want, and could not deny that it was not by his own choice that he had filled so conspicuous a station. It made Allen very miserable to hear her talk in this manner, sobbing between almost every word she said; especially when little Martha looked wistfully from one to the other, not understanding the grounds of the dispute, but hoping that it would end in father's leaving off walking about the room in that manner, and in mother's stopping her sobs, and in there being something better than those nasty potatoes for dinner. Once or twice she tried to make her bulfinch sing so loud that they could not hear one another speak; but this did not do, for her mother twitched off her apron and flung it over the cage, so that the poor bird cowered down in a corner for the whole day afterwards.

One morning when Allen had persuaded his wife that he was immovable, and that the best thing she could do was to go out and buy some potatoes with what money they had, he came and leaned over the table to see Martha feed her bird.

"You are as fond of that bird as ever, Martha."

"Yes, – and I have so much time to teach him things now."

"Had you rather play with him or be at the factory all day?"

"I don't know. My knees are so much better since I have been at home, and I like playing with Billy; but mother has got to cry so lately; and, father, we are all so tired of potatoes, we don't know how to eat them."

"Poor child! I wish we could give you anything better. But, Martha, do you think you could bear to stay at home without Billy?"

Martha's countenance fell.

"You see, my dear child, we have sold almost everything we have; and when we can scarcely get food for ourselves, it does not seem to me right to keep animals to feed. This was why I sold the dog so many weeks ago."

"But, father, it is only just a halfpenny now and then. Mother has always found me a halfpenny now and then for Billy."

"A halfpenny is as much to us now, child, as a guinea is to some people; besides we could get money by Billy. Ah! I knew it would make you cry to say so."

And he left her and walked about the room in the way which it always frightened Martha to see. She sobbed out a few words, –

"I can't – I can't help crying, father, but I don't mean – I wish you would take Billy and sell him."

"Listen to me, my dear child," said Allen sitting down by her, and putting his arm round her waist. "You were always a very good little girl in working industriously as long as you had work. Now you cannot earn money by working, but you can get some by giving up your bird. Now, you know I always tried to make you as comfortable as I could when you earned money, and I promise you, that I will do the same if you will let me sell your bird. The very first money that I can properly spare, when better days come, shall go to buy you a bird, and this very bird if we can get it back again."

Martha thanked him, and said the bird should go for certain; but if this very bird could not be got back again, she would rather have a triangle like Hannah's, and then, she thought, they might all grow rich. Allen smiled and said they would see about that when the time came; in the meanwhile, if Billy was to go, the sooner the better, and all the more as she had just cleaned the cage; and he took his hat.

Martha struggled with her tears, and asked if she might go too. Her father thought she had better not; but she said nobody could make Billy sing all his songs so well as herself; so her father kissed her, and let her follow him down stairs, asking Field's wife who happened to be in good humour, to have an eye to the children till their mother came home.

It was a sad trial to Martha to hear the bird-fancier speak slightingly of her pet, and remark that the cage was very shabby. She had a great mind at first to make Billy seem dull, which she knew how to do; but remembering that this would punish nobody but her father, she put away the evil thought, and made Billy sing his best songs in his clearest tone. The bargain was made; her father bade the bird-fancier pay the money into her hand, and whispered that he wished he had anything which would sell for so much. When they were on the threshold, she once more turned round. The man was twirling the cage in a business-like manner, between his hands. "O, once more!" cried Martha, running back. Once more Billy fluttered at the sight of her, and put out his beak between the wires to meet her lips; and then she went away without looking back any more. Every day for the next fortnight, however, little Martha lingered about the bird-fancier's door, doing all she could without being observed, to set Billy singing. One day she was remarked by her parents to be very silent; and after that she went out less. She had missed Billy, though his empty cage still hung in the shop; and having made bold to ask, had found that he was sold to a country customer; really gone for ever. This hope destroyed, Martha tried to comfort herself, as she had proposed, with visions of a triangle.

Chapter XI

FINAL DELIBERATION

The spirits of the people were sunk, not only by poverty, but by a more bitter disappointment than had attended any former strike. The Combination Laws having formerly been the great object of dread and hatred, it had been too hastily supposed that the repeal of these laws would give all that was wanted; whereas the repeal only left the people free to make the best bargain they could for their labour, without its having any thing to do with the grounds of the bargain. The repeal could not increase the supply of capital, or diminish the supply of labour; it could not therefore affect the rate of wages.

One more event was looked to with hope; the arrival of the delegates who had travelled in search of support. They had remitted money as they had received it, and the remittances had fallen off much of late; but it was still hoped that the messengers might bring such assurances of sympathy and support, as might justify the people in holding out a little longer. These men, who returned nearly all at the same time, were met some miles out on the road, greeted with cheers, carried to the Committee-room, and with difficulty left alone with the Committee to tell their business.

These men brought advice and intelligence so various as might have perplexed the most discerning and prudent of all managers of public affairs. There were exhortations from some places to hold out to the very last shilling; and from others to retreat, while retreat could be managed with honour. Some distant friends gave them a kindly warning to look for no more contributions from that quarter; and others were sorry to send so little at present, but hoped to raise such and such sums before they should be much wanted. Some sent word that it had always been a bad case which they could not in conscience support, while so many more promising needed help; others declared that if ever there was a righteous cause, this was it, and that they should brand with the name of traitor the first who quailed. While the members of the Committee sighed and inquired of one another what they were to think of such opposite advice, and each delegate was vehement in urging the superior value of that which he brought, Allen proposed that they should abide by the advice of the London delegates, who had been in communication with persons who understood more of the matter in hand, than any who occupied a less central situation. All agreed to this, and the consideration of the matter was deferred till the next morning, when the delegates were expected to have arrived from London.

Every member of the Committee was in his place the next morning, and the expected messengers appeared at the foot of the table, and delivered in their report, which was brief enough. Their London friends believed their strike to be in a hopeless condition, and advised their making the best terms they could with their masters, without any further waste of time and capital. Not that all combinations were disapproved of by their London advisers; there were cases in which such union was highly desirable, cases of especial grievance from multiplication of apprentices, or from unfair methods of measuring work, or from gross inequality of wages, &c.; but for a general and permanent rise of wages, no strike could ultimately prevail, where there was a permanent proportion of unemployed labour in the market. A proportion of three per cent. of unemployed labour must destroy their chance against the masters.

"Just what Wentworth told us," observed a committee-man. "Pray did you inquire whether it is possible to get a rate of wages settled by law?"

"Of course, as we were instructed so to do; and the answer is what you probably expect, – that unless the law could determine the amount of capital, and the supply of labour, it cannot regulate wages. The law might as well order how much beef every man shall eat for his daily dinner, without having any power to supply cattle. If there be not cattle enough, men cannot have law beef. If there be not capital enough, men cannot have law wages."

"Besides," observed the other delegate, "wages-laws involve the same absurdity as the combination laws we are so glad to have got rid of. Every man who is not a slave has a right to ask a price for his labour; and if one man has this right, so have fifty or fifty thousand. What is an innocent act in itself, cannot be made guilt by being done by numbers; and if Government treats it as guilt, Government treats those who do it as slaves. Government then interferes where it has no business. This was the argument in the case of the combination laws, and it holds in this case too: Government is neither buyer nor seller, and has nothing to do with the bargain; and having nothing to do with it, could neither pass a just wages-law, nor enforce it when passed, any more than in the case of the combination laws, which we all know to have been unjust and perpetually evaded."

As it was now clear that the turn-out must come to a speedy end, the committee decided to waste no more time in discussion, but to proceed to immediate action. Allen begged to produce the accounts, which were balanced up to the present day, and the sight of which would, he thought, quicken their determination to let all get work who could. He had for some time found it difficult to get a hearing on the subject of the accounts, as his brethren were bent on holding out, and would listen to nothing which opposed their wishes; but they were now completely roused. "How much have we left?" was their first question.

"Left!" exclaimed Allen. "You know I have been telling you for this fortnight past that we are deficient 70*l.*, without reckoning the bills for advertisements, which had not then come in, and which, I am sorry to say, swell the amount considerably."

This declaration was received with murmurs, and on the part of some, with loud declarations that there must have been mistake or bad management.

Allen passed his hand over his forehead, while enduring the bitter pang caused by this outcry; but he recovered himself instantly.

"There are the accounts," he said. "See for yourselves whether there has been any mistake, and bring home to me, if you can, your charge of bad management. You pressed the task upon me in the first instance against my will; you referred it to my disinterested-ness to resume it, when, fearing that I had lost the confidence of the people, I would have resigned it. At your call, I have done my best, and – this is my reward!"

There was a cry of "Shame, shame!" and two or three friends rose in turn to say for Allen what he was too modest to say for himself; that the unthankful office had been repeatedly forced upon him, because there was no other man who could discharge it so well; that he had never been detected in a mistake, never found in the rear of his business, never accepting fee or reward, never –

This eulogium was interrupted by objections. He *had* erred in involving the Union with the editor of a newspaper, who now unexpectedly brought an enormous charge for the insertion of notices, intelligence, &c., which it had been supposed he was glad to print gratuitously. Allen *had* also claimed fee and reward in a way which, to say the best of it, was shabby.

Allen calmly related the facts of the transaction with the editor, leaving it to his judges to decide whether the misunderstanding arose from carelessness on his part, or from some other cause. As to the other charge, what fee or reward had he taken?

"The clothes, the clothes!" was the cry. "To send for them privately to sell, after pretending to give them back in the face of the people. Fie! Shabby!"

Allen looked on his thread-bare dress with a smile, supposing this a mistake which a moment would clear up. He went to the press belonging to the committee, where the clothes had been deposited, and flung open the doors. He looked very naturally surprised at their having disappeared, and turned round with an open countenance to say.

"I see how it is. Some dishonest person has used my name to obtain possession of the clothes. I give you my word of honour that I have never seen the clothes, or known that they were not here, since the hour that I gave them back in the face of the people."

All believed him, and some had consideration enough to command silence by gesture; but before it could take effect, the fact was out, that Allen's own wife was the "dishonest person." While he silently walked to the window, and there hid his face in his hands, his friends called on business which attracted attention from him. It was pay-day, and what was to be done? What funds were in hand?

Allen returned to his seat to answer this question; and, as all were just now disposed to do as he pleased, he carried his point of honesty, and obtained authority to lessen the allowance one-half, and give advice to every applicant to attend the afternoon meeting for the purpose of voting for the dissolution of the strike.

Of these applicants, some were glad, and some were sorry to receive the advice of the paymaster; but there was a much greater unity of opinion about the reduction of the allowance. Some murmured, some clamoured, some silently wept, some sighed in resignation; but all felt it a great hardship, and wondered what was to become of them either way, if it was true, as Mr. Wentworth had said, that the wages-fund of the masters and the Union-fund of the men were wasting away together. Some were ready with bad news for Allen in return for that which he offered to them.

"You will be worst off, after all, Allen; for there is not a master that will give you work."

"Did you hear, Allen, what Elliott said about you? He hopes you will go to him for work, that he may have the pleasure of refusing you."

"Mortimer has got a promise out of his cowardly partner, that he will not let you set foot on the premises, Allen, on account of the part you have taken."

"They say, Allen, that you are a marked man in Manchester, and that no master in any trade will take you in among his men. What do you think of doing, I wonder?"

This question Allen could not have answered if he had wished it. It was again put to him by his wife, who waited for him in the street to tell him through her tears all the evil-bodings which a succession of Job's comforters had been pouring into her ears since the news of the probable dissolution of the strike had got wind. "What do you think of doing, I wonder?" was still the burden of her wail.

"Do you know that man?" replied her husband, pointing to a wasted and decrepit man who was selling matches; "that man was once a well-paid spinner. He lost his health in his employment, and now, at forty years of age, is selling matches from door to door. He has submitted to God's will. I too will submit to sell matches, if it be God's will that I should lose my good name as innocently as that man has lost his health."

"I told you how it would be. I told you –" cried Mary.

"I too foresaw it, Mary, and prepared myself for much; – but not for all."

He reproached her no further for the injury she had done to his good name than by declaring his unalterable will that not an article should be purchased by her beyond a bare supply of daily food till the clothes were bought back again and restored to the Committee, or their full value, if they could not be recovered.

Chapter XII

HOPE EXTINCT

There had been a lingering hope among some who would fain have stood out longer, that this day's post would have brought the wherewithal to build up new expectations and prolong the struggle. The wiser ones had resolved that not even the receipt of 200*l.* should shake their determination to return to work; but there was no question about the matter, for no money came. – A prodigious amount of business was done in the few hours preceding the final meeting. The masters met and settled that they would give no more than the medium wages, – that is, the rate given by Wentworth; Elliott carelessly consenting to lower his, and Mortimer being with difficulty persuaded to raise his. Rowe was consulted only as a matter of form, and the other firms had to make slight differences or none at all. They agreed to yield the point of their men belonging to the Union, since it appeared vain to contest it while of importance, and needless when not so. – The men settled that they must agree to a medium rate of wages, and make what they could of having obtained an equalization, such as it was, and of being permitted to adhere to the Union. – Clack agitated for his own private interest, – to get himself appointed to some salaried office in the Union, as he was no more likely to obtain employment from the masters than Allen. – So much was settled beforehand as to leave little to be done at the meeting but to make a public declaration of agreement.

With dark countenances and lagging steps the people came, – not in proud procession, with banners and music and a soldier-like march, but in small parties or singly, dropping into the track from by-streets and lanes, and looking as if they were going to punishment rather than to consultation. There was a larger proportion than usual of ragged women and crying babies; for, as the women had been all along opposed to the strike, they were sensible of a feeling of mournful triumph in seeing it dissolved. Bray was present without his pipe and his bells, for this was no time for lively music; but he carried his drum to be used as a signal for silence if the speakers should find any difficulty in obtaining a hearing. He beat a roll between each proposition submitted and agreed to; and thus did his last service to the turn-out he had watched from its commencement.

Proposed: – That as the masters are represented to be inclined to concession, the men shall do their part towards promoting an adjustment of their differences, agreeing to take such and such a rate of wages, provided that the masters pay all alike, and that the men be not disturbed in their peaceable adherence to the Union. – Agreed.

Proposed: that the men shall set apart a portion of their weekly earnings, as soon as able to do so, and in proportion to the size of their families, in order to liquidate the debt incurred on account of the strike now about to be closed. – Murmurs.

Allen came forward to state the gross amount of subscriptions and expenses, intimating that the account-books would be left at the Committee-room for one month, open to the inspection of all who could prove themselves to belong to the Union. It would be seen through what unavoidable circumstances a debt had been incurred, and how essential it was to the honour of the body that it should be liquidated as soon as possible.

No reasonable exception could be made to any of the items of expenditure. The people could only wonder that there should be such crowds of children to receive pay, so many lying-in women to be relieved, so many sick persons to be aided, and so much to pay for printing and advertising. They could not deny that the expenses of the Committee had been very small.

This explanation finished, Allen's part was done. He had neither faults of his own nor favours of theirs to acknowledge. He spoke not of himself, but, when he had rendered his account, gravely made his bow and retired.

Clack then came forward, and, supported by a powerful party of friends near the waggon, succeeded in obtaining the public ear. With more success than delicacy, he enlarged upon his public services, pleaded his betrothment to one who was now suffering under the persecution of the masters, as a title to their support, as well as the certainty that he should not again be employed by any firm in Manchester. He declared that were it only through zeal for their rights, he would marry Ann Howlett as soon as she came out of prison –

"If she will have you," cried somebody; and the crowd laughed.

Clack repeated his declaration without noticing the doubt, and moreover declared his willingness to travel into every county in England, Scotland, and Ireland, in behalf of the Union. He boasted of his connexions in all places, and pointed out the wisdom there would be in employing him as a missionary of the Union, in preparation for any future struggle. – This proposal went a degree too far in impudence, or Clack might, perhaps, have gained his object; for he seemed to have recovered his hold on the people in proportion as that of better men had been weakened. A plain statement from the Committee that, as they were in debt, they had no power at present to appoint a missionary, served, however, to disappoint Clack's hopes. He skilfully laid hold of the words "at present," and left it an understood matter between himself and the people that the office was to be his by and by.

Within half an hour, not a trace of the meeting was left but the trampled grass and the empty waggon. The people seemed to try who could flee the fastest, some to obtain the first access to the masters, some to get out of sight of a scene which had become disagreeable, and some few to talk big at the Spread-Eagle of what might have happened if this cowardly Committee would but have stood out a little longer.

Allen's steps were directed to Mr. Wentworth's counting-house. "I will ask work of him and of him only, in this line," thought he. "If I fail, I must take to some other occupation. They can hardly be all shut against an honest man."

"I am sorry for you, Allen," was Mr. Wentworth's reply when, with some difficulty, Allen had made his way through a crowd of people on the same errand with himself. "But you shall pronounce upon the case yourself. I can employ now only two-thirds of the number who turned out from me. Of these, at least half left me unwillingly, and have therefore the first title to employment; and the rest have worked for my firm for many years. At the best, I must refuse many whose services I should be glad to keep; judge then whether I can take on a stranger, be he who he may."

Allen bowed and had no more to say.

"If the firm you worked under cannot take you on, I fear you have little chance, Allen; for all are circumstanced like myself, I believe."

Allen shook his head, and would trespass no longer on Mr. Wentworth's time.

In the street he met Bray, who was looking for him to say farewell, while Hannah was doing the same to little Martha. Where were they going, and why so soon?

There was nothing to stay for now, Bray thought; for he had no liking to see honest men stand idle in the labour-market, except by their own choice. Choice made the entire difference in the case. As for where he was going, – he and Hannah must find out where people were most fond of street music and dancing, and would pay the best for it. And this put him in mind of what he had to say. He was as much obliged as Hannah herself, and more, by the hospitality with which she had been received at Allen's house; but his friend could not suppose he meant his daughter to be any charge upon the family in times like these. On this account, and for old friendship's sake, and from the sympathy which one proscribed man should feel for another, he hoped Allen would do him the favour to pocket this little bit of paper and say no more about it. – Allen agreed so far as to deter saying much about it till better times should come. He only just told Bray that the bank note was most acceptable at present for a very particular purpose, wrung his friend's hand, and ran home to fetch his wife, that the suit of clothes might be rebought without loss of time. They proved a dear bargain; but that was a secondary consideration, poor as Allen was. He went to rest that night, satisfied that his honour was redeemed, and that his wife would scarcely venture to put it in pawn again.

His wife said to herself that she had no idea he could have been so stern as he was all this day; she scarcely knew him for William Allen. – Many people made the same observation from this time forward. His sternness only appeared when matters of honour were in question, and no one who knew by what means he had been made jealous on this point wondered at the tone of decision in which a once weak and timid man could speak. But there were other circumstances which made them scarcely able to believe him the same William Allen. He no longer touched his hat to the masters, or appeared to see them as they passed. He no longer repaired to the Spread-Eagle to hear or tell the news, or to take part in con-sultation on the affairs of the workmen of Manchester, though he was ever ready to give his advice with freedom and mildness when called upon. He stated that he was a friend to their interests, and therefore anxious to avoid injuring them by being one of the body. He would not even represent his children, who grew up one after another to be employed in the factories, while their father toiled in the streets with his water-cart in summer and his broom in winter; enduring to be pointed out to strangers as the leader of an unsuccessful strike, as long as his family were not included with himself in the sentence of proscription.

When will it be understood by all that it rests with all to bring about a time when opposition of interests shall cease? When will masters and men work cheerfully together for their common good, respect instead of proscribing each other, and be equally proud to have such men as Wentworth and William Allen of their fellowship?

Summary of Principles illustrated in this Volume

COMMODITIES, being produced by capital and labour, are the joint property of the capitalist and labourer.

The capitalist pays in advance to the labourers their share of the commodity, and thus becomes its sole owner.

The portion thus paid is WAGES.

REAL WAGES are the articles of use and consumption that the labourer receives in return for his labour.

NOMINAL WAGES are the portion he receives of these things reckoned in money.

The fund from which wages are paid in any country consists of the articles required for the use and consumption of labourers which that country contains.

THE PROPORTION OF THIS FUND RECEIVED BY INDI-VIDUALS MUST MAINLY DEPEND ON THE NUMBER AMONG WHOM THE FUND IS DIVIDED.

The rate of wages in any country depends, therefore, not on the wealth which that country contains, but on the proportion between its capital and its population.

As population has a tendency to increase faster than capital, wages can be prevented from falling to the lowest point only by adjusting the proportion of population to capital.

The lowest point to which wages can be permanently reduced is that which affords a bare subsistence to the labourer.

The highest point to which wages can be permanently raised is that which leaves to the capitalist just profit enough to make it worth his while to invest his capital.

The variations of the rate of wages between these extreme points depending mainly on the supply of labour offered to the capitalist, the rate of wages is mainly determined by the sellers, not the buyers of labour.

Combinations of labourers against capitalists (whatever other effects they may have) cannot secure a permanent rise of wages unless the supply of labour falls short of the demand; – in which case, strikes are usually unnecessary.

Nothing can permanently affect the rate of wages which does not affect the proportion of population to capital.

Legislative interference does not affect this proportion, and is therefore useless.

Strikes affect it only by wasting capital, and are therefore worse than useless.

Combinations may avail or not, according to the reasonableness of their objects.

Whether reasonable or not, combinations are not subjects for legislative interference; the law having no cognizance of their causes.

Disturbance of the peace being otherwise provided against, combinations are wisely therefore now left unregarded by the law.

The condition of labourers may be best improved, –

1st. By inventions and discoveries which create capital.

2d. By husbanding instead of wasting capital: – for instance by
making savings instead of supporting strikes.

3d. BY ADJUSTING THE PROPORTION OF POPULATION TO
CAPITAL.

Charlotte Elizabeth Tonna

1790-1846

Charlotte Elizabeth Tonna's *Helen Fleetwood* (1839–40) is the first English novel to be entirely concerned with the lives of industrial workers, and to be so on the basis of data collected by Parliamentary Commissioners and contemporary publicists in their investigations of working-class conditions.[1] Although Mrs Tonna, too, primarily wanted to present the public with the facts of the situation, she realized that the Blue Books had more chance to move the hearts and stir the conscience of middle-class readers if turned into fiction, and this consideration induced her to take up the writing of fiction.

Charlotte Elizabeth Tonna's commitment to the Evangelical faith determined her views on political economy; it led her to reject the comfortable explanations of the existing social crisis offered by exponents of the theory of *laissez-faire*. Guided by the principle of Christian brotherhood, she imposed upon herself the task of exposing the inhuman suffering inflicted on large sections of the nation to ensure industrial progress. That the members of the working class led miserable lives was obvious to her, and from this she derived the conclusion that their moral degradation was a direct consequence of their appalling situation. Hunger, she argued, could induce not only a spirit of revolt but also the total extinction of any sense of values, so that a man can be reduced to a bestial state in his fight for survival. In Mrs Tonna's opinion the great sin of industrial society was the complete disregard for the body and the soul of the individual whom it employed. Since this was her persuasion, the main aim of her fiction was to display the process of moral and spiritual disintegration which accompanies the gradual undermining of the basis for human existence in a competitive industrial society.

Charlotte Elizabeth was the only daughter of Michael Brown, a clergyman of Norwich, where she was born in 1790. She died of cancer in 1846. At the age of ten she lost her hearing and almost her eyesight as well; her delicate health made her turn to books, her favourite reading being the plays of Shakespeare. In her *Recollections*[2] she admits that these encouraged her to develop her own imagination, and she resolved to become a writer on the death of her father, when her mother faced financial difficulties. Later on, however, after her religious conversion, she came to regret her youthful addiction to Shakespeare and romantic fiction as a sinful waste of time, and to express her gratitude that it had pleased God to save her from the temptation of seeking personal fame and fortune as a writer of light fiction. God secured this rescue through the timely appearance of a husband, a Captain Phelan, whom she accompanied to Nova Scotia for two years and then to his post in Ireland. It was there that her reading of religious tracts for the poor gave her the idea of using her literary talents in the service of Protestantism. The Dublin Tract Society was soon paying her liberally for her immediately successful stories and tracts, and among her fellow Evangelicals she became a polemical writer of some importance. When her husband deserted her, she returned to England, where she supported herself by writing. Four years after Captain Phelan's death in 1837, Charlotte Elizabeth married Lewis H. Tonna, Secretary of the Royal United Institution, and a religious writer of some standing. Her activities at this time were manifold; she wrote numerous prose narratives, poems, tracts and articles and she also worked as editor of *The Christian Lady's Magazine* in the years from 1843 to 1846, of *The Protestant Magazine* from 1841 to 1845 and of *The Protestant Annual* from 1841 to her death in 1846. She contributed amply to the journals she edited, usually anonymously or signing herself 'Charlotte Elizabeth'.

This record of the principal events in her life cannot convey the liveliness and intensity of her nature. Her tremendous vitality, in spite of lifelong frailty, is revealed in her *Recollections*. Although ostensibly an account of her conversion to Evangelicalism and a discussion of religious issues, the *Recollections* also afford a vivid picture of an immensely active existence devoted to many worthy causes – the Irish poor, English factory children, deaf mutes, Zionism, and the poor and friendless everywhere.

Her success as an author is shown by the fact that frequent new editions of her works were called for, and the 11 volumes of her collected edition testify to her productivity. In view of her condemnation, for religious reasons, of imaginative writing, her writing of novels requires an explanation. The reason has already been suggested: Mrs Tonna had recourse to fiction the better to reach the hearts of her readers. As she puts it herself, the "abstract idea of a suffering family does not strongly affect the mind", but let the people be known to us and "we are enabled much more feelingly to enter into their trial" ('The Forsaken Home', V).

Charlotte Elizabeth's most important work, *Helen Fleetwood*, first serialized in *The Christian Lady's Magazine* (1839–40), was published in 1841 in one volume at seven shillings.[3] This is a moving documentary narrative showing how industrialism leads to moral disintegration in the social class employed to operate the machines. The plot centres on a single family, the Greens, consisting of a grandmother, her four grand-children and an adopted granddaughter, Helen Fleetwood, and it out-lines their downhill progress from the moment they are forced to leave their native village to seek employment in Manchester. The move has tragic consequences for them all. The parish guardians, who persuade pauperized families to migrate to avoid having to support them, depict life in the fast-growing industrial centre in glowing colours, and the device succeeds. This is how the Greens come to Manchester and to the cotton-mill where Helen and Mary work to earn their living. This cotton-mill is a synthesis of all the factories condemned as inhuman by wit-nesses called by official investigators. The novel exposes the culpability of those who refuse to consider the cost, in terms of human lives, of industrial prosperity. These were the men denounced by Dickens for seeing "figures and averages, and nothing else". But Mrs Tonna was completely indifferent to statistics; what she fought for was a re-establishment of a spirit of Christian fellowship – an ideal adopted and developed later on by Frederick Denison Maurice and his Christian Socialists, one of whom was Charles Kingsley, the novelist.

The story told in *Helen Fleetwood* requires a tragic end, and the action moves painfully but plausibly towards its conclusion. By the time we reach the last chapter the city of Manchester has taken little more than a year to destroy the simple rural family. The author's straight-forward and generally skilful presentation of the various situations allows the tension to mount toward its tragic climax without any of the false pathos found in the stories of many of her better-known contem-poraries. The function of her characters is limited to the part they play in the routine events in the lives of the working poor. Since the author was less interested in character analysis than in explaining what happens to her characters as members of an exploited class, her protagonists are portrayed not as complex individuals but rather as actors in a pageant the purpose of which is to show one part of the nation – the rich – how the other part – the poor – lives. But Helen Fleetwood and her asso-ciates are more than mere abstract socio-economic cases of the kind that we meet in Frances Trollope's *The Life and Adventures of Michael Armstrong, the Factory Boy,* which appeared in the same year as *Helen Fleetwood.* Michael scarcely reminds one of a factory worker, while the other characters in Frances Trollope's story are mere shadows. But in Mrs Tonna's novel the workers – children and adults alike – are distinctly marked as individuals. Their idiosyncracies are such that they do not strike the reader as being either eccentrics or stereotypes.

One of the most successful portraits in *Helen Fleetwood* is that of Tom South, a character who in many ways foreshadows John Barton in Mrs Gaskell's *Mary Barton, a Tale of Manchester Life* (1848).[4] South is a revolutionary trade unionist who reads seditious literature. As a skilled worker he is sufficiently well paid, but he deplores the condition of his own class and his anger is strongly stirred by the merciless exploitation of child labour. Equally convincing and moving is Mrs Tonna's presentation of working-class family life as illustrated by the story of the Wright family in the same novel. Here the relationship between parents and children is devoid of natural affection. Like so much else in the daily lives of the workers this basic human relationship has been destroyed, and the destruction extends to families that are better off. This is seen when the Green family, on arriving in Manchester, turn to working-class relatives who receive them with little enthusiasm. These relatives earn enough from factory work to live in relatively easy circumstances, in rooms furnished with some pretension to elegance, with bright pictures in gaudy frames on the walls. Although there is here no real poverty, the children are sent into factories as a matter of course, but this is not all. The mother reveals a callous indifference to the young breadwinners, and the children on their side have neither respect nor affection for her.

Helen Fleetwood never idealizes poverty and those who suffer from it, and so there is no easy way out for readers who feel uncomfortable. Unlike Dickens, Mrs Tonna does not present the poor as an embodiment of her vision of what man ought to be. Her purpose was to convince the reader of what she herself believed to be true: that poverty causes degradation as well as suffering. Hence she compels her readers to watch the process whereby this is made to happen. Dickens may again serve to point the contrast, since he permitted his young protagonist in *Oliver Twist* (1837) to remain unharmed by his evil environment. Mrs Tonna's fictional characters, moreover, are true to their class and to human nature to an extent that must be denied to better-known fictional characters like Alton Locke in Charles Kingsley's novel of that name (1850), or Gerald in Benjamin Disraeli's *Sybil* (1845), who turns out to be an aristocrat, or again Stephen Blackpool in Dickens's *Hard Times* (1854), who acts completely out of character.[5]

To the singleness of vision and purpose which explains Mrs Tonna's achievement must also be attributed the most obvious artistic flaw in her novel: its total lack of humour. She has none of Dickens's subtle and often poignant understanding of man's rudimentary need for laughter; her seriousness is unrelieved.

Helen Fleetwood illustrates the amazing extent to which Charlotte Elizabeth Tonna's fiction rests on a basis of fact. The very substance of the conversations carried on by characters like Tom South, Richard Green and Hudson can be referred back to official documents like the *Sadler Committee Report*, or to pamphlets by reformists like Peter Gaskell, Richard Oastler, James Kay-Shuttleworth and R. D. Granger, the speeches of Lord Shaftesbury and sources like Hansard's Parliamentary debates. The story told in *Helen Fleetwood*, of the tragic experiences of the Green family, is actually a detailed and informative digest of contemporary reports on the industrial poor in the 1830s; and almost all the events narrated – from the recruitment of new hands for industry to the placing of old Mrs Green in the workhouse – are based on testimony taken from the Blue Books if not from personal observation. We do not know if the author herself ever visited a factory. Had she done so, however, she would surely have mentioned it, for she was a careful recorder of events and facts. It seems reasonable to assume, therefore, that she depended on her own imaginative powers to transfer fact into fiction, as in the following haunting passage on the terror with which a child experiences the machinery in a cotton mill.

Everything is done by machinery: you see, they are great things, ever so high and big, all going about and about, some on wheels running up and down the room, and some with great rollers turning about as fast as the steam can drive them; so you must step back, and run forward, and duck, and turn, and move as they do, or off goes a finger or an arm, or else you get a knock on the head, to remember all your lives. As to sitting down there's no such thing.
. . . Move, move, everything moves. The wheels and the frames are always going, and the little reels twirl round as fast as ever they can; and the pulleys, and chains, and great iron works overhead, are all moving; and the cotton moves so fast that it is hard to piece it quick enough; and there is a great dust, and such a noise of whirr, whirr, whirr, that at first I did not know whether I was not standing on my head.

(chap. VI)

One incident shows how a young girl loses an arm because of this unfenced machinery, a topical issue indeed since Parliament had been busy for years debating the legality or propriety of compelling employers to install fencing.[6] The novel is at its most topical when it dramatizes problems connected with labour legislation, and the most important of these issues was the inadequate enforcement of the law when adopted.[7] It was apparently easy to circumvent existing Factory Acts. As one of Mrs Tonna's working-class characters puts it: "The inspector comes once a year, and is bound to advertise his coming in the newspapers: so they take care to have all right just then" (chap. VI). And even should an owner be found guilty, the penalty imposed would be the lowest one permitted.

The members of the Green family in *Helen Fleetwood* are not the only victims, in contemporary fiction, of factories operated with indifference to the welfare of the workers. In Elizabeth Gaskell's *North and South* (1854) a girl who is dying of tuberculosis accuses her master of refusing to invest twenty pounds in a ventilator which would have made the air much less harmful to breathe. Another Manchester author, Geraldine Jewsbury (*Marian Withers*, 1851), describes in graphic detail the unhealthy nature of some of the tasks performed in a cotton factory. Cruelty to children is described by Frances Trollope in *Michael Armstrong* (1839–40) as well as by Mrs Tonna. A worker explains to the latter's old Mrs Green, when her granddaughter has been beaten, that the children have no legal redress: "In the case of ill-usage, you see, the master usually contrives to shift the blame from himself to the managers or overlookers, or spinners: *he* don't order the children to be beat; *he* don't see them beaten; and so he gets off and the poor things have no real protection anywhere." (Chap. VI.)

But the author of *Helen Fleetwood* looked beyond the physical cruelty of hard blows and long hours of work to what she saw as the greatest cruelty of all: the dehumanizing effect of work which consists merely in watching machinery, a process which alienates man from himself:

> Seen at their work they are a community of automata. Nothing seems to animate them. The cold listlessness of their looks sends a chill to the heart of the spectator, who, if he feels rightly, must feel it a degradation to his species to be chained, as it were, to a parcel of senseless machinery, confused by its din, and forced to obey its movements with scarcely an interval for thought or repose.

(chap. XIX)

As a writer of fiction Charlotte Elizabeth Tonna's most important contribution to the genre was to show how it could be developed so as to serve the cause of social reform. Next to *Helen Fleetwood* must be placed a series of shorter narratives originally published in her *Christian Lady's Magazine* and subsequently collected in a volume entitled *The Wrongs of Woman* (1843–4).[8] As indicated by the titles – 'Milliners and Dress-makers', 'The Forsaken Home', 'The Little Pin-Headers' and 'The Lace-Runners' – each focusses on conditions in a particular line of work where women were employed, often together with children. The workers in 'Milliners and Dress-makers' belong to what one would call the 'shabby-genteel' rather than the working class, and the appeal here is not so much for legislative action as for greater consideration on the part of the fashionable ladies who patronized the unscrupulous sweatshop owners or operators. 'The Forsaken Home' describes the tragedy of a family where the mother is the only one to obtain employment. The story shows how the position of working women becomes unbearable during pregnancy, and is not much better once the baby is born, since the work takes all their time and strength. The baby is kept quiet by means of the sinister 'Godfrey's Cordial', a tranquillizer made of opium mixed with treacle. The women who have to see their children die from the effects of this drug, seek relief in strong drink.

'The Little Pin-Headers', the best of these four stories, rivals *Helen Fleetwood* in power, which is why it is included in our Anthology. 'The Lace-Runners' describes a family employed in the manufacture of lace on their own premises. The whole family engage in this work, even a three-year-old child, and several children from the neighbourhood. The picture is one of unrelieved gloom: no talk is allowed, and work is carried on till late at night when one or more of the children will faint from hunger and fatigue. Everything is sacrificed to the overriding necessity of producing enough lace to secure physical survival and the sacrifice includes the baby that dies after too frequent doses of the fatal cordial. Sympathy for these lace-runners prompts Mrs Tonna to vehement denunciation of the middle classes; the gulf between the rich and the poor is widened by their demand for unnecessary luxuries and by their culpable ignorance of the conditions under which these luxury articles are produced. Unless the process is stopped, England will be brought to the brink of revolution.

In her treatment of the juvenile workers Mrs Tonna differs from the majority of her Evangelical fellow-writers. The latter were inclined to sentimentalize the last moments of pauper children who never murmur against their fate, and face death with fortitude thanks to their faith in the Scripture. Consequently, pious and submissive little boys and girls were in great favour with the writers of didactic tales, who demonstrated their admiration by sending many a pauper child betimes to Heaven. *The Annals of the Poor* (1814) by the Rev. Legh Richmond is the best-known specimen of homiletic stories exhorting exemplary young Christians on their death-beds. Mrs Tonna, however, did not write in emulation of this Evangelical stereotype. A pauper child who must work even when it is ill excites her compassion, and the destruction of a child employed in industry she compares to the discarding of a piece of machinery: the sick factory child is like a "broken wheel thrown into the lumber room to fall to pieces."

One of Mrs Tonna's non-fictional works ought to be mentioned because of its close connection with her favourite fictional themes. This is *The Perils of the Nation: An Appeal to the Legislature, the Clergy, and the Higher and Middle Classes* (1842), a tract not usually associated with Mrs Tonna because her publisher preferred anonymous publication. It presents a terse and well-documented argument in favour of government intervention to regulate conditions in factories, mines, small workshops and distressed agricultural areas. It also calls for new laws concerning sanitary conditions, urban housing, rampant pauperism and better educational opportunities for the poor. Like her conservative Evangelical friends, Mrs Tonna combined her championship of legislative reform with staunch opposition to Free Trade and Whig policies in general. Thus her pamphlet denounces the doctrines of political economy held by the free-traders, holding up to ridicule the idea that workers could be considered as free agents under such a system. As she puts it in *Helen Fleetwood*, with irony reminiscent of Dickens, the workers "of course were under no compulsion, save that of poverty", and were entirely at liberty to starve, if they so chose.

However loudly Mrs Tonna denounced the exploitation of the working classes, she in no sense supported political action on the part of the workers. She may have opposed the principle of *laissez-faire*, but like Carlyle and Dickens, she was equally opposed to trade unionism because it was a Socialist movement. Thus she remarks in *Helen Fleetwood* that "some half dozen of the young men" had become Socialists, whereupon she adds the following Apocalyptic judgment:

> Beyond this it was impossible to go – Socialism is the *ne plus ultra* of six thousand years' laborious experience on the part of the great enemy of man[9] – it is the moral Gorgon upon which whomsoever can be compelled to look must wither away: it is the doubly denounced woe upon the inhabitants of the earth – the last effort of Satanic venom wrought to the madness of rage by the consciousness of his shortened time. (chap. XX)

It is an ironical paradox that although she opposed the Socialist critics of the capitalist system with a fervour amounting almost to frenzy, she arrived at many of the same conclusions.

To love the proletarian and hate his organization – this was the ambiguous position of Charlotte Elizabeth Tonna. This characteristically Victorian inconsistency places her work in an intermediate position among writers of fiction concerned with social problems. Her narratives

constitute a link between the school of the highly rational, unsenti-
mental and propagandistic fictional tracts on the one hand and, on the
other, the later group of social novelists who treated similar subjects
more emotively, more dramatically, and – in the larger and deeper sense
– more realistically. Mrs Tonna possessed the objectivity of the first
group, best represented by Hannah More and Harriet Martineau, but
without their frequent ambivalence of attitude; she never condoned the
evil aspects of the early phases of industrialization. On the other hand,
she had the personal compassion with human suffering characteristic
of Elizabeth Gaskell and Charles Dickens, but without their occasional
sentimentality and melodrama. 'The Little Pin-Headers' suggests the
kind of achievement that might have been hers, had she also possessed
the artistic power of her greater contemporaries.

Notes

1. See Ivanka Kovačević and Barbara Kanner, 'Blue Book into Novel:
   The Forgotten Industrial Fiction of Charlotte Elizabeth Tonna',
   Nineteenth-Century Fiction, 25 (Sept. 1970), 152–73. Parts of this
   article have been included here with minor changes. For a list of
   secondary sources bearing on Mrs Tonna and her work, readers are
   recommended to consult this article.
2. *Personal Recollections of Charlotte Elizabeth, Continued to the Close of
   Her Life*, published by R. B. Seeley and W. Burnside (1847). Her
   husband, L. H. J. Tonna, added a few supplementary chapters to
   Mrs Tonna's account.
3. Published by R. B. Seeley and W. Burnside. All my quotations are
   from this edition.
4. There is no evidence indicating whether Elizabeth Gaskell had in
   fact read *Helen Fleetwood*, which would account for the similarity.
   It is unlikely, however, that anyone so interested in, and familiar
   with, the condition of factory workers in that city would have
   failed to read this earlier "tale of Manchester life".
5. See my comments, p. 111.
6. See above, p. 219.
7. On this particular issue Mrs Tonna appears to have made use of
   Leonard Horner's 'Open Letter to Nassau Senior' of May 1837,
   the argument of which is repeated in Horner's subsequent *Report*
   included in the evidence given before the Commission of 1840.
8. Published in four parts by W. H. Dalton of London.
9. The Apocalyptic references need glossing to be understood today.
   The great enemy of man is, of course, Satan, who has been given

all of time in which to ruin the design of God. But all of time was traditionally compressed into a span of 6,000 years at the end of which would follow the Millennium when the 'dragon' (Satan) would be bound, and Christ would be sole ruler.

Bibliographical Details

'The Little Pin-Headers' first appeared in Mrs Tonna's *Christian Lady's Magazine*, and was subsequently published as the third story in a volume entitled *The Wrongs of Woman* (1843–4), from which edition the text given here is taken.

In the preceding story, 'The Forsaken Home', the Smiths, a rural family in search of employment, arrive in an industrial town. Unfortunately, the mother is the only one to obtain employment. But despite her desperate struggle to support the whole family on her meagre wages, the Smiths are ruined before long. The husband changes from a decent farm labourer to a mere idler and drunkard. In the end, his wife dies from overwork and illness, and he soon brings a step-mother to his children, who are now sent to work in a pin workshop.

THE
WRONGS OF WOMAN

Part III
'The Little Pin-Headers'

Chapter I

THE CHILDREN'S FRIEND

There was a time when God manifest in the flesh walked this earth among the creatures whom he had made. Many wonderful acts were then wrought in the sight of man; divine wisdom proceeded from his lips, miracles of mercy were dispensed by his hands. Great multitudes followed him, pressing on his path: the wise, the scribe, the disputer of this world, hung watchfully on all his words, for they hoped to catch something whereof they might accuse him: the ignorant came to be taught, the sick and lame to be healed, the hungry to be fed; and his own disciples, tenacious of the precious privilege, maintained their station nearest to his sacred person. The angry complaint of the rulers was true; "All men go after him."

In the midst of this mingled throng, some were seen, boldly endeavouring to force a passage, even to the very feet of the majestic Teacher. They reached at last that innermost circle where the immediate followers of the Lord enclosed him, listening to the gracious words that proceeded out of his lips; and here the intruders were met by a repulse, a rebuke, from which they would naturally shrink; for the reprovers were men, rough and rude; and the reproved were timid women. A pause ensued: the advancing party were no doubt preparing to retreat, or to remain stationary until such time as the Master's eye might perchance be cast towards the quarter where they stood. Ah! they knew not yet the love that filled the Master's heart, the omniscient mercy to which their secret desire was known, by which their bosom's unuttered prayer was already granted. The

Lord turned; and he, the meek and lowly One, showed himself exceedingly displeased: he rebuked the disciples who had been rebuking them; and as the too officious guards shrank back, the words that conveyed reproof to them fell as sweetest music on the ears of that group of mothers, and elder sisters, and gentle friends, for he said, "Suffer the little children to come unto me, and forbid them not; for of such is the kingdom of heaven."

Perhaps you have looked upon some fanciful painting, intended to represent the scene, where the Saviour's gentle smile invited the little wondering Israelites to approach; where the good Shepherd gathered those lambs in his arms, and carried them in his bosom: where the young babe nestled in the folds of his robe, and the less helpless caught its hem, or clung round his knees, or pressed the glad head beneath the hand laid on it in solemn benediction: – you would have called it beautiful; and your heart has melted, perhaps it melts even now, at the picture your own fancy is painting of what no mortal tints can adequately portray. Why do you feel it thus? Because little children are so engaging, their comparative innocence is so touching, their relative harmlessness, and unacquaintance with the woes of life appeal so eloquently to the tenderer sensibilities of our nature; because, too, you attach, as well you may, a real, though as yet not a fully explained significancy to the solemn words, "Of such is the kingdom of heaven."

Ah, lady, take from any part of your apparel that very trivial though indispensable appendage, a common pin: look well upon it, and then I will show you another picture: I will show you the professed disciples of the Lord Jesus not merely barring the way by which mothers might bring their little ones to HIM for the blessing that he waits to bestow, but opening a way, and forcing the mothers into it, by which they must carry those little ones to the brink of a pit, and fling them, helpless, hopeless, succourless, into the iron grasp of Satan.

But first let us pause, and inquire where now is He, who, when the young children of Judea were brought to him, "took them up in his arms, and put his hands on them, and blessed them;" what is he doing, and what is he saying? He is in heaven, gone to fulfil the purpose for which he then came down from thence: our great High Priest, having offered up the all-sufficient sacrifice of himself on the altar of the cross, as a propitiation of your sins and mine, has entered the Holy of holies, there to appear before God for us, presenting the tokens of that atoning sacrifice, ever living to make intercession for such as we are, who come to God by him. He pleads for us as a Mediator, he governs us as a King; and to effect these two great operations he must be cognisant of all that concerns us. At what moment of our lives could we feel content to believe that our Lord and Master forgets us – that he ceases to feel for our infirmities, to have compassion on our weakness, to plead his sacrifice for the pardon for our continual offences? If you know Jesus as a Saviour, you must be able to realize this more powerfully than I can express it; if you know him not, away with every other topic, until you have grounded yourself in the faith on which the salvation of your own soul depends. But, while thus employed, in heaven itself, what does he say to us, his disciples? To each and all he says, "I know thy works." To some he addresses the encouraging language, "I know thy works . . . and service;" or, "I know thy works, and where thou dwellest, even where Satan's seat is; and thou holdest fast my name, and hast not denied my faith." To others he utters the startling rebuke, "I know thy works, that thou hast a name that thou livest, and art dead;" and, alas! to how many the menace of rejection, "I know thy works, that thou art neither cold nor hot!" To us, collectively, he speaks, without distinction, without reservation, "All the churches shall know that I am he which searcheth the reins and hearts; and I will give unto every one of you according to your works."

And for a rule of life, for a plain standard of the works that he requires of us, we have in every possible situation that accountable beings can be placed in, the surest of all guides – his unchangeable words, concerning which he has declared of every man, "The word that I have spoken, the same shall judge him in the last day." In the case now before us, where children are concerned, we have not only the directions given by the Holy Ghost through the holy men of old, prophets and apostles, commanding us to train them up in the way that they should go, but we have the Lord Jesus Christ himself admonishing us, "Suffer little children to come unto ME, and forbid them not." Forbidding a thing is not confined to a verbal prohibition: blocking up the way of access, turning them by force, or by deceit alluring them into a different way – concealing from them the fact of the Saviour's nearness, of his willingness to bless them, or their great need of that blessing, – all these and various other modes of interposing, amount to what is so plainly denounced as forbidding their approach; and a fearful prospect is theirs who stand in this position when the Lord proceeds to give unto every one of us according to our works. What testimony did he demand of the surpassing love in which the pardoned disciple professed to hold him? "Feed my lambs." We know that, on earth, the Lord repeatedly evinced his especial tenderness for the little ones; and can we for one moment suppose that his "bowels of compassion" are less moved towards them, now that the rich purchase-money is fully paid for their redemption, and in heaven itself he waits to be gracious to every creature who will seek his help? We cannot so imagine: we may contrive to forget, but deny it we may not. Throughout the short, sad sketch that must now be drawn, let us keep in view the objects and the incident with which we set out: the Saviour inviting their approach; the disciples who own his Name surrounding both him and them; and the young children waiting to be led forward by such as know the way to that Saviour's feet.

From the royal lady who wields the sceptre of England, down to the most squalid female beggar who prowls about the street for the prize of a half-gnawn bone, or ragged shred, none can dispense with the produce of the pin manufactory. The demand is so universal, the articles so insignificant both as to size and cost, and their wasteful loss so incessant, that it is a matter of wonder to any who take the trouble to think about it, how such a consumption can be supplied. By minute investigation, too, we may perceive that there is a good deal of nice workmanship bestowed upon it, to furnish its many indispensable qualities; to render it at once so slender and so firm; so smooth and tapering; to fix its round, flat head with sufficient steadiness; to give its sharp point an edge that will not rend the most delicate fabrics; and so to whiten it that no unseemly coarseness of the original metal may remain. In the very small size that it can be made to assume, it is really a marvellous piece of delicate workmanship, overlooked only because it is proverbially worthless from the immense quantities perpetually tossed about; but little do the majority of those who use it know of the heart-rending circumstances under which its manufactory is carried on. It will not be the writer's fault, if a tongue is not henceforth added to the silent appendage of each reader's toilet, pleading for those who, immured in the dingy receptacles of infant labour, misery, and wrong, cannot speak for themselves, save only as their sorrows and sufferings cry aloud to him whom they know not – whom they are not permitted to approach – whose loving invitation never reaches them, because it falls unheeded or rejected on the cold ear of paternal and mercantile speculation, intent only, the one on a present supply of craving wants, the other on accumulating capital, to be expended in widening the gulf between the unfeeling rich man and his poverty-stricken brother of the dust!

We enter at once on a new scene – the interior of a pin manufactory.

It is winter: the chilliness of a November day, while the fog and frost divide the rule between them; and the comfort of a warm wrapper, aided by the prospect of a bright fire in our well-curtained and carpeted room, when the very short day shall have closed, is not only a welcome but an essential element in the contentment with which we endure these ills of our climate. Pass on, through the misty, slippery street, and turn into yonder building. It does, indeed, look more like an outhouse in a state of dilapidation than a place where artizans assemble to pursue a thriving trade; but the interior will prove that the latter is its real purpose. We proceed through several departments of busy employment: in one there are children winding slender wire, which, being passed through a machine by steam-power, is drawn out by men. Here, the boys work, generally, under their fathers; and whatever we may think of their close, protracted confinement, the labour itself is not severe. In the next room we find many little fellows, more fatiguingly employed, being perpetually on foot, walking to and fro, assisting their seniors by the operation of straightening the coiled wire furnished by the drawers, which the men cut into lengths and point. Next we find a third part of boys, mixed with about an equal number of men: they spin, by a very exact, monotonous process, some wire into a spiral shape, which is subsequently cut into rings, forming heads for the pins. Hither to, we have found no girls, nor very little children; but enter the next department, and the scene will change.

Here is a room, if we can call it by that name, eight yards in length, by six in breadth, and about nine feet high. A row of small, dingy windows, along each side, admit such light as there is; and here, seated before machines unlike any that we have yet surveyed, are about fifty children, of whom the eldest may be thirteen; but the general age is less, much less – they are mere babes. Near each of them is placed a quantity of the prepared heads, from which they pick out one with the pointed head of the wires, also supplied to them, and passing it up the shank, they fix it at the blunt end; and holding the pin obliquely under a small hammer, turn it round until, with four or five smart strokes, it is properly secured in its place. Such is the general aspect of the apartment, such the employment of its inmates, and just as we now behold them they have been engaged since eight o'clock in the morning, with the certainty of carrying it on till eight in the evening: how much longer they may, on any pretext, be detained, no one can tell.

Stunted in their growth, bony, pallid, and most wretchedly unhealthy in their looks; filthy beyond expression in their persons, with scarcely rags enough to hold decently together, these miserable little beings appear conscious of but two objects capable of attracting their notice beyond the work about which their poor dirty little hands are incessantly moving. One of these is the very small fire-place, where an exceedingly scanty portion of fuel is just emitting smoke enough to prove that fire smoulders beneath. Towards this, many a longing look is cast, while the blue lips quiver, and the teeth chatter, and the fingers are well-nigh disabled from moving by the benumbing influence of cold. One might suppose that the crowding of so many living creatures within that confined space, would en-sure heat enough; but oppressive as the air feels, it evidently brings no warmth to them. Empty stomachs, and curdling blood, never set in motion by exercise or play, will produce a chill not to be over-come by these damp exhalations, even if the frequent entrance of a draught of colder though not purer air from neighbouring work-shops did not increase it: and as to the fire, it may serve to speak of, to think about, to look towards, but for any purpose of warmth, such as these poor infants require, the grate might just as well be empty.

But another object divides their attention: a woman on whose hard features many violent passions have conspired to plough in-delible lines, whose inflated nostril, compressed lip, and restless eye, bespeak alike a cruel disposition, and watchfulness for means to gratify it, stalks to and fro, with a supple cane in her hand, intent to catch at a case of delinquency – a false movement, a momentary flagging of energy, a slight indication of the drowsiness peculiarly inevitable in children, when limb and spirit are fatigued, the mind unoccupied, and natural playfulness wholly restrained – sufficient to warrant the application of the well-known weapon to their poor little heads or shoulders. Occasionally she disappears, as if to in-vite a feeling of momentary security; and then, perhaps, some of the small hammers will tap less vigorously on the heads of the pins; some cramped fingers are stretched, and some half-frozen ones are held in the mouth for the comfortable refreshment of a warm breath: some little bare feet are briskly rubbed together, or perhaps some kind-hearted brother might take his baby-sister on his knee, and chafe her arms and ancles, numbed with the bitter cold of such unnatural stagnation: but, noiselessly, yet rapidly, the watcher re-enters, the cane is uplifted, and in the sudden acceleration of machinery something is gained by the traffickers in infant life; while only a few among the deliquents get any blows worth speak-ing of; and perhaps a lock or two of flaxen hair may be twitched out by her left, while her right hand administers the passing switch to some culprit, flurried by the sudden surprise into a blundering movement!

In the far corner of this prison-house sits one whose features are not quite strange to us, though greatly altered for the worse. It is Betsy, the second daughter of Alice Smith, and of all that family the one who most resembles her mother. Her anxious looks are frequently, though stealthily, sent along the line of her workmates, whenever the overlooker's back is fairly turned; and if we follow them, we shall find that they rest on one whom we should scarcely have expected to find here – her little curly-headed brother Joe, who is no longer allowed to sit next her, because she was several times detected helping him in his work, to the unavoidable neglect of her own, in order that the blows reserved for him might fall on herself. In vain was her own allowance of strict discipline increased, while his was not diminished: in vain was a weal of considerable size raised across her neck for thus transgressing: so incorrigible is the temper of this girl, that she actually interposed her own head between her brother's and the hand lifted to strike him; and for this he was removed into a very different neighbourhood, where two older hands understood the value of such a scapegoat, and made ample use of the manager's spite against him, to purchase exemption from punishment, not unfrequently deserved, by themselves. All this was very dreadful to Betsy, and her frequent cries of entreaty on his behalf proved it; but she is wiser now: she finds that by appearing indifferent to his sufferings, she can better mitigate them; and those stolen looks are all the sign she gives of unchanged solicitude about him.

But where is their mother? Surely the warm-hearted Alice Smith would at all hazards rescue her little one from such ill-usage. Do not put that question to Betsy: she saw her mother die, the victim of what would have been a trifling indisposition, had it fallen on her before her frame was so toil-worn, her heart so broken; and scarcely was the grave closed over her, when, in a half-drunken fit, the father of her helpless children gave them the curse of a most profligate step-mother, who sent them all out to work on such terms as their weak efforts were deemed worth, while she, by her outrageous conduct, drove Smith to enlist as a soldier. She now subsists on the wages of these poor children's labour, added to what her own abandoned course of life may bring in; and having none to contradict her, or to attempt any sort of control over her words or actions, she is no worse to the destitute little ones than she would be to her own, had she any. It is true, they have no vestige of what their mother once deemed indispensable comforts: they are not washed, nor combed, nor indulged, as formerly, with a weekly change of linen, or rather of rags; neither is any kind or degree of instruction, religious, moral, or social, ever placed within their reach; but their condition is really better than that of many working beside them, who are exposed at home to the ebullitions of drunken rage, or spiteful cruelty, from which there is no escape. The two youngest, as yet incapable of earning anything, have, on the step-mother's pathetic representation, been received into the union workhouse; and Polly has employment in another line, where she has made acquaintance more to her liking than any she can find at home. Thus, deserted on all sides by their natural associates, the two children before us are thrown completely upon each other's affection, and very touching it is to witness the strength of that concentrated attachment. Betsy has a more womanly mind than many nearly twice her age: she has looked upon the objects that have crossed her early path of sorrows with an observing eye; and this has induced a sort of tact that might pass for cunning contrivance, if any selfish object was to be gained by it; but all self being, on her part, wrapped up in her little brother, it is never brought to bear upon any other point than his well-being: in all that concerns her, individually, she is a simple child. He, poor little fellow, from being the spoiled pet of the house, has passed under such harsh discipline, and endured so many buffetings, that his spirit is completely broken: he is not now the bold, bright-eyed boy, who, even when tumbling among cinders, or splashing in the liquid mud before his father's door, attracted notice by his energetic bearing and unflinching gaze, and merry, shouting tones; but a trembling, shrinking, hesitating whisperer, afraid, as it would seem, of trusting his own step, or hearing his own voice, or encountering the look of any eye save Betsy's. One idea seems to have taken possession of his mind, and that one relates to his mother; but of its exact nature neither he nor any one about him is conscious.

It is fatiguing to prolong the observation of these wretched little automata, with their small hammers, so monotonously sounding on the dirty-looking manufacture before them. The pins are not yet whitened or polished, and nothing here looks neat, nothing feels comfortable. You might be tempted to stroke the head of some pretty, engaging child, and to try whether a smile would not call up some answering expression of gladness in its heavy countenance, but your hand shrinks from the contact of that uncleanly hair, and you *cannot* smile with such an aggregate of infant misery before you. Yet, the pain produced by the contemplation is transient: you are not obliged to remain here a minute longer than your own free choice may prompt you to stay. This spectacle of wretchedness, this close, unwholesome, fœtid air, may at once be changed for any enlivening, refreshing spot that it may please you to repair to. But they must remain: their hours of slavery will not expire till the glare of gas shall have long shone upon their work, and the heated atmosphere have prepared them to meet with a more sensitive shudder the sudden gust of a November night's wind. They must persevere; and if drowsiness steals on their heavy little eyelids, the monitory switch is at hand to chase it away. No friend will look upon them then; none but He whose eyes as a flame of fire pierce the deepest shades that cruelty can draw around to hide her impious work; and the disregarded invitation of whose gracious lips yet stands recorded on the page that they dare not look upon: "Suffer the little children to come unto me, and forbid them not: for of such is the kingdom of heaven."

Chapter II

A SUNDAY STROLL

We are now to take a Sunday stroll in the suburbs of this industrious town. The country being a christian land, and most of the large employers being attendants on some place of worship where the Word of God is read, and the precepts therein set forth inculcated, we might expect that when the industrious poor have fulfilled that part of the commandment which tells them, "Six days shalt thou labour, and do all that thou hast to do," it would be considered a duty by their well-taught employers to see that they enjoyed means for observing the remainder – for keeping the seventh day holy, as a season both of spiritual refreshment and of bodily rest. Considering the vast profits realized by their means, the masters might be supposed to set apart a fair proportion of such gains, for the erection of a place of worship, and the support of faithful teachers; and as regards the little children, for a very effective system of Sunday-school instruction. Considering the intense anxiety that they manifest for the proper education of their own families, and the horror with which they would recoil from the bare idea of leaving one of them in utter ignorance, we may picture to ourselves their christian solicitude to see their little labourers making the most of the only day allowed them for the acquisition of even the first rudiments of the most common instruction: but everybody knows that such expectations are perfectly absurd, save only where one stands out, in despised notoriety, from the great mass, and devotes himself to a cause utterly over-looked, yea, scorned by the generality of his brethren. We will just look about us on this, the day when, by the law of the land, all shops and manufactories are closed, all churches opened, and all classes are supposed to assemble together before His throne of grace, at whose throne of judgment they must and shall meet, to render an account of all that has been done, and all that has been evaded.

But lest we be suspected of drawing a fanciful sketch, untrue to nature, we will only in thought accompany a gentleman, one officially deputed to investigate those things, from whose note-book we copy the following entries, *verbatim*, as made at the time.

"*Sunday, March 14.* Walked about the town – streets and outskirts – during church-time. Met men, singly and in groups, wandering about in their working aprons and caps, or with dirty shirtsleeves tucked up, and black, smithy-smutted arms, and grimed faces. Some appeared to have been up all night – probably at work to recover the time lost by their idleness in the early part of the week; perhaps drinking. Lots of children seen in groups at the end of courts, alleys, and narrow streets – playing, or sitting upon the edge of the common dirt-heap of the place, like a row of sparrows, and very much of that colour, all chirruping away. Groups of children, all in their working dresses, playing about on the open waste at the back of the new church and parsonage now building at the end of —— street. Boys, from nine to seventeen years of age, playing at marbles, in groups of five, and from that to ten. Adults of about twenty, and from that to thirty years of age, looking on – some smoking, vacant, listless – not really attending to the game. Boys fighting; bad language, and bloody noses. Women in their working dresses, standing about at doors or ends of passages, with folded arms. Little boys sitting in holes in the ground, playing at mining with a small pick-axe. Girls playing about in various ways; all dirty, except one group of about half-a-dozen girls, near —— lane, of the age of from nine to fifteen, who are washed and dressed, and are playing, with continual screams and squeaks of delight, at jumping from the mounds of dirt, dung, and rubbish-heaps, which are collected there, and cover a considerable space. Some fell with a sprawl; in a moment, all were scuttling up the dirt-heaps again. Scarcely any houses with children sitting at the doors washed and dressed. A few small houses, not in courts and yards, but facing the streets, were cleansed, i.e. had the brick-floor washed and sanded; but most of these sold cakes, oranges, sugar-sticks, and small-beer; the cleaning a part of the business, and a sort of rare attraction to their tribe of dirty little customers. Adults seated smoking, or with folded arms, on the threshold of their door, or inside their houses, evidently not intending to wash and shave. Many of them sitting or standing in the house, with an air of lazy vacancy – they did not know what to do with their leisure or with themselves. . . . No working men walking with their wives, either to or from church or chapel, or for the sake of the walk. No brothers and sisters. Until the issuing forth of the children from the Sunday-schools, with all those adults who had attended some place of worship, nothing seen but squalid disorder, indifference, and utter waste, in self-disgust, of the very day of which, in every sense, they should make the most. With all this, no merriment – no laughter – no smiles. All dulness and vacuity. No signs of animal spirits, except with the girls on the dust-heaps."

These memoranda, it will be observed, were noted down, as the writer moved past the various spots; – a plain sketch from nature, or rather from the unnatural perversion of all that God has made; of all that man, in his moral, social, intellectual capacity, has undertaken to frame into a civil community. Darker features belong to the picture, even as respects mere children, but these we forbear to introduce: our present business is with such little ones as labour at the pin-heading; and we will once more call at the squalid dwelling where Alice Smith had hoped to establish all the comforts belonging to a poor but well-ordered home.

Two only of its former inmates are there: Polly has been called, by a boy somewhat older than herself, to join a strolling party of companions, whose steps we do not wish to trace. The step-mother has not yet roused herself from the heavy sleep that usually follows her long Saturday night's debauch; and Betsy steals now and then a fearful glance towards the dirty bundle of rags on which she lies snoring, while she heaps a few sticks and cinders on a spark of fire communicated to the torn leaf of a bible; given probably by some compassionate visitor to the wretched woman, who received it for the sake of the accompanying shilling, and then used it as so much waste-paper.

"Own mammy wouldn't have let us burn a bible," murmurs the little boy, as the sacred words rapidly disappear in a spreading tinge, which, however, yield no flame: "own mammy called it a holy book, and said we should all learn to read in it."

"Hush, dear: if she hears you talk of own mammy, she'll set out abusing daddy – I don't like to hear her."

"Daddy kicked me sorely when he was drunk, but he never hurt me when he wasn't. I love my own mammy best, and I wish she'd make haste back."

"I'm always telling you, Joey, that she can't come back; for they put her into a pit, ever so deep, as you might remember, for it wasn't so long ago."

"I remember it well enough; but I know the parson said something over her about sleeping and waking – waking at last, he said. Depend on it, she'll wake, and come up again."

"If I thought she'd wake," says Betsy, with a sigh, "'twould be a trouble to me; for they screwed that coffin down over tight for her to open, and the men stamped upon the clay as fast as they shovelled it in over her. She could never get through it all, if she did wake: and she'd better sleep on."

"No, I sha'n't sleep any longer," exclaims the shrill voice that always, even in its kindest tone, makes those little ones start. "It's proper enough of you to wish I might; for I have a hard time of it, taking such trouble about other people's brats. You can't help that. Where's Poll? Gone off, I dare say, for no good: that girl will bring me and my honest family to shame. Well, blow away, and heat the kettle while I dress."

Her orders are obeyed with the alacrity of secret dread; and the motherless children are glad that she so completely mistook what, in the earnest feeling of the moment, was spoken so distinctly as to catch her waking ear.

Another hour sees them wandering among dirt-heaps, desirous to find play-fellows, but with so little heart for play, that they want to be roused to the very mood for it. At a loitering pace, they scramble on, Joe every now and then jumping over some trifling obstruction, and crying "Hollo!" in a tone the very ghost of what it has been in former days. Nakedness, cold, hunger, may damp the mirthful spirits of childhood; but to quench them, nothing operates so rapidly and effectually as protracted labour in a confined spot, even without the super-addition of such cruelty and fear as these poor children have known by daily experience, and look for on the morrow, even as they endured it yesterday. Thus they stroll along, until the last row of dirty hovels is left behind, and they are alone in a narrow lane, bordered by hedges.

"Here's a gap," says Betsy; "let's get through, and find out what's on t' other side."

Nothing but a thick covering of dead leaves on the ground, while the naked branches of a tree hung over their heads, rewarded this search. The leaves were damp and dirty, yet they might serve as playthings, and the poor little creatures busy themselves in the idle amusement of kicking and tossing them about; occasionally pushing each other down, and laughing at the exploit. In this way, half an hour is passed, and Joe, having made his way from under a mass that his sister had flung upon him, suddenly calls out, "I say, Betsy, a' done, a' done; I want to talk about own mammy."

"Well, it's no use talking about her, for we can't get her back."

"That's more than we know: it's come in my head that daddy said to Richards, she was gone to heaven; and I don't believe heaven is at the bottom of that grave, is it?"

Betsy muses, with a look of recollection, and says, "No, for certain, Joey, its overhead. I've a notion, Polly can tell us about that: but it's so long since I heard any talk, I quite forget. It's a bonny place, too; I heard speak of it for a very bonny place."

"She's there," says the boy, confidently; "and if she got out of the coffin to go there, she can very well get out of heaven to come here; so you needn't say any more to me about her not coming back. I wonder how *she'll* look, when own mammy comes again to turn her out of doors, neck and crop!"

Betsy gazes on her little brother, for a flash of his native fire has appeared again; and he stands quite erect, with his head thrown back, and his dirty, but beautiful features all alive with unwonted animation. His voice too – poor child! the fond vision of a returning mother, in whose bosom he may once again nestle, has produced this strange effect. Betsy is secretly convinced that he is wrong, but does not know how to undeceive him. The lessons that reached their ear from the village pulpit had not penetrated any farther; they were considered too young for the schools; and neither father nor mother could read. The little girl's heart is full, and her voice falters as she remarks, "I can't think own mammy will ever come back: daddy may, for he's only gone to Ingee, they say; but mammy won't get out of heaven – it's so far off."

"So you say, but you don't know. Look, look, here's some boys and girls coming from towards the school! They'll be sure to know, and I'll ask them. Hollo! come this way!" and he runs to meet them, followed by Betsy.

Some of the party pass on; they have other sport in view, and this very short holiday must not be trifled with: two or three, however, are willing to stop, and the child asks, "Can you tell me how far it is to heaven?"

"No, I can't: I don't know where 'tis, nor nothing about it."

"Don't you hear about it at the school?" asks Betsy.

"No: they talk about London, and other places, and like enough that's one; but I never trouble my head to listen."

"It's no place at all," observes another, "but a great, rich man.

I heard my granny say sometimes, when the wages was spent, and nothing to eat, 'Heaven help us!' "

"No, no, it's a place," cries Betsy, anxiously; "for when mammy was going to die, she looked at us, and said, 'God in heaven bless ye.' "

"Like enough: they often talk of *him* in master's workshop." And here the boy repeats some forms of imprecation, and other blasphemous expressions, that must be passed over.

"If I went to school," says Joe, fretfully, "I'd get more learning than you; I'd mind what they said there, and remember it.'

A box on the ear, from the biggest boy, cuts short his speech; the little fellow's momentary excitement is past, and he begins to sob and cry, while Betsy throws her arms round him, and begs for mercy.

"The impudent young cur," says another, kicking up a heap of wet leaves into his face, "to think he'd be a better scholar than us, that's twice his age;" and as they move off, the two orphan children slink away in the contrary direction.

Late in the evening Polly comes home; and, as it had been agreed on, they ask her the question that perplexes them; "Whereabouts is heaven, where own mammy is gone to?" A very deep colour rises to the girl's face; then, casting down on them a look of supreme contempt, she mutters, "What a couple of great fools you must be to believe there's any such place!" and hurries to her own corner.

The step-mother presently returns from gossiping at the door, and attacks her, not for staying out, but for coming home hungry, and asking for supper. Polly recriminates, and the children hear much of language similar to that quoted in the morning, but nothing to throw any light on the matter so interesting to them. They nestle in their miserable bed, and are soon asleep, to open their eyes on another week of toil, and unpitied suffering. The frequent start, and half-uttered cry of imaginary torment, betray how busily fancy is occupied with dreams of the future, grounded, as they are, on bitter experience of the past; and in order to account for the reluctance with which their heavy eyes will open to the morrow's dawn, we will accompany them throughout a day's work at the seemingly light employment of sticking heads on the pins that are placed in shallow trays before them.

Chapter III

A DAY IN THE WORKSHOP

Although the little headers do not go to their work till near eight
o'clock, Polly starts for her's much earlier; and the step-mother
does not think of rising till long after they are all gone. The children, therefore, must leave their beds before the dull light of a
November morning has prevailed over the lingering shades of night,
and having put on their soiled rags, without any attempt at cleans-
ing their equally soiled persons, they kindle a fire, and commence
cooking the miserably thin porridge, or rather gruel, that forms
their breakfast. The supply of meal is very scanty; and the elder
girl, calculating that she requires more nourishment than those
junior to herself – particularly as Betsy looks younger and Polly
older than their real ages would lead us to suppose – secures her
share, by making the mixture tolerably thick, then subtracting her
own portion, and diluting the rest for the little ones. In addition to
this, a kettle has to be placed on the fire, and the latter roused to
tolerable briskness, that whenever Mrs. Smith chooses to rise, she
may be able to make her tea. A new penny loaf is procured, and a
slice of butter placed beside it, for her use; and the children, by
whose toil these indulgences are mainly provided, sit eyeing the
tempting provisions while swallowing down the watery, tasteless,
unsubstantial stuff, that their mother, even when most pressed by
poverty, would have deemed it a wrong to serve out to them. This
done, they eagerly press close to the little fire; for long hours must
pass before they may again enjoy that luxury; and a cold drizzle
without warns them of the state in which they will reach their place
of labour. But the time is short; Betsy soon puts on the remains of
her mother's old bonnet, and ties the fragment of a cap on her
brother's head with a piece of a handkerchief, taking him by the hand
for the walk. They go forth, unnoticed and uncared-for, to make
their way through the filthy streets, until, benumbed with cold, and
wet with the fine but penetrating rain, they reach the manufactory.
Here they stand, side by side, with a lurking hope that they may
once more be permitted to sit down together; but the approach of
the woman extinguishes that hope, as she pushes them in contrary
directions: they take their posts, and commence the work, as
already described. Such a collection of cold, hungry, half-naked
children, is scarcely to be found in any other department. Shoes and
stockings are very rare among them; a whole garment no less so;
and an instance of warm clothing suited to the season, it would be

vain to seek. They are not the children of decent mechanics, very few of whom would send their little ones here, but of street beggars, casual vagrants, and those Irish poor who have wandered over to what they hear is a richer country than their own, and find themselves perishing in it. Hence there are few instances of regular attendance, a week's work being often all that is sought; but each batch appears so like the preceding, that the difference is hardly noticed; and some are regular in their attendance, even for a long while together. The employer never comes here: the management is vested exclusively in the "master" placed over the shop, who renders no account of his conduct to the children; and who delegates his authority, on equally irresponsible terms, as regards everything but the amount and quality of the work done, to the female overlooker, whose cane he frequently borrows to inflict a harder blow on some defenceless culprit. In a horde of little strangers, untaught, and ungoverned at home, it can hardly be doubted that occasional demands would be made on the patience and forbearance of even the most benevolent disposition: but where no such feeling exists, and where the sole object is to see the utmost done in the shortest time, it may readily be supposed that the ill-humour occasioned by one instance of awkwardness or perverseness finds many a victim on which to vent itself.

Next to little Joe Smith sits a boy not much bigger than himself, but several years older: his parents are poor Irish people, and this child, unable to bear the close confinement, after his free life in the bogs, had run away some weeks before. However, he found his sick mother's sufferings so greatly aggravated by the loss of the weekly fifteen-pence, that on this morning he ventured to place himself near the door, where the master seeing him, ordered him in to work. He is a giddy fellow, fond of looking about him; and in spite of hunger, and rags that will scarcely hold together, he is full of restless vivacity. At this time, he is scanning the assembled party, to discover how many old acquaintances are there; but he keeps his fingers going with the hammer; and looking another way, he gets his thumb severely pinched, and cries out, though by no means loudly, "Och, murder!"

"You little Irish vagabond!" exclaims the dreaded woman, who had glided close behind him; and at the same time hits him a severe stroke over the head with her cane: "what business has the likes of such lazy beggars as you to be sitting here?"

The boy cries out again; for the poor little head had already been bruised by a fall or a blow, and the pain is very great. For the offence of so doing, he receives another, and heavier rap, which makes him roar for mercy, and hold up his hands to protect his head. Just at this moment the "master" enters – not the proprietor, as we have before explained, but the man who managed the concern – and while the female overlooker makes a violent complaint to him, little Joe whispers, "Hush, hush! the more you cry, the more they'll lick you."

This friendly caution only involves the poor child in his comrade's punishment: the man, having a heavy rod in his hand, goes up to the Irish boy, and telling him he had earned a thrashing by running away, which he may as well get now, along with his present desert, proceeds to chastise him most severely, until his cries subside into the suffocated sobs of complete exhaustion; then turning to Joe, who was pointed out to him by the woman as a confederate, who had whispered encouragement to the noisy rebel, he gives him two or three cruel strokes, under the last of which he falls off his seat, either from weakness or terror.

"And now," continues the governor, "I'll keep ye all a good twenty minutes past the time, to make up for the loss, and riot, and trouble, you've treated us to. Keep a sharp look out over them, Kitty, and don't spare the switch."

Poor little Betsy! the effort by which she suppressed both the scream and the tear, and refrained from even moving to her brother's assistance, was a terrible one. It convulsed her tender frame, and made her hand tremble as with an ague. She now sits, apparently quiet, but with a film over her eyes, and a choking in her throat, and a pain in her side, often experienced by adults of a nervous temperament, but a strange concomitant of early childhood. All is outwardly still again; terror has paralyzed the minds, but quickened the mechanical movements of those poor little slaves. Some have fathers or mothers, who love them dearly, and bitterly grieve over the hard necessity that compels them, perhaps in sickness or other infirmity, or the total inability to find employment themselves, to send their children out to labour; others have selfish, unfeeling parents, who gladly use them as machines to make money for their own indulgence; and others, again, are orphaned or deserted creatures, feeling themselves alone in the world, toiling for strangers; or to earn the price of a scanty meal for themselves, if they be above the earliest age. But all are laid under the same benumbing spell, in a place where the light of day never falls broadly and cheerily through the narrow, dirty panes of dull glass; where fresh air is excluded, where freedom never comes, where cleanliness is unknown, and mirth, the very element of a childish spirit, would be punished as a crime.

Day wears on, and those who came hungry at eight o'clock are sick from exhaustion by noon; but few indeed look forward to the luxury of a dinner. It has been observed that this department is supplied from the very poorest of the poor, many of whom have no home, creeping under carts, or into gateways, for shelter at night, or owing the comfort of a share in some filthy bundle of straw and rags to the compassion of such as let beds at two or three pence a night, or that of the miserable tenants who occupy them. These have no home by day except the workshop; and unless they have begged or stolen a scrap besides their mouthful at breakfast, they have nothing to eat till they get away to forage at night. These children are the most pitiable objects imaginable; their sunken, glassy eyes, hollow cheeks, and the general fall of their features, tell a tale that man may find it convenient to turn from, but which is ever prolonging its sad, silent appeal to Him whose eyes are in every place. Others have brought with them lumps of bread, with perhaps a bit of cheese, or bacon, which they devour on the spot, and then go out to lounge in the street, for they have no heart to play; and a few repair to homes, where a welcome sweetens the poor fare set before them, and a parental ear is open to their tale of trouble or alarm.

But the hour has slipped away, and the machinery, sensible and insensible, is again set a-going, to cease no more till six or seven hours have elapsed. It is now that childish endurance is put to the test: those who have not had their hunger appeased, or, at best, not satisfied, begin to droop; the back bends to a more decided curve, the shoulders rise higher, and the head declines on one side, while a confused giddiness renders even the monotonous process of heading difficult. In other cases, where nature has been tolerably well satisfied, the restlessness inevitable among growing children, increased by the temporary stimulus of food and drink, becomes a source of misery to themselves, and of torment to their languid comrades. Many a naked foot is stealthily kicked out under the board; many a ragged elbow jerked in half-nervous, half-mischievous invasion of a neighbour's confined space; and some, in the imprisoned state of their limbs, indulge in the liberty of making hideous faces, provoking a smothered titter from the observer, and a smart blow from the overlooker, should she detect what is of course construed into a premeditated insult. Thus they go on, hour by hour, until all is weariness – a weariness inconceivable by any who have not endured the imprisonment of a protracted sedentary occupation – a weariness that makes the bones feel as though grated on by some harsh, foreign substance, and the flesh endure alternately the deadening numbness of obstructed circulation, and the tingling pain of inflammatory action, while the limbs seem preternaturally stretched, and every perception confused into indistinct bewilderment – a weariness that it is vain to attempt describing; because those who have not experienced cannot imagine it; and those who have, know it to be indescribable.

What a luxury it would be, even for a few minutes, to lie stretched at full length on that dirty floor; or to take two or three brisk runs from end to end of the narrow room; or to rub the stiffened fingers before the fire which emits no warmth for them, however efficacious it may be for the comfort of Kitty, the overlooker, as she seats herself at will right before it, or stirs the sluggish embers into a transient glow! But heat will not long be lacking, for the daylight has declined, and a blaze of gas falls upon the scene, producing a rapid rise in the temperature, accompanied with suffocating smells, and a closeness that operates like a narcotic on the poor children, who, to counteract its effects, gaze into the gaslights, round which their sleepy eyes picture a circle of diverging rays, and then again experience the increased difficulty of hitting aright the diminutive aperture of the pin-heads, frequently so minute as to be a trial for the strongest sight under the steady beam of noon. The playfulness of childhood has utterly disappeared: mischief, before comparatively harmless, as a practical joke, has become the ebullition of quarrelsome ill-humour, and the malice of a revenge that would fain wreak itself somewhere; and, being unable to reach the tyrants who provoked it, finds vent on its fellow-sufferers. "Hateful and hating one another," now indeed is shown to be the inbred character of unregenerated mankind; and as that character prematurely unfolds itself under the cruel influences of premature exaction of toil, who does not long to obey the gentle invitation, and ere the heart is utterly hardened, to place these poor little children at the foot of him who says, "Forbid them not to come unto me," though, alas! they have passed too suddenly from the stage of existence to which the sequel was applied; and we are compelled to feel that of such is not the kingdom of heaven.

"Can't you be a little brisker?" fearfully whispers Joe Smith to his Irish neighbour, while Mrs. Kitty is known to be taking her tea in the next room, and therefore off her watch: "I'm afraid she'll see you, and be over cross."

"Sorra a bit faster can I move, then, dear. My head's too sore, and it aches so; and my arms drop. I can't stand it."

"Why did you come back?"

"Mother's so sick, and hasn't food to eat."

"Ah, if you've a mother to work for, it's worth bearing a good lot of hardship to help *her*. My poor mammy is dead and gone."

"The heavens be her bed!" ejaculates the good-natured Irish boy, while his swollen eyes turn compassionately on his little friend.

"Do *you* know where heaven is?" asks Joe, in an almost breathless whisper.

"It's somewhere beyond purgatory; and the souls that the priests get out of that go there."

"Purgatory!" mutters Joe, to whom the word is wholly new; and then, with the timidity that has become a second nature, he shrinks from further discourse, and pursues his work. But curiosity prevailing again, or rather, solicitude about his lost parent, he soon turns to his comrade, intending to ask another question, and encounters the eye of the master, who has stolen into the room to detect any undue advantage taken of Kitty's absence; and who, catching the little fellow in the very act of addressing the condemned culprit beside him, bestows a pinch on his ear that turns it to purple, while his nail penetrates the tender skin, saying, "You young dog, I'll teach you to choose your company better;" and at the same time commands another boy to change places with him, in order to separate him from one of whom he seems fond.

But this manœuvre has placed Joe so near his little sister, that her heart bounds with joy; and a sly look of gratulation is exchanged between the children. A few minutes, however, bring Kitty back, whose careful eye discovers the new arrangement, and in a moment her hand is on the ragged collar of Joe's little coat, whom she drags back over his seat, and rapping his head with her cane, calls out, "How durst you do such a thing, you impudent jackanapes?"

The boy who had exchanged with him, anxious to escape a similar infliction, eagerly explains how and why it was done; and Joe, instead of being returned to his former station, is put further than ever from the only two beings who can feel for his desolate condition; all the rest being fully engrossed by their own share of suffering. One short, broken sob is all that escapes the child throughout this double exercise of petty tyranny, which has done service in one or two respects, by changing the course of his perplexing thoughts, and rousing several of the lookers-on from their half-dormant state, thereby saving them from the cane.

But the scene becomes more painful every moment: the unnatural efforts of the poor children to combat at once fatigue, heat, drowsiness, and the exhaustion that fasting brings, superadded to so many hours of unvaried toil, produce among other effects so much awkwardness, so many blunders, and retarding of the work, that neither the scolding tongue nor ever active arm of the woman can keep up with the demands on their continued exercise. She is herself very much tired, heartily sick of her task, and under the influence of something stronger than tea, which she felt it but reasonable to add to that beverage. *She* gains nothing by the additional twenty minutes' toil exacted by the master: it is a prolongation of her own confinement to the spot; and those who are pointed out as its cause must expect to endure a full share of her resentment, along with that of their companions.

"I'll give you a right good milling for this, as soon as I get you outside," muttered a big boy to little Joe Smith, at the same time suddenly jarring the child's elbow, so as to make him hurt his fingers among the pins; and Joe shrank from him.

"I'll make your head ache for you twice more nor it does now," growled another to the Irish boy, who, looking up sideways in the face of the threatener, replies,

"More power to your elbow, then. Once I'm free to handle my own fists, I'd like to see the fellow that'll touch my head against my will."

"You dirty Irish beggar!"

"You're not over clane, for an English one, any how."

"Go it, Bill," "Go it, Jerry", was the encouraging counsel of mischievous neighbours, who felt quite cheered by the prospect of a fight in the street; while a sensible little fellow, scarcely out of petticoats, observes, "I think we get knocks enough in doors, and might find better fun outside."

But even this excitement presently subsides, as the overlooker lounges behind them; and the raps that the cane audibly gives on many a devoted head justify the little boy's remark. Some relieve their minds by a long string of curses deliberately pronounced when the woman is out of hearing; and too often a regular trial ensues of which among the demoralized young creatures shall apply the foulest names, the most dreadful maledictions, to this miserable official. The master comes in for his share, because they often feel his power and willingness to make them smart; and if they look not beyond him – if their eyes penetrate not the decorated walls of mansions where every luxury is revelled in at their expense, or that of some equally helpless, equally injured class, it is because their knowledge extends no farther than their bodily senses can lead them. There is an eye that looks farther: a hand that, sooner or later, will deal even justice to all: and while such as are wrongfully blamed have the comfort of knowing that "the curse causeless shall not smite," others, who never appear as the direct oppressors of the infant poor, have a lesson to study, which, theoretically or practically, they MUST learn: – "As the partridge sitteth on eggs and hatcheth them not, so he that getteth riches, and not by right, shall leave them in the midst of his days, and at his end shall be a fool."

The hour-glass has been turned and turned all day long. It is preferred to a clock, and some of the elder children say they have seen it with the sand fully run out for some minutes before it was turned; and that they would rather have a clock, which goes tick, tick, without any intermission, and cannot count wrong. At home, indeed, from elder people, they hear of hands put back, and clocks regulated to go slow, as occasion may require; but it is all matter of talk – by clock, or by hour-glass, as the progress of either may be interpreted by superior authority, the poor must labour on to the stipulated moment of release.

On the present night, there is a press of work in the pin manufactory; and long before the misdemeanor of our young friends settled that point, it had been predicted that the children would not get out at the regular time. No one can tell what an amount of suffering is contained in a quarter of an hour's extra work when eight o'clock has passed. Nature seems just capable of sustaining the effort up to the point to which it is habitually screwed; and then the human machinery stops of its own accord – it can no more. *Can!* What has can to do with factory toil? *Must* is the word. Ay, they must go on for another twenty minutes, reckoned by the same infallible interpretation of the sand's movement in the glass; and tears are falling down many a babyish face, because of this intolerable strain on weary eyes, this agonizing stretch of over-wrought muscles. The twenty minutes are worth a long hour to them; but even they have passed, and forth go the little straggling herd, right out of that heated room into the piercing wind, the cutting frostiness of a sullen November night, in a locality where even frost does not clarify the air, but hangs, as it were a sharp edge on a dusky fog. In a moment the skins still dripping with perspired moisture pucker into the knotted surface that intense cold produces: a smart is felt about the eyes, too often the precursor of blindness; teeth chatter; and feet stumble in the sudden darkness that succeeds a glare of light; or the feeblest are pushed down by the more strong. Betsy has wrapped up, as well as she can, her shivering little brother, and keeps her arm round his bare neck, where the rough grasp of the woman had torn away the poor remnant of a collar; and the Irish boy, after lingering awhile to ascertain whether his challenger meant to make good his threats, and seeing him scamper off in the direction of a gin-shop, hastens towards the cellar where his sick mother has found a temporary rest, in the corner spared to her by the hospitality of a countrywoman, a very few degrees richer than herself.

Betsy and Joe proceed to their step-mother's home. The rain that was falling in the morning has continued, with some intermission, through the day, causing every filthy puddle to overflow its regular boundaries; and sending a broad stream of water, thickened by all possible varieties of foul additions, through the gutters that divide the streets into two roughly-paved and unequal portions. Spouts obstructed by long neglect, send their contents dripping and splashing from the eaves of many a house; and between the two, our poor children become thoroughly soaked, even before they can reach the covered passage, the ground under which is one continued pool of dirty water, while beyond it a strong light would scarcely suffice to guard the passenger from frequently slipping ancle-deep into the little pits of mud and slime that break up the path in every direction. Light, however, there is none in this region of wretchedness, save where the red glare of a forge shows the labourers at their night work within, and further dazzles the bewildered sight of the pedestrian without. Once or twice Betsy has tried to lift her brother over some of the more formidable obstructions, but her stride, so encumbered, falls short of the distance, and she has found her anxiety to protect him only a means of aggravated suffering to both. The intense cold of the all-but frozen element which now steeps the limbs so lately perspiring from artificial heat produces a sickening sensation; and they encourage each other with the prospect of a cup of warm gruel, a huddle into the chimney-corner, and such covering as may remain to their miserable bed after Mrs. Smith and Polly shall have taken what they may want to defend themselves from the cold of that inclement night.

Chapter IV

VICISSITUDES

One of the most common events that befal the poor is a seizure of the few articles of furniture that they may possess for arrears of rent; and a summary ejectment from the premises occupied. Alice Smith had been very careful to see the landlord regularly paid, while she lived; but her successor took no thought about it. Her husband paid up the first half-year after her death, at the same time that he added several articles (how come by we need not inquire) belonging to the person whom he had married; but no further payment was thought of. Some threats had been uttered, which at last reached the ear of this woman, and the necessity of seriously exerting herself was felt as a most grievous annoyance. The poor children, hastening under the shelter of the roof, are soon made to feel its effects, in reproaches, pushes, and blows: while their humble request for a little supper is treated as an aggravation of her wrongs. After going on for some time venting her ill-humour on the weeping creatures, she suddenly turns her attention to a new object, and commences packing up, in small bundles, the various articles of bedding, and other portable matters; after which she goes out, locking the door, and taking the key.

Hard as their case was, it was not altogether new to the children: they had gone supperless to bed before now, and though the sickness induced by the cold damp is added to that of long fasting, and renders the want of a little warm nourishment more trying, they know there is no remedy. Afraid to go to bed, until the stepmother's return, they roll themselves up in a corner, and after some bitter lamentations about their own mammy, sleep overpowers them. In the same place they awake next morning, wondering to find the room so bare, the bundles all gone, and Mrs. Smith herself busily occupied in preparing their morning mess. They find, too, that they have been allowed to sleep beyond the time, and must run to their work the moment their breakfast is swallowed down. Two thick slices of bread, and a piece of cheese for their dinner, are quickly put into their hands; and they are pushed, not roughly but hastily, from the door, with an injunction to run fast – no easy matter, so much their little limbs are stiffened by the miserable cold of the night, and the incrustations of mud on their feet and apparel.

The day passes as its predecessor did: a like amount of unvaried labour, capricious tyranny, severity, and pain. At night, the two little ones of Alice Smith repair homeward, comforting themselves with the recollection of the comparative attention bestowed on them in the morning, and hoping for a better reception than on the preceding night; but the door is fast, and a shutter is up against the window, which was never known to be there before; and while they, at intervals, repeat the humble rap that they are accustomed to give, no answer is returned. A neighbour, however, comes out from her house, and says, "Poor bairns! you may spare your knocking;

the landlord's been, and seized the few sticks of things that cunning hussey didn't slip away, and now you may shift for yourselves.''

The frightened children stare in her face, not well able to comprehend her meaning; and she adds, 'You'd best go at once to the overseer, and he'll take you into the workhouse for the night.''

A man who had stopped to listen to her story, moved by the helplessness of the children, observes that they cannot get in at that late hour without somebody to speak for them; and he will go. But on being told to follow, Betsy bursts out crying, and says she is sure if she sits on the step a while, mammy Smith will come home, or else Polly, and let them in.

"Don't be a little fool," says the woman; "but be glad of your luck to have a friend in need. Neither Polly nor anybody else can get into the house. Go away with you, or you'll have to sleep in the street.''

With some difficulty, they are induced to move on; and through the kind persuasions of this strange man, a night's lodging in the workhouse is afforded, till inquiry can be made respecting their step-mother's proceedings. At the same time, a messenger is dispatched to caution their employer against paying any part of their wages to the woman who has cast them off – a measure of no avail now; for she had been there, and by a tale equally false and plausible, had actually won on the under master to depart from his customary rule, and out of his own pocket to advance several months' wages, on account of the two children, who, ill as they were treated, were secretly admitted to be two of the most punctual attendants, and best workers in the manufactory.

Betsy and Joe have now a new trial to undergo: they must be separated. She is given in charge to a woman for the night, and he turned into the boys' room. A good fire, a fair mess of hot milk-and-water, with bread-and-butter to eat, and a merry set of little fellows in the corner assigned to him, presently reconcile Joe to his situation; more especially as he is too sleepy to be able to reflect much. For otherwise is it with poor Betsy: the sudden rending of every tie is too much for her. Miserable as her home had long been, even before her mother died, still the memory of that mother, particularly in her last illness and death, hung around it; and it seems as if the recent conversations about her with the little boy had been ordered on purpose to add bitterness to her present grief. Then Joe himself! how *could* they take him from her? Her fancy pictured a thousand wrongs and cruelties inflicted on him, and the idea of never seeing him again took fast hold on her mind. The women in vain offer her hot tea, and toast: she can only sob and moan, and has not a word to answer either their soothings or reproaches. One woman, who has just lost a little girl of her age, seeing her so filthy and wretchedly clad, resolves to wash her, and put on some few things that belonged to her child; and while thus employed, she obtains from Betsy a whispered confession that it is after her brother she is fretting so much. The assurance that she will see him in the morning, and go to work with him as usual, tranquillizes her a little; but she is too sick to eat, and a feverish headache renders her insensible to the comforts of such a bed as she has not for a long time lain down on.

Here let us pause. What would be the position of this little girl if christian principles were carried out, or common justice rendered, where the infant poor are concerned? As the child of a village labourer, she would be employed in light field work, or sewing for the family, or helping her mother in such easy tasks as suited her age and capacity. She would be gratuitously receiving an education to ground her in the principles of christian faith and knowledge, with the Bible placed in her hands, and all the appointed means of grace within her reach. She would be kept cleanly in person and habits, and taught that female respectability does not depend on wealth or station, but that the humblest of English maidens may establish as strong a claim to it as the proudest peeress in the land. She would be practically learning in early childhood what was to fit her to be the wife, the manager, the mother, in her own humble rank; a comfort and a blessing to all around her, without even taking one step beyond that rank. Her body's growth would be promoted by fresh air and exercise, her mental faculties brought into play, and her habits formed on a model of frugal, patient diligence in that state of life into which it had pleased God to call her.

But regarding Betsy as an orphan, and in a town, necessarily debarred from many of these advantages, and with no natural friends to provide for her, what, on the same principle of Christianity and justice, would be the difference of her situation from that in which we behold her? She would be the more amply provided with all needful instruction because of having no mother to learn from at home: she would enjoy longer and more frequent opportunities of out-door exercise, because she had further to go for the freshening air of heaven, which could not visit her in the alley of a town as in a country cottage. She would be the more carefully watched over, in regard to her health, because to her own industry alone she must look forward for support. She would be more diligently instructed in the nurture and admonition of the Lord, because in Him are the fatherless children specially to trust;

and because temptations to evil were multiplied around her. Every one would shrink from laying a heavy burden on her, because HE has said, whose word never faileth, "Ye shall not afflict any widow or fatherless child: if thou afflict them in any wise, and they cry at all unto me, I will surely hear their cry; and my wrath shall wax hot, and I will kill you with the sword, and your wives shall be widows, and your children fatherless." As one who had no parent's helping hand to lean on for future provision, and with three little orphaned companions, younger than herself, who might look to her as their senior, and natural guide, she would be more perfectly instructed in whatsoever branch of industry promised the best returns for her labour; and care would also be taken to prepare her for the domestic management that might early devolve upon her.

All these particulars combined amount to no more than a simple act of justice, the plain carrying out of a universally recognized principle of christian duty. It is a duty, too, from which none can plead exemption. The church owes it as an act of obedience to the divine command, "Feed my lambs." Each minister of the church owes it, in his respective sphere, as the fulfilment of his ordination vow; the state owes it, as a minor part of its office, being the appointed minister ordained of God to govern the people right-eously – a terror to evil-doers, and for the praise of them that do well. The child whose parents neglect it, in matters where it cannot judge for itself, or who are removed by death or absence from their posts, becomes a powerful claimant on the sympathizing help of all who witness its forlorn condition; and howsoever habit, custom, selfishness, blind us to this fact, the claim is registered in the book of God's remembrance, and a strict note taken of the manner in which it is responded to.

Some excellent societies are in operation for promoting educa-tion, of a scriptural and industrial character, among the female children of India and the East, the wilds of America, and every quarter of the globe where Christianity is not established. The distinctly avowed purpose of these institutions is to supply the lack of what we so abundantly enjoy – they are the out-goings of christian benevolence from an enlightened people to nations who sit in darkness still. Very great is the zeal and very commendable is the diligence evinced by English ladies to promote this work, and to enlist the sympathies of all around them for its extension. Still we must ask, how do these ladies contrive to overlook the objects perishing so near them, and to confine their compassionate cares to others, so very far removed? The misery, the wretchedness, the sufferings, the degradation of young English girls, far exceed those of the little heathen abroad; nor is the foulest system of pagan demoralization, cruelty, and crime, second in atrocity to that which varnishes itself over with the name of Christianity, and seizes for its victims the free-born children of Britain, baptized into a faith of which they live and die in soul-destroying ignorance.

Proceeding on our plan of embodying facts, as they are proved to exist in daily occurrence, we will now return to Betsy Smith – the fictitious representative of a host of real living sufferers, under the dreadful system pursued in all our manufacturing districts. Among the hundreds of poor little children who, from one cause or another, are suffering sickness, but without enjoying, on that account, any exemption from toil, we see this little girl rendered feverish and ill by causes, to the operation of which the majority of her companions are also liable: alternate cold and heat; wet clothes not shifted; exposure in a fasting state to the malaria of a most revoltingly offensive atmosphere, loaded with putrid effluvia; and the debility consequent on long fasting. The poor inmates of a workhouse ward could not offer much to tempt the sick stomach of an ailing child, though what they could they had done; but in addition to her illness, the poor little creature had to endure great misery of mind. She secretly dreaded that the promise of her brother's restoration to her might not be fulfilled: experience had taught her two facts – one was, that in whatever way an additional penny might be wrung from their premature toil, in that way they would certainly be employed; the other was, that the world contained no human being to whom she might make appeal, or from whom she could hope to gain the smallest alleviation of any hardship allotted to her or to the comrade of her early sorrows. This, preying on a spirit depressed yet more by real illness of body, kept her silent, shrinking, and utterly unable to make any return for the many proffers of kindness, sweetened tea, thinner bread, and even a dust of sugar stealthily strewn over the butter that was scraped upon it, from the private hoard of an old woman, except a faint, "No thank ye." Some resented this: one called her ungrateful, another, a stupid little fool; a third, proud and fanciful; but the person who had taken charge of her, and cleaned her, still repeated, with a shake of the head, "The bairn is sick."

At last the decisive moment arrives; and Betsy, having received injunctions to repair straight to her place of work, while descending the narrow stone steps that lead to the door, sees the smiling face of little Joe peeping up from the bottom. The joyous "Ah!" that bursts from her pale dry lips, is the first happy tone that has issued from them for a long while; and, hand in hand, the children skip forward, each relating the wonders that had occurred during their long separation, and forming vague guesses as to what had become of mammy Smith, and of Polly. But this was a temporary excitement of mind only; Betsy, on taking her place, feels uncommonly faint and giddy: the machinery appears to move in unwonted confusion, and the occasional hum of voices, whispering in the absence of the overlooker, to form such sounds as she never heard before. But a watchful eye is following the movements of her unsteady hand; and a few raps from the cane, each more severe than its predecessor, admonish her that, well or ill, she is there to labour.

They were ordered to run to the workhouse for their dinner; but before they can proceed many steps, a violent fit of shivering obliges the little girl to sit down on a stone, declaring that it will do her more good to rest there than to go to dinner. Joe, hungry, and elated at the prospect of a hot meal, does not require much persuasion to leave her, and she sits wondering, not at being very cold, but at the hot feeling that every now and then shoots over her.

If little Betsy had been born into a gentleman's family, with what anxious care would she now be put into a soft bed; all the curtains drawn, every voice hushed, every foot commanded to fall lightly; the best medical attendance summoned, and, perchance, a kind mother kneeling beside her downy couch, at once to watch and to pray over the alarming symptoms. Yes, Betsy Smith might have been the very same individual, body, soul, and spirit; of the same age, features, complexion, and feelings – if only her *station* were different, how very different would be her fate! But there is no respect of persons with God; except that with a very peculiarly jealous care he deigns to watch what shall befall the fatherless and poor at the hands of the wealthy.

And what befalls little Betsy Smith, the pin-header! Nothing, as yet. She sits upon the stone, her knees drawn up, and her chin resting on her hands, with a very sick headache, and a very vacant look. Nobody minds her: why should they? She has no recognized claim on anybody. A drunken men reels against her, and she falls off, but soon recovers herself, with only a slight sprain of the wrist and bruise on the temple; and when Joe returns, she slides down from her damp seat, walking so unsteadily as to draw on her the jeering rebukes of licentious passers-by, who observe, she is o'er young to be tippling at that time o' day.

Meanwhile, the parish officer has been to the deserted hovel, to the landlord of it, and finally to the pin manufactory. The result of all is, that the woman Smith has outwitted and defrauded every party; and as the master will maintain his right to be repaid out of the children's labour, there is no remedy left for the parish: they must feed and lodge them until the money advanced by the master is earned back; and then they may hope to send them into the labour market on their own account. The evening of that day is one of agony to poor little Betsy: fits of stupor, from which she is only roused by blows, or by twitching out of her weak flaxen hair, are succeeded by passing moments of positive though silent delirium. Her wild thoughts betray themselves in looks alone, which nobody heeds: and as, at last, she makes her way homewards, Joe can scarcely persuade her that their path lies in a new direction. The bitter night-air brings some refreshment, however; and her sick fancy completely settles on the kind face and soothing voice of the good woman to whom she was returning; with some anticipations of the comfort she shall feel in nestling in that nice bed. She resolves to be very communicative to her new friend; and to look to her as a sort of mother, very different from mammy Smith, though not to be loved like "own mammy."

At the door, however, they are met by one of the porters, who, without any explanation, tells them to "come along!" and going round to another entrance, delivers Joe up to a man smoking near it: then bidding Betsy "move on," makes her walk through a pretty long street, into a very narrow lane, and knocks at a door, which is opened by an aged and not very prepossessing woman.

"You see, missus, the girls' room's full; and this here pauper child must stop with you."

"To be sure: there's lots of room. Go in, child, up them stairs."

This is all the explanation poor Betsy receives of a change so sudden. She creeps, shivering and gasping, up a sort of a ladder, and finds herself in a long- low-roofed room, very miserable in appearance, but tolerably airy from its size; while grouped in knots are about a score of girls, varying in age, bearing on them the marks of all the dirty occupations in the town; some pressing round a candle's end, examining a farthing print, or other rubbish; all looking miserably poor, ill-fed, and heavy-hearted. Articles in the shape of beds, but as destitute of cleanliness and comfort as could be imagined, mark this long room as a dormitory; but the accommodations are so scanty, compared with the number to be accommodated, that Betsy expects to sleep on the floor, to which she is near falling from exhaustion. However, the old woman comes up, and succeeds in finding a small bed, where only two have a claim, and Betsy is told to make a third. By this time she is nearly insensible, and one of the biggest girls goes to report her case to the "missus," who hobbles up, feels her pulse, looks at her tongue, and pronouncing her to be not bad enough to want the doctor, but in want of medicine, administers a nauseous draught, and bids her lie down.

Too light-headed to comprehend anything clearly, poor Betsy only feels that she cannot sleep; but whether from the ruggedness of the bed, the rapid talking of her companions, or the severe pain in her own bones, she cannot tell. She passes the night in feverish tossings; and in the morning, being wholly unable to rise, she is told to lie still till the doctor calls, on his way to the workhouse. Anxious thoughts of Joe, and fears for him, oppress her; but all is confused. The doctor pronounces it a feverish cold – very feverish – and she must remain quiet, take another dose, and drink gruel very thin.

She is left quite alone; the very loud noise made by very little children below, convincing her that the old woman is going through the ceremony of pretending to keep a dame school. She is dreadfully thirsty; but in the bustle below the gruel has been forgotten; and she is helpless, till the dinner hour brings home some of the pauper girls, and her parched throat is moistened from the jug of water, that had stood all night far out of her reach, at the utmost end of the room.

Towards dusk she feels considerably better, asks to sit up, and wants to see her brother. She is told that boys never come there, and it would be of no use inquiring for him. She also learns something of her present situation from a girl who had been at the workhouse during the morning; and who tells her that the way to see Joe again is to get well as fast as she can; that they may go to work together.

Chapter V

THE SICK PAUPER

At all times comparatively helpless and dependent, childhood in sickness becomes doubly so; and hardened, indeed, must be the heart that can resist its touching plea for compassion and succour. Yet to this extent is the heart of man, and of woman too, hardened by the all-absorbing principle of selfishness. The hireling who is paid for rendering attentions which are peculiarly the office of a mother, sister, or other near connexion, will too frequently be found faithful in their discharge only so far as the eye of the party holding the purse is upon her, even where the charge is a fondled child of wealth, and the remuneration abundantly large: but in the case of friendless pauper children, for whom a compulsory provision is made by law, and a niggardly allowance is doled out to the grumbling recipient, for undertaking to look after the troublesome brat, what can we expect? The official considers herself ill-paid, even for the modicum of attention that she is obliged outwardly to bestow; and the poor aching little head is less likely to be lulled on its hard pillow by the soothings of kindness, than to be further racked and bewildered, and frightened, by noisy outbursts of splenetic ill-humour, and complaints of the trouble imposed. The comforts of cleanliness, ventilation, fumigation, cool drinks, and encouragements to sleep, that in other cases are deemed indispensable, must not be dreamed of here. Loud tones, heavy tramping, slamming of doors, and neglect in every possible form, are matters of course. Long sickness in a pauper child is not to be tolerated: if it does not quickly get well, without any fuss being made about it, better it should die and be done with: more will be left than anybody knows how to provide for.

But there is another class from whom little mercy can be hoped: those who having a certain quantity of work to be done, and requiring it to be done within the shortest possible time, at the least possible cost, hire pauper children to do it. These employ two sorts of machinery in their business: one being made of flesh, the other of wood and iron. If a wheel or strap becomes entangled, it is set to rights by the proper workman; if so injured as not to allow of speedy repairing, it is thrown by, and a new one substituted, to avoid any delay. Just so it is with the human department. Why should any difference be made? Why should not a child be worked as long as it can be compelled to go on, with a little occasional quick patching, and when it cannot, be thrown into the street, just as a broken wheel is thrown into the lumber room, to fall to pieces? It is not to be expected that the master's profits of a few hundred or thousands per annum, should be decreased to the amount, now and then, of one and sixpence, by allowing a little creature, that has worked itself ill in his service, to lie by for a week without forfeiting its eighteen pence; or to retain its claim to re-admission on recovery. But add to this the fact, that what the child earns is not at its own disposal, going to remunerate the person who has charge of it, for such food and such clothing as it gets, we may believe the little labourer must be in the position of a shuttlecock, struck alternately from one battledore to the other, until, escaping a stroke, it falls to the ground, and is trampled into kindred dust.

Our little Betsy Smith's situation is that of thousands upon thousands in this land. One parent lost by premature death, through merciless exaction of labour beyond her strength, the other by total desertion, first of his duties, and then of his home; It is a small matter for whom she toils, or who is to deal out to her the very scanty portion of this world's good that falls to her lot. Under a different system – under the protection of christian laws, administered in a christian spirit, – no doubt such helpless beings would find a fitting asylum, where their bodies would be allowed to grow, their minds to expand, their constitutions to acquire some stamina, and their hands to become both active and strong for the various burdens of labour to which, at a proper age, they might be destined. But, alas! as respects the most numerous class of her people, the Christianity of England is a name, and her boasted laws of equal right and privilege are a farce.

Betsy Smith's employer having been cheated out of the price of toil, not yet performed, by the craft of her step-mother, and having had, on the preceding day, a little altercation with the parish authorities, as to their comparative claims on the child's future earnings, in which, with some trouble, he established his own, might naturally look with a suspicious eye on her absence. She was, perhaps, kept away to work for them under pretence of illness; for Joe had been ordered to report her sick. After trying in vain the effect of cross-interrogation, enforced with a few heavy blows, (for the "question" is sometimes administered in that way without the superintendence of a grand inquisitor,) and ascertaining that the boy really knew nothing more than he had repeated, it was resolved, if she did not appear on the morrow, to send Kitty the overlooker on a mission of inquiry.

This woman, indeed, could have borne testimony that the little girl was so ill on the preceding day, as scarcely to get through her work; and that she had even fallen from her seat through exhaustion; but the temptation of a walk, and a gossip, and a confidential office in the eyes of the workhouse people, more than counterbalanced any inclination to tell the truth, or any compunction for what she was helping to inflict on the innocent boy; especially as no one of the children would dare to volunteer a testimony, so long as she gave none. Accordingly, at noon the next day, Mrs Kitty puts on her bonnet, a warm cloak, and showy apron, and proceeds to investigate the mysteries of the workhouse. She happens to find at the door the very man who had conducted Betsy to her present abode; and he, unwilling to be kept from his dinner, by starting any difficulties, tells her at once where to find the child, adding with a wink, "You needn't say who told you."

The female overlooker of the pin-headers is not more willing to pay a gossiping visit than is the old woman at the pauper child's lodging to receive one. They soon become very sociable; and after comparing notes, and relating a variety of concurrent anecdotes, they arrive at the conclusion that there is not upon earth such another set of plagues and torments as beggar-children; nor any class of respectable persons so ill-paid and oppressed as those who have the charge of them; whether in a workshop or a domestic institution. Having settled this, and partaken of "something warm," they mount the stairs, enter the long room, and find little Betsy in a sound sleep, flushed, indeed, and breathing painfully, but still in what might be called a luxury of rest, compared with any thing she has known for a long while.

"The lazy little hussey!" says Mrs. Kitty, roughly pulling away the clothes that shaded her eyes from the light of an opposite window in that curtainless room, "there's nothing the matter with her, I'll be bound."

The rude jar, the harsh voice, at once wake the child, and to her terrified sight the apparition of her task-mistress, scowling over her, is the signal of something worse than either words or looks. She starts up in her bed, and sits, trembling and panting, with a broad stare fixed on the object of her dread.

"O you're wonderfully brisk all on a sudden," remarks the old woman of the house; "a while ago, it was all lack-a-daisy! and you couldn't lift your head from the bolster, not you!"

"It's all a sham," observes Mrs. Kitty, "and she shall smart for it. Indeed, she ought to catch it on both sides her face, for she's deceived you, and robbed us. Only think of our suspecting you of keeping her to work, and whipping her poor little brother for not telling what he didn't know, poor child!"

At hearing this, Betsy bursts into a most piteous cry; her sobs gradually increasing in violence, till she becomes so convulsed as almost to alarm the two women, who stand looking at her and at each other, muttering, "What's to be done?" At this moment, a young lad, the parish doctor's apprentice, who has been sent to call in on the slighter cases among the paupers, and report, but not to interfere further, runs up the ladder, and exclaims, "Who is in a fit here?"

"It's a fit of passion, sir," answers Kitty.

The young gentleman feels the pulse, and shakes his head. "No, 'tis something serious, and she must be bled: fetch a basin, my good woman." Then, taking out his new case of pocket instruments, he adds, "In such an emergency as this, I must not be too strictly attentive to the letter of my directions, as a life may be lost. However, you need not say anything about it;" looking inquiringly at the old woman, whose grin of acquiescence shows that she understands she will lose nothing by indulging the young practitioner in a trial of his skill on this insignificant pauper child.

But Kitty has more at stake: she is resolved to have Betsy back in the shop, in proof of her own discernment, and to gain some indulgence that she wants, in reward for the good service so discreetly performed. She therefore says, "I beg your pardon, sir, but this girl belongs to us, and is wanted at her work. I'm morally sure she is ailing little or nothing; and I can't agree to her being bled unless the workhouse doctor himself says 'tis needful."

"Well, I'm sure I don't care. The child is ill, and unfit to work, but she is in excellent hands here. You may call for a draught in the evening; till then, my good woman, keep her quiet, give her cooling drink, and all that." So saying, he ran off.

"Fine work some of them chaps make among the beggars, trying their hands, when the master is away," says Kitty. "I was sorry to thwart such a nice young gentleman."

"I never do, if I can help it," observes the other. "They are often as clever as their masters, and if they do make a mistake now and then, among people that ain't of no consequence, it helps them to be more skilful and careful when they come to practice openly."

By this time, Betsy had sobbed herself into a state of insensibility, and lay quite still. The old woman threw the bed-clothes over her shoulders again, saying, "There, let her be till morning, and I'll send her off to you in working order."

Night arrives, and a cluster of shivering girls take possession of the cold room. Something has happened to put the old woman out of temper, and their poor supper is served out with a double allowance of scolding, while an inch only of rushlight is allowed them to take upstairs. The girls who sleep with Betsy are inclined to grumble at the miserable condition of the bed in which she has been tossing all day; but finding her more distressed about it than at her own sufferings, they kindly bid her not to mind.

Having gathered a party about her, Betsy says, "Will you listen to me a bit? I'd a own mammy not long ago; and she died, and I think I'm going to die too; and I want to know where mammy is gone to, now she's dead; so can you tell me?"

Various replies were given. One said, "I suppose she went into the grave." Another, "When a body dies, there's an end of 'em – the worms eat 'em up." A third remarked, "I never heard such a rum speech." And a fourth, "Ghostesses is dead people: they come up, whiles, and walk, and frighten folk."

This draws the whole party instinctively together; particularly as the last ray of light is glimmering in the dirty socket. It expires; but immediately a cloud that had obscured the full moon also passes away, and from a sky of the deepest blue that beauteous orb looks out, displaying its broad clear disc directly opposite the window, and throwing a stream of light upon the bed, and the group who cower and crowd about it. The sight seems to revive in Betsy's mind some long dormant recollection.

"I know," she says, "there's more in it than that. I used to pray some pretty prayers once, and I wish I could remember them now. Do any of you know any prayers?"

"O yes," was the answer of several voices, while some laughed; and a fair little girl half whispers, "I very often say, 'Our Father!'"

"That's it!" cries Betsy: "say it now, will you dear?"

The child settles her face to a serious look, joins her hands, bends her knees against the side of the bed, and devoutly repeats the words "Our Father!"

"Go on," says Betsy.

"That's all: I don't know no more." And several of the girls agreed that they used the same form of prayer, consisting of the same two words, and no more.

"Yes, there *is* more," exclaims the sick child: "Our Father – our Father *which art in heaven*, – that's it! that's it! and there's more too, if I could remember it."

"It isn't true, if I said it," remarks one of the girls; "my father an't in heaven, he's in prison, and going to be transported."

"My own mammy is in heaven, though," says Betsy, "and I want to go too, but I can't find out anything about it. O who," she adds, in the most touching tone of entreaty, "who will tell me and Joey something about heaven?"

Poor child! there are many daily passing you by in the street, who could both tell you, and instruct you in the only way to that blessed place. But their thoughts are otherwise engaged; their zeal has more distant objects; and for allowing *you* to perish in ignorance they must answer to Him who said, "Suffer little children to come unto me, and forbid them not; for of such is the kingdom of heaven."

Chapter VI

AUTHENTICATIONS

"If all this were true, it would be frightful; but it is a mere story of the imagination, to be received with due allowance for the writer's exaggerating fancy." To obviate such remark, we are bound now to adduce a few statements of facts which have appeared in the best authenticated form. We will first quote from the report of Mr. Grainger, and evidence collected by him on a spot where such things do not even wear so bad an aspect as elsewhere they are known to do. He thus speaks of the pin-headers: –

"The work in which they are engaged being entirely of a sedentary and monotonous character, affords none of those changes of occupation and position which in the case of most other pursuits allow the children a certain degree of relaxation and exercise. At this kind of irksome work, the children, many of whom are of a most tender age, seven or eight years, are kept without any relaxation for twelve or thirteen hours, out of which but one hour, or a little more, is allowed for meals. . . . A fraud is in some cases committed, by which these poor children are made to continue a quarter of an hour or longer at their work at night, when, being already exhausted, they feel severely any addition to their labour; for this overwork they receive no remuneration, but are at this time frequently punished. Whilst at work, the overlooker is constantly watching them, and the least relaxation is punished with the cane; towards evening, this is particularly the case, and the children were often heard crying by the porter."

Here we will give a few extracts from the evidence, actually rendered. One of the "*masters*" makes these admissions: – "The children are left entirely to his care: the proprietor does not at all interfere in the management of them. Thinks the workshop is too dark, too small, and too close for fifty-one persons to inhabit from eight in the morning till seven in the evening. No other means than the fire are taken to ventilate the shop: the windows are not set open at night, or in the morning before work. 'Indeed there is no need, as there are plenty of broken panes.' The windows are capable of being opened. In the sharp winter weather, the children are cold at their work; and at night when the candles are lighted, the shop gets very warm. There is no place for the children to wash after work. There is no proper provision made for the children as to out-houses – that place is not in a fit state for any one to enter.

Many of the children have not sufficient food or clothes. Does not make any provision for those children who come without their dinner. Cases have occurred of children staying from eight in the morning till seven at night without having food. The children generally are at task-work; if this is not done, they are corrected. Those who work at this trade learn nothing which is useful to them as mechanics. . . . Thinks the children are occasionally neglected by their parents. No care is taken by the witness or the proprietor to improve their condition."

So much was admitted by the very person who by his own account had fifty-one of these little labourers under his own, sole, irresponsible charge. If they failed of their exact task, he says, "They are corrected." How corrected they may be or have been, we proceed to show. The following is the evidence of a respectable, well-informed woman, who had been eleven years at work in the different branches.

"Towards the evening, the children are both tired and hungry, theirs being 'very hungry work.' They are in the evening, as in the day, kept at their work by the cane; they require a great deal of caning; some of them not being able to stand the work, run away. Some of these will come back, and stand at the entry of the manufactory, and the master seeing them, will bring them into the shop. On these occasions they are sometimes beaten. A former overlooker of this manufactory, Satchwell by name, has taken witness, then a child, by the hair, and beat her with his fists on the head. This man did not use a cane, but a strap; has seen him fetch blood 'by using weapons,' such as a file, or anything that came near him. Has herself many times been beaten till the blood came. . . . The mothers of the children have often taken out a summons against this man, but he was never taken before a magistrate for this offence, having compromised the charge by giving money to the mothers!! Her own mother took out a summons, for cutting her head open with a pin-tray. At present the children are corrected on the back with a cane."

Another young woman, who had worked at the pin-heading thirteen years, heard this evidence, and fully confirmed it; adding, that she had herself been beaten by Satchwell, so that the blood ran down her back. "On one occasion, when he was beating her over the head, a long pin-shank was driven into the skin so deeply that the pincers were used to extract it. Thinks that Bramer, another master here, was worse than Satchwell; he was a very savage person, and beat the little children, boys and girls, as much as the larger ones."

Another witness, the wife of a police constable, was formerly overlooker in a pin manufactory. She adds fresh testimony to the savage cruelty of Satchwell and Bramer. She also states, "If the worker asked for it, a certain number of pins were weighed out in proportion to the wages. If, after this, the pins were not finished in the usual hours of work, the child was kept extra time, till eight P. M., and also at the dinner-hour, till the lost work was made up. It occasionally happened that the children were set more work than they could perform; they were sometimes beaten for this. Children often complained of cold, the shop being long, and there being only one small fire-place. Has known the children to be so cold that they would not do more than three days' work in the week. Headers often came without their breakfast, and knows that many of them were often all day at the shop without food, especially on the Saturday, when they always staid from eight A. M. till five P. M. No time on the Saturdays allowed for dinner, all the years witness was at the manufactory. Children on this day were frequently detained till eight P. M. for their wages; they were never paid before seven."

With regard to one particular part of the premises which was unavoidably frequented by some fifty boys and girls every day, the female overlooker used the words: 'It is not in a fit state for any human being to go into: it is not in a fit state for a dog to enter."

Mr. Grainger says, that, "Most of them were pale and sickly-looking; they generally were more or less in rags, or without shoes or stockings: many of them complained of want of food. . . . A custom prevails of the masters lending money to the parents, which is repaid out of the labour of their children. One of these masters states, that in most weeks he lends money to the parents, – that this is regularly done, – that most parents are always in debt, – and that the children are kept to work out the debt of their parents. The same witness further states, that it is common for parents to hire their children as headers usually for twelve months, or rather 'it is common to make the hiring for three years.' No similar instances came under my notice in other trades. Considering that so many very young children are employed in these establishments, it might have been reasonably expected that the principals, who derive the benefit of their labour, would have felt a moral obligation to afford them efficient protection; such, however, is not the case; one proprietor 'does not in any way interfere in the shop, except as regards the quality of the work.' At another manufactory, where the most severe cruelty took place, the principals did not interfere effectively to prevent the ill-treatment. In the whole of my inquiries," concludes Mr. Grainger, "I have met with no class more urgently requiring legislative protection than the unhappy pin-headers."

Legislative protection, however, appears as far off as when the sufferings of these poor little creatures were first brought before the public eye: so recently as the 30th of August last, the following fact was stated, by unquestionable authority, in Manchester, respecting the increased labour which factory children had to sustain in the mills: "The velocity of the machinery has been increased fourfold since 1819, and the child who had then to walk eight miles a day has now to travel thirty-two!"

But another point brought forward in our preceding pages must also be established. We refer to the utterly incredible extent of ignorance prevailing not only in the heart of an English town, but among children who actually, and for a prolonged period, have attended Sunday-schools. This is really the most fearful branch of the subject: we must give the evidence as it appears on the face of the reports themselves.

Mary Field, aged between ten and eleven, was at a day-school "about six months, every day; went to a Sunday-school besides; can use a needle; could not hem a handkerchief, nor darn a stocking; could not put a patch upon a hole in her clothes. Never heard of another world, nor of heaven, nor of another life; has looked up at the stars very often; thinks there's a good many on 'em; that's all she ever thought, looking at 'em."

A boy of fourteen, able to read, and having been regularly at a Sunday-school for three years, states that he "has never heard of St. Paul or St. Peter; has heard of Adam – he was the first-born son. Has heard of Jesus Christ – he was an angel in heaven."

John Wood, aged nearly eighteen, who could read easy words, deposed that he "never heard of St. Paul, or St. John the Baptist; never heard of king Herod. Has heard of Jesus Christ, the Saviour's Lord's Son."

Walter Brindley, aged seventeen, having attended various Sunday-schools for *seven years*, and able to read easy words of one syllable, "has heard of the apostles; does not know if St. Peter was one, or if St. John was one, unless it was St. John Wesley; does not know anything about Job; never heard of Samson – knows about Jack Sheppard."

Stephen Hart, aged seventeen, "knows his letters; never heard of the twelve apostles; never heard of Solomon, nor Job, nor Samson; has heard of Pontius Pilate; thinks he was one of the twelve apostles; thinks he has heard that read at the free-school."

Another boy, of the same age, who had attended a Sunday-school regularly for five years, "Does not know who Jesus Christ was, but has heard the name of it. Never heard of the twelve apostles," &c.

William Southern, also aged seventeen, able to read, and having regularly attended a Sunday-school for nearly six years, "Knows who Jesus Christ was, he died on the cross to shed his blood to save our Saviour. Never heard of St. Peter or St. Paul."

Another, nineteen years old, regularly attending a Sunday-school for five years, says, "There were twelve apostles; St. Peter was one, Moses was another, Jonah was another, Job was another; cannot mention any more that he recollects."

Henry Ward, near seventeen, from the workhouse at Birmingham, able to read a little in the Testament: "Does not know how many disciples there were; does not know who Jesus Christ was – thinks he was an apostle; they don't learn the catechism here, else he could tell about him, but thinks he was a king of some kind, of London, a long time ago."

Eliza Baff, aged fifteen: "Never heard of Jesus Christ; never heard the name; never heard of our Saviour; never says any prayers; does not know one."

The following answers were taken from pupils in the various Sunday-schools; that is to say, during the hours of their attendance there, and upon the very spot.

George Canser, age above sixteen, had regularly attended a Sunday-school upwards of four years, and able to write a little, said, "There were twelve apostles; thinks Adam was one, and Eve was two; and Jesus Christ was another. Cannot recollect any more."

Samuel R. Horton, near twelve, "Cannot read, only in the six-penny book. Is not afraid of any boy or man either. Thinks he *is* of the devil, but not particularly."

These are painful exposures indeed; but where lies the fault? teachers, often willing and always gratuitous teachers, are themselves frequently but very little advanced in knowledge beyond their pupils; and wholly unable to command the attention of such a wild, unruly, overworked, burdened, or stultified little crowd of noisy children, assembled in a close room, and longing to be at full liberty again. View it as we may, in its origin, its present aspect, or its future results, it is a most appalling spectacle for the eye of a Christian to rest on; and one for the continuance of which no English Christian can render a satisfactory account to his God. One more particular must be stated, in the words of Mr. Horne, who collected the foregoing and a vast number of similar evidence.

"Many of the children told me they always said their prayers at night, and the prayer they said was 'Our Father.' I naturally thought they meant that they repeated the Lord's Prayer, but I soon found that few of them knew it. They only repeated the two first words: they knew no more than 'Our Father.' These poor children, after their laborious day's work, lying down to sleep with this simple appeal, seemed to me inexpressibly affecting. Having nothing but harsh task-masters in this world, or 'working under their father,' it was probably the only true sense in which they could use the words."

But, ignorant as these miserable little slaves were proved to be of all that related to holiness, all that belongs unto their peace, it was too plain that they were wise concerning evil. Cursing and blasphemy abound among them, and they were almost universally found to be acquainted with the names and histories of Jack Sheppard, Dick Turpin, and other felons, whose vile courses have been recorded in popular story-books, for the emolument of two or three individuals – the hopeless perdition of thousands. Of the Eternal Father and his holy law, of Jesus Christ and his blessed gospel, of the divine Spirit and his renewing, guiding influences, they knew nothing: the words in which they were interrogated concerning them appear scarcely to have conveyed a meaning to the minds of these wretched children, or of the more advanced youths whose long attendance on what are called schools might have led us to expect a far higher degree of information than could be looked for among the former class: but that they were capable of receiving and retaining any information in which they could be induced to take an interest was manifested by their ready replies when questioned concerning the infamous characters who had perished on the gibbet. Scarcely one of them knew the queen's name, or who or what she might be, or where she dwelt; but with 'Jim Crow' they were all familarly acquainted, brightening up at the name. To infer from the replies noted down, of which the above are but a very scanty specimen, that the mental faculties of these young victims to the demon of covetousness were indeed utter blank, and their intellectual perceptions lost in idiotcy through the operation of such destructive causes, would indeed furnish another, and a tremendous count, in the indictment against their task-masters; but it would not be capable of sustaining proof while the facts just noticed stood recorded to show the retentive and reflective powers engaged by themes of viciously exciting interest. No, the crime committed is that, the very first and faintest approach to which was so severely rebuked by the Lord – his nominal disciples place a barrier between Him and the little children. What object can they have in so doing?

The matter is plain enough. In the first place, they do not themselves serve God whose hearts are set on the accumulation of worldly wealth. They do not – they cannot. The declaration stands indelibly engraven where it can neither be erased, nor hidden, nor misunderstood: "No man can serve two masters. . . . YE CANNOT SERVE GOD AND MAMMON." They have no agreement whatever with heavenly things; it is impossible that they should have; for thus again saith the imperishable word: "Covetousness is idolatry;" to believers it says, "Ye are the temple of the living God;" and "What agreement hath the temple of God with idols?" Not only does the grasping worldling decline to serve God, and cut himself off from any agreement with Him, but he shuns and hates the truth. "He that doeth evil hateth the light, neither cometh to the light, lest his deeds should be reproved." But are we authorised to point to any man or body of men, and judge them to lie under such fearful condemnation as this? We do and must apply it to all who voluntarily, deliberately, and publicly exhibit themselves, before the whole world, in the character of men so greedy of gain as to sacrifice to its acquisition the bodies and the souls of their fellow-creatures. If any man considers himself aggrieved by having such a stigma affixed to his name, the remedy is within his reach – let him cast it off; let him begin to do justly, and to love mercy; to care for the poor, and to render unto all their dues – not excluding from that comprehensive ALL the humble beings by whose toilsome services he is enabled to meet every other demand on his probity.

There is no department of labour now filled by children which could not be occupied by adults; there is no task in any department so heavy that it might not be lightened by reasonable subdivision. Supposing that the business is such as to make it easy work to a child, and at the same time gainful to the parents, what a change might be wrought in the whole scene, what a blessing shared by all parties, if even the wish existed to deal out a common measure of justice to those whom God has made dependent on their wealthier brethren! We will suppose a case in this very department of pin-heading: what is there to prevent a proprietor who might choose to furnish a good-sized, airy room, with all the needful implements of the business, and a duly qualified person to act as instructor in the first rudiments of education, placed either in that or in an adjoining apartment, so as to combine teaching with manual labour as is done, in fact, in all our girls' schools, where sewing in its different branches constitutes a great part of the daily routine.

Let us but imagine such a provision made, with just so many more children admitted than might be required to fill the working seats as to allow of relays, however small; each party going up in turn to the teacher, to read, to spell, to receive a lesson for the next half hour's conning, while engaged at the pins; let us suppose a decent amount of personal cleanliness enforced, and means to ensure it supplied, as in all schools; let us take it for granted that the confinement would not be prolonged beyond what childhood can well support, and a fair remuneration given, after deducting, if so it must be, a portion for the attendant expenses – and under how new an aspect would even infant labour appear to us!

Is this impracticable? Must the whole creature, body and mind, be engrossed by the employment for which the child is hired? Must that employment be so protracted, and the confinement so unbroken, and the restraint so complete, and the discipline so severe, as we now behold them? Then the continued existence of such a system is a crime against God and our brethren; one that cannot fail to bring down a punishment as lasting as are the effects of that crime – as lasting as are the woes of immortal beings who close a life of sin by a death of impenitence and despair. Will God become a liar to accommodate the speculatists in a commercial market? Will He set aside both his law and his gospel, to abet the very deeds that, alike under both, He has vowed to punish in the sight of all men? Will He cease to be the Judge of the widow, the Father of the fatherless, the God of the poor, because Messrs. So-and-so could not increase their capital at the present ratio, and prosper according to their wish, unless it were so? No person can be mad enough to calculate thus; and if not, what remains? "Go to now, ye rich men, howl and weep."

But perhaps these employers will not admit that they are rich: they gain only a moderate competence by their traffic in infant flesh, and bone, and sinew, and health, and mind, and soul. Their losses in trade are frequent and severe; their profits doubtful and inadequate; they often question whether they shall realize a decent provision for their own children; and therefore they will not plead guilty to the charge of enriching themselves by unlawful or cruel means. So long as unlawful and cruel means are used, the Judge of all the world will not inspect their balance-sheet, nor overhaul their ledgers, preparatory to passing sentence. Whether the employer is compelled to walk afoot, or whether he splashes about with his chariot wheels the mud through which his poor little baby-labourers crowd to their miserable homes, they and their sufferings, not the amount of wealth that he may wring out of them, must be the theme when the great day of reckoning comes. O that, knowing the terrors of the Lord, we could persuade men to consider what refuge they have to flee to, when the world and all its wretched baits disappear from before them, and they are compelled to know that He who is the Truth lied not, when he said, in reference to the scriptures which reveal his will to man, "The word that I have spoken, the same shall judge him in the last day."

Not long ago, a gleam of hope dawned on the region of darkness and the shadow of death. The British legislature was roused to a sense of its duty, and provision was made for a supply of educational aid, where the lack of it sends up a continual cry of accusation to heaven. We enter not into the particulars of its failure: every man must give account of himself to God, and there is a fearful item standing against some men in this matter. It has pleased God to rouse the hearts of many individuals to effect by a combined effort what the government failed of accomplishing; and if these humble but truthful pages may help to warm one heart, to strengthen one hand, to encourage one benevolent mind in a work so sacred, it will be a crown of rejoicing to her who has penned them; and who, in the absence of other means to help it forward, would fain feel that, in thus using the one talent committed to her, "she hath done what she could."

THE END

Richard Henry Horne

1802-1884

Richard Henry Horne (or, as he called himself, Richard Hengist Horne) is remembered today mainly as one of Dickens's collaborators on *Household Words* and as the friend of Elizabeth Barrett Browning, yet he enjoyed some measure of popularity in his own time.[1] He caught the attention of the public when he challenged the widespread indifference to epic poetry by advertising that his *Orion, an Epic Poem in Three Books* (1843) would be sold for a farthing. The scheme succeeded beyond his expectations, and subsequent editions made up for his initial loss. His fame, however, proved of short duration; never again was he able to please his readers in the same manner. A bohemian by nature, adventurous, and impulsive, Horne could not limit himself to one occupation only or to one particular literary field. He was a man possessed of many gifts but with no genius and no perseverance, and so he became an amateur who dabbled in poetry, fiction, and drama, rather than a true artist.[2] It is not clear why he changed his name Henry to Hengist in 1867. He travelled widely and to distant parts of the globe such as Mexico and Australia. Horne had many friends,[3] but he outlived his fame and seems to have been a forgotten figure by the time he died in 1884, in a shabby two-room apartment in London.

To quote the words of Horne's biographer, Cyril Pearl, he was a late Romantic, "flamboyant, vain, pretentious", yet at the same time "liberal-minded, generous, and compassionate".[4] Horne's easily moved mind and heart made him uniquely qualified to serve both as reporter, in fictional terms, of working-class conditions and as one of the 20 Assistant Commissioners appointed in 1841 to inquire into the 'Employment of Children in Mines, Collieries, and other Occupations not Regulated by the Factory Act of 1833'. The final report of the

Committee appeared in 1843 in 18 large volumes. The story of how Horne came to be appointed Parliamentary Commissioner has been told by Ann Blainley in her biography of "the farthing poet". Horne was genuinely interested in the condition of working children, and he had a number of friends among the Radicals and among the liberal-minded educationalists associated with W. J. Fox of Craven Hill. One of these was Southwood Smith, a Parliamentary Commissioner, who, together with his daughter Caroline Hill, made Horne wish to serve on a new Royal Commission appointed to investigate the condition of children working in mines and in the non-textile industries. Southwood Smith may have helped Horne to obtain this appointment. Horne paid his first visit to a nail factory in the Wolverhampton area on 6 March 1841, and we may learn from the Blue Book referring to the Report of 1843 what factories he visited later on. Thus Horne's name is mentioned in connection with the discussion of glass manufacture in Worcestershire and the manufacture of iron in south Staffordshire, Shropshire and parts of Worcestershire. And as I have myself observed, the name of Horne has been added by hand in a copy of the Blue Books in a section dealing with the morals of children employed in mines and collieries, and in the manufacture of bricks in the neighbourhood of Stourbridge.[5]

Horne's talent as a journalist makes his reports on the physical and moral condition of these children fascinating to read. The testimonies of his juvenile witnesses are presented in a lively manner: he has succeeded in reproducing their own idiomatic speech, and in selecting impressive details from their daily lives. All the children and young people whom he interviewed, whether in screw factories, bell foundries or tin workshops, struck Horne as being under-sized, under-nourished and intellectually starved. It is incredible to read that some children were actually sent to work at the age of three or four, and that they could be obliged to remain at work for 22 hours at a stretch. Horne underlines the appalling ignorance of the children, their miserable homes and poor health.

When the Reports were published during the early 1840s the public conscience was stirred once again, and as one of the Commissioners responsible for these Reports, Horne received a letter of praise from Lord Ashley, the Tory advocate for factory legislation. Complaints were heard, however, from the industrial areas where the masters resented the publicity given to the findings of the Commissioners, and some Members of Parliament protested against the pathetic account, written by Horne, of apprentices deformed by overwork.[6]

Horne's accounts affected the sensitive Elizabeth Barrett (not yet Mrs Browning) so strongly that she wept, and they provided the inspiration for her two poems dedicated to working children. The well-known anthology piece, 'The Cry of the Children', appeared as early as 1844, a few months after Thomas Hood's 'The Song of the Shirt' (published in *Punch*). As Cyril Pearl has shown, passages from Horne's reports were taken over almost verbatim by Elizabeth Barrett as she wrote her famous poem. This happened again in 1860 in 'A Curse for a Nation' (*Poems before Congress*), where the conscience of her generation speaks through her plaintive lines: [7]

Evermore
My heart is sore
For my own land's sins: for little feet
Of children bleeding along the street.

In 1844 she collaborated with Horne in his social studies *A New Spirit of the Age*. The close association between the two writers can be studied in their correspondence which lasted for several years, from 1839 to 1846. [8]

Horne recorded his experiences as Parliamentary Commissioner in his novel, *The Dreamer and the Worker, A Story of the Present Time*, serialized in 1847 in Douglas Jerrold's *Shilling Magazine* and published in two volumes by Henry Colburn in 1851. Douglas Jerrold complained privately to a friend that the serial was not of the kind to attract readers, [9] and no wonder since the story has no unity, whether of action, purpose, or style. It mixes ingredients from two conflicting literary modes, the romantic and the realistic. Passages describing elevated emotions in Romantic isolation from the world are combined with passages marked by a spirit of strict matter-of-fact utilitarianism without any effort to ease the transition, or fuse the two into a rounded whole. They simply co-exist in an undigested and indigestible compound.

The story begins with a shipwreck, and although Horne had experienced one himself, this can scarcely be inferred from his description. Notwithstanding the threatening circumstances, ten people rescued on a raft amid the angry seas engage in a lively philosophic debate. This theatrical situation was apparently contrived to permit the introduction of various topical issues of interest to the author. It also serves to bring together the two heroes of his narrative, the Dreamer (Archer, a poet) and the Worker (Harding, a shipyard mechanic). The two become friends and the Dreamer tries to improve the Worker's mind by telling him what to read, but the friendship is clouded when the Worker falls in love with the Dreamer's fiancée. The dreaming poet is himself torn between his love for two women and finally chooses the one to whom he is not engaged. In the end the Worker, who has educated himself, succeeds in gaining the affections of the woman he loves, and with these two marriages Horne somehow brings the story to a conclusion without bothering to tie up a number of loose ends. The following episode, for example, serves no particular purpose: the father of the heroine advocates an enterprise called Associate Homes designed to simplify the problems of running working-class households. The building project is postponed, however, and he is attracted instead to a business venture in Ireland, and in order to obtain the necessary capital he plans a performance of *Titus Andronicus* with a cast of amateurs. In the course of the performance one of the actors has a nasty accident by falling through a hole in the floor, but the fact that the performance is a complete artistic failure does not prevent it from being a commercial success. The Irish fishing enterprise, however, is unsuccessful because of the hostility of the local Irish fishermen who burn the five boats belonging to the English. The episode carries on in this rambling, haphazard manner and reads like a last-minute effort to meet the deadline for a new instalment.

The ideas subscribed to by Horne reflect what Dickens's Stephen Blackpool would have called a 'muddled' social philosophy. He mixes truly fundamental issues with purely private preoccupations, more or less casual reflections with firmly held principles. His novel bristles with schemes for the reformation of society, which makes it an excellent illustration of the spirit of the age. This was the age of the Chartists when social schemes of all kinds were advanced from all quarters, and few of Horne's ideas are at all original. His passionate support of National Education reflects the influence of his friends at Craven Hill and their *Monthly Repository*, to which he contributed several pieces. The editor, W. J. Fox, placed all his hope for the working classes in mass education, while his attitude to trade unions and proletarian organization was one of suspicion. Horne's novel similarly advocates a free, state-provided educational system, but he was more tolerant of trade unionism than his philosophically-minded radical friends. He is at one with them, however, when he sings the praise of PROGRESS in the hope that improved machinery will benefit the workers as well as the masters. It is also part of his argument that the masses will rise in revolt to secure their rights; the concessions made to them by the privileged few in an effort to preserve the old constitution are bound to prove inadequate. This and similar statements may seem revolutionary, but their radicalism is essentially modified by the conclusion that the required reformation "will come gradually, peacefully; let us hope that the triumph will be the triumph of opinion, with its gentle yet irresistible power." One must not forget that this view of *The Coming Reformation*, expressed in the publication of that name, was voiced at a time when the threat of Chartism was strongly felt.

In *The Dreamer and the Worker* Horne revived his memories of south Staffordshire, the place where he sends his heroine, Mary. The young girl is made to re-live the shock that he had himself experienced on being confronted by the grimness of this district; she is appalled to observe the degradation of the adult workers and the ignorance of the young hands. The former, she believes, are past remedy, but the young must be enabled to escape from the brutality of their environment by means of education.[10] Oddly enough, Horne's fictionalized account of working-class conditions is less impressive than the records he compiled for the official Reports. These abound with telling details, and the direct simplicity of the testimony offered by children makes a strong impression. In contrast it is the novel which reads as flat as an official report, as in the following passage comparing children to slaves: "How many of these poor children were in a condition no better than that of slaves . . . The wretched, ragged, half-starved, and spirit-crushed appearances of numbers of these children showed Mary that all the facts which had been duly reported to the Government by their own Commissioners, had produced no effect whatever upon the condition of the sufferers".[11] Although Benjamin Disraeli had no personal experience to draw on, he put the same Reports to very good use when he wrote *Sybil* (1845), but Horne was apparently incapable of turning an item from the Reports into dramatic narrative. He was content to discuss the children impersonally as mere social cases, as when he mentions a girl of 15 "who had never known the joy of such a thing as a dance, or a holiday; and many a little boy of ten or eleven who had never once seen a butterfly, nor a flower, nor a green field".[12] In view of the topical nature of the subject of child labour in 1847 it is strange to discover that Horne concerns himself with it for only a couple of pages in his long-drawn-out two-volume novel. His tardiness is remarkable; both Charlotte Elizabeth Tonna and Disraeli made ample use of the Reports to which Horne had contributed before he did so. Moreover he failed to honour the work of these novelists, although his preface to the 1851 edition of *The Dreamer and the Worker* contains a reference to Mrs Gaskell's novel *Mary Barton* (1848) and to Charles Kingsley's *Alton Locke* (1850). In 1844, in *A New Spirit of the Age*, Horne dismissed Frances Trollope as "constitutionally coarse" and unprincipled.[13] His radicalism must have made it impossible for him to stomach the work of a Tory writer; the fact that she, too, sponsored the cause of working children in *The Life and Adventures of Michael Armstrong, the Factory Boy* (1840) could not bridge the gap between them.

But despite his obvious shortcomings as a social novelist, Horne was capable of true insight when his romantic bent enabled him to rise above the matter-of-fact attitude of the social reformer. And Horne's insight into the basic need of the working man has not lost its relevance. Bread alone is certainly not enough, as Horne tells his readers, the working man wants "to get some beauty into his soul. His nature needs this, whether the man is aware of his want or not."[14] And on occasion Horne's rhetoric achieves true pathos and dignity in a manner not unworthy of Charles Dickens himself, as we may see in the following passage describing the "city within the city" reserved for the poor:

> What a city – not quite a city under ground, but a staggering series of holes and corners, and side-lanes and attics, and lofts and cellars, and nooks behind dark walls, and dung-heaps, and hovels and dens close to cess-pools and slushy passages, and the dirty people crowded and jammed together in these family-places – far behind and round about and out of the sight of the city which gentlemen and travellers walk through and admire. *This* is the second city of all great capitals – the city kept out of sight – the unknown town within the famous town.[15]

In passages like this, one feels the spirit of Engels' *The Condition of the Working Class in England in 1844* (1845).

By the time when he wrote *The Dreamer and the Worker* Horne was in daily contact with Charles Dickens, who hired him as a reporter for his *Daily News* on its inception in 1846. And when publication of *Household Words* began in 1850 Horne became a member of the permanent staff on a salary of five guineas a week. It was for this journal that Horne wrote 'The True Story of a Coal Fire'. Dickens liked Horne and the two families were on visiting terms. When Horne left England for Australia to join the gold-rush, he promised Dickens to contribute accounts of his experiences to his journal, but Horne's futile quest for easily-acquired riches kept him in Australia for nine years, and when he finally returned to England, Dickens did not again take him on as member of his staff.

Little need be said about the story reproduced here; it is in all respects a much finer literary performance than the novel which preceded it. The restricted scope enabled the author to achieve a more closely-knit narrative and display a major theme of considerable poetic power. The form of the short story suited Horne's artistic talents, incapable as he was of sustained literary efforts. His moments of true inspiration may have been of short duration, but 'The True Story of a Coal Fire' proves their genuine character. His subject-matter permitted the full exercise of his romantic imagination; he could indulge in a dream-like vision without imperilling the unity of his narrative. The circumstance that he presented the story as a dream liberated his creative powers so that he presented vividly scenes observed while serving as a Commissioner. Moreover, his experience as a writer of tales for children played its part in the happy process, since 'The True Story of a Coal Fire' was a story for the young.

Notes

1. *The Cambridge Bibliography of English Literature,* ed. G. Watson (1969), lists 38 items by Horne. Among these are: *Cosimo de Medici: an Historical Tragedy* (1837), in verse; *The Death of Marlowe: a Tragedy in one Act* (1837), chiefly in verse; *The History of Napoleon* (1841), in two volumes; *Orion: an Epic Poem in Three Books* (1843); *A New Spirit of the Age* (edited and largely written by Horne) (1844), in two volumes; *Complete Works of Shakespeare* edited by Horne; *Letters of E. B. Browning addressed to Horne,* ed. S. R. T. Mayer (1877), connecting narrative by Horne.

2. For biographical information see Ann Blainley, *The Farthing Poet, Biography of Richard Hengist Horne 1802–1884, A Lesser Literary Lion* (1968). The standard bibliography is E. J. Shumaker's *Concise Bibliography of the Complete Works of Richard Henry (Hengist) Horne* (Granville, Ohio, 1943). Histories of Literature and biographical dictionaries sometimes give 1803 as the year of his birth, but Horne wrote a poem on his eightieth birthday which proves that he was born on 31 December, 1802.

3. Among these were Charles Dickens, Douglas Jerrold, Leigh Hunt, William Charles Macready, and W. J. Fox.

4. Cyril Pearl, *Always Morning. The Life of Richard Henry "Orion" Horne* (Melbourne, 1960), vi.

5. P.P. 1840 (203) vol. X, 153; Appendix Pt I Q.18, par. 208 *et seq.*; Appendix Pt II p.Q. 16, par. 122 *et seq.*; Appendix to the First Report of Commissioners (Mines) Pt 1, P.P. vol. XVI for 1842; P.P. 1843 (430) XIII, 307 (where Horne's name has been written in by hand); P.P. 1843; Appendix to the Second Report Pt 2, vol. XV, 561–738, and P.P. 30 1843 B–H vol. I, 21; 1845 vol. XLII, 247–8.

6. Blainley, *op.cit.,* 113.

7. Pearl, *op.cit.,* 60f.

8. See S. R. Townshend Mayer (ed.), *Letters of Elizabeth Barrett Browning Addressed to R. H. Horne* (1887), and George Gilfillan, *Galleries of Literary Portraits* (1856), 193.

9. Blainley, *op.cit.,* 173.

10. "She became more and more convinced that the only hope of change was in the adoption of a rigid system of National Education, apart from all special religious sects." Quoted from the 1851 edition, vol. II, 279.

11. *Ibid.,* vol. II, 276f.

12. *Ibid.,* 277.

13. Quoted from the edition of 1844, vol. VII, 239–41.

14. *The Dreamer and the Worker*, vol. I, 223.
15. *Ibid.*, vol. I, 266f.

Bibliographical Details

'The True Story of a Coal Fire' appeared in three parts in Dickens's magazine *Household Words*, the first part in the issue for 13 April 1850. The text given here is from *Household Words*.

THE TRUE STORY
OF A COAL FIRE

Chapter I

One winter's evening, when the snow lay as thick as a great feather-bed all over the garden, and was knee-deep in the meadow-hollows, a family circle sat round a huge fire, piled up with blocks of coal of that magnitude and profusion which are only seen at houses in the neighbourhood of a coal-mine. It appeared as if a tram-waggon had been "backed" into the room, and half its load of great loose coal shot out into the enormous aperture in the wall which lies below the chimney and behind the fire-place in these rural abodes. The red-flames roared, and the ale went round.

The master of the house was not exactly a farmer, but one of those country personages who fill up the interval between the thorough farmer and the 'squire who farms his own estate, – a sort of leather-legged, nail-shoed old gentleman, whose elder sons might easily be mistaken for gamekeepers, and the younger for plough-boys, but who on Sundays took care to "let un see the difference" at church. Their father was therefore never called Farmer Dalton, but old Mr. Dalton, and almost as frequently Billy-Pitt Dalton – the coal mine in which he held a share being named the "William Pitt." His lands, however, were but a small matter; his chief property was a third share he had in this coal mine, which was some half a mile distant from the house. His eldest son was married, and lived close to the mine, of which he acted as the charter-master, or contractor with proprietors for the work to be done.

Among the family group that encircled the huge coal fire was one visitor, – a young man from London, the nephew of old Dalton. He had been sent down to this remote coal country by his father, in order to separate him from associates who dissipated his time, and from pursuits and habits that prevented his mind settling to any fixed occupation and course of life. Flashley was a young man of kindly feelings and good natural abilities, both of which, however, were in danger of being spoiled.

Various efforts were made from time to time to amuse the dashing young fellow "from town." Sometimes the old gentleman related the wonders of the coal-mines, and the perilous adventures of the miners; and on more than one occasion the curate of the village endeavoured to interest him in the grand history of the early world, and especially of the period of antediluvian forests, and their various transmutations. All in vain. He paid no attention to them. If anything they said made any impression at all, it was solely due to the subtle texture of the human mind, which continually receives much more than it seeks, or has wit enough to desire.

"You don't find the coal countries quiet so bright and merry as London town, do ye, Flashley?" said old Dalton, with a good-natured smile.

"I can't say I do, uncle," answered the youth, frankly. "As to merriment, that is all very well at the present moment, in front of that great family bonfire; but all the rest of the day –" and here Flashley laughed with easy impudence and no small fun; "the house and garden are in a state of dingy mourning, so are all the roads, and lanes, and hedges, – in fact, the passage of lines of little black waggons to and fro, rumbling full of coals, or rattling by, empty, seems like the chief business of life, and the main purpose for which men came into the world."

"And so they be!" ejaculated old Dalton, jocosely; "so far as these parts are concerned. You know, Flashley, the world is made up of many parts, and this be the coal part. We be the men born to do the world's work of this sort; and we can't very handsomely pass all our time a-sitting before a shiny fire, and drinking ale, – though, that's good o' nights, after the work's done."

With this laconic homily, old Billy-Pitt Dalton rose smiling from his chair, emptied his mug of ale, and, shaking the young man kindly by the hand, trudged off to bed. With much the same sort of smiling "good night," the sons all trudged after him. The good dame and her daughter went last. Flashley remained sitting alone in front of the great fire.

He sat in silence for a long time, watching the fire decline into great dark chasms, black holes, and rugged red precipices, with grim smouldering chaotic heaps below.

A word or two about this young man. Flashley Dalton had some education, which he fancied was quite enough, and was very ambitious without any definite object. His father had proposed several professions to him, but none of them suited him, chiefly because, to acquire eminence in any of them, so long a time was needed. Besides, none seemed adequate to satisfy his craving for distinction. He looked down rather contemptuously on all ordinary pursuits. The fact was, he ardently desired fame and fortune, but did not like to work for either. One of the greatest injuries his mind had sustained, was from a certain species of "fast literature," which the evil spirit of town-life had squirted into the brains of our young men during the last three or four years, whereby he had been taught and encouraged to laugh at everything of serious interest, and to seek to find something ridiculous in all ennobling efforts. If a great thing was done, he endeavoured to prove it a little one; if a profound truth was enunciated, he sought to make it out a lie; to him a new discovery in science was a humbug; a generous effort, a job. If he went to see an exhibition of pictures, it was to sneer at the most original designs; if to see a new tragedy, it was only in the hope of its being damned. If a new work of fiction were admirable, he talked spitefully of it, or with supercilious patronage; and as to a noble poem, he scoffed at all such things with some slang joke at "high art;" besides, he *wrote* himself, as many a young blade now attempts to do, instead of beginning with a little study and some decent reading. To Flashley all knowledge was a sort of absurdity; his own arrogant folly seemed so much better a thing. He therefore only read books that were like himself, and encouraged him to grow worse. The literature of indiscriminate and reckless ridicule and burlesque had taught him to have no faith in any sincere thing, no respect for true knowledge; and this had well-nigh destroyed all good in his mind and nature, as it unfortunately has done with too many others of his age at the present day.

After sitting silently in front of the fire for some half an hour, Flashley gradually fell into a sort of soliloquy, partaking in about equal degrees of the grumbling, the self-conceited, the humorous, and the drowsy.

"So they're all snoring soundly by this time – all the clodpole Billy Pitties. Uncle's a fine old fellow. Very fond of *him*. As for all the rest! – Wonder why the mine was called the William Pitt! Because it is so black and deep, I suppose. Before *my* time. Who cares for him now, or for any of the bygones! Why should we care for anybody who went before us? The past ones give place to the fast ones. That's *my* feather.

"But a pretty mess I've made of my affairs in London! My father does not know of half my debts. Hardly know of half of them

myself. Incontinent contractions. Tavern bills, sixty or seventy
pounds – may be a hundred. Tailors? can't calculate. Saloons and
night-larks, owing for – don't know how much, besides money paid.
Money borrowed, eighty or ninety pounds. Books – forget – say
sixpence. Like Falstaff's ha'pennyworth of bread to all that quantity
of sack! Think I paid ready money for all the light reading, and
young gent's books."

The fire sank lower and lower, and so did the candles, one of
which had just gone out, and began to send up a curdling stream of
yellow smoke.

"What a place this is for coals. What a smutty face Nature
wears! From the house upwards, all alike, – dull, dusky, and
detestable. Pfeu! Smell of fried mutton fat! Now, then, old Coal-
fire, hold up your head. I'm sleepy myself. This house is more like
a hearse than a dwelling-place for live stock. The roadway in front
of the house is all of coal-dust; the front of the house is like a sweep's,
it only wants the dangling sign of his "brush." The window-ledges
have a constant layer of black dust over them; so has the top of the
porch; so have the chimney-pieces inside the house, where all the
little china cups and gimcracks have a round black circle of coal-
dust at the bottom. There is always a dark scum over the water of
the jug in my bedroom. How I detest this life among the coals!
Where's the great need of them? Why don't the stupid old world
burn wood?"

The fire had by this time sunk to dull red embers and grey ashes,
with large dark chasms around and behind. The shadows on the
wall were faint, and shifting with the flickering of the last candle,
now dying in the socket. Flashley's eyes were closed, and his arms
folded, as he still continued to murmur to himself. Sooth to say, the
ale had got into his head.

"Margery, the housemaid has large black eyes, with dark rings
of coal-grime round them. Her hair is also black – her cap like a
mourning mop – and she has worn a black patch on one side of her
nose since last Friday, when I gave her a handful from the coal-
scuttle for comparing me to the lazy young dog that lay asleep
before the fire. Margery Daw! – you shall slide down to the lower
regions, – on an inclined plane, as the Useful Knowledge books
would say.

"Ale is a good thing when it is strong; but a coal-mine is all
nonsense. Still, they seem to make money by it, and *that's* some
excuse – some reason for men wasting in work lives which ought
to be passed in pleasure. Human time – human – I thought something touched my elbow.

"Human time should not be passed – why there it came again! I must be dreaming.

"Old Billy-Pitt Dalton understands brewing. But human time should not be passed in digging and groping, and diving and searching – whether to scrape up coals, or what folks call "knowledge." For the fuel of life burns out soon enough of itself, and, therefore, it should not be wasted over the baser material; because the former is all for one's self, while coal-fuel, and the search after it, is just working for other people. Something *did* touch my elbow! There's something astir in the room out in the darkness! It was standing at my side!"

Flashley made an effort to rise; but instead of doing so, he fell sideways over one arm of the chair, with his arms hanging down. Staring up helplessly from this position, he saw a heavy dwarfed figure with shining eyes, coming out of the darkness of the room! He could not distinguish its outline; but it was elf-like, black, and had a rough rocky skin. It had eyes that shot rays like great diamonds; and through its coal-black naked body, the whole of its veins were discernible, not running with blood, but filled with stagnant gold. Its step was noiseless, yet its weight seemed so immense, that the floor slowly bent beneath it; and, like ice before it breaks, the floor bent more and more as the figure came nearer.

At this alarming sight, Flashley struggled violently to rise. He did so; but instantly reeling half round, dropped into the chair, with his head falling over the back of it. At the same moment the ponderous Elfin took one step nearer; and the whole floor sank slowly down, with a long-drawn moan, that ended in a rising and rushing wind, with which Flashley felt himself borne away through the air, fleeter than his fast-fleeing consciousness.

In the progress of generations and cycles – in that wealth and dispensation of Time ordained by HIM, before whose sight "one day is as a thousand years, and a thousand years as one day" – mere grains of sand running through the glass that regulates the operations of never-ending work – the bodies of all living things, whether animal or vegetable, fulfil their destinies by undergoing a gradual transmutation into other bodies and things of the most opposite kind to their own original being. Original being, accurately to speak, there is none; but we must call that thing original to which some other thing is traced back as to its ultimate point, or starting place, and at which we are obliged to stop, not because it is the end, but because we can go no further; nevertheless, up to that antediluvian period, and during a great part of it, we are moving in the dusky yet demonstrable regions and tracts of substantial facts, and scientific knowledge.

Not daring to unclose his eyes, Flashley gradually returned to consciousness, and heard a voice speaking near to him, yet in tones that seemed like the echoes of some great cavern or deep mine.

"Man lives to-day," said the voice – and the youth felt it was the black Elfin, with the diamond eyes and golden veins, that was speaking – "man lives to-day, not only for himself and those around him, but also that by his death and decay fresh grass may grow in the fields of future years, – and that sheep may feed, and give food and clothing for the continuous race of man. Even so the food of one generation becomes the stone of another. And the stone shall become a fuel – a poison – or a medicine. Awake, young man! – awake from the stupor of an ignorant and presumptuous youth – and look around you!"

The young man, with no little trepidation, opened his eyes. He found he was alone. The strange being that had just spoken was gone. He ventured to gaze on the scene that surrounded him.

The place in which he found himself seemed to partake, not in distinct proportions, but altogether, so far as this was possible, of a wild forest of strange and enormous trees – a chaotic jungle – a straggling woodland, and a dreary morass or swamp, intersected by a dark river, that appeared to creep towards the sea which embraced a part of the distant horizon with a leaden arm. The moist mound whereon he stood was covered with ferns of various kinds – the comb-fern, the wedge-fern, the tooth-fern, the nerve-fern – and of all sizes, rising from a crumpled crest bursting through the earth, to plants of a foot high, of several feet, and thence up to lofty trees of forty or fifty feet in height, with great stems and branching crowns. The green-stemmed and many-pointed mare's-tail was also conspicuous in number and in magnitude; not merely of two or three feet high, as in the present period of the earth, but large green-jointed trees, shooting up their whisking spires to fourteen or fifteen feet. Thickly springing up in wild and threatening squadrons over the morass, they bent their heads in long rows after rows over the edge of the muddy river, with sullen, moveless, and interminable monotony. Here and there, enormous sombre shrubs oppressed the scene. The collective clumps resembled the inextricable junction of several of our thickest-foliaged trees, as though several oaks had agreed to unite their trunks, and make one – several beeches, the same – several poplars – several limes – though not one of them bearing likeness in trunk or foliage to oak, or beech, or poplar, or lime, or any known tree of present date.

Clumps also were there, of a rank undergrowth, out of which limp bare stems shot up to a great height, covered with a sickly white mealy powder, and terminating, for the most part, in coarse brown swollen heads, or gigantic black fingers, varied with dull red bosses at the tops of the great stems, broken cups, or red and grey forks and spikes – a sort of monstrous club-moss and cup-moss, with lichens, coarse water-weeds, and water-grasses at the base.

Uncouth and terrible as were the forms to the young man's eyes, there were some things not without grace. Large trees, having their entire trunks and boughs elegantly fluted, bearing leaves at regular intervals on each fluting upwards and along every bough, rose up amidst the disordered vegetation. Where the leaves had fallen from the lower part of the trunk, marks were left, like seals, at regular intervals on the flutings.*

In many places, close to the trees just described, huge tortuous succulent roots† protruded from the ground, as if anxious to exchange their darkness and want of air for the light, and for the warm atmosphere, attracted by the strong gases with which it was impregnated.

Round the feet of the young man lay intertangled bunches and bundles of wood-weeds, river-weeds, and other weeds that seemed to partake equally of the river and the sea; long rank grasses, sword-like, spear-like, or with club-like crowns of seeds, and fungi, of hideous shapes, gross, pulpy, like giants' heads, hairy and bearded, and sometimes bursting and sending forth steamy odours that were scarcely to be borne, and which the youth felt to be a deadly poison, but that for the time he, somehow, was endowed with a "charmed life."

Spell-bound, he turned from these dismaying sights, to trees that rose to altitudes of from sixty to eighty feet, having leaves in long rows upon all the boughs, from which they shot forth direct, and without the intervention of any small twigs or other usual connecting medium of foliage. The same course of leaves had existed on the trunk, from which they had fallen as the tree rose up to maturity, and had left scars or scales, like a Mosaic ornament, and a sign of their progressive years.‡

Gazing through and beyond all these lofty trunks, Flashley beheld in the distance a sort of palm-like and pine-like trees, standing against the pale blue sky, which far transcended all the rest in altitude, and seemed indeed, here and there, to rise to a

---

* These trees are known in fossil botany as the *Sigillariæ*.

† The *Stigmaria*.

‡ The *Lepidodendron*.

hundred feet above the whole range of other lofty trees! His eyes ached as he stared at them. It was not their altitude alone that caused a painful impression, but the feeling of their unbroken solitude – a loneliness unvisited by a single bird, and with nothing between them and the heavens, to which they seemed to aspire for ever and in vain.

No flowers on any of the trees and shrubs around him were to be seen – and no fruits. The tone of colour was grave, sullen, melancholy. It was a solitude that seemed to feel itself. Not only no bird was visible, but no quadruped, insect, creeping thing, or other form of animal life. The earth was devoted solely to the production of enormous vegetation.

To complete the pregnant solemnity of the scene, there were no sounds of life or motion in the air; all was silence.

Looking round with a forlorn and overawed yet enquiring face, he discerned something like two keen stars of arrowy light at the foot of a gigantic fern-tree, at some distance from him. The darting rays seemed directed towards him. They were eyes; they could be nothing else! He presently perceived that the rough black elfin figure, with the veins of stagnant gold, was seated there, and that its eyes were fixed upon him!

"The scene amidst which you stand," said the Elfin in his echo-like voice, and without moving from his seat beneath the tree, "is the stupendous vegetation of the elder world. The trunks and stems of the antediluvian earth erect their columns, and shoot up their spires towards the clouds; their dull, coarse foliage overhangs the swamps, and they drink in, at every pore, the floating steam impregnated with the nutriment of prodigies. No animal life do you behold, for none is of this date, nor could it live amidst these potent vapours which feed the vegetation. And yet these vast trees and plants, this richly poisoned atmosphere, this absence of all animal life of man, and beast, and bird, and creeping thing, is all arranged in due order of progression, that man may hereafter live, not merely a savage life, but one civilised and refined, with the sense of a soul within – of God in the world, and over it, and all around it – whereof comes man's hope of a future life beyond his presence here. Thus upward, and thus onward ever.

"And all this monstrous vegetation above ground shall be cast down and embedded deep in the dark bowels of the earth, there under the chemical process of ages to become a fuel for future generations of men, yet unborn, who will require it for their advance in civilisation and knowledge. Yes; these huge ferns, these trunks, and stems, and towering fabrics of trees, shall all crash down – sink deep into the earth with all the rank enfolding mass of undergrowth – there to be jammed and mashed up between beds of fiery stone and grit and clay, and covered with oozy mud and sand, till stratum after stratum of varied matter rises above them, and forms a new surface of earth. On this surface the new vegetation of the world will commence, while that of the old lies beneath, – not rotting in vain, nor slumbering uselessly in darkness, but gradually, age after age, undergoing transmutation by the alchemy of Nature, till verdure becometh veriest blackness, and wood is changed to coal.

"Then man is born, appearing on the earth only when the earth is ready to receive him, and minister to his wants. At first he useth wood for his fuel; but as his knowledge expands and deepens he penetrates far below the surface, and there finds forests of fuel almost inexhaustible, made ready for his various needs and arts. And when, in far-off ages, these vast stores become exhausted, others will be discovered not only of the same date, but which have been since accumulated; for the same process of transmutation is constantly going on. Thus present time always works for future ages.

"Slowly as moves the current in *my* veins," – the Elfin rose up as he said this – "veins which seem to your eye to contain a stagnant gold, but whose metallic current, in its appointed period of years, performs each several circulation within me, – yea, slowly as this, or any other invisible progression, move these mighty forest trees towards their downward course, to rise again in coals, – in fire, – and thence ascend to air. Yes, this invisible motion is as certain withal, as that immediate action which mortal nature best can comprehend."

As the Elfin uttered these last words, the great trees around sank with crashing slant one over the other! – then came rushing, like a sudden tempest, down upon the earth; and the young man was overwhelmed with the foliage, and instantly lost all further consciousness.

The traveller who has journeyed for many days across the fertile levels and shining flats of Holland, must often have bethought him that all this was surging ocean, but a few years ago; in like manner, by an inverse process, the voyager up the Mississippi or Missouri rivers, or the wayfarer for many days through the apparently interminable and dense forests of North America, might look forward to a period when all these masses of vegetation would become coal, if left to be dealt with by the regular process of nature.

The rapid advances of civilisation into these wooded solitudes may prevent the transmutation to which they were otherwise destined; and the same may be said of the forests even on many of the vast tracts, as yet scarcely trodden by the foot of man, in New Zealand and Australia; but many other giant forest tracts exist in unknown regions, which are destined to follow the law of transmutation, and secretly become a carbonic fuel for future ages of discovery.

But what does young Flashley now behold? He is aroused from his trance, and is again conscious of surrounding objects. He is seated, so that he cannot move, on a little wooden bench beneath a low wooden shed, such as labourers "knock up" by way of temporary shelter in the vicinity of some great works. Great works are evidently in hand all around him.

Labourers with pick-axes and spades came hurrying to the spot, and began to dig a circular hole of some seven feet in diameter. Then came others with a great wooden roller on a stand, with a thick rope, like a well-rope, wound round it; and fixing this across the top of the hole, they let down a basket, ever and anon, and brought it up filled with earth and stones. It was evident that they were employed in sinking a shaft.

They worked away at a prodigious rate, the descending baskets continually taking down men with pickaxes and spades; and next with carpenter's tools and circular pieces of wood-work, with which they made an inner frame round the sides of the shaft below. Bricklayers, with hods of bricks, were next let down in the baskets, and with the support of the circular frame beneath, they rapidly cased the inside of the shaft with brickwork up to the top. More and deeper digging out then took place – more wooden frame-work below, with more brickwork round the sides, and gradually sinking lower and lower. This was continued again and again, till suddenly loud cries from below announced some new event. The diggers had arrived at springs – water was gushing in upon them!

Up came the rope and basket with three men standing up inside and holding on the rope, and two men and a boy clinging round rope and basket, and round each other as they best could, and with no small peril to all. Leaping, scrambling, or lugged to the side, they relieved the basket, which rapidly ran down again to bring up others.

Meanwhile came labourers heavily trotting beneath the weight of pumps and pump-gear; and they rigged up the pump, and as soon as all the men and boys were out of the shaft, up came the water pouring in a thick volume, now mud-coloured, now clay-coloured, and now grey and chalky. At length the volume became less and less, and soon there was no more. Down again went basket after basket, with men or boys in them. Flashley shuddered, as something within him seemed to say "*Your* turn will come!" Up came the clay, and the sand, and the gravel, and the chalk as before; and soon a mixture of several earths and stones. Thus did they toil and toil below and above, winding up and winding down, till at last a shout of success was heard faintly echoing from the deep pit beneath, and presently up came a basket full of broken lime-stone, and grit, and red sandstone – and coals!

Flashley now observed a great turmoil above, but all with definite intention, and preparations for new and larger works. A steam-engine was fitted up in a small brick edifice at a hundred yards distance, from which came a strong rope that passed over a large drum or broad wheel. The rope was then extended to the shaft, over the top of which a small iron wheel was erected; and over this they carried the rope, which was to take down men and bring up coals. A larger measure than the basket, called a *corve*, was fastened to this rope by chains, and up and down it went bringing great heaps of coals to the surface. After a time, wood-work and iron-work of various kinds were sent down, and sledges and trucks with little wheels; and then broad belts were put round horses, by means of which they were raised, kicking and capering wildly in the air, and staring with horrified eye-balls into the black abyss, down which they were lowered, every limb trembling, and their ears sharpened up to a single hair.

At this sight Flashley's ears began to prick and tingle in sym-pathy, for he felt that he should not much longer remain a mere spectator of these descents into the lower regions of the earth.

And now corve after corve full of coals rose in regular succession from the mine, and tram-roads were laid down, upon which little black waggons constantly ran to and fro, carrying away the coals from the pit's mouth. While all this had been going on, a second shaft was sunk at no great distance; but no coals were seen to issue from it. It was for air, and ventilation of the mine.

The men sometimes went down standing up in the corve, but generally each man sat in the loop of a short chain which he hooked on to the rope; and, in this way, six or seven went swinging down together in a bunch; sometimes ten or twelve in a bunch; and now and then, by some using longer chains than the others, in a double bunch, amounting to as many as twenty, men and boys.

A voice, which seemed to come from beneath the earth, but which poor Flashley recollected too well as that of the Elfin who had carried him so recently into the antediluvian forests and swamps, now called him by his name, with a familiarity that made him shudder. Instantly he found himself borne away from the wooden shed, and placed on the brink of the first shaft. A strange apparatus, composed of a chain with a loop at bottom, and an iron umbrella over head, was now attached to the rope by three chains. It had very much the look of some novel instrument of torture. Into this loop Flashley's legs were placed in a sitting posture.

"Straddle your legs!" cried an old black-visaged miner, as the young man was swung off from the brink, and suspended over the profound abyss below. Not obeying, and, indeed, not instantly understanding the uncouth injunction, Flashley had omitted the "straddling;" in consequence of which the chain loop clipped him close around, and pinched his legs together with a force that would have made him utter a cry, but for the paramount terror of his position. Down he went. Round and round went the shaft-wheel above – faster and faster – and lower and lower he sank from the light of day between the dark circular walls of the shaft.

At first the motion was manifestly rapid. It took away his breath. It became more rapid. He gave himself up for lost. But presently the motion became more smooth, and more steady – then quite steady, so that he thought he was by no means descending rapidly. Presently, again, he fancied he was not descending at all – but stationary – or, rather, *ascending*. It was difficult to think otherwise. The current of air rising from below, meeting his swiftly descending body, gave him this impression.

He now saw a dim light moving below. It became stronger, and almost immediately after he saw three half-naked demons of the mine, as he thought, who stood ready to receive him.

For the first time he ventured to cast a forlorn look upwards. He beheld the iron umbrella with a light from beneath flashing upon it. Again, he turned his eyes below. He was close down upon the demons. One of them held a lamp up to his face as he descended among them. Whereupon these three demons all uttered a jovial laugh, and welcomed him.

"Oh, *where* am I?" exclaimed Flashley, in utter dismay.

"At the first 'workings' of the Billy-Pitt Mine!" shouted a voice. "Steady the chains!"

The chains were steadied, and in a moment Flashley felt himself launched into a new abyss, down which he descended in utter darkness, and in utter silence, except from the rushing of the air-currents, and the occasional grating of the iron umbrella against the sides of the shaft.

Chapter II

Down the lower shaft the young man continued to descend in silence and darkness. He did not know if he descended slowly or rapidly. The sense of motion had become quite indefinite. There was a horrible feathery ease about it, as though he were being softly taken down to endless darkness, with an occasional tantalising waft upwards, and then a lower descent, which made his whole soul sink within him. But he grasped the chain in front of him with all his remaining force, as his only hold on this world – which in fact it *was*.

From this condition of helpless dismay and apprehension, poor Flashley was suddenly aroused by a violent and heavy bump on the top of his iron umbrella! He thought it must be some falling miner, or perhaps his ponderous-footed elfin abductor, who had leaped down after him. It was only the accidental fall of a loose brick from above, somewhere; but the dead bang of the sound, coming upon the previous silence, was tremendous. The missile shot off slanting from the iron umbrella – seemed to dash its brains out against the side of the shaft – and then flew down before him, like a lost soul.

Flashley now felt a wavering motion in his descent, while an increasing current of air rose to meet him; and almost immediately after, he heard strange and confused sounds beneath. Looking down into the darkness, he not only saw a reddening light, but, as he stared down, it became brighter, until he saw the gleam of flames issuing from one side of the shaft. He fully expected to descend into the midst, and "there an end;" but he speedily found he was reserved for some other fate. The fire was placed in a large chasm, and appeared to have a steep red pathway sloping away behind it. He passed it safely. From this moment he felt no current of air, but his ears were assailed with a variety of noises, in which he could distinguish the gush of waters, the lumbering of wood, the clank and jar of chains, and the voices of men – or something worse. Three black figures were distinctly visible.

In a few seconds more, his feet touched earth – which seemed to give a heave, in answer. His descent from the upper surface had not occupied longer time than has been necessary to describe it, but this was greatly magnified to his imagination by the number, novelty, and force of the emotions and thoughts that had attended it. He was now at the bottom of the William Pitt Coal Mine, nine hundred and thirty feet below the surface of the earth.

A man all black with coal-dust, and naked from the waist upwards, took hold of Flashley, and extricating him from the chain

girdle and iron umbrella, led him away into the darkness, lighted
only by a candle stuck in a lump of clay which his conductor held
in the other hand.

Over all the various sounds, that of rushing waters predomi-
nated at this spot; and very soon they turned an angle which
enabled Flashley to descry a black torrent spouting from a narrow
chasm, and rushing down a precipitous gully on one side of them to
seek some still lower abyss. Another angle was turned; the torrent
was no longer seen and its noise grew fainter almost at every step.

The passage through which they were advancing was cut out of
the solid coal. It was just high enough for the man to walk upright, though with the danger of striking his head occasionally
against some wedge of rock, stone, or block of coal, projected down-
wards from the roof. In width the sides could be reached by the
man's extended hands. They were sometimes supported by beams,
and sometimes by a wall of brick, and the roof was frequently sustained by upright timbers, and limbs or trunks of trees. In one
place, where the roofing had evidently sunk, there stood an irregular row of stunted oak trunks, of grotesque shapes and shadows,
many of which were cracked and gaping in ragged flaws from the
crushing pressure they had resisted; showing that, without them,
the roof would certainly have fallen, and rendering the passage
more "suggestive" than agreeable to a stranger beneath. Here and
there, at considerable distances, candles stuck in clay were set in
gaps of the coaly walls, in the sandstone, or against the logs and
trunks. The pathway was for the most part a slush of coal-dust,
mixed with mud and slates, varied with frequent nobs and snaggs
of rock and iron-stone. In this path of intermittent ingredients, a
tram-road had been established, the rails of which had been laid
down at not more than 15 inches asunder; and moving above this
at no great distance, Flashley now saw a dull vapoury light, and
next descried a horse emerging from the darkness a-head of them.
It seemed clear that nothing could save them from being run over,
unless *they* could run over the horse. However, his guide made him
stand with his back flat against one side of the passage – and presently the long, hot, steamy body of the horse moved by, just
moistening his face and breast in passing. He had never before
thought a horse's body was so long. At the creature's heels a little
low black waggon followed with docility. The wheels were scarcely
six inches high. Its sides were formed by little black rails. It was
full of coals. A boy seemed to be driving, whose voice was heard on
the other side of the horse, or else from beneath the animal's body,
it was impossible to know which.

They had not advanced much further when they came to a wooden barricade, which appeared to close their journey abruptly. But it proved to be a door, and swung open of its own accord as they approached. No sooner were they through, than the door again closed, apparently of its own careful good will and pleasure. The road was still through cuttings in the solid coal, varied occasionally with a few yards of red sand-stone, or with brick walls and timbers as previously described. Other horses drawing little black coal-waggons were now encountered; sometimes two horses drawing two or more waggons, and these passed by in the same unpleasant proximity. More *Sesame* doors were also opened and shut as before; but Flashley at length perceived that this was not effected by any process of the black art, as he had imagined, but by a very little and very lonely imp, who was planted behind the door in a toad-squat, and on this latter occasion was honoured by his guide with the title of an 'infernal small *trapper*,' in allusion to some neglect of duty on a previous occasion. It was, in truth, a poor child of nine years of age, one of the victims of poverty, of bad parents, and the worst management, to whose charge the safety of the whole mine, with the lives of all within it, was committed; the requisite ventilation depending on the careful closing of these doors by the trapper-boys, after anybody has passed.

Proceeding in this way, they arrived at a side-working close upon the high-road, in which immense ledges of rocks and stones projected from the roof, being embedded in the coal. In cutting away the coal there was danger of loosening and bringing down some of these stones, which might crush the miners working beneath. A "council" was now being held at the entrance, where seven experienced "undergoers" were lying flat on the ground, smoking, with wise looks, in Indian fashion, and considering the best mode of attack, whereby they might bring down the coals without being "mashed up" by the premature fall of the rocks and stones together with the black masses in which they were embedded.

Among all the gloomy and oppressive feelings induced by this journey between dismal walls – faintly lighted, at best, so as to display a most forbidding succession of ugly shadows and grotesque outlines – and sometimes not lighted at all for a quarter of a mile; there was nothing more painful than the long pauses of silence; a silence only broken by the distant banging of the trappers' doors, or by an avalanche of coal in some remote working. After advancing in a silence of longer duration than any that had preceded it, Flashley's dark conductor paused every now and then, and listened – then advanced; then stopped again thoughtfully, and listened. At length he stopped with gradual paces, and turning to Flashley, said in a deep tone, the calmness of which added solemnity to the announcement, –

"We are now walking beneath the bed of the sea! – and ships are sailing over our heads!"

Several horses and waggons were met and passed after the fashion already described. On one occasion, the youth who drove the horse, walked in front, waving his candle in the air, and causing it to gleam upon a black pool in a low chasm on one side, which would otherwise have been invisible. He was totally without clothing, and of a fine symmetrical form, like some young Greek charioteer doing penance on the borders of Lethe for careless driving above ground. As he passed the pool of water, he stooped with his candle. Innumerable bubbles of gas were starting to the surface. The instant the flame touched them, they gave forth sparkling explosions, and remained burning with a soft blue gleam. It continued visible a long time, and gave the melancholy idea of some spirit, once beautiful, which had gone astray, and was for ever lost to its native region. It was as though the youth had written his own history in symbol, before he passed away into utter darkness.

"You used to be fond," observed Flashley's companion, with grim ironical composure, after one of these close encounters with horseflesh – "You *used* to be fond of horses."

Flashley made no reply, beyond a kind of half-suppressed groan of fatigue and annoyance.

"Well, then," said the other, appearing to understand the smothered groan as an acquiescence – "we will go and look at the stables."

He turned off at the next corner on the left, and led the way up a narrow and steep path of broken brick and sandstone, till they arrived at a bank of rock and coal, up which they had to clamber, Flashley's guide informing him that it would save a mile of circuitous path. Arriving at the top, they soon came to a narrow door, somewhat higher than any they had yet seen. It opened by a long iron latch, and they entered the "mine stables."

A strong hot steam and most oppressive odour of horses, many of whom were asleep and snoring, was the first impression. The second, was a sepulchral Davy-lamp hanging from the roof, whose dull gleam just managed to display the uplifting of a head and inquiring ears in one place, the contemptuous whisking of a tail in another, and a large eye-ball gleaming through the darkness, in another! The stalls were like a succession of narrow black dens, at each side of a pathway of broken brick and sand. In this way sixty or seventy horses were "stabled."

"This is a prince of a mine!" said the guide; "we have seven hundred people down here, and a hundred and fifty horses."

They emerged at the opposite end, which led up another steep path towards a shaft (for the mine now had four or five) which was used for the ascent and descent of horses. They were just in time to witness the arrival of a new-comer, – a horse who had never before been in a mine.

The animal's eyes and ears became more frightfully expressive, as with restless anticipatory limbs and quivering flesh he swung round in his descending approach to the earth. When his hoofs touched, he made a plunge. But though the band and chain confined him, he appeared yet more restrained by the appalling blackness. He made a second plunge, but with the same result. He then stood stock-still, glared round at the black walls and the black faces and figures that surrounded him, and instantly fainted.

The body of the horse was speedily dragged off on a sort of sledge, by a tackle. The business of the mine could not wait for his recovery. He was taken to be "fanned." Flashley of course understood this as a mine joke; but it was not entirely so. A great iron wheel, with broad fans, was often worked rapidly in a certain place, to create a current of air and to drive it on towards the fire in the up-cast shaft, assisting by this means the ventilation of the mine; and thither, or at all events, in that direction, the poor horse was dragged, amidst the laughter and jokes of the miners and the shouts and whistles of the boys.

How silent the place became after they were gone! Flashley stepped forwards towards the spot immediately beneath the shaft. It was much nearer to the surface than any of the other shafts, and the daylight from above-ground just managed to reach the bottom. Under the shaft was a very faint circle of sad-coloured and uncertain light. The palest ghost might have stood in the middle of it and felt "at home."

The "streets" of the mine appeared to be composed of a series of horse-ways having square entrances to "workings" at intervals on either side, and leading to narrow side-lane workings. Up one of these his guide now compelled Flashley to advance; in order to do which they were both obliged to stoop very low; and, before long, to kneel down and crawl on all-fours. While moving forward in this way upon the coal-dust slush, where no horse could draw a waggon, a poor beast of another kind was descried approaching with his load. It was in the shape of a human being, but not in the natural position – in fact, it was a boy degraded to a beast, who with a girdle and chain was dragging a small coal-waggon after him. A strap was round his forehead, in front of which, in a tin socket, a lighted candle was stuck. His face was close to the ground. He never looked up as he passed.*

These narrow side-lane passages from the horse-road, varied in length from a few fathoms, to half-a-mile and upwards; and the one in which Flashley was now crawling, being among the longest, his impression of the extent of these underground streets and by-ways, was sufficiently painful, especially as he had no notion of what period he was doomed to wander through them. Besides, the difficulty of respiration, the crouching attitude, the heated mist, the heavy sense of gloomy monotony, pressed upon him as they continued to make their way along this dismal burrow.

From this latter feeling, however, he was roused by a sudden and loud explosion. It proceeded from some remote part of the trench in which they were struggling, and in front of them. The arrival of a new sort of mist convinced them of this. It was so impregnated with sulphur, that Flashley felt nearly suffocated, and was obliged to lie down with his face almost touching the coal-slush beneath him, for half-a-minute, before he could recover himself. Onward, however, he was obliged to go, urged by his gruff companion behind; and in this way they continued to crawl till a dim light became visible at the farther end. The light came forwards. It proceeded from a candle stuck in the front of the head of a boy, harnessed to a little narrow waggon, who pulled in front, while another boy pushed with his head behind. A side-cutting, into which Flashley and his companon squeezed themselves, enabled the waggon to pass. The hindermost boy, stopping to exchange a word with his companion, Flashley observed that the boy's head had a bald patch in the hair, owing to the peculiar nature of his headwork behind the waggon. They passed, and now another distant light was visible; but this remained stationary.

As they approached it, the narrow passage widened into a gap, and a rugged chamber appeared hewn out in the coal. The sides were supported by upright logs and beams; and further inwards, were pillars of coal left standing, from which the surrounding mass had been cut away. At the remote end of this, sat the figure of a man, perfectly black and quite naked, working with a short-handled pickaxe, with which he hewed down coals in front of him, and from the sides, lighted by a single candle stuck in clay, and dabbed up against a projecting block of coal. From the entrance to

* Young women and girls were also used in this way till the Report of the Children's Employment Commission caused it to be forbidden by Act of Parliament.

this dismal work-place, branched off a second passage, terminating in another chamber, the lower part of which was heaped up with great loose coals apparently just fallen from above. The strong vapour of gunpowder pervading the place, and curling and clinging about the roof, showed that a mass of coal had been undermined and brought down by an explosion. To this smoking heap, ever and anon, came boys with baskets, or little waggons, which they filled and carried away into the narrow dark passage, disappearing with their loads as one may see black ants making off with booty into their little dark holes and galleries under ground.

The naked miner in the first chamber, now crept out to the entrance, having fastened a rope round the remotest logs that supported the roof of the den he had hewed. These he hauled out. He then knocked away the nearest ones with a great mallet. Taking a pole with a broad blade of iron at the end, edged on one side and hooked at the other, something like a halbert, he next cut and pulled away, one by one, by repeated blows and tugs, each of the pillars of coal which he had left within. A strange cracking overhead was presently heard. All stepped back and waited. The cracking ceased, and the miner again advanced, accompanied by Flashley's guide; while, by some detestable necromancy, our young visitor – alack! so very lately such a dashing young fellow "about town", now suddenly fallen into the dreadful condition of receiving all sorts of knowledge about coals – felt compelled to assist in the operation.

Advancing with great wedges, while Flashley carried two large sledge hammers to be ready for use, the miners inserted their wedges into cracks in the upper part of the wall of coal above the long chamber that had just been excavated, the roof of which was now bereft of all internal support. They then took the hammers and began to drive in the wedges. The cracks widened, and shot about in branches, like some black process of crystallisation. The party retreated several paces – one wide flaw opened above, and down came a hundred tons of coal in huge blocks and broad splinters! The concussion of the air, and the flight of coal-dust, extinguished the candles. At this the two miners laughed loudly, and, pushing Flashley before them, caused him to crouch down on his hands and knees, and again creep along the low passage by which they had entered. A boy in harness drawing a little empty waggon soon approached, with a candle on his forehead, as usual. The meeting being unexpected and out of order, as the parties could not pass each other in this place, Flashley's special guide and "tutor" gave him a lift and a push, by means of which he was squeezed between the rough roofing and the upper rail of the empty waggon, into which he then sank down with a loud "Oh!" His tutor now set his head to the hinder part of the waggon, the miner assumed the same position with respect to the tutor – the boy did the same by the miner – and thus, by reversing the action of the wheels, the little waggon, with its alarmed occupant, was driven along by this three-horse power through the low passage, with a reckless speed and jocularity, in which the ridiculous and hideous were inextricably mingled.

Arriving at the main horse-road, as Flashley quickly distinguished by the wider space, higher roofing, and candles stuck against the sides, his mad persecutors never stopped, but increasing their speed the moment the wheels were set upon the rails, they drove the waggon onwards with yells and laughter, and now and then a loud discordant whistle in imitation of the wailful cry of a locomotive; passing "getters," and "carriers," and "hurryers", and "drawers," and "pushers," and other mine-people and once sweeping by an astonished horse – gates and doors swinging open before them – and shouts frequently being sent after them, sometimes of equivocal import, but generally *not* to be mistaken, by those whom they thus rattled by, who often received sundry concussions and excoriations in that so narrow highway beneath the earth.

In this manner did our unique *cortège* proceed, till sounds of many voices a-head of them were heard, and then more and more light gleamed upon the walls; and the next minute they emerged from the road-way, and entered a large oblong chamber, or cavern, where they were received with a loud shout of surprise and merriment. It was the dining-hall of the mine.

This cavern had been hewn out of the solid coal, with intervals of rock and sandstone here and there in the sides. Candles stuck in lumps of damp clay, were dabbed up against the rough walls all round. A table, formed of dark planks laid upon low tressels, was in the middle, and round this sat the miners, nearly naked, – and far blacker than negroes, whose glossy skins shine with any light cast upon them, – while these were of a dead-black, which gave their robust outlines and muscular limbs the grimness of sepulchral figures, strangely at variance with the boisterous vitality and physical capacities of their owners. These, it seemed, were the magnates of the mine – the "hewers," "holers," "undergoers," or "pickers," – those who hew down the coal, and not the fetchers and carriers, and other small people.

Before he had recovered from his recent drive through the mine, Flashley was seated at the table. Cold roast beef, and ham, and slices of cold boiled turkey were placed before him, with a loaf of bread, fresh dairy-butter, and a brown jug of porter. He was scarcely aware whether he ate or not, but he soon began to feel *much* revived; and then he saw a hot roast duck; and then another; and then three more; and then a great iron dish, quite hot, and with flakes of fire at the bottom, full of roast ducks. Green peas were only just coming into season, and sold at a high price in the markets; but here were several delphic dishes piled up with them; and Flashley could but admire and sit amazed at the rapidity with which these delicate green pyramids sank lower and lower, as the great spoonfuls ascended to the red and white open mouths of the jovial black visages that surrounded him. He was told that the "undergoers" dined here every day after this fashion; but only with ducks and green peas at this particular season, when the miners made a point of buying up all the green peas in the markets, claiming the right to have them before all the nobility and gentry in the neighbourhood.

While all this was yet going on, Flashley became aware of a voice, as of some one discoursing very gravely. It was like the voice of the Elfin who had wrought him all this undesired experience. But upon looking forwards in the direction of the sound, he perceived that it proceeded from one of the miners – a brawny-chested figure, who was making a speech. Their eyes met, and then it seemed that the miner was addressing himself expressly to poor Flashley. Something impelled the latter, averse as he was, to stand up and receive the address.

"Young man – or rather gent!" said the miner – "You are now in the bowels of old mother Earth – grandmother and great grand-mother of all these seams of coal; and you see a set of men around you, whose lives are passed in these gloomy places, doing the duties of their work without repining at its hardness, without envying the lot of others, and smiling at all its dangers. We know very well that there are better things above ground – and worse. We know that many men and women and children, who are ready to work, can't get it, and so starve to death, or die with miserable slowness. A sudden death, and a violent is often our fate. We may fall down a a shaft; something may fall upon us and crush us; we may be damped to death;* we may be drowned by the sudden breaking in of water; we may be burned up by the wildfire,† or driven before it to destruction; in daily labour we lead the same lives as horses and other beasts of burden; but for *all* that, we feel that we have some-

* *The choke-damp*, carbonic acid gas.
† *Fire-damp*, also called *the sulphur* – hydrogen gas.

thing else within, which has a kind of tingling notion of heaven, and a God above, and which we have heard say is called 'the soul.' Now, tell us – young master, you who have had all the advantages of teachers, and books, and learning among the people who live above ground – tell us benighted working men, how have *you* passed your time, and what kind of thing is your soul?"

The miner ceased speaking, but continued standing. Flashley stood looking at him, unable to utter a word. At this moment, a half-naked miner entered hurriedly from one of the main roads, shouting confused words – to the effect that the fire which is always placed in the up-cast shaft to attract and draw up the air for the ventilation of the mine, had just been extinguished by the falling in of a great mass of coal, and the mine was no longer safe!

"Fire-damp!" – "The sulphur!" – "Choke-damp!" ejaculated many voices, as all the miners sprang from their seats, and made a rush towards the main outlet. Flashley was borne away in the scramble of the crowd; but they had scarcely escaped from the cavern, when the flame of the candles ran up to the roof, and a loud explosion instantly followed. The crowd was driven pell-mell before it, flung up, and flung down, dashed sideways, or borne onwards, while explosion after explosion followed the few who had been foremost, and were still endeavouring to make good their retreat.

Among these latter was Flashley, who was carried forwards, he knew not how, and was scarcely conscious of what was occurring, except that it was something imminently dreadful, which he momentarily expected to terminate in his destruction.

At length only himself and one other remained. It was the miner who had been his companion from the first. They had reached a distant "working," and stopped an instant to take breath, difficult as it was to do this, both from the necessity of continuing their flight, and also from the nature of the inflammable air that surrounded them. Some who had arrived here before them, had been less fortunate. Half-buried in black slush lay the dead body of a miner, scorched to a cinder by the wild-fire; and on a broad ledge of coal sat another man, in an attitude of faintness, with one hand pressed, as with a painful effort, against his head. The black-damp had suffocated him: he was quite dead.

Beyond this Flashley knew nothing until he found himself placed in a basket, and rising rapidly through the air, as he judged, by a certain swinging motion, and the occasional grating of the basket against the sides of the shaft. After a time he ventured to look up, and to his joy, not unmixed with awe, he discerned the mouth of the shaft above, apparently of the size of a small coffee-

cup. Some coal-dust and drops of water fell into his eyes; he saw no
more; but with a palpitating heart, full of emotions, and prayers,
and thankfulness, for his prospect of deliverance, continued his
ascent.

Chapter the Last

The air blew freshly over the bright waving grass of a broad sloping
field, on which the morning dews were sparkling and glancing in the
sun. The clouds moved quickly over head, in clear grey and golden
tints on their upper edges and foamy crests, with dark billows beneath, and their shadows chased each other down the green slopes
of the field in rapid succession. Swiftly followed them – now in the
midst of them – now seeming to lead them on, a fine bay horse with
flying mane, wild outspreading tail, and dilated nostrils, dashed onward exulting in his liberty, his strength, his speed, and all the
early associations and influences of nature around him! He was a
coal-mine horse, and had been just brought up the shaft for a
holiday.

All this Flashley saw very distinctly, having been hastily landed
at the top of the shaft, lifted into a tram-cart, and trundled off, he
knew not by what enginery, till he was suddenly shot out on the top
of a green embankment, and rolling down to the bottom, found
himself lying in a fresh green field. He enjoyed the action, the spirit,
and every motion of the horse. It was the exact embodiment in
activity of his strongest present feelings and impulses. He jumped
up to run after the horse, and mount him if he could, or if not,
scamper about the field with him in the same fashion. But while he
sought to advance, he felt as if he were retreating – in fact, he was
sure of it; – the grass ran by him, instead of his running over it – the
hedges ran through him, instead of his passing along them – the
trees sped away before him into the distance, as he was carried
backwards. He lost his legs – he sank upon the air – he was still
carried backwards – all the landscape faded, and with a loud splash
he fell into the sea!

Down he sank, and fancied he saw green watery fields rolling on
all sides, and over him; and presently he heard a voice hoarsely
calling as if from some bank above. He certainly had heard the
voice before, and recognised it with considerable awe, though the
words it uttered were homely and unromantic enough. It shouted
out "Nancy, of Sunderland!—boat ahoy!"

By some inexplicable process – though he clearly distinguished

a boat-hook in the performance – Flashley was picked up from beneath the waves, and lifted into a boat. It was a little, dirty, black,
thick-gunnelled jollyboat, rowed by two men in short black over-
shirts and smutty canvas trowsers. In the stern sat the captain
with his arms folded. A broad-brimmed tarpaulin hat shaded his
face. They pulled alongside a ship as black as death, but very
lively; and a rope being lowered from the side, it was passed under
Flashley's arms in a noose, and the next moment he was hoisted on
deck, and told to attend to his duty.

"My duty!" ejaculated Flashley, "Attend to my duty! Oh, what
is my duty?" His eyes wandered round. Nothing but hard black
planks and timbers, and masts with reefed sails, and rigging all
covered with coal dust, met his gaze. The sky, however, was visible
above him – *that* was a great comfort.

"Scrape these carrots and parsnips," said the Captain solemnly,
"very clean, d'ye mind! – and take them to the cook in the galley,
who'll let you know what's next. When he has done with you, clean
my sea-boots, and grease them with candle-ends; dry my pea-
jacket, pilot-coat, and dreadnoughts; clean my pipe, and fill it –
light, and take three whiffs to start it; mix me a glass of grog, and
bring it with the lighted pipe; then, go and lend a hand in tarring
the weather-rigging, and stand by, to go aloft and ease down the
fore-top-gallant mast when the mate wants her on deck."

"Oh, heavens!" thought Flashley, "are these then my duties!
This hideous black ship must be a collier – and I am the cabin-boy!"

A mixed impulse of equal curiosity and apprehension (it certainly was from no anxiety to commence his miscellaneous duties)
caused him to "inquire his way" to the cook's galley. He was
presently taken to a square enclosure, not unlike a great black
rabbit-hutch, open at both sides, in which he was received by a man
of large proportions, who was seated on an inverted iron saucepan
smoking. The black visage gave a grim smile and familiar wink. It
could not be the miner who had acted as his guide and companion
underground! And yet –

Flashley stepped back hastily, and cast an anxious look towards
the after-part of the deck. There stood the Captain. A short yet
very heavily-built figure, – a kind of stunted giant. He was not an
Indian, nor a Mulatto, nor an African, – and yet his face was as
black as a coal, in which several large veins rose prominently, and
had a dull yellow tinge, as if they had been run with gold, or some
metallic substance of that colour. Who could he be? Some demon
incog.? No, not that – but some one whom Flashley held in equal
awe.

How long poor Flashley continued to perform his multifarious duties on board the "Nancy" he had no idea, but they appeared at times very onerous, and he had to undergo many hardships. This was especially the case in the North Sea during the winter months, which are often of the severest kind on the coast between Sunderland and the mouth of the Thames. The rigging was all frozen, so that to lay hold of a rope seemed to take the skin off his hand; the cold went to the bone, and he hardly knew if his hands were struck through with frost, or by a hot iron. The decks were all slippery with ice, so were the ladders down to the cabins, and the cook's galley was garnished all round with large icicles, from six inches to a foot and a half in length, which kept up a continual drip, drip, on all sides, by way of complimentary acknowledgment of the caboose-fire inside. Sometimes the wind burst the side-doors open – blew the fire clean out of the caboose, and scattered the live and dead coals all over the deck, or whirled them into the sea. One night the galley itself, with all its black and smutty paraphernalia, was torn up and blown overboard. It danced about on the tops of the waves – made deep curtseys – swept up the side of a long billow – was struck by a cross-wave, and disappeared in a hundred black planks and splinters. That same night Flashley was called up from his berth to go aloft and lend a hand to close-reef the main-topsail. The sail was all frozen, and so stiff that he could not raise it; but as he hauled on one of the points, the point broke, and something happened to him, – he did not know what, but he thought he fell backwards, and the wind flew away with him.

The next thing he remembered was that of lying in his berth with a bandage round one arm, and a large patch on one side of his head, while the cook sat on a sea-chest by his side reading to him.

A deep splashing plunge was now heard, followed by the rapid rumbling of an iron chain along the deck overhead. The collier had arrived off Rotherhithe, and cast anchor.

"Up, Flashley!" cried the cook; "on deck, my lad! to receive the whippers who are coming alongside."

"What for?" exclaimed Flashley; "why am I to be whipped?"

"It is not you," said the cook, laughing gruffly, as he ran up the ladder, "but the coal-baskets that are to be whipped up, and discharged into the lighter."

The deck being cleared, and the main hatchway opened, a small iron wheel (called *gin*) was rigged out on a rope passing over the top of a spar (called *derrick*) at some 18 or 20 feet above the deck. Over this wheel a rope was passed, to which four other ropes were attached lower down. These were for the four whippers. At the other end of the wheel-rope was slung a basket. A second basket stood upon the coals, where four men also stood with shovels – two to fill each basket, one being always up and one down. The whippers had a stage raised above the deck, made of five rails, which they ascended for the pull, higher and higher as the coals got lower in the hold. The two baskets-full were the complement for one measure. The "measure" was a black angular wooden box with its front placed close to the vessel's side, just above a broad trough that slanted towards the lighter. Besides the measure stood the "meter," (an elderly personage with his head and jaws bound up in a bundle-handkerchief, to protect him from the draughts,) who had a piece of chalk in one hand, while with the other he was ready to raise a latch, and let all the coals burst out of the measure into the trough, by the fall of the front part of the box. The measure was suspended to one end of a balance, a weight being attached to the other, so that the weighing and measuring were performed by one process under the experienced, though rheumatic, eye of the meter.

The whippers continued at their laborious work all day; and as the coals were taken out of the hold, (the basket descending lower and lower as the depth increased,) the "whippers" who hauled up, gave their weight to the pull, and all swung down from their ricketty rails with a leap upon the deck, as the basket ran up; ascending again to their position while the basket was being emptied into the trough.

The lighter had five compartments, called "rooms," each holding seven tons of coals; and when these were filled, the men sometimes heaped coals all over them from one end of the craft to the other, as high up as the combings, or side-ridges, would afford protection for the heap. By these means a lighter could carry forty-two tons, and upwards; and some of the craft having no separate "rooms," but an open hold, fore and aft, could carry between fifty and fifty-five tons.

A canal barge or monkey-boat (so called we presume from being very narrow in the loins) now came alongside, and having taken in her load of coals, the friendly cook of the "Nancy" expressed an anxiety that Flashley should lose no opportunity of gaining all possible experience on the subject of coals, and the coal-trade generally, and therefore proposed to him a canal trip, having already spoken with the "captain of the barge" on the subject. Before Flashley had time to object; or utter a demur, he was handed over the side, and pitched neatly on his legs on the after-part of the barge, close to a little crooked iron chimney, sticking blackly out of the deck, and sending forth a dense cloud of the dirtiest and most unsavoury smoke. The captain was standing on the ladder of the cabin, leaning on his great arms and elbows over the deck, and completely filling up the small square hatchway, so that all things being black alike, it seemed as if this brawny object were some live excrescence of the barge, or huge black mandrake whose roots were spread about beneath, and, perhaps, here and there, sending a speculative straggler through a chink into the water.

The mandrake's eyes smiled, and he showed a very irregular set of large white and yellow teeth, as he scrunched down through the small square hole to enable the young passenger and tourist to descend.

Flashley, with a forlorn look up at the sky, and taking a good breath of fresh air to fortify him for what his nose already warned him he would have to encounter, managed to get down the four upright bars nailed close to the bulk-head, and called the "ladder."

He found himself in a small aperture of no definite shape, and in which there was only room for one person to "turn" at a time. Yet five living creatures were already there, and apparently enjoying themselves. There was the captain, and there was his wife, and there was a child in the wife's right arm, and another of five years old packed against her left side, and there was the "crew" of the barge, which consisted, for the present, of one boy of sixteen, of very stunted growth, and with one eye turning inwards to such a degree that sometimes the sight literally darted out, seeming to shoot beneath the bridge of his nose. They were all sitting, or rather hunched up, at "tea." The place had an overwhelming odour of coal-smoke, and tobacco smoke, and brown sugar, and onions, to say nothing of general "closeness," and the steam of a wet blanket-coat, which was lying in a heap to dry before the little iron stove. The door of this was open, and the fire shone brightly, and seemed to "*wink*" at Flashley as he looked that way.

"Here we are!" said a strange voice.

Flashley looked earnestly into the stove. He thought the voice came from the fire. The coals certainly looked very glowing, and shot out what a German or other imaginative author would call *significant* sparks.

"Here we are!" said the voice from another part of the cabin, and, turning in that direction, Flashley found that it proceeded from the "crew," who had contrived to stand up, and was endeavouring to give a close imitation of the "clown," on his first appearance after transformation. This, by the help of his odd eye, was very significant indeed.

And here they were, no doubt, and here they lived from day to

day, and from night to night; and a pretty wretched, dirty, monotonous life it was. Having once got into a canal, with the horse at
his long tug, the tediousness of the time was not easily to be sur-
passed. From canal to river, and from river to canal, there was
scarcely any variety, except in the passage through the locks, the
management of the rope in passing another barge-horse on the
tow-path, and the means to be employed in taking the horse over a
bridge. The duty of driving the horse along the tow-path, as may
be conjectured, fell to the lot of our young tourist. Once or twice,
"concealed by the murky shades of night," as a certain novelist
would express it, he had ventured to mount the horse's back; but
the animal, not relishing this addition to his work, always took care,
when they passed under a bridge, or near a wall, or hard embankment, to scrape his rider's leg along the side, so that very little good
was got in that way. And once, when Flashley had a "holiday," and
was allowed to walk up and down the full length of the barge upon
the top of the coals, a sudden bend in the river brought them close
upon a very low wooden bridge, just when he was at the wrong end
of the barge for making a dive to save his head. Flashley ran along
the top as fast as he could, but the rascally horse seemed to
quicken his pace, under the captain's mischievous lash, so that
finding the shadow of the bridge running at him before he could
make his leap from the top of the coals, he was obliged to save himself from being violently knocked off, by jumping hastily into the
canal, to the infinite amusement and delight of the captain, his
wife, and the "crew." The horse being stopped, the captain came
back and lugged him out of the bulrushes just as he had got
thoroughly entangled, and immersed to the chin; knee-deep in mud,
and with frogs and eels skeeling and striking out in all directions
around him.

After a week or ten days passed in this delightful manner,
Flashley found the barge was again on the Thames, no longer
towed by a horse and rope, but by a little dirty steam-tug. They
stopped on meeting a lighter on its way up with the tide, and
Flashley being told to step on board, was received by his grim but
good-natured companion and instructor, the cook of the "Nancy",
now going up with a load to Bankside, and performing the feat of
managing two black oars of enormous length and magnitude. They
were worked in large grooves in each side of the lighter, one oar
first receiving all the strength of this stupendous lighterman (late
cook) with his feet firmly planted on a cross-beam in front, so as to
add to the mighty pull of his arms, all the strength of his legs,
as well as all the weight of his body. Having made this broad

sweep and deep, he left the oar lying along the groove, and went to the one on the other side, with which he performed a similar sweep.

"Here's a brig with all sails set, close upon us!" cried Flashley.

"She'd best take care of herself;" said our lighterman, as he went on deliberately to complete his long pull and strong.

Bump came the brig's starboard bow against the lighter; and instantly heeling over with a lift and a lurch, the former reeled away to leeward, a row of alarmed but more enraged faces instantly appearing over the bulwarks – those "aft" with eyes flashing on the lighterman, and those "for'ard," anxiously looking over to see if the bows had been stove in. A volley of anathemas followed our lighterman; who, however, continued slowly to rise and sink backward with his prodigious pull, apparently not hearing a word, or even aware of what had happened.

In this way they went up the river among sailing-vessels of all kinds, and between the merchants' "forest of masts," like some huge antediluvian water-reptile deliberately winding its way up a broad river between the woods of a region unknown to man.

"But here's a steamer!" shouted Flashley. – "We shall be run down, or she'll go slap over us!"

The man at the wheel, however, knew better. He had dealt with lightermen before to-day. He therefore turned off the sharp nose of the steamer, so as not merely to clear it, but dexterously to send the "swell" in a long rolling swath up against the lighter, over which it completely ran, leaving the performer at the oars drenched up to the hips, and carrying Flashley clean overboard. He was swept away in the rolling wave, and might have been drowned, had not a coalheaver at one of the wharfs put off a skiff to his rescue

So now behold Flashley at work among the wharfingers of Bankside.

Before the coals are put into the sack, they undergo a process called "screening." This consists in throwing them up against a slanting sieve of iron wire, through which the fine coal and coal-dust runs: all that falls on the outer side of the screen is then sacked. But many having found that the coals are often broken still more by this process, to their loss, (as few people will buy the small coal and dust, except at breweries and waterworks), they have adopted the plan of a round sieve held in the hand, and filled by a shovel. The delightful and lucrative appointment of holding the sieve was, of course, conferred upon Flashley. His shoulders and arms ached as though they would drop off long before his day's work was done; but what he gained in especial, was the fine coal-dust which the wind carried into his face – often at one gust, filling his eyes, mouth, nostrils, and the windward ear.

In the condition to which this post soon brought his "personal appearance," Flashley was one morning called up at five to go with a waggon-load of coals a few miles into the country, in company with two coalheavers and a carman. Up he got. And off they went.

Flashley, having worked hard all the previous day, was in no sprightly condition on his early rising; so, by the time the waggon had got beyond the outskirts of London, and begun to labour slowly up hill with its heavy load, he was fain to ask in a humble voice of the head coalheaver, permission to lay hold of a rope which dangled behind, in order to help himself onwards. This being granted with a smile, the good-nature of which (and how seldom do we meet with a coalheaver who is not a good-natured fellow) shone even through his dust-begrimed visage, Flashley continued to follow the waggon till he had several times nearly gone to sleep; and was only reminded of the fact by a stumble which brought him with his nose very near the ground. The head coalheaver, observing this, took compassion on him; and being a gigantic man, laid hold of Flashley's trowsers, and with one lift of his arm deposited the young man upon the top of the second tier of coalsacks. There he at once resigned himself to a delicious repose.

The waggon meanwhile pursued its heavy journey, with an occasional pause for a slight moistening of the mouth of men and horses. At length the removal of one or two of the upper tier of sacks caused Flashley to raise his drowsy head, and look round him.

The waggon had pulled up close to a garden-gate, on the other side of which were a crowd of apple-trees. The ripe fruit loaded the branches till they hung in a vista, beneath which the sacks of coals had to be carried. All the horses had their nose-bags on, and were very busy. It was a bright autumn day; the sun was fast setting; a rich beam of crimson and gold cast its splendours over the garden, and lighted up the ripe apples to a most romantic degree.

The garden gates were thrown open; the passage of coal-sacks beneath the hanging boughs commenced.

Not an apple was knocked down, even by the tall figure of the leading coalheaver. Stooping and dodging, and gently humouring a special difficulty, he performed his walk of thirty yards, and more, till he turned the shrubbery corner, and thence made his way into the coal-cellar. His companion followed him, in turn, imitating his great example; and, if we make exception of three lemon-pippins and a codlin, with equal success. But where these accidental apples fell, there they remained; none were promoted to mouth or pocket.

It was now half-past four, and "the milk" arriving at the gate, was deposited in its little tin can on a strawberry bed just beyond the gate-post. The head coalheaver's turn with his load being next, he observed the milk as he approached, and bending his long legs, by judicious gradations, till he reached the little can with the fingers of his left hand, balancing the sack of coals at the same time, so that not a fragment tumbled out of the open mouth, he slowly rose again to his right position, holding out the can at arm's length to prevent any coal-dust finding its way to the delicate surface within. In this fashion, with tenfold care bestowed on the ounce and a half in his left hand, to that which he gave to the two hundred weight of coals on his back (not reckoning the sack, which, being an old and patched one, weighed fifteen pounds more) the coalheaver made his way, stooping and sideling beneath the apple-boughs as before, all of which he passed without knocking a single apple down, and deposited the little can in the hands of an admiring maid-servant, as he passed the kitchen window on his way to the coal-cellar.

After the sacks had all been shot in the cellar, and the hats of each man filled with apples by the applauding master of the house, the counting of the empty sacks commenced. Having been thrice exhorted to be present at this ceremony by a wise neighbour, who stood looking on anxiously, from the next garden, with his nostrils resting on the top of the wall, the owner of the apple garden went forth to the gate, and with a grave countenance beheld the sacks counted. Orders for beer being then given on the nearest country alehouse, the coalheavers carefully gathered up all the odd coals which had fallen here and there, then swept the paths, and with hot and smiling visages took their departure, slowly lounging after the waggon and stretching their brawny arms and backs after their herculean work.

As the men thus proceeded down the winding lane, crunching apples, and thinking of beer to follow, the carman was the first to speak.

"How *cute* the chap was arter *they* sacks!" said he with a grin, and half turning round to look back.

"There's a gennelman," said the head coalheaver, "as don't ought to be wronged out of the vally of *that*!" the amount in question being a pinch of coal-dust which the speaker took up from one side of the waggon, and sprinkled in the air.

"He allus gives a ticket for beer," said the second coal-heaver, "but last time the apples warn't ripe."

"He counted the *sacks* nation sharp, howsever," pursued the carman with a very knowing look.

At this both the coal-heavers laughed loudly.

"Ah!" said the second coalheaver; "people think that makes all sure. They don't think of the ease of bringing an empty sack with us, after dropping a full one by the way. Not they. Nobody yet was ever wise enough to count the full sacks when they first come."

On hearing this, the carman's face presented a confounded and perplexed look of irritated stupidity, marked in such very hard lines, that the coalheavers laughed for the next five minutes with the recollection of it.

Towards dusk the waggon returned to the wharf, and next day Flashley resumed his usual duties.

One morning, after several hours' work with the sieve in "screening," when his face and hands were, if possible, more hopelessly black than they had ever been before, Flashley was called to take a note to a merchant at the Coal Exchange. This merchant's name seemed rather an unusual one to meet with in England – being no less a person than Haji Ali Camaralzaman and Co.

The merchant was a short, solid-built figure, and stood with a heavy immobility that gave the effect of a metallic image rather than a man. He was a Moor, though nearly black, and with very sparkling eyes. He was dressed in a long dark blouse, open at the breast, and displaying a black satin waistcoat, embroidered with golden sprigs and tendrils. It seemed to Flashley that he spoke a foreign language; and yet he understood him, though without having any idea what language it was. Something passed between them in a very earnest tone, almost a whisper, about Sinbad the Sailor, and a sort of confused discussion as to the geographical position of the Valley of Black Diamonds; also, if coals were ever burnt in the east; then a confused voice from within the hall called out loudly, "The North Star!" to which a chorus of coal-merchants responded in a low chant, "What money does he owe the divan?"

"Yes," said the great Camaralzaman, "and what lost time does he owe to nature and to knowledge? Let the North Star look to it."

"It does, great Sir!" responded the chorus of coal-merchants, in the same low chant. "It shines directly over the shaft of the William Pitt mine."

"Enough," said Camaralzaman.

At this all the merchants fell softly into a heap of white ashes.

Then the Moor, turning to Flashley, said, "You must reflect a little on all these things. Coals are more valuable to the world than the riches of other mines – more important than gold and silver, and diamonds of the first water, because they are the means of advancing and extending the comforts and refinements of life – the industrial arts, the trades, the ornamental arts. Are not these great things? Behold, there are greater yet which are indebted to the coal-fires. For, may I not name Science, Agriculture (in the making of iron, and the steam-ploughs which are forthcoming), Commerce and Navigation. Moreover, do they not tend, by the generation of steam, to annihilate space and time, and are they not rapidly carrying knowledge and civilisation to the remotest corners of the habitable globe? By myriads of jets, in countless forms, they turn the dark night into the brightness of day. Their history commences from the infancy of the earth; they proceed through gradations of wonders; are no less wonderful in the varieties and magnitude of their utility, and do not cease to be of use to man, even when the bright fire is utterly extinguished, and its materials can no more be re-illumined, but are claimed for the garden and the brickfield, not by the dinging and tolling of the bell-man of your grandsires, but by the longdrawn wail of the queer-kneed dusky figure in the flaphat, who wanders down your streets yowling " 'Sto – e! o – e!"

"And is it then all over? Verily, it doth appear when the coal fire is fairly burnt out to cinders and ashes, that it hath performed its complete circle, and is for ever ended. It is *not* so. The antediluvian forests absorbed the gases of the atmosphere; much of these have been drawn off, and appropriated, but some portions have remained locked up and hidden in the depths of the earth ever since. Lo! the coal-fire is lighted! – flames, for the first time, ascend from it. Then, also for the first time, are liberated gases which are of the date of those primæval forests; they ascend into the atmosphere, and once more form a portion of those elements which are again to assist in the growth of forests. The Coal-Spirit has then performed his grand cycle – and recommences his journey through future cycles of formation."

A great blaze of light now smote across the hall, in which everything vanished. Then passed a rushing panorama through Flashley's brain, wherein he saw whirling by, the stage of a saloon theatre, with a lighted cigar and two tankards dancing a ridiculous reel, till the whole scene changed to a melancholy swamp, out of which arose, to solemn music, an antediluvian forest. The Elfin of the Coal-mine came and stood in the midst, and some one held an iron umbrella over Flashley's head, which instantly caused him to sink deep through the earth, and he soon found himself crawling in a dark trench terminating in a chasm looking out upon the sea. He was immediately whisked across by a black eagle, and dropped in a bright-green field, where he met a tall dusky figure carrying a sack of coals and a "ha'p'orth" of milk; but just as he was about to speak to him, a voice called out "Nancy!" and all was darkness, while through the horrid gloom he saw the glaring eye-ball of a horse. "Camaralzaman!" cried the voice again: "Have you been sleeping here all night in the arm-chair?" Then a vivid flame shot over Flashley's eyelids – there was a great fire blazing before him, in the midst of which he saw the head of the Elfin, who gave him a nod full of meaning, and also like bidding farewell, and disappeared in the fire, – while at his side stood Margery with the carpet-broom.

It was six in the morning, and she had just lighted the parlour fire. Without replying to any of her interrogations of surprise, Flashley slowly rose, and went out to take a few turns round the garden; where he fell into a train of thought which, in all probability, will have a salutary influence on his future life.

Bibliography

A strictly selective principle has been adopted in the composition of this bibliography. Readers interested in background material are referred to section 1, which lists relevant bibliographies. More space has been given to section 2, covering contemporary sources. Section 3 lists only the most obvious critical studies.

The place of publication is London if not otherwise indicated.

1. Bibliographies and Anthologies

Witt Bowden, *Industrial Society in England Towards the End of the Eighteenth Century* (New York, 1925).

Early English Pamphlets on Machinery and Employment of Labour 1780–1830 (California State Library, San Francisco, 1939).

Henry Fishwick, *Lancashire Printed Books* (The Lancashire Library, 1975).

James Orchard Halliwell, *A Catalogue of Chap-books, Garlands and Popular Histories* (1849).

Yuri V. Kovalev, *An Anthology of Chartist Literature* (Moscow, 1958).

William Matthews, *British Diaries* (Los Angeles, 1950).

Michael Sadleir, *Nineteenth-Century Fiction: A Bibliographical Record Based on his Own Collection* (1951).

R. C. Slack, *Bibliographies of Studies in Victorian Literature from 1955–1964* (Urbana, Ill., 1967).

William Templeman, *Bibliographies of Studies in Victorian Literature from 1932–1944* (Urbana, Ill., 1945).

J. E. Tobin, *Eighteenth Century English Literature and its Background, a Bibliography* (New York, 1939).

Harry B. Wiess, *A Catalogue of Chapbooks in the New York Public Library* (New York, 1936).

Austen Wright, *Bibliographies of Studies in Victorian Literature from 1945-1954* (Urbana, Ill., 1956).

2. Primary and Secondary Sources of the Period

Where necessary, an explanation has been inserted in square brackets following the entry.

John Aikin, *A Description of the Country from Thirty to Forty Miles round Manchester* (1795).

—— *England Delineated, or a Geographical Description of Every County in England and Wales* (1778). [For the young.]

William Harrison Ainsworth, *Mervyn Clitheroe* (1858). [Novel.]

Alfred [pseudonym], *The History of the Factory Movement* (1857).

James Anderson, *Observations on the Means of Exciting a Spirit of National Industry of Scotland* (Edinburgh, 1777). [533 pp.]

Anonymous, *Annals of the Poor, Chambers's Miscellany* (Edinburgh, 1844).

—— 'The Art of Candle-Making', *The European Magazine*, XLII (December 1802). [Satire in verse.]

—— 'The Birmingham Button-Maker' (n.d.). [In verse.]

—— 'The Case of the Woollen Manufacturers in the West Riding of the County of York', n.p. (1774). [Against factories.]

—— 'Character, Object and Effects of Trade Unions' (1834). [Against the trade unions.]

—— 'Chilmarke Quarries', *Gentleman's Magazine*, XXIX (1759). [Descriptive poem of "subterranean wealth".]

—— 'The Clothier's Delight, or the Rich Man's Joy, and the Poor Man's Sorrow' (n.d.). [Verse, probably from the end of the seventeenth century.]

—— 'A Dialogue between an Associator and a Well-Informed Englishman on the Grounds of the late Associations, and the Commencement of War with France' (1793). [Pro-French.]

—— 'A Dialogue between a Gentleman and a Mechanic' (Dublin, 1798). [Against egalitarian ideas.]

—— 'A Dialogue between Mr. Worthy and Simple on some Matters relative to the Present State of Great Britain', n.p. (1792). [Against egalitarian ideas.]

—— ' Dialogues on the Rights of Britons, between a Farmer, a Sailor and a Manufacturer' (1793). [Against egalitarian ideas.]

—— 'The Factory Girl' (Providence, R.I., 1854). [Short story, set in America; Puritan.]

—— *Hugh Vernon, the Weaver's Son*, serialized in *The True Briton* (1854). [Novel.]

—— [G.E.S.], 'The Incendiary', *Bradshaw's Manchester Journal* (1842). [Short story.]

—— 'A Journey to Nottingham in a Letter to a Friend', *Gentleman's Magazine*, XIII (1743). [Descriptive verses.]

—— 'Lilly Crossland', *Eliza Cook's Journal* (1851). [Short story.]

—— [R.D.], 'Lines Written on Entering a Coal-Pit at Wollaston in Nottinghamshire', *Gentleman's Magazine*, LV (1785). [In verse.]

—— 'Little Mary, a Tale of the Black Year', *Household Words* (1851). [Misery in Ireland.]

—— *Memoirs of a Working Man* (1845).

—— 'Minerva, or the Art of Weaving' (1677). [In verse.]

—— 'Socialism', *The Cottage Magazine* (1842). [Anti-Socialist.]

—— 'The Strike, or a Dialogue between Andrew Plowman and John Treadle' (1834). [Against strikes.]

—— 'A Tale of Self-Denial', *Bentley's Assurance Magazine* (1847).

—— 'Ten Minutes Caution from a Plain Man to his Fellow Citizens' (1792). [In favour of introducing machinery into factories.]

—— 'The Three Homes; a Tale of the Cotton Spinners', by one who has been among the spindles, *The Working Man's Friend* (1850–1).

—— 'A True Story', *The Cottage Magazine* (1843). [Anti-Socialist.]

—— 'The Working Man's Wife' (Religious Tract Society, 1844).

—— 'The Young Working Man; or a Few Words to a Farm Labourer' (Religious Tract Society, 1850). [128 pp.]

[Rev. Joseph Armstrong], 'The Life and Confession of the Factory Boy' (1833). [Price 1*d*.]

Richard Ayton, *A Voyage Round Great Britain, 1813* (1814); illustrated by William Daniel. [Section on Lancashire very interesting.]

Edward Baines (jun.), *On the Manufacturing Districts* (Leeds, 1843).

Samuel Bamford, *Homely Rhymes, Poems and Reminiscences* (1843).

—— *Passages in the Life of a Radical and Early Days* (1893). [1844–9.]

—— *Walks in South Lancashire and on its Borders* (Blackley, near Manchester, 1844).

John Banks, *The Weaver's Miscellany*, or Poems on Several Subjects by J. B., now a Poor Weaver in Spittle-Fields (1730).

Anna Laetitia Barbauld, 'To the Poor', 'Eighteen Hundred and Eleven', in *The Works of Anna Laetitia Barbauld, with a Memoir*, by L. Aikin (1825). [In verse.]

Thomas Haynes Bayly, *The Spitalfields Weaver*, a burletta in one act (1838).

Henry Beighton, 'Description of the Invention and Progress of the Engine for Raising Water out of Mines by the Force of Fire', *The Ladies' Diary* (1725). [Prize enigma in verse.]

R. Beatniffe (ed.), *The Norfolk Tour* (Norwich, 1795).

William Bell, 'A Dissertation on the Following Subject: What Causes

Principally Contribute to Render a Nation Populous? etc. . . .'
(Cambridge, 1756). [Advocates increase of population.]

Thomas Biddulph, 'Seasonable Hints for the Poor on the Duties of
Frugality, Piety and Loyalty', A Sermon (Bristol, 1797).

James Bisset, 'A Poetic Survey round Birmingham' (Birmingham, 1800).

William Blake, 'Holy Thursday', *Songs of Experience* (1794).

—— *Vala or the Four Zoas* (1795–1804), Night VII ("Wheel without
wheel"); Night VIII ("Then sang the sons of Eden"); Night IX
("Let the slave, grinding at the mill').

Robert Blincoe, *Original Biography, Memoir of Robert Blincoe, an
orphan boy*, serialized in *The Lion* (1828). [The plight of apprentices
in the early factories. The memoir was supposedly written by one
J. Brown.]

Robert Bloomfield, *Rural Tales, Ballads and Songs* (1802).

John Brand, *The History and Antiquities of the Town and County of
Newcastle upon Tyne* (1789).

[William Bray], *Sketch of a Tour into Derbyshire and Yorkshire* (1778).

Charlotte Brontë, *Shirley* (1849).

Elizabeth Barratt Browning, 'The Cry of the Children' (1844).

—— 'A Curse for a Nation', *Poems before Congress* (1860).

George S. Bull, 'Faithful Appeal to the Inhabitants of Bradford on the
Behalf of the Factory Children' (Bradford, 1832).

James Dawson Burn, *The Autobiography of a Beggar Boy* (1855).

James Butterforth, *Trade of Manchester* (Manchester, 1822).

Richard Carlile, *Journal of Mr. Carlile's Tour through the Country*,
serialized in *The Lion* (1828).

Thomas Carlyle, 'Chartism' (1839); 'Latter-Day Pamphlets' (1850);
'Past and Present' (1843); 'Signs of the Times' (1829).

[Edward Clarke, Dean of Cambridge], *A Tour through the South of
England, Wales and Part of Ireland, made during the Summer 1791*
(1793).

[Frederick Richard Chichester], Lord B[elfast], *Masters and Workmen,
Illustrative of the Social and Moral Condition of the People* (1851).
[3-volume novel.]

John Cleveland, 'News from Newcastle, or Newcastle Coal-Pits' (1659).
[In verse.]

John Cobden, *The White Slaves of England* (American edn, 1854).

William Cobbett, *Rural Rides* (1830).

George Cockings, *Arts, Manufacture and Commerce, a Poem*, Dedicated
to the Society for the Encouragement of Arts, Manufacture, and
Commerce (1766).

—— *Benevolence and Gratitude, a Poem* (1772). [Advocates philanthropic works.]

Samuel Taylor Coleridge, *Addresses to the People* (Bristol, 1795). [Revolutionary.]
—— *First and Second Circular* (1818) addressed to the public on behalf of the factory children, in L. E. Watson (ed.), *Coleridge at Highgate* (1925).
William Combe, 'A Word in Season to the Traders and Manufacturers of Great Britain' (1792). [Against egalitarian ideas.]
W. Cook-Taylor, *Notes on a Tour in the Manufacturing Districts of Lancashire* (1842).
Thomas Cooper [the Chartist], *The Life of Thomas Cooper by Himself* (1783).
Charles Cotton, *The Wonders of the Peake* (1681). [Verse description of lead-mine.]
William Cowper, *The Task* (1785). [Praise of London commerce.]
Rev. George Crabbe, *The Village* (1783).
—— *The Parish Register* (1807).
John Dalton, 'A Descriptive Poem addressed to Two Ladies at their Return from Viewing the Mines near Whitehaven' (1755).
Erasmus Darwin, *The Botanic Garden* (1789–91).
Daniel Defoe, *A Tour thro' the Whole Island of Great Britain* (1724).
Charles Dickens, *Hard Times for these Times* (1854).
—— *The Old Curiosity Shop* (1841).
—— 'A Poor Man's Tale of a Patent', *Household Words* (October 1850).
—— 'The Chimes' (1844).
—— 'On Strike', *Household Words* (1854).
Benjamin Disraeli, *Sybil, or the Two Nations* (1845).
Sir John Denham, *Cooper Hill* (1642).
John Dryden, *Astraea Redux* (1600).
Stephen Duck [the Thresher-Poet], *Curious Poems on Several Occasions* (1738).
George Dyer, *The Complaints of the Poor People of England* (1793). [Radical.]
John Dyer, *The Fleece* (1757).
Ebenezer Elliott, *The Corn-Law Rhymes* (1828).
Frederic Morton Eden, *The State of the Poor, or an History of the Labouring Classes in England* (1797). [In 3 volumes.]
Frederick Engels, *The Condition of the Working-Class in England in 1844* (1845).
William Enfield. 'A Sermon Preached at Norwich' (1788). [Praise of English Constitution.]
John Evelyn, *Fumifugium* (1661). [Pamphlet on air pollution in London.]
Benjamin Fawcett, *The Religious Weaver, or Pious Meditation on the Trade of Weaving* (1773). [Didactic.]

John Fielden, *The Curse of the Factory System* (1836).
John Galt, *Annals of the Parish* (1821). [Country life in Scotland.]
R. G. Gammage, *History of the Chartist Movement* (1854).
Elizabeth Gaskell, 'Bessy's Troubles at Home' (1852).
—— 'Christmas Storm and Sunshine' (1848).
—— 'Hand and Heart' (1849).
—— 'Libbie Marsh's Three Eras' (1847).
—— *Mary Barton, a Story of Manchester Life* (1848).
—— *North and South* (1855).
—— *Ruth* (1853).
Mary Leman Gillies, 'Blighted Homes', Sounders's *People's Journal* (1847). [Short story.]
John Gisborne, *The Vales of Wever* (1797). [Descriptive poem, 1120 lines.]
George Robert Gleig, *The Chronicles of Waltham* (1835). [Novel.]
Gloucester [Bishop of], *Sermon* preached in Holborn (1730). [On pauper children.]
William Godwin, *Fleetwood, or the New Man of Feeling* (1805). [Chapters 11–14.]
William Goldwin, 'A Description of the Ancient and Famous City of Bristol, a Poem' (1751). [Glorifies commerce.]
Oliver Goldsmith, *The Deserted Village* (1770).
[Mrs] C. G. F. Gore, *Men of Capital* (1857). [Novel.]
T. H. Hair, *Sketches of the Coal Mines in Northumberland and Durham* (1839). [Little mention of miners, no mention of women or children at work.]
John Vine Hall, 'The Sinner's Friend' (Maidstone, n.d.). [64 pp, mention of 110 editions of the work in 650,000 copies.]
[Mrs] S. G. Hall, *Tales of Women's Trials* (1835).
Jonas Hanway, *Virtue in Humble Life*, . . . in two hundred and nine conversations . . . intended as an amusing and instructive library to persons of certain conditions (1774). [523 pp, ten editions in 60 years.]
T. Harpley, *The Genius of Liverpool*, a drama in one act (Liverpool, 1790). [Glorifies commerce.]
Rowland Hill, *Journey through the North of England and Parts of Scotland, with Remarks* (1799). [Refers only to religion.]
—— *Village Dialogues* (1810). [Preaches religion.]
[Mrs] Barbara Hofland, *Tales of the Priory* (1820). [Didactic.]
John Holland, *The Mechanics' Festival* (Sheffield, n.d.). [In verse.]
Thomas Hood, 'The Song of the Shirt' (1843).
Richard Hengist Horne, *The Dreamer and the Worker* (1851). [Novel.]
—— 'The True Story of a Coal Fire', *Household Words* (1850).
Leonard Horner, *Letters on the Factory Acts* (1837).

Mary Howitt, *Work and Wages* (1842). [Didactic short stories.]

William Howitt, 'The Miner's Daughters', *Household Words* (1850).

William Hutton, 'A Journey from Birmingham to Caernarvon', *Gentleman's Magazine*, LXIX (1799). [Descriptive verses.]

——— *An History of Birmingham* (Birmingham, 1795).

——— *The History of Derby* (1791). [Autobiographical, interesting.]

——— *Life of Hutton* (2nd edn 1817). [Child labour in 1730.]

Richard Jago, *Edge-Hill*, or the Rural Prospect Delineated and Moralized, a Poem in four books (1767). [Industrialization praised.]

G. P. R. James, *Margaret Graham*, a Tale founded on Facts (1848). [2-volume novel about the poor in the country.]

Geraldine Jewsbury, *Marian Withers* (1851). [3-volume novel about industrialists and workers in Manchester.]

Ernest Jones, *Woman's Wrongs: A Series of Tales* (1855).

James Kay-Shuttleworth, *Moral and Physical Condition of the Working Classes* (2nd edn 1832).

Charles Kingsley, *Alton Locke, Tailor and Poet: an Autobiography* (1850).

——— *Politics for the People* (1848). [Contributor.]

——— *Yeast* (1848). [Novel.]

Rev. Richmond Legh, *Annals of the Poor* (1828). [Short stories.]

John Leslie, *Phoenix Park*, a Poem (1772). [Refers to Irish linen manufacture.]

John Liddon, *Sermon* preached for the benefit of Sunday-schools (1792).

Elizabeth Lynn Linton, *Realities, a Tale* (1851). [3-volume novel on the London poor.]

William Lovett, *Autobiography* (1876).

William McGill, *A Sermon* on the Fear of God and the King (1795).

Jane Marcet, *Conversations on Political Economy* (1816). [499 pp.]

——— *John Hopkin's Notions on Political Economy* (1833). [For the young.]

——— *Rich and Poor* (1851). [Dialogue between teacher and pupil.]

Harriet Martineau, *Autobiography*, ed. M. W. Chapman (1877).

——— *The Factory Controversy* (Manchester, 1855). [Polemical pamphlet.]

——— *Health, Husbandry, and Handicraft* (1861). [Descriptive.]

——— *A History of England during the Thirty Years' Peace 1816–1846* (1850). [Completed by Charles Knight.]

——— *Illustrations of Political Economy* (1832–4). [9 volumes.]

——— 'The Rioters' (1827). [Short story.]

——— 'The Turn-Out' (1829). [Short story.]

Henry Mayhew, *London Labour and the London Poor* (1851). [Documentary].

[Fanny Mayne], *Jane Rutherford, or a Miners' Strike* (1854). [Novel.]

Rev. E. Monro, *The True Stories of Cottagers* (1849). [Religious didacticism.]

Hannah More, *Cheap Repository Tracts* (1795). [Signed 'Z'.]

—— *Village Politics* (1893). [24-page refutation of Tom Paine's *The Rights of Man*.]

Charles P. Moritz [Karl Philip Moriz], *Travels Chiefly on Foot, through Several Parts of England in 1782* (1795). [Translated from the German original.]

Dinah Maria Mulock [Mrs Craik], *John Halifax, Gentleman* (1857).

Thomas Nicholson, *The Warehouse Boy of Manchester*, a metrical tale in four parts (Manchester, 1852).

Caroline Norton, 'A Voice from the Factories' (1836). [Poem.]

—— 'The Child of the Islands' (1845). [Poem.]

Robert Owen, *The Life of Robert Owen by Himself* (1857).

Francis Paget [rector of Elford], *Tales of the Villages* (1840–1). [240 pp; in favour of the Church, against Dissenters, Catholics and the Infidel.]

—— *Warden of Berkingholt; or Rich and Poor* (1843). [Novel of 299 pp; little about the Poor: advocates charity.]

William Paley, 'Equality as Consistent with the British Constitution, in a Dialogue between a Master-Manufacturer, and one of his Workmen' (Carlisle, 1793).

—— *Reasons for Contentment* (Carlisle, 1793). [Religious pamphlet.]

Peter Parley, 'A Wintry Night', *Peter Parley's Annual* (1840). [Misery of a hand-loom weaver.]

Parliamentary Reports:

Report of the Committee on the State of Children Employed in the Manufacturies of the United Kingdom (1816), vol. 1.

Report of the Select Committee on the Bill to Regulate the Labour of Children in Mills and Factories; Sadler Report (1832), vol. XV.

Report of the Select Committee on the Bill to Regulate the Labour of Children (1835), vol. V.

Minutes of Evidence Taken before the Select Committee on Mills and Factories (1840), vol. X.

Royal Commission on the Employment and Condition of Children and Young Persons: First Report – Mines and Collieries (1842); Second Report – Trade and Manufacture (1842–5).

Thomas Love Peacock, *Headlong Hall* (1816). [Chapter VII.]

Archibald Prentice, *Historical Sketches and Personal Recollections of Manchester* (1851).

John Reid, *Illustrations of Social Depravity* (Glasgow, 1834). [Short stories.]

John Robinson [of Norwich], *The Village Oppressed*, a Poem Dedicated to Dr Goldsmith (1771). [Against the "extension of commerce".]

John Rook, *The Silk Worms*, a Poem in two books, translated from the Latin of Hieronymus Vida (1725).

Charles Rowcroft, *Fanny, the Little Milliner, or the Rich and the Poor* (1846). [Novel.]

James Malcolm Rymer, *The White Slave* (1844). [Very cheap novel.]

John Sargent, *The Mine*, a Dramatic Poem (1778). [About the lead mine in Idria, province of modern Yugoslavia.]

Richard Savage, *London and Bristol Delineated*, Chalmers's *English Poets*, XI (1744). [Praise of commerce.]

John Scott, 'Amwell, a Descriptive Poem' (1776). [Country life idealized.]

David Service, 'The Caledonian Herd-Boy, a Moral Poem' (Yarmouth, 1802).

Anna Seward, 'Colebrook Dale' (1785). [Spread of industry.]

William Sewell, *Hawkstone: a Tale of and for England* (1845). [Condition-of-England novel by a clergyman.]

G. Whorton Simmson, 'Colliers and Coal Mining', *The Working Man's Friend* (1850). [Short story.]

Henry Skrine, *The Successive Tours in the North of England and Great Part of Scotland* (1795). [Industrial scenery described casually.]

Samuel Smiles, *Self-Help, with Illustration of Character and Conduct* (1859). [Didactic.]

Alexander Somerville, *The Autobiography of a Working Man* by one who has whistled at the Plough (1848). [Scottish labourer.]

Robert Southey, 'The State of the Poor; the Principle of Mr. Malthus's Essay on Population and the Manufacturing System 1812', *Essays Moral and Political*, IV (1832).

Rev. Shaw Stebbing, *A Tour to the West of England* (1789). [In praise of technical progress.]

Elizabeth Stone, 'The Widow's Son', *Chambers's Miscellany* (Edinburgh, 1844).

—— *William Langshawe, the Cotton Lord* (1842). [Novel of Manchester life.]

Sir Richard Joseph Sullivan, *Observations Made during a Tour through Parts of England, Scotland and Wales* (1780).

Rev. Charles Tayler, *Social Evils, and their Remedy* (1833). [Short stories – refutes Harriet Martineau's message, preaches subordination.]

John Thelwall, 'On Leaving the Bottoms of Glostershire, August 1797', from *Poems Chiefly Written in Retirement* (1801). [Disapproval of child labour in factories.]

James Thomson, *The Seasons* (1728). [Praise of commerce.]

—— *The Castle of Indolence* (1748). [Praise of imperial expansion.]

John Throsby, *The Memoirs of the Town and County of Leicester* (1777).

Charlotte Elizabeth Tonna, *Helen Fleetwood* (1841). [Novel.]
—— *The Perils of the Nation* (1843). [Pamphlet, 399 pp.]
—— *Remedies suggested for some of the Evils which constitute the Perils of the Nation* (1844). [Pamphlet, 472 pp.]
—— *The Wrongs of Woman* (1843). [Four short stories.]
Camilla Toulmin, 'A Story of the Factories', *Chambers's Miscellany* (Edinburgh, 1846).
—— *Toil and Trial* (1849). [The plight of shop-assistants.]
Sarah Trimmer, *The Economy of Charity, or an Address to Ladies Concerning Sunday-Schools* (1787). [183 pp.]
—— *Instructive Tales* (1815). [22 very short stories.]
—— '*Reflections upon the Education of Children in Charity Schools*' (1792).
Frances Trollope, *Jessie Phillips, a Tale of the Present Day* (1844). [Novel.]
—— *Life and Adventures of Michael Armstrong, the Factory Boy* (1840). [Novel.]
Josiah Tucker [rector of St Stephen's, Bristol], *Instruction for Travellers* (1757). [Concentrates on the effects of mechanization, condition of work, class relationship.]
John Walker, *The Factory Lad*, a domestic drama (n.d.). [Wrecking of machinery.]
Rev. Richard Warner, *A Walk through Wales in August 1797* (Bath, 1798). [Description of lead mines.]
F. A. Wendeborn, *A View of England towards the Close of the Eighteenth Century*, translated from the German by the Author. [930 pp, in favour of "sentiments of philanthropy".]
John Wesley, *The Journal of John Wesley*, ed. N. Curnock (1909–16).
George Woodley, *Cornubia*, a Poem in Five Cantos (1819). [On mining.]
William Wordsworth, *The Excursion* (1814). [Books VIII and IX.]
Thomas Yalden, *On the Mines*, Chalmers's *English Poets*, XI (1710).
Arthur Young, *An Enquiry into the State of the Public Mind among the Lower Classes* (1798).
—— *A Six Months Tour through the North of England* (1771).
Edward Young, *The Merchant, an Ode on the British Trade and Navigation* (1729). [In imitation of Pindar.]

3. Literary Studies

This select bibliography is limited to works having an immediate bearing on the subject or providing useful bibliographical information. For other works mentioned in this book see the Index.

Ralph Everett Adams, *The Industrial Novel in England, 1832-1851* (unpublished dissertation, University of Illinois, 1965).

Richard D. Altick, *The English Common Reader*, A Social History of the Mass Reading Public (Chicago, 1957).

Robert Arnold Aubin, *Topographical Poetry in 18th Century England* (Modern Language Association of America, 1936).

William O. Aydellotte, 'The England of Marx and Mill as Reflected in Fiction', *Journal of Economic History*, suppl. VIII (1948).

Myron Brightfield, *Victorian England and its Novels 1840-1870* (xerox copy, University of California, 1950).

Louis Cazamian, *Le roman social en Angleterre*, 1830-1850 (Paris, 1903).

Raymond Chapman, *The Victorian Debate, English Literature and Society 1832-1901* (1968).

Bart Anne Coenroad, *Social Elements in English Prose Fiction 1700-1832* (Amsterdam, 1929).

Robert A. Colby, *Fiction with a Purpose*, Major and Minor Nineteenth-Century Novels (Indiana, 1951).

Margaret Dalziel, *Popular Fiction 100 Years Ago* (1957).

Paul Benjamin Davis, *Industrial Fiction 1827-1850* (unpublished dissertation, University of Wisconsin, 1961).

Dwight D. Durling, *Georgic Tradition in English Poetry* (New York, 1935).

Louis James, *Fiction for the Working Man 1830-1850* (Oxford, 1963).

A. S. Karminski, *Writers in Manchester 1831-1854* (unpublished dissertation, University of Oxford, 1955).

P. J. Keating, *The Working Classes in Victorian Fiction* (1971).

Arnold Kettle, 'The Early Victorian Social-Problem Novel', in *From Dickens to Hardy*, ed. Boris Ford (1958).

Ivanka Ćuković Kovačević, *Romanopisac i čartizam* (Beograd, 1968). [Summary in English, 25 pp.]

Robert D. Mayo, *The English Novel in the Magazines 1740-1815* (Oxford, 1962).

David Shusterman, *The Victorian Novel of Industrial Conflict 1832-1870* (unpublished dissertation, University of New York, 1953).

Morris E. Speare, *The Political Novel* (Oxford, 1924).

L. Herbert Sussman, *Victorians and the Machine*, The Literary Response to Technology (Harvard, 1968).

J. M. S. Tomkins, *The Popular Novel in England 1770-1800* (1932).

Jeremy Warburg, *The Industrial Muse*, The Industrial Revolution in English Poetry, An Anthology with introduction and comment (Oxford, 1958).

R. K. Webb, *The British Working-Class Reader 1790-1848* (1955).

Index